THE
QUALITATIVE
INQUIRY
READER

THE
QUALITATIVE
INQUIRY
READER

NORMAN K. DENZIN
YVONNA S. LINCOLN
EDITORS

Sage Publications
International Educational and Professional Publisher
Thousand Oaks ▪ London ▪ New Delhi

For information:

Sage Publications, Inc.
2455 Teller Road
Thousand Oaks, California 91320
E-mail: order@sagepub.com

Sage Publications, Ltd.
6 Bonhill Street
London EC2A 4PU
United Kingdom

Sage Publications India Pvt. Ltd.
M-32 Market
Greater Kailash I
New Delhi 110 048 India

Printed in the United States of America

Library of Congress Cataloging-in-Publication Data

02   03   04   05   06   10   9   8   7   6   5   4   3   2   1

The qualitative inquiry reader / editors, Norman K. Denzin and
  Yvonna S. Lincoln.
    p. cm.
  Includes bibliographical references and index.
  ISBN 0-7619-2491-4 (c) — ISBN 0-7619-2492-2 (p)
    1. Sociology—Field work. 2. Qualitative research.
  3. Ethnology—Field work. 4. Sociology—Methodology.
  5. Ethnology—Methodology. I. Denzin, Norman K.
  II. Lincoln, Yvonna S.
  HM517 .Q35 2002
  301'.07'23—dc21   2001004186

Acquiring Editor:	Margaret H. Seawell
Editorial Assistant:	Alicia Carter
Production Editor:	Claudia A. Hoffman
Typesetter/Designer:	Marion Warren
Indexer:	Molly Hall
Cover Designer:	Ravi Balasuriya

CONTENTS

——

EDITORS' INTRODUCTION

——

The goals of *The Qualitative Inquiry Reader* are three-fold. The first goal is to introduce scholars and students to cutting-edge work in the field of qualitative inquiry. Second, we seek to present a critical framework for interpreting this new work. Third, chapters in this collection show how reflexive methodological work can contribute to critical political and moral discourse.

Qualitative inquiry is a name for a "reformist movement that began in the early 1970s in the academy" (Schwandt, 2000, p. 189). The interpretive and critical paradigms, in their several forms, are central to this movement, encompassing complex epistemological and ethical criticisms of traditional social science research. The field of qualitative inquiry now has its own journals, scientific associations, conferences, and faculty positions (Denzin and Lincoln, 2000a, p. x). The movement has made significant inroads into many social science disciplines, including education, sociology, nursing, business, organizational studies, communications, anthropology, political science, advertising, marketing, and consumer research.

Properly understood, qualitative inquiry becomes a civic, participatory, collaborative project, a project that joins the researcher with the researched in an on-going moral dialogue. This form of research has roots in liberation theology, neo-Marxist approaches to community development, and human rights activism in Asia and elsewhere (Kemmis & McTaggart, 2000, p. 568). This project presumes a moral ethic. It demands that interpretive work provide the foundations for social criticism and social action. As a cultural critic, the researcher is anchored in a specific community of moral discourse. The moral ethnographer is politically engaged.

The readings in this collection draw from the first seven years of *Qualitative Inquiry*. In 1995 (Denzin & Lincoln, 1995) we proudly launched *Qualitative Inquiry*, the first interdisciplinary, international journal to provide a forum for qualitative methodology and related issues in the human sciences. We sought cutting-edge manuscripts that transcended disciplinary, racial, ethnic, gender, national, and paradigmatic boundaries, including manuscripts that experimented with nontraditional forms, content, and modes of representation. The success of that early invitation is evidenced in this reader.

Over the past decade, the field of qualitative research has mushroomed in the social sciences, professional disciplines, and, to a lesser extent, in the humanities and the arts. Qualitative research has become an umbrella term encompassing a wide range of epistemological viewpoints, research strategies, and specific techniques for understanding people in their natural contexts.

We believe that qualitative research is an interdisciplinary field that crosscuts the humanities and the social and physical sciences. Qualitative research is many things at the same time. It is multiparadigmatic in focus. Its practitioners are sensitive to the value of the multimethod approach. They are committed to the naturalistic perspective and to the interpretive understanding of human experience. At the same time, the field is inherently political and shaped by multiple ethical and political positions.

Qualitative research is characterized by a tension between two areas of research. On one hand, it is drawn to a broad, interpretive, postmodern, feminist, and critical sensibility. On the other hand, it is drawn to more narrowly defined, positivist and postpositivist, humanistic, and naturalistic conceptions of human experience and its analysis.

Elsewhere we have argued that qualitative research operates in a complex sociocultural field that intersects seven historical moments (Denzin & Lincoln, 1994; 2000b, p. 2). These seven moments, all of which operate in the present, are the **traditional** (1900-1950), the **modernist** (1950-1970), **blurred genres** (1970-1986), **the crisis of representation** (1986-1990), **postmodern** or experimental (1990 to 1995),

post-experimental (1995-2000), and the **future** (2000-). The present period continues to be defined by a new sensibility, the core of which "is doubt that any discourse has a privileged place, any method or theory a universal and general claim to authoritative knowledge" (Richardson, 1991, p. 173).

It is in the seventh moment that *QI* and the *QI Reader* enter the dialogue. Today we understand that the researcher is not an objective, neutral observer. We know that this individual is always historically situated, never able to give more than a partial rendering of any situation. The present moment is defined by messy, experimental and multi-layered texts, cultural criticism, new approaches to the research text, new understandings of old analytic methods, and evolving research strategies. New interpretive communities are on the horizon, as are novel approaches to presenting the other's voice. And others are creating forms and modes for their own participation and representation, occasionally rejecting postmodern and postcolonial theoretical stances for problems which must be worked in the modern (L. Smith, 1999). Scholars are now reworking old understandings of what the qualitative text can and should do. The authors represented in this reader are helping shape and define these new tasks and their meanings for the human disciplines.

The transformations in qualitative inquiry that gained momentum in the 1990s continue into the new century. Today, few look back with skepticism on the narrative turn. Many have told their tales from the field. Further, it is now understood that writing is not an innocent practice. Men and women write culture differently. Sociologists and anthropologists continue to explore new ways of composing ethnography, and more than a few are writing fiction, drama, performance texts, and ethnographic poetry. Social science journals are holding fiction contests. Civic journalists are experimenting with various forms of critical ethnography.

The appeal of critical cultural studies across the social sciences and the humanities increases. This is a period of ferment and explosion. It is defined by breaks from the past, a focus on previously silenced voices, a turn to performance texts, and a concern with moral discourse, with critical conversations about democracy, race, gender, class, nation, freedom, and community (Lincoln & Denzin, 2000, p. 1048).

In the seventh moment, in the first decade of the twenty-first century, there is a pressing demand to show how the practices of critical, interpretive qualitative research can help change the world in positive ways. It is necessary to examine new ways of making the practices of critical qualitative inquiry central to the workings of a free democratic society. This is the charge of the *QI Reader*.

THIS WORK

The *Reader* is divided into five sections: Reflexive Ethnography, Autoethnography, Poetics, Performance Narratives, and Assessing the Text.

These divisions are not arbitrary. (We briefly define them here.) They reflect the ways in which contemporary researchers have implemented the narrative turn in their writing. Interpretive ethnographers make the world visible through their writing practices. The **reflexive ethnographer** is morally and politically self-aware, self-consciously present in his or her writing, often speaking with the first-person voice. Reflexive ethnographers experiment with different writing forms, what Richardson (2000) calls creative analytic practices.

Reflexive ethnography merges with **autoethnography.** In autoethnography, the researcher is the subject of the text (Ellis & Bochner, 2000, p. 739). In autoethnography, researchers conduct and write ethnographies of their own experiences. Many now argue that we can study only our own experiences. The researcher becomes the research subject. This is the topic of autoethnography (see Shelton, 1995).

Ivan Brady (2000) argues that anthropologists have been writing experimental, literary, and **poetic ethnographic texts** for at least 40 years. Such work reflects another version of the narrative turn. We use the phrase ethnographic poetics to describe this form of writing (see Marcus & Fischer, 1986, p. 73). We distinguish three poetic forms: *ethnopoetics*, "the emics of native poetries that are midwifed by western poets" (Rose, 1991, p. 220); *native poetry*, the poetry of traditional, native poets; and *ethnographic poetics*, the poetic productions of ethnographers. Within this last category, following Rose (1991, p. 221) we distinguish between personal poetry, which is unshaped by the anthropological experience, and those poetic productions that meditate on this experience and re-articulate it within the poetic frame.

In the literary, poetic form, ethnographers enact a moral and writing aesthetic that allows them to say things they could not otherwise say. In so doing, they push the boundaries of artful ethnographic discourse. Thus are the boundaries between the humanities and the human sciences blurred. This is a dialogical process. In this blurring, our moral sensibilities are sharpened.

Performance narrative or **performance ethnography** is a genre within ethnography, what Paget (1993, p. 42) calls ethnoperformance, Mienczkowski (1995; 2001) labels ethno-drama, and McCall (2000), Turner (1986), and Turner and Turner (1982) term performance and reflexive anthropology, the rendering "of ethnography in a kind of instructional theater" (1982, p. 41). We connect this textual form to the move that sees culture as a performance, as theater. Performance ethnographies are messy, they exist in the spaces where rhetoric, performance, ethnography, and cultural studies come together.

In the seventh moments, there are multiple **ways of assessing the interpretive text**. In the social sciences today, there is no longer a God's eye view that guarantees absolute methodological certainty (Smith & Deemer, 2000, p. 877). Indeed, as the readings in Part Five indicate, there is considerable debate over what constitutes good interpretation in qualitative research. Nonetheless, there seems to be an emerging consensus that all inquiry reflects the standpoint of the inquirer, that all observation is theory-laden, and that there is no possibility of theory-free knowledge. The days of naïve realism and naïve positivism are over. In their place stand critical and historical realism and various versions of relativism. The criteria for evaluating research are now relative. The injunction to pursue knowledge can not be given epistemologically; rather, the injunction is moral and political (Downing, 1987, p. 80; Christians, 2000; Collins, 1991).

IN CONCLUSION

It is clear that interest in qualitative research, alternative paradigm research, and ethnographic fieldwork has grown exponentially in recent years. This is demonstrated by the launching of several recent journals in this area (*Qualitative Studies in Education, Qualitative Health*

Research, Journal of Life History and Narrative, Ethnography, Qualitative Research, Fieldwork) and the phenomenal sales of publishers' books on this topic.

Still, attempts to create a unified interdisciplinary field have been almost nonexistent. A few conferences cross disciplinary boundaries and several disciplinary interest groups include a handful of scholars from other disciplines. While recent years have seen the beginnings of small, special interest groups on this topic, to date no major national association has a formal section specifically designed to nurture qualitative or interpretive work.

Few cross-disciplinary publishing enterprises have been tried, with the notable exceptions being Sage's *Qualitative Research Methods* series and the *Handbook of Qualitative Research* edited by Denzin and Lincoln (1994, 2000c). At this point, there is a need for ongoing interdisciplinary publications that will provide a forum for critical innovative publications on qualitative methods. We want the *QI Reader* to be one of those publications. We believe this edited volume has the potential to reshape the disciplinary discourses around qualitative research for the next generation of scholars, researchers, and practitioners. Indeed, because this field is developing so rapidly, we envison regular revisions and new editions of the *QI Reader*.

We view the audiences for the *QI Reader* to be those scholars, practitioners, and advanced students interested in qualitative research methodology. Most readers, we expect, will come from the following fields: sociology, anthropology, educational research, psychology, nursing, management, communication, cultural studies, gerontology, family studies, health and medicine, social work, and evaluation.

Welcome to the *QI Reader*. We hope to hear from you.

Norman K. Denzin and Yvonna S. Lincoln

REFERENCES

Brady, I. (2000). Anthropological poetics. In N. K. Denzin & Y. S. Lincoln (Eds.), *Handbook of qualitative research* (2nd ed., pp. 949-980). Thousand Oaks, CA: Sage.

Christians, C. (2000). Ethics and politics in qualitative research. In N. K. Denzin & Y. S. Lincoln (Eds.), *Handbook of qualitative research* (2nd ed., pp. 133-155). Thousand Oaks, CA: Sage.

Collins, P. H. (1991). *Black feminist thought.* New York: Routledge.

Denzin, N. K., & Lincoln, Y. S. (1994). Introduction: Entering the field of qualitative research. In N. K. Denzin & Y. S. Lincoln (Eds.), *Handbook of qualitative research* (2nd ed., pp. 1-17). Thousand Oaks, CA: Sage.

Denzin, N. K., & Lincoln, Y. S. (1995). Editor's introduction. *Qualitative Inquiry, 1*(1), 3-6.

Denzin, N. K., & Lincoln, Y. S. (2000a). Preface. In N. K. Denzin & Y. S. Lincoln (Eds.), *Handbook of qualitative research* (2nd ed., pp. ix-xx). Thousand Oaks, CA: Sage.

Denzin, N. K., & Lincoln, Y. S. (2000b). Introduction: The discipline and practice of qualitative research. In N. K. Denzin & Y. S. Lincoln (Eds.), *Handbook of qualitative research* (2nd ed., pp. 1-29). Thousand Oaks, CA: Sage.

Denzin, N. K., & Lincoln, Y. S. (Eds.). (2000c). *Handbook of qualitative research* (2nd ed.). Thousand Oaks, CA: Sage.

Downing, D. B. (1987). Deconstruction's scruples: The politics of enlightened critique. *Diacritcs, 17*, 66-81.

Ellis, C., & Bochner, A. P. (2000). Autoethnography, personal, narrative, reflexivity. In N. K. Denzin & Y. S. Lincoln (Eds.), *Handbook of qualitative research* (2nd ed., pp. 733-768). Thousand Oaks, CA: Sage.

Kemmis, S., & McTaggart, R. (2000). Participatory action research. In N. K. Denzin & Y. S. Lincoln (Eds.), *Handbook of qualitative research* (2nd ed., pp. 567-606). Thousand Oaks, CA: Sage.

Lincoln, Y. S., & Denzin, N. K. (2000). The seventh moment: Out of the past. In N. K. Denzin & Y. S. Lincoln (Eds.), *Handbook of qualitative research* (2nd ed., pp. 1047-1065). Thousand Oaks, CA: Sage.

Marcus, G., & Fischer, M. (1986). *Anthropology as cultural critique.* Chicago: University of Chicago Press.

McCall, M. M. (2000). Performance ethnography: A brief history and some advice. In N. K. Denzin & Y. S. Lincoln (Eds.), *Handbook of qualitative research* (2nd ed., pp. 421-435). Thousand Oaks, CA: Sage.

Mienczkowski, J. (1995). The theatre of ethnography: The reconstruction of ethnography into theatre with emancipatory potential. *Qualitative Inquiry, 1*(3), 360-376.

Mienczkowski, J. (2001). Ethnodrama: Performed research—limitations and potential. In P. Atkinson, A. Coffey, S. Delamont, J. Lofland, & L. Lofland (Eds.), *Handbook of ethnography* (pp. 468-476). London: Sage.

Paget, M. A. (1993). *A complex sorrow.* M. L. DeVault (Ed.). Philadelphia: Temple University Press.

Richardson, L. (1991). Postmodern social theory. *Sociological Theory, 9*, 173-179.

Richardson, L. (2000). Writing: A method of inquiry. In N. K. Denzin & Y. S. Lincoln (Eds.), *Handbook of qualitative research* (2nd ed., pp. 923-948). Thousand Oaks, CA: Sage.

Rose, D. (1991). In search of experience: The anthropological poetics of Stanley Diamond. In I. Brady (Ed.), *Anthropological poetics* (pp. 219-233). Savage, MD: Rowman & Littlefield.

Schwandt, T. A. (2000). Three epistemological stances for qualitative inquiry. In N. K. Denzin & Y. S. Lincoln (Eds.), *Handbook of qualitative research* (2nd ed., pp. 189-213). Thousand Oaks, CA: Sage.

Shelton, A. (1995). Foucault's madonna: The secret life of Carolyn Ellis. *Symbolic Interaction, 18*, 83-87.

Smith, J. K., & Deemer, D. K. (2000). The problem of criteria in the age of relativism. In N. K. Denzin & Y. S. Lincoln (Eds.), *Handbook of qualitative research* (2nd ed., pp. 877-896). Thousand Oaks, CA: Sage.

Smith, L. T. (1999). *Decolonizing methodologies.* London: Zed Books.

Turner, V. (1986). *The anthropology of performance.* Performing Arts Journal Publications.

Turner, V. (with E. Turner). (1982). Performing ethnography. *The Drama Review, 26,* 33-50.

PART ONE

— —

Reflexive Ethnography

Reflexive ethnography, as argued in our Introduction, is that ethnographic form that privileges the presence of the writer in the text. In *Fictions of Feminist Ethnography* (1994), Kamala Visweswaran argues that the authority of the ethnographer is challenged in reflexive ethnographies. In reflexive ethnography, the ethnographer becomes part of the inquiry (Kincheloe & McLaren, 2000). Reflexive ethnographers use their own experiences in a culture "reflexively to bend back on self and look more deeply at self-other interactions" (Ellis & Bochner, 2000, p. 740).

According to Ellis and Bochner (2000), reflexive ethnographies "range along a continuum," starting with texts that focus solely on the writer's experiences to ethnographies "where the researcher's experiences are actually studied along with other participants, to confessional tales where the researcher's experiences of doing the study become the focus of investigation" (p. 740). Reflexive ethnographers anchor their experimental (and traditional) writing in an ongoing moral dialogue with the members of a local community.

Richardson (2000) observes that, in the last decade, the narrative genres connected to ethnographic writing have been "blurred, enlarged, altered to include poetry, drama, conversations, readers'

1

theatre and so on" (p. 929). She uses the term *creative analytic practice* to describe these many different narrative forms, which include autoethnography, fiction-stories, poetry, performance texts, polyvocal texts, reader's theatre, responsive readings, aphorisms, comedy and satire, visual presentations, allegory, conversation, layered accounts, writing-stories, and mixed-genres. Creative nonfiction, memoirs, personal histories, and cultural criticism may be added to this list of narrative forms that are used by the reflexive ethnographer.

This shift in writing form means that many ethnographers have abandoned the traditional ethnography, that writing form that distanced the writer from the text. The traditional ethnography, in qualitative research's classic period, was written under the guise of objectivism and observer neutrality. The field worker, during this period, was lionized, made into a larger-than-life figure who went into and then returned from the field with stories about strange people.

Rosaldo (1989, p. 30) describes this as the period of the Lone Ethnographer, the story of the man-scientist who went off in search of his native in a distant land. There this figure "encountered the object of his quest . . . [and] underwent his rite of passage by enduring the ultimate ordeal of 'fieldwork.'" Returning home with his data, the Lone Ethnographer wrote up an objective account of the culture studied.

These accounts were structured by the norms of classical ethnography. This sacred bundle of terms (Rosaldo, 1989, p. 31) organized ethnographic texts in terms of four beliefs and commitments: a commitment to objectivism, a complicity with imperialism, a belief in monumentalism (the ethnography would create a museum-like picture of the culture studied), and a belief in timelessness (what was studied never changed). This model of the researcher, who could also write complex, dense theories about what was studied, holds to the present day.

The myth of the Lone Ethnographer depicts the birth of classic ethnography. The texts of Malinowski, Radcliffe-Brown, Margaret Mead, and Gregory Bateson are still carefully studied for what they can tell the novice about fieldwork, taking field notes, and writing theory. At this moment, however, these texts serve as histories of how fieldwork was conducted in the classical period of ethnography. We see their presumptions of authority, legitimation, and rights of representation as a claim to timeless truth. We are no longer so innocent. Today this image has been shattered. The works of the classic ethnographers are seen by many as relics from the colonial past (Rosaldo, 1989, p. 44). While many feel nostalgia for this past, others celebrate its passing.

The four chapters in Part One celebrate this passing, and reflect the variations on the reflexive ethnographic form discussed above. **Deborah Ceglowski**, in a semi-confessional mode, presents a series of stories about her multiple relationships with the Head Start staff and children at Wood River. She is the reflexive focus of these ethnographic stories.

Christopher Dunbar presents three short stories about the experiences of five African-American male students enrolled in a Midwest alternative school. Dunbar is present in this story, both as narrator and as reflexive participant. Using this narrative form allowed him to bring a sense of immediacy and urgency to this educational setting. Like Ceglowski, he uses reflexive ethnography to write social criticism.

In "Skirting a Pleated Text," **Laurel Richardson** reflexively comments on her academic and writing career. She shows how her evolving writing style grew out of her negative experiences with the academy. She argues that writing is a form of inquiry. The academy disciplines and polices the writing styles it allows. If we change the way we write, we challenge the academy's control over us. In so doing, we help form alternative interpretive communities that nurture our emergent selves.

Elizabeth Adams St.Pierre shows how her understandings of a group of older White southern women shifted and changed as she took up different writing practices. Drawing on Foucault and using Deleuze and Guattari's notions of the rhizome, the fold, the nomad, and the haecceity, she outlines a set of ethical-writing practices for the seventh (and sixth) moments. Reworking Foucault, these practices and ethical principles direct the scholar to abandon negative, unitary thinking while developing political practices based on processual action models. Such models value disjunction, and difference, and see individuals as the products of systems of power.

Positioning herself as a nomadic researcher, she rediscovers Richardson's insight that writing is a way of knowing. Drawing on Ruth Behar (1996), St.Pierre observes that rhizomatic, nomadic writing practices, in fact, write their authors, producing "hybrid genres like self-ethnography and ethnobiography" (Behar, 1996, p. 26), in short reflexive ethnography. St.Pierre reminds us that writing is not an innocent practice. It is always ethical, and always political.

REFERENCES

Behar, R. (1996). *The vulnerable observer: Anthropology that breaks your heart.* Boston: Beacon.

Ellis, C., & Bochner, A. (2000). Autoethnography, personal, narrative, reflexivity. In N. K. Denzin & Y. S. Lincoln (Eds.), *Handbook of Qualitative Research* (2nd ed., pp. 733-768). Thousand Oaks, CA: Sage.

Kincheloe, J. L., & McLaren, P. (2000). Rethinking critical theory and qualitative research. In N. K. Denzin & Y. S. Lincoln (Eds.), *Handbook of Qualitative Research* (2nd ed., pp. 279-313). Thousand Oaks, CA: Sage.

Richardson, L. (2000). Writing: A method of inquiry. In N. K. Denzin & Y. S. Lincoln (Eds.), *Handbook of Qualitative Research* (2nd ed., pp. 923-948). Thousand Oaks, CA: Sage.

Rosaldo, R. (1989). *Culture & truth.* Boston: Beacon.

Visweswaran, K. (1994). *Fictions of feminist ethnography.* Minneapolis: University of Minnesota Press.

CHAPTER 1

Research as Relationship

——

Deborah Ceglowski
University of Minnesota

This article explores the author's multiple relationships with the Head Start staff and children at Wood River. The text is presented in a story-narrative form. Interspersed are the Head Start teacher's comments about an earlier draft of this article. There are three aspects of these relationships that the author explores. The first is the relationships among researchers' multiple community memberships when conducting research. The second is the relationships with mentors who guide researchers in how they conduct their investigations. The third entails the author's relationships with the Wood River staff and children. These relationships do not follow a smooth path; rather, they shift over time and from one moment to the next based on the context at hand.

A year before I begin my research at the Wood River Head Start in a rural midwestern town, I am sitting in a classroom at the University of Illinois. The windows are open because it is warm and we all know that Norm will want a smoke. A few minutes after 2 o'clock, Norman Denzin, unkempt long gray hair, dressed in old baggy shorts and shirt and $2 rubber thongs, reading glasses around his neck, pack of Camels hanging out of his pocket, enters and sits down. His watercolor blue eyes study those of us sitting in front of him. He pulls out a cigarette, lights it, and in his booming voice, tells us this story:

> Right after I think it was Kennedy died, I was sent out to interview people. As I went house to house, I met people crying, unable to talk. Christ, I didn't have the heart to ask them the survey questions. I realized that I didn't believe in what I was doing. It was then, in this epiphany, that I decided there had to be a different way of doing research. It was then that I started to think about qualitative work.

As Norm finishes this story, he looks out and smiles at me. Perhaps it is the combination of the story, the smile, and the autumn leaves rustling through the open windows that make this memory so vivid. Yet, I now know that Norm's story calls me to enter the lived experience of those I study. With his help, I plan to conduct my study about how Head Start staff interpret policies by participating in the daily events at a local center. What I do not realize is what doing research in this way entails. I do not understand what it feels like to enter into the lives of Head Start families and staff.

My previous writing focuses on my research at Wood River Head Start and uses short stories as a research writing genre (Ceglowski, 1997, 1998a, 1998b). My study investigates how Head Start staff interpret and implement official policies and create a local set of policies. I use short stories to invite the reader into the mundane and extraordinary events at the program. The stories are evocative texts (Richardson, 1994) that expand traditional policy analysis writing genres.

These accounts hint at, but do not specifically address, the emotional pulls I encounter during this study. They are masks that partially hide my behavior and feelings about activities at Wood River and my attachment to the children and disagreements with the staff. The emotional memories of my work with the children and staff draw me now to examine in greater depth how I conduct research. They do not let go.

My experiences at Wood River force me to think in "personal terms about the social science I do" (Krieger, 1991, p. 2). I am flooded with feelings of caring and concern, guilt, insensitivity, and deceit. My research training does not erase or lessen these feelings (Bochner, 1997). These feelings draw me to talk about my relationships with the Wood River Head Start program staff. They draw me back to talk in more honest and forthright ways with Judy Roberts, the Wood River teacher, about how I behave as a researcher/volunteer/friend/consultant and what she learns from participating in a research project.

Some might call it a confessional tale (Van Maanen, 1988). I prefer the term *unofficial text*. Unofficial texts (Bloom, 1998; Bochner, 1997; Ellis, 1995; Richardson, 1995; Ronai, 1992; Whyte, 1996) present the researchers in much the same way as they portray those they study—human and fallible, good and bad. Researchers no longer escape their own ruthless gaze. The gaze is turned inward. Instead of asking others about their lives, researchers begin to ask others about our lives as researchers. We take seriously the challenge "how we can learn from other people's descriptions of ourselves" (Rosaldo, 1987, p. 91). Those at the research site begin to tell us juicy tales about our work.

This article is titled "Research as Relationship" because ethnographic research is based on relationships. There are three aspects of these relationships that I explore in this article. The first is the relationships among researchers' multiple community memberships when conducting research. Some of my community memberships include teacher, parent, Head Start consultant, researcher, and volunteer. As I work at Wood River, these memberships influence my viewpoint of the children and staff. These memberships shape my emotional, physical, and cognitive experiences with the Head Start staff and children (Bochner & Ellis, 1996).

Second, researchers have relationships with mentors that guide them in how they conduct their research. Denzin (1997), my research director, and Graue (1993), a member of my dissertation committee, encourage me to join in the lived experience of the staff. Others with whom I study instruct me to maintain distance (Glesne & Peshkin, 1992).

The other aspect of research relationships entails my relationships with the Wood River staff and children. These relationships do not follow the smooth path, as often is portrayed in the literature, of gaining access and developing rapport and trust (Glesne & Peshkin, 1992; Lincoln & Guba, 1985). Rather, they shift over time and from one moment to the next based on the context at hand. There is no continuity in these relationships. They reflect the complexity of other human endeavors—emotions, contradictions, dilemmas, and tensions. These three aspects of relationships intertwine in the following narrative. They are not separate strands but rather vines that entangle each other.

I use the present tense throughout the article. Research texts are written in the past tense, indicating that the studies are complete. By using the literary present tense, I invite the reader into the present moment. I am creating this text now. It represents my present-day understanding.

A RESEARCHER'S NIGHTMARE

My story begins when I finish my graduate courses and return home to begin my research. I talk to the Head Start director about my plan to study how Head Start staff interpret policies. I ask for a job as an aide in one of the programs. An aide position is an ideal way in which to get the inside scoop on staff's perceptions of policy. After 10 years of consulting with this Head Start agency, I think that the agency owes this to me. It is unfathomable that the director will refuse this request. The director hesitates. She does not want me to come in for a year. She is not interested in a pseudo-aide/researcher. She needs someone at the program that can wash the dishes and ride the bus.

I am familiar with the arguments that research in my "backyard" entails certain risks. My previous alliances with program administrators and some staff, and my prior knowledge about the program, might skew what I observe. My former identities with the program might influence what is shared or hidden from me (Glesne & Peshkin, 1992). On the other hand, I have a sense of long-term connection and commitment to Head Start, and these relationships draw me to this program as a research site. These "collaborative, reciprocal, trusting, and friendly relations" (Denzin, 1997, p. 275) might prove to be solid base for this investigation.

The director worries about what I will write. She asks whether she can comment on it. I do not answer her. That is because I know there are things that I will not want to share. I have just completed an interview study with Head Start administrators and teachers at her agency. I do not share the study with the administrators because the director would not approve of what I wrote. Although I present the administrators' viewpoints, my sympathies are with the teachers. I sometimes wake up at night in a sweat worrying what would happen if she or the executive director would read the article. It is published in a journal. I do not tell her. Head Start directors do not read research journals, but the uneasiness stays with me.

I recall Ellis's (1995) haunting story of returning to the fishing community where she conducts research. The residents learn about what she writes from a professor. Many residents are angry with her for sharing personal details about their lives. Her relationships are shattered, and the friends that welcome her do so in a different manner. She breaks the trust with the community. My worry is that I broke the trust with the Head Start administrators when favoring the teachers' viewpoint in my salary study.

My friend and program administrator, Martha Calle, intervenes and argues that I am entitled to apply for an aide position. She supports her position by citing the high turnover in these low-level positions. An aide job is open in Wood River, and I am called for an interview. I walk into the interview self-assured and confident that I will get the position.

Everything is going just as I had planned. Then a parent member of the interview team asks me, "Why are you applying for this job with all your qualifications?"

I fumble, "I believe in Head Start and what goes on here. I want to be a part of it." I do not tell the interview team about my research project. Only the administrators know about that.

Martha adds, "During the year, Deb will conduct research. If she isn't offered the job, she will volunteer her time."

I freeze, caught in a researcher's nightmare. If there had been a deep hole in the room, I would crawl in. As soon as the interview is over, I quickly exit the room. Martha calls me later to say that they offered the job to someone else. Judy Roberts, the teacher, "is more comfortable with you as a volunteer, not an aide."

I am ashamed of my behavior. My bubble of arrogance bursts into pieces. But I do not call Judy and the parent to apologize for fooling them. The thought briefly enters my mind. I treated them badly, but I do not want to dwell on it. Let it pass. Lie under the carpet. I will make amends by volunteering at Wood River.

WHO AM I?

In September, I drive to Wood River and volunteer. The former teacher/volunteer/research community memberships are not good matches. I am used to being in charge, not following someone else's directions. I cringe when Judy reprimands a child harshly. "This is not how to talk to children!" I say to myself. It is hard to participate in this. Other times, we are walking outside and I am holding a child's hand as we look at Halloween decorations. This is comfort. It feels good.

Judy knows of my work with the agency and worries that the administrators will expect me to keep an eye on things. She tells me, "They won't come around as much. They expect you to report back." She is right. I am a resident spy. The administrators say to me, "I know you can't say much, but how are things going?" I tell them something, but not much: "We are still waiting for the room divider in the gym."

Judy tells me now, "Happy that you didn't go back and spy for the administrators." Her comment comforts me.

The administrators' questions make me uneasy. I am on a tightrope, worried that if I don't tell the administrators something, they will withdraw their support for my research. On the other hand, I don't want to report on the Wood River staff. We all know this is a research no-no.

As I help out at Wood River and talk with the staff, I align myself with their understanding of how the program operates. They are frustrated by the lack of administrative response to their needs and concerns. We have to cancel the program during the first week because the office cannot find a sub for the bus driver. Everyone at Wood River is fuming. I join in the complaining.

My alignment with the administrative perspective is weakening. If I were to be honest in responding to the administrators' queries about the program, then I would advocate for the Wood River staff. I would tell them how difficult it is to share rooms with another program. How we wait in the hallway for the other program to finish up. When we enter the classroom, there are dirty dishes in the sink and stinky diapers in the trash. The other programs in the building treat us like second-class citizens. We are powerless. But the administrators make these arrangements. If I talk in this honest way, then I question their decisions. They will not like what I say. I hold back.

I think about McLaren's (1991) study within a school system. There is controversy among the teaching staff about his work, and he ends up leaving the site. I worry that this could happen to me as well. When I am at Wood River, I align myself with the staff. When the administrators see me, I feel my stomach churn. My answers to their questions often are evasive. Even though they know that I cannot say much, they keep asking.

At the end of the 2 weeks, Judy adds my name to the staff list. She says that it is much easier with me around. She calls me the "extra pair of hands." Throughout the year, Judy relies on my presence to help out. I sub for her and other staff, prepare materials, lead children's games, monitor the boys' room, clean up, and help with art projects and lessons. Adding my name to the staff list signals the permanence of my presence during the 1st year. It also signals to me that Judy has expectations that I will show up consistently. It is both a privilege and a commitment to join the staff in this way.

I feel like an accepted part of the staff. But I really am not. I hide my research from the staff. I run to the women's room during the day to take a few notes. I worry that the notebook will fall out of my pocket. One day in the midst of my mad jotting in the women's room, I look around and start to laugh. Here I am, sneaking off for a few quick notes. Sneaking off and hiding my research. It reminds me of trying to hide my research during the interview. I leave the notebook at home.

Judy now tells me, "Didn't feel you were being deceitful being there. Didn't know that you felt that you had to sneak off and keep notes. Why did you have to sneak off and do it? Would be better if had told me and kept them in the classroom." I tell her that I wanted to fit in and that Head Start folks don't stop and make notes all day long.

Leaving the notebook at home makes me queasy. I search the literature for help. I find that Lubeck (1985), in her study of a Head Start program, did the same thing. She tries keeping notes on-site and realizes, like I do, that it interferes with understanding what is going on. She tells the staff that if they will let her, she will just help out. Her words comfort me. At the same time, I rush to my computer as soon as I finish my daily volunteering. My afternoon is consumed with fieldnotes and logs. It is like two different monkeys on my back, chatting incessantly. One argues, "Join in the fun. Don't worry about the fieldnotes." The second monkey warns me that I must keep accurate notes and maintain objectivity while at Wood River (Ceglowski, 1993).

Tedlock (1991) states that ethnographic fieldwork is in a period of transition. Participant observation, joining in the experiences of others and then writing about it from an objective stance, is making way for the observation of participation. New ethnographers enter the lived experience of others and write from that mutual perspective. "Ethnographers both experience and observe their own and others' coparticipation within the ethnographic encounter" (p. 69). There are no firm guidelines for this new way of conducting research.

But the new version lacks guidelines. It does not provide the security of well-established methods. Some argue that it is not solid or valid research. Those who venture on this path face more difficulties than do researchers who adhere to traditional mores. This new version demands that "we chart new paths rather than constantly return to well-worn roads and point out that they will not take us where we want to go" (Tierney, 1998, p. 68).

I feel torn by the old and new versions. The need to create an "accurate" record and the wish to "actively enter the worlds of the interacting individuals and to render those worlds understandable from the point of view of those studied" (Denzin, 1989, p. 270). The new version is more appealing. It is the higher and nobler ground. The old version is safer. I am steeped in certain research protocols about obtaining access, developing trust, and conducting studies (Rose, 1990). This is how successful researchers operate. The older version produces more publishable texts.

I do not talk about my research with the Wood River staff. The staff never ask me about what I am doing. I rationalize my silence. Ellis (1995) writes that even when people know about what a researcher does, it has little relevance to their everyday lives. But this really is a mask to hide behind. I did not want to have an ongoing conversation about my research. I am supposed to know what I am doing. The truth is that most of the time I do not have a clue. I am embarrassed to share this with the staff. They share their frustrations and troubles with me. I am silent about my research troubles. How would they judge this confession? I hold onto my fragile sense of control and plow ahead, often aimlessly.

FALLING IN LOVE

I get to know the children and families including a 4-year-old farm boy who lives outside of Wood River. The summer before my volunteering begins, I pass him as I walk with my friend Martha. He plays outside with his two brothers. The farm has the look of rural poor—graying wood and older vehicles parked in a dirt driveway alongside the house.

Martha and I wave to the boys. They sometimes stop and look at us, but they don't wave back. They are part of the landscape. In the fall, I start volunteering at Wood River. The bus driver, Gary Neilson, and I talk about the Head Start families, and he describes a farm family that lives along the Wood River. Suddenly, the nameless farm boy is transformed into Steven, who sits next to me at breakfast. He is in the boys' room with me every morning. I hold the water on for him and pass him a paper towel. I watch him in music class when he hides his head in his lap and doesn't sing. I worry about him, and Judy reassures me, "He was like that when he first came here. He will get over it in time."

Judy tells me that Steven's father is away at college and his mother deserted her husband and sons several months ago. The boys live with their elderly grandparents. Steven tells Judy and me that he "misses his mom every day." We do not know what to tell him. What do you say to a 4-year-old who wants to see his mom? We pray that his absent mother will set up a visit with her sons. Halfway through the year, Steven tells us that he will get to see her for a weekend visit. We are relieved.

When Martha and I walk by the farmhouse later in the fall, I wave at Steven's brother. The next day, I tell Steven that I went by his house. He says, "I know. I saw you walking there too."

Steven humbles me. After 20 years of consulting with Head Start administrators and staff, I think I know the program. Until then, Steven and his family were Head Start statistics. Numbers that are used politically to support more services for more nameless impoverished families. But they are faceless children and families. The faceless children do not sit next to me day after day saying that they "miss their moms."

I ride the bus with Gary, the bus driver. My hometown, where I have lived for 13 years, is transformed. The Head Start families live up the street from me. I "discover the once invisible [people] who lived throughout" (Weinstein-Shr, 1992, p. 166), in my case children and families living in poverty. My small town community, reminiscent of Garrison Keiller's Lake Wobegon, is gone. The outward appearance of middle-income lifestyle is ruptured by this new knowledge. The town no longer is a middle-class haven from the midsized city 3 miles away. There are people living in poverty.

Their quiet poverty invades my neighborhood. I no longer am ignorant.

Then I meet 4-year-old Brian, and he invades my heart. With his long blonde curly hair and deep blue eyes, he is a look-alike version of my own son.

Judy leads us on a walk in the woods behind the classroom. There is a steep section, and Brian holds tightly to my hand. He says, "I'm gonna fall." I tell him, "I'll hold you. It will be okay." I encircle his back with my left hand and stoop down to help him over the steep parts. I remember what it was like to walk with my son, Jim, years ago. I glance down at this Jim look-alike. I am confused. Brian is both my son and the child who lives with his mother and brothers in a run-down apartment. He is the child whose mother often is not home when Gary returns him at the end of the day. Ruth tells us of the bus driver, "You should just see his face when we pull into the yard and she is not there." Ruth and Gary ride around town until they can find someone on Brian's emergency list to leave him with.

I hold him in my lap during story time. Judy looks at Brian and says, "Couldn't you just take him home and keep him?"

He comes home with me. He is there as I look at my adolescent son. Brian pulls at my "mother-heart." But wait! I am a researcher, not his mother. [Bracket these feelings.] I write down what Brian says. When I tell my husband how it felt to hold Brian's hand, I start to cry. I tell him how Brian asks about Disneyland. "Mom says Mickey Mouse lives there. Right, Deb?" I tell him that's right. He tells me, "I wanna go there." I want to pack him up and take him there.

I feel guilt about my own son, who at Brian's age had been to the Magic Kingdom twice. I write a story about Brian and my son. I give it to Judy to read. When she gives it back to me, she says, "You are a real soft heart." She is right. Despite my researcher training and 20 years of teaching experience, I am a soft heart. But it wasn't until volunteering at Wood River that I experienced what it means to be a soft-hearted researcher. I am back in the classroom at the University of Illinois again listening to Norman Denzin telling me that he did not have the heart to ask people questions following Kennedy's death. I am walking with him now.

This is not something that you read about in a journal. It is a "my-connection" to the children and the staff. It gets under your skin. I am peeling back the layers of my formal Self, the researcher Self (Ronai, 1992). The feelings well up in my throat when Brian asks me to hold his hand. It's the gut reaction to hearing Ruth tell about Brian's expression when they pull into his yard and his mother isn't there. It is the caring connection of sitting next to Steven and hearing him say, "I miss my mom."

I had little preparation to understand how personally attached I become to the Wood River children. I know that long-term studies draw researchers emotionally, physically, and intellectually (Bochner & Ellis, 1996) into the lives of others. Researchers make themselves available for interactions with those studied to form relationships and friendships and to listen to the stories told and retold at the research site (Denzin, 1994). From this perspective, researchers write about the world as they experience it. These explanations are merely words. They strip away Steven's smile and his head bent into his lap during music time.

I search the research and educational philosophy literature for words to describe my feelings for Brian and Steven. I cannot find any concepts that are adequate. Years later, I stumble across the concept of caring relation. A caring relation "assumes a relational, or connective, notion of the Self, one that holds that the Self is formed and given meaning in the context of its relations with Others" (Witherell & Noddings, 1991, p. 5). A caring relation assumes a sense of connected knowing, a knowing that "carries with it an intimacy that presumes a sharing of Self and Other, a felt relation between knower and known" (Helle, 1991, p. 54).

This concept is the closest one that I can find. Yet, the words read hollow—"a relational, or connective, notion of the Self." This is pure antiseptic compared to listening to Brian and Steven. This is scholarly text. These abstract words strip away the feelings. Richardson (1995) states that theory and lived experience are at odds. The power of lived experience lies in our feelings and emotions. It is deeply personal and comes from our inner being. Yet, the world of theory is abstract. Theories are about ideas, not personal stories. They homogenize the experiences of many into concepts. The stories are gone.

CAUGHT IN A RESEARCHER MUDDLE

I worry that my attachment to the children will unduly influence my interactions at Wood River and how I write about the program. It smacks of the forbidden researcher identity "gone native." "In the process, the investigator's objectivity is weakened, if not destroyed" (Shaffir & Stebbins, 1991, p. 145). To what will this attachment lead? Can I learn to trust it "to guide me to do what is right in relation to those I study?" (Hatch, 1995, p. 221). I do not know.

Mark, the finicky eater, illuminates the difficulty of this attachment. Mark, a redheaded 3-year-old, enters school hungry and eats most of his breakfast food. At lunch, 2½ hours later, he often announces, "I am not gonna eat it." Mark likes breakfast foods better than lunch foods. These items seldom are served. Although other children do not eat much at lunch, Mark is the most vocal about his complaints. Two other girls eat practically nothing at lunch. But they are quiet. They do not complain loudly the way in which Mark does. When he asks for seconds of a favorite food, especially fruit, we tell him that he has to try another food before he gets more. Judy tells Mark that he has to try one of the food items before he can have dessert. If he does not eat, then she does not give him dessert and tells him that he "can't have one today."

On a day when I am visiting another Head Start program, Judy starts an eating program for Mark. When I return, she tells me, "Yesterday Mark ate a bit of potatoes and meat. I told him if he didn't eat, he couldn't go outside. He put the potatoes in his mouth and looked like he was going to gag. I told him, 'If you gag and throw up, you can't go outside either.' He chewed it, and then I gave him a piece of meat. Later, when he came back to the room, he told a friend that I had given him some more meat and that he drank his milk too."

Judy explains that she thinks it is important for Mark to have a "bite of protein" every day. I go numb. Just a few days ago, we share how we ignore our own children's finicky eating behavior. Before lunch that day, Mark starts to cry in the classroom. At lunch, he gags when Judy cuts a small slice of meat and tells him that he has to eat it. During the next week, Mark gags and vomits during lunch. He often cries in the classroom before we go to the cafeteria. It is difficult to sit next to him, and whenever I have the choice, I choose not to sit at the table with Judy and Mark.

I come face to face with the dilemma that my friend, Mary Starr Whitney, poses: "What will you do if you see something that you don't agree with?" I respond, "My job is to understand what is going on. Not to change it." Perfect researcher response. It misses the mark completely. I am now sitting beside Mark. No matter how many pages of fieldnotes I write or how many entries I make in my log, I cannot escape my feelings (Hatch, 1995).

I call my adviser, Daniel Walsh, for advice. I expect that he will agree with me that Judy's approach is wrongheaded. He, the experienced researcher, will know exactly what to do and set me straight. My head throbs as I tell him what is happening. Daniel tells me a story about a child he once had in his classroom. He tells me that the child was sickly and did not eat well, so Daniel set up an eating program for this child. The child reacted as Mark does, gagging and vomiting. Over time, the child's eating behavior changed, and he became healthier. Daniel challenges me to rethink my personal reaction to Judy's approach and take a broader view of the situation. I understand Daniel's rationale. But he is not in my shoes, sitting next to Mark crying and gagging.

Judy tells me now, "Love the part when you called Daniel and he agreed with me. But what Daniel did was different. I had Mark taste the food." She is right. What they did was different. But in my discomfort, I place them both in the "force the kids to eat" camp.

Torn between what Daniel tells me, my discomfort in watching Mark, and the larger aim to write my dissertation, I decide to halfheartedly go along with Judy's approach.But there is no halfhearted way in which to participate in this plan. Judy goes on vacation, and Mark sits next to me. Although I am tempted to forget the new eating program, I know that it will make it more difficult for Mark when

Judy returns. I tell him that he has to try a bite of a new food, and I hold his hand. He gags and cries. The tears stream down his face. His voice cracks, "Deb, I don't wanna eat it." I sit with him after the other children have left the lunchroom. When he finishes, I give him stickers and write to his mother, telling her that he tried a new food.

The finicky eater incident raises for me the difficulty in separating my researcher Self from my other Selves (e.g., teacher, parent, consultant) that I bring with me to the study (Ronai, 1992). It disrupts the notion that the researcher has one identity (Rodriguez, 1998). My researcher Self focuses on interchanges with Mark and the changes in his eating pattern. I talk with Judy and listen to her rationale for the plan. At the same time, I don't want to be implicated in witnessing Mark's struggles. It is painful to see him. I co-conspire in this new plan. I work against myself and what I think is right. I justify this in the name of the research project. I turn the anger inward against myself.

The outcome of Judy's plan is just as Daniel predicts. Mark learns to taste foods on his own. Six weeks after the program begins, he samples most of the foods on his plate. However, my discomfort with the plan does not diminish. The outcome does not justify the process.

From a researcher perspective, I can observe and write about how the staff (including me) handle Mark. My stance as a researcher might be correct, but from a human perspective, it feels wrong (Bochner, 1997).

Judy tells me forcefully, "No idea that you were so upset about Mark. Why the hell didn't you tell me? Why didn't you tell me that you thought it was wrong?" I tell her, because then I would not be a good researcher.

What it means to be a good researcher depends on your points of reference. Bloom (1998) suggests that researchers often are pulled by different research paradigms. Oakley (1981) encourages researchers to engage in friendly, honest, and forthright conversations. From this perspective, I could share my feelings with Judy. Yet another discourse, which includes feminist phenomenologists, admonishes researchers to be restrained in their responses and listen carefully to site workers.

The difference between researchers and Judy is that we write our own research autobiographies. We get to leave out when we act dishonestly, arrogantly, or harshly. These autobiographical tales are not censured. Typically, our research texts discuss research procedures, not process, and they describe the research site, not the complexity of our relationships with site workers.

How I decide what to share and keep secret from Judy is not addressed in methodology literature. Bloom (1998) states that interpretive researchers do not write about this issue but focus instead on the power that researchers have to exploit those they study. She continues by arguing that this silence must be analyzed and disrupted if feminist researchers are to write honestly about women's lived experience and the challenges of participatory research.

My fear is that Judy will ask me to leave.

RESEARCHER POWER

But I do not turn away from this struggle within me. I seek redemption. Although I do not directly challenge the eating plan for Mark, I do have the power to write about it. The authority of the researcher rises up within me. Using a story format and accompanying text, I explain my version of the story. I present the paper at three national research conferences. Before the first two conferences, Judy tells me that she worries that the audiences will see her as an "ogre." Although she does not come out and say it, I know that Judy does not want me to present the story. I do it anyway. Judy plans to come with me to the third research conference and talk about the story. A family conflict interferes with her plans, and I go alone.

Judy tells me, "When you went to the conference, I was afraid they would think I was an ogre. Maybe [I was] having a bad day. Not right not to bring out the story. [Some] 75% of teachers don't like some kids. [She is referring to Mark.] [I] shouldn't have sounded so harsh."

I explain why Judy starts the plan, but my sympathies lie with Mark. I cover my version with the objective description of the eating incidents and Judy's rationale for developing the "bite of protein" plan. The research audience knows my agenda. They question Judy's approach. I objectively explain her reasons. I tell them that Mark is eating foods on his own. This rationale masks my feelings. I don't fool anyone.

The dual discomforts of sitting next to Mark and my unresponsiveness to Judy's concerns stay with me. I am there again at the lunch table sitting next to Mark. He is crying, his hand in mine. I remind him, "You have to have a bite." It is a time when I disagree with Judy. I want to shout, "This is wrong!" I disappoint myself. I sit back and watch. I perform the very acts I abhor. That eating plan becomes my eating plan. My hands are busy writing fieldnotes and holding out a fork to Mark telling him, "You have to try this."

Judy's voice calls out, "They'll think I'm an ogre." She really is saying, "You think I am an ogre." That is closer to the truth. I don't like who Judy is in this story. I take my power as a researcher/writer and share my story. This is the traditional power identity of researchers. I miss the opportunity to acknowledge my power as a researcher and question how I use it (Tierney, 1998).

Ellis (1995) suggests that researchers ask themselves how they would feel if their descriptions were applied toward them. Judy's worry about being called an ogre is valid. I miss an opportunity to discuss more openly with her and other staff what and how I portray the daily events at Wood River. This discussion differs from merely asking staff to comment about the stories I write. The staff could "challenge my interpretations" and negotiate with me "the ultimate decision about whether to include sensitive information" (Ellis, 1995, p. 88).

Judy remarks, "You said that it was a hollow victory when you brought the story to the conferences."

Judy is right. It is a hollow victory. It is hollow because I fear her anger if I tell her my reaction to her eating plan. Likewise, Bloom (1998) doesn't share her anger at a respondent's remarks about Israel and Jewish Americans. In her writing, Bloom now questions whether her bonds with the respondent are so fragile. Perhaps there is space to share these emotions with others. It is chancy.

JUDY'S LEARNING AND ADVICE

When I ask Judy about talking about the research project when I was there, she tells me, "Glad that you didn't talk about the research. It would have made me nervous. Would have thought you're the one doing the research. Why are you asking us?"

If I talk about my research every day, then perhaps Judy and I would share our nervous feelings. Perhaps I would tell her that I often do not know what I am doing. I would ask Judy for her feedback. Yet,

Judy tells me that might have made her nervous. Sharing our unpleasant feelings on a daily basis might have been uncomfortable. It might have been more honest.

I ask Judy, "If I talked about the research with you at the end of each day, what could have happened?" She responds, "[I] would have discouraged you from writing some things. This would have missed the point. I would not have wanted to sound so harsh. I would have asked you to take out stuff that made me uncomfortable so that I would be more like the perfect teacher, not the human teacher."

I admire Judy. She wants to read my version of the story and reflect on it. Although she feels uncomfortable about what I write, she does not dismiss the descriptions as inaccurate or exaggerated. Although the descriptions sometimes are painful, she is open to learn from them. She does not hide from my version.

And how did my writing help Judy? She tells me after reading my book, "Sounded like a bitch to the kids sometimes in the book. Harsh. A couple of sentences. Wish hadn't said those things. Maybe the tone of voice was different. Wish I would have used a different choice of words. This is not hard to admit person to person, but reading it makes it harder. I think now before reacting. The book made me think about this. Helpful to me. More aware of how to react to things."

I am humbled that my writing provides Judy insight into her practice. I am struck that the times that are most difficult for me at Head Start, such as sitting next to Mark, help Judy to reevaluate her own practice. I learn to be more honest in sharing my reactions to her. She learns to think more about her reactions to the children. Our paths are not the same. This is not reciprocity as I imagine it to be. But it might be the beginning of a new journey.

NEW DIRECTIONS

To me, this new journey means talking with those we study in different ways. We bring to research sites skills and talents associated with the research process, but that does not prepare us for the task of developing relationships with those at the research site. Not only will people such as Judy teach me to interpret the phenomena I study, they will teach me how to research. And just as Judy teaches me about conducting research, my insights into her practice help her to understand her own practice.

When I ask Judy what she would tell me to do differently if I were to come again, she tells me, "Don't sneak off to do the writing. Want you to be more honest."

I take her words to heart, but they are difficult to hear. Would I now have the courage to tell her that I thought her plan for Mark was wrongheaded? I hope so. But I am not certain. I would face the fear again that I might be asked to leave the program. Will I have the courage to face that moment and fear? Only time will tell.

For Judy, the silent approach is not "more honest." Judy's anger is not that I disagree with her. She is angry because I do not have the courage to tell her about my feelings. During my years at Wood River, I expect Judy to be honest with me. I fail to return her trust. I cheat Judy and myself out of more fully feeling and understanding our different perspectives about children such as Mark.

Bracketing my feelings runs against the human grain. Fully human as I observe and interact with Judy, I produce manuscripts that appear as if I am sitting on the side, observing others. I inoculate my writing against my own feelings and emotional reactions. I often write about others' hardships and triumphs through a dream-like veil. It is time now to walk through the veil and tentatively grasp the hands that I study so closely.

REFERENCES

Bloom, L. R. (1998). *Under the sign of hope: Feminist methodology and narrative interpretation*. Albany: State University of New York Press.

Bochner, A. (1997). It's about time: Narrative and the divided Self. *Qualitative Inquiry, 3,* 418-438.

Bochner, A., & Ellis, C. (1996). Taking ethnography into the twenty-first century. *Journal of Contemporary Ethnography, 25,* 3-5.

Ceglowski. D. (1993). *Moving from observer to participant: Issues of distancing and subjectivity.* Paper presented at the Fifth Annual Qualitative Research in Education Conference, Amherst, MA.

Ceglowski, D. (1997). "That's a good story, but is it really research?" *Qualitative Inquiry, 3,* 188-201.

Ceglowski, D. (1998a). *Inside a Head Start center: Developing policies from practice.* New York: Teachers College Press.

Ceglowski, D. (1998b). Writing short stories. In M. E. Graue & D. J. Walsh (Eds.), *Studying children in context: Theories, methods, and ethics* (pp. 228-238). Thousand Oaks, CA: Sage.

Denzin, N. (1989). *The research act*. Englewood Cliffs, NJ: Prentice Hall.

Denzin, N. (1994). The art and politics of interpretation. In N. K. Denzin & Y. S. Lincoln (Eds.), *Handbook of qualitative research* (pp. 500-515). Thousand Oaks, CA: Sage.

Denzin, N. (1997). *Interpretive ethnography*. Thousand Oaks, CA: Sage.

Ellis, C. (1995). Emotional and ethical quagmires in returning to the field. *Journal of Contemporary Ethnography, 24*, 68-96.

Glesne, C., & Peshkin, A. (1992). *Becoming qualitative researchers: An introduction*. New York: Longman.

Graue, M. E. (1993). *Ready for what? Constructing meanings of readiness for kindergarten*. Albany: State University of New York Press.

Hatch, J. A. (1995). Ethical conflicts in classroom research: Examples from a study of peer stigmatization in kindergarten. In J. Hatch (Ed.), *Qualitative research in early childhood settings* (pp. 213-222). Westport, CT: Praeger.

Helle, A. (1991). Reading women's autobiographies. In C. Witherell & N. Noddings (Eds.), *Stories lives tell: Narrative and dialogue in education* (pp. 48-66). New York: Teachers College Press.

Krieger, S. (1991). *Social science and the Self: Personal essays on an art form*. New Brunswick, NJ: Rutgers University Press.

Lincoln, Y. S., & Guba, E. G. (1985). *Naturalistic inquiry*. Beverly Hills, CA: Sage.

Lubeck, S. (1985). *Sandbox society*. Philadelphia: Falmer.

McLaren, P. (1991). Field relations and the discourse of the Other: Collaboration in our own ruin. In W. Shaffir & R. Stebbins (Eds.), *Experiencing fieldwork: An inside view on qualitative research* (pp. 149-163). Newbury Park, CA: Sage.

Oakley, A. (1981). Interviewing women: A contradiction in terms. In H. Roberts (Ed.), *Doing feminist research* (pp. 30-61). London: Routledge.

Richardson, L. (1994). Writing: A method of inquiry. In N. K. Denzin & Y. S. Lincoln (Eds.), *Handbook of qualitative research* (pp. 516-529). Thousand Oaks, CA: Sage.

Richardson, L. (1995). Writing stories: Co-authoring "The Sea Monster"—A writing-story. *Qualitative Inquiry, 1*, 189-203.

Rodriguez, M. (1998). Confronting anthropology's silent praxis: Speaking of/from a Chicana consciousness. *Qualitative Inquiry, 4*, 15-40.

Ronai, C. (1992). The reflexive Self through narrative: A night in the life of an erotic dancer/researcher. In C. Ellis & M. Flaherty (Eds.), *Investigating subjectivity: Research on lived experience* (pp. 102-144). Newbury Park, CA: Sage.

Rosaldo, R. (1987). Where objectivity lies: The rhetoric of anthropology. In J. Nelson, A. Megill, & D. McCloskey (Eds.), *The rhetoric of the human sciences* (pp. 87-110). Madison: University of Wisconsin Press.

Rose, D. (1990). *Living the ethnographic life*. Newbury Park, CA: Sage.

Shaffir, W., & Stebbins, R. (Eds.). (1991). *Experiencing fieldwork: An inside view of qualitative research*. Newbury Park, CA: Sage.

Tedlock, B. (1991). From participant observation to the observation of participation: The emergence of narrative ethnography. *Journal of Anthropological Research, 47*, 69-94.

Tierney, W. (1998). Life history's history: Subjects foretold. *Qualitative Inquiry, 4*, 49-70.

Van Maanen, J. (1988). *Tales of the field: On writing ethnography*. Chicago: University of Chicago Press.

Weinstein-Shr, G. (1992). Learning lives in the post-island world. *Anthropology & Education Quarterly, 23,* 166-171.

Whyte, W. (1996). On the evolution of street corner society. In A. Lareau & J. Shultz (Eds.), *Journeys through ethnography* (pp. 9-74). Boulder, CO: Westview.

Witherell, C., & Noddings. C. (1991). Prologue: An invitation to our readers. In C. Witherell & N. Noddings (Eds.), *Stories lives tell: Narrative and dialogue in education* (pp. 1-12). New York: Teachers College Press.

— —

Deborah Ceglowski is an assistant professor of early childhood education in the Department of Curriculum and Instruction and is outreach coordinator for the Center for Early Education and Development at the University of Minnesota. She recently has published Inside a Head Start Center: Developing Policies From Practice. *Her research interests include interpretive studies of the impact of policies on Head Start teachers, parents, and children and employing alternative writing genres in research texts. She currently is partnered with three Head Start programs to study the impact of full- and half-day services on families transitioning from welfare to work.*

CHAPTER 2

Three Short Stories

— —

Christopher Dunbar, Jr.
Michigan State University

The following three short stories are part of a collection of stories writ-ten about the experiences of five African American male students enrolled in a Midwest alternative school. This alternative school was established to house students who have been described as incorrigible, disruptive, social misfits, and academically incompetent. The collec-tive stories included in this text are about students who have lived diffi-cult lives. This text reveals the "experiences of a sociologically con-structed category of people in the context of larger social-cultural and historical forces."[1] It is about students who have been forgotten; writ-ten off; and placed in foster care, detention centers, alternative schools, and, for some, juvenile prison. This approach provides insight into the lives of an increasing number of African American male students placed in alternative school environments.

NO NEW JORDANS

Roger was hyped up more than usual. Today, after school, his bio-logical parents were going to take him to buy a pair of the new Michael Jordan basketball sneakers (MJs) as well as other items that he desperately needed. His eager anticipation and anxiety reminded me of my youthful days just before Christmas. In his case, however, there was an additional twist involved. Roger was more excited that his "real" parents were going to pick him up because Roger lives in a foster home. In fact, his biological parents were ordered by the court not to have any contact with him. They were deemed unfit parents.

For many of us, it is a given that our parents would provide our needs. Consequently, this notion is taken for granted by many. I didn't sense this same vibe coming from Roger. I think two things were going on here with him that caused this heightened excitement. First, he wanted to have the new Jordans because they were expensive and *anybody* who was *anybody* as far as he was concerned had a pair. I am almost certain that these sneakers didn't represent anything having to do with improving his basketball game. The sneaks made a statement. With these sneakers he would become somebody. He may not necessarily become the next Michael Jordan; however, he would become somebody in his own eyes. Furthermore, he would become somebody in the eyes of his peers. Owning a pair of MJs served as a social and economic status indicator.

However, I think what is most important here is his perception that getting these sneakers from his "real" parents meant (to him) that they cared for him. His foster parents for whatever reason didn't buy the sneakers for him.

On this particular day, Roger was running around school, blurting out answers in class, talking about other kid's shoes, and being simply out of control. Many teachers were concerned that he was setting himself for a hard fall in the event that his parents didn't show up. It wouldn't have been the first time.

"My Mom's gonna' buy me those Jordans when skool let out. Dey gonna' pick me up afta' skool and buy me anythin' I want. Aa-ha look at yo' shoes dey all toe' up. Wait 'til yu see me tomorra' with my new shit and none a yaw niggas better step on em either," Roger said.

Soon the day had gone by and everybody, including most of the kids, had had just about enough of Roger. He had managed to get on the nerves of even the cafeteria lady who rarely says anything to anyone. I think it was his arrogance at just the idea of owning a pair of the Jordans. Oh the power of advertisement!

Most of the kids had left school by now but Roger was unaffected by the fact that his parents had not yet arrived to take him on his shopping spree. Soon Roger, the teacher's aid, and the assistant director were the only ones left in the building.

"Don't worry, dey comin'. Dey toll me dey was," he could be heard telling the teacher's assistant as she offered to walk with him to the bus stop.

It was time to leave the building. His parents were 2 hours late and it didn't appear that they were coming. Roger was angry and crying now because once again, they had let him down.

"Why do dey keypon doin' dis shit?" he cried.

Ms. C (support staff) walked him to the bus stop and waited until he boarded the bus and was headed in the direction of home.

The next morning Roger was one of the last students to arrive and he was wearing the same shoes he had on the day before. No new Jordans, no new jacket, no new nuthin'.

Most of the kids were smart enough not to say anything to him about it. I'm not sure whether it was because they too have been victims of constant broken promises or if they feared his response if anyone inquired or simply if they just didn't care. Most of the teachers had geared themselves up for an uproar knowing his possible reaction at yet another disappointment. As a result, the teachers were not saying much either.

"Where yo' new Jordans nigga. You talked all dat shit yestida'. I don't see yu wit' none on," blurts out Ticco. Ticco is a little bigger and unafraid of Roger. Now that Ticco has the issue stirred up, the rest of the kids begin to laugh and taunt Roger.

Roger charged toward Ticco and in a fit of anger grabbed a chair and tossed it in his direction. Ticco moved out of the way and a fight ensued. A staff member separated the two but the tone for the day had been set. Roger had problems in every class, including fights and cursing teachers. In general, he was completely out of control.

Was it Jordans or mom?

I last saw Roger in juvenile court, where he was given a sentencing date for his part in the crime of aggregated restraint using a deadly weapon. His attorney told me that he would be sentenced to juvenile prison for up to 5 years or until he reached the age of 21. Roger was 14.

DONE DEAL BABY BOY

It's 10:55 a.m. when I arrive at the courthouse. This building, only a few months back, was the scene of a fire bombing. An African American man, upset with a judge's decision, went into the courtroom and discharged firebombs. I walked in wondering if I would smell the remnants of a bomb. Would it smell anything like the gutted buildings I walked through after the Los Angeles riots? Memories of the event came to mind quickly as I placed keys, pen, and wallet into the plastic bread holder that served as a tray just before I walked through the metal detectors. Only once through this time, I thought, as I made it through without the buzzer going off, which would have resulted in the guards waving the magic wand across my person.

I wondered if I had anything in my pocket that could have been construed as a weapon as I walked through the door before reaching the archway housing the metal detectors. Such a strange thought in my head, considering the fact that I hadn't carried as much as a pocketknife in 30 years. Clearly, courtrooms, police, and attorneys, in most instances, have not been viewed as friends to many African Americans. This must account for the strange feelings going on in my head. I don't remember any visit to court as cause for comfort. This time was no exception!

The court officer pointed in the direction of Courtroom H, where Peter's sentencing hearing was to be held. I wasn't sure of the process. I came here because Peter asked me to. I saw a young Asian guy sitting alone holding a stack of manila folders with writing all over the cover. He wore a dark colored suit, lawyer shoes, and thick glasses that made him appear as though he had done a great deal of reading. I remember thinking about an undergraduate buddy who wore thick glasses and the way we used to tease him about reading every book in the library. He also became a lawyer. I'd choose him to represent me just on the strength of the thickness of his glasses.

The Asian guy had to be the attorney. He had that lawyer persona. In fact, he was the only person up there that fit the bill. The rest of the people were African Americans waiting for court to begin. They clearly were not dressed for the part, and none of them wore glasses.

African Americans were standing or sitting waiting for court to begin. This seems to be the case in any courthouse that I've ever visited. Anguish is generally the look and feel of the moment. It often drapes the faces of African Americans like a wet T-shirt as it accompanies us into courtrooms. There is a sense of impending doom.

"Is this where Peter Williams' hearing is?" I ask.

"Yes, I'm representing him. Are you his father?" the Asian man said.

"No, I'm a graduate student at the university doing research at the alternative school. I met Peter while doing research there. He asked me to come today for his hearing," I said.

"What is your relationship with Peter? What is the nature of alternative school? How long have you done work in this area? Do you think Peter is savable?" the attorney questioned.

I sensed that he wanted me to testify on Peter's behalf as a last ditch effort to save him from juvenile prison. Juvenile prison—hmm— at first when the fellas referred to juvenile detention as prison, I thought they were simply embellishing the term or simply adding the word *prison* to it (rather than using the word camp or youth authority) to make it sound tougher than it really is. However, the attorney also used the term juvenile prison. A frightening thought: juvenile prison. Kinda' throws out the notion of rehabilitation, innocence, redeemability, savability, or second chance! The attorney asked if I would say a few words on Peter's behalf.

"Certainly I would," I responded.

Peter's father appeared and a few minutes later, Peter's mother and grandmother arrive. The parents are not together. The father lives in a neighboring town. The attorney spoke with them briefly, then introduced us.

"Peter has talked about you. It is nice to meet you," Peter's mom said.

"I've asked Mr. Dunbar to speak on Peter's behalf and he has agreed to do so," the attorney said.

I spoke briefly with Peter's father who said, "Peter's not a bad kid. I think that if he's given another chance he'll straighten out. He knows this is it for him. If he gets another chance I believe he'll do right."

Court was running about 30 minutes late that morning. We sat still while our emotions ran rampant; we were filled with anxiety about the impending decision. Peter had been found guilty of gun possession. In addition, he was on probation and had a horrendous school report. Court convened and all of us took our seats. Peter's family sat on benches adjacent to the judge's podium while I found a seat on the back row facing the judge. The chamber was slightly larger than a matchbox. The judge sat above all of us and peered over his glasses while he looked down at his notes. He never appeared to look up to make eye contact with any family member or with me.

Moments later, Peter was escorted into Courtroom H by an officer that I recognized from the local school district. He was handcuffed and wearing an oversized coat with a look of despair riding on him like a saddle. Father, mother, and grandmother sat side by side silently praying that their boy would be given another chance while deep down inside they knew his chances were slim; he had no chance of being set free. The lawyer talked to me about the options.

"The best-case scenario is Peter getting intensive probation. The worse case would be that he could get up to 3 years in juvenile prison. Once sentenced, it is up to the institution to determine how much of the sentence Peter must serve. We're trying to dig ourselves out of a hole here," the lawyer said.

I was called to the witness stand.

"Do you swear to tell the whole truth and nothing but the truth?" the clerk said.

"I do," I answered.

"You may be seated."

The attorney began to ask a battery of questions about my research and other issues, many of which we'd discussed in the lobby.

Peter's lawyer: Mr. Dunbar, in light of the fact that Peter is 13 years old, do you think he is savable?

Author: Yes, I do. There are a number of programs for kids just like him where they can receive positive behavior reinforcement. They can learn to be responsible. They can interact with positive role models. I have made contact with the local Urban League and another agency and they both indicate that he could participate in their respective programs.

Peter's lawyer: Is there anything that you'd like to add, Mr. Dunbar?

Author: Only that of all the students that I interviewed, Peter seemed to be the most mature. He answered all my questions and was very helpful with respect to shedding light on issues around this alternative school environment. The other kids seem to look up to him. If his energy was directed in a positive vein, I think he could become a responsible youngster.

Judge: Are there any more questions for Mr. Dunbar?

State attorney: No your Honor.

Judge: You may take a seat.

The judge motioned with a nod in the direction that I should go to step down from the elevated witness stand. He never made actual eye contact with me; rather, he peered over the top of his glasses.

The attorneys presented their closing remarks.

State attorney: Your Honor . . . in light of the current charges and for the safety of the community as well as Peter's own safety, the state recommends that Peter Williams be remanded to the custody of the Department of Corrections.

The state rests its case.

Peter's lawyer: Your Honor, Peter is 13 years of age. We recognize the severity of the crime; however, the gun was not loaded. . . . Peter, except for the time when he lived with his father, obeyed the conditions of his probation. In light of the information about community agencies with programs to help mentor Peter, we ask that the sentence be intensified probation so that this youth can have an opportunity to become a responsible person.

The defense rests.

Judge: I have heard both arguments.

Tears began to roll down the faces of both parents and the grandmother. I studied the judge as he went on with his decision. Never once did he look at the parents. It was as though they were invisible. Peter's family already knew the verdict. So did I.

Judge: Peter has a good report from the detention center while he was locked up.

My ears fix on the words *locked up* because I sensed that the judge was trying to convey a message. We all knew that when Peter was in the detention center he was locked up. For the judge to say "good report . . . while locked up" clearly indicated that he intended to keep him locked up.

Judge: However, his public school record from last May before he was sent to the alternative school is atrocious.

I remember thinking about an interview with Peter when he indicated that the security guards from his home school used to harass and taunt him, talking about his mother and family. But there was no mention of this. This boy does not wear a halo by any means, but clearly only one side of the story was being told here. The judge then read his school record from the alternative school.

Judge: His record there is abominable: on September 4 . . . insubordinate, on September 8 . . . cursing, on September 10 . . . fighting.

And on and on. I sat there reflecting on the behavior of the 20 or so kids who attended the alternative school. This same report could be used to describe the behavior of at least 15 of those kids by simply changing the name on the top of the page. Peter was made to appear as a menace to society, an aberration of the worst kind, a child that was not worth redeeming. When the judge read his report from the alternative school, my head began to pound because the description of Peter's behavior indicated by the report was the same behavior exhibited by most of the students most of the time. Everything inside me screamed, "Judge, most of the kids at the school fit this bill."

Judge: It is the opinion of this court that gun possession is a serious offense, loaded or unloaded. He is a danger to the community, to himself, and to the police, who would have no way of knowing whether a gun is loaded or not. Further, it is clear that Peter has no intention of cooperating in school, as indicated by his record, and his parents are unfit or unable to provide, other than financially, the care necessary to guide this boy. Therefore, it is the decision of this court that he be remanded to the custody of the Department of Corrections. You have the right to appeal pursuant . . .

Peter's family stood as soon as court was adjourned. They filed past me as I sat dumbfounded thinking about what I could have said differently or additionally to save this boy from prison. I didn't know that I would be asked to speak. Maybe I could have been better prepared. Perhaps I could have brought in some statistics on what happens to kids when they get caught up in the penal system at this age.

How it's almost inevitable that they end up with an adult criminal record before the age of 30.

"Judge, you're helping him become a real criminal," my insides screamed.

Somehow, I knew that I would be more involved than I had envisioned. I just wasn't prepared. I don't believe it would have made a difference anyway. This notion helps me better deal internally with this whole scene. My words fell on deaf ears. It was a done deal!

As the family walked in the direction of Peter, I could see the expression on his once young face. This was a youngster of 13 being treated as an adult (in the sense that he was held responsible for his actions) and wearing a stoic expression as though it had been painted on with the artistic touch of a Rembrandt.

I remembered the past Monday when we had talked and he had commented on the prospect of going to prison.

Peter: I ain't scared, I'll do the time. I ain't never cried. Usually kids start to cry. I won't cry, I'll do the time.

He appeared, this time, to have more creases in his forehead than a man 4 times his age. This kid was aging before my very eyes like a script out of the Twilight Zone. He stood and faced his escort so that the handcuffs could be placed around his small wrist and he mouthed the words, "Yaw gon' com' se' me for I go," to his father.

"When they taking ya?" Peter's dad asked.

Peter turned to his escort and asked, "When Ima leavin'?"

"Tomorrow morning," the escort replied.

His father nodded yes and the two of us walked toward the door. I paused for a minute and said, "Hang in there Peter, take care of yourself," while thinking, how do you tell a 13 year old on his way to prison to take care of himself?

His father thanked me for my feeble effort. I felt a sense of emptiness inside like my very soul had been gutted. A severe case of helplessness and a touch of hopelessness girdled me like a suit too small. As I walked down the stairs, Peter's grandmother was standing in the foyer, hands clasped, looking toward the sky. Her face depicted signs of horror, fear, pain, and worry concerning the well-being of her grandson. After all, it wasn't that long ago that she must have been teaching him how to walk.

"He really needs strict probation. That way, he'll take it seriously," I remembered her saying before we entered the courtroom.

It was a cold morning when I entered the courtroom, but now, as I darted past the metal detector and the double doors leading to the outside, the temperature felt as if had dropped another 20 degrees. I scurried to my car, unlocked it, hopped in, and drove in the direction of home. I felt my eyes swelling as I thought about the 13 year old that had just been sentenced to prison. Soon, tears rolled down my face thinking about all the things that had gone wrong in this boy's life. Thinking about the unsympathetic judge who viewed this child as a responsible adult. Thinking about what must have been going through the parents' minds as they watched their flesh and blood being sent away. Could they have been thinking about what they could have done to make the outcome different? Were they blaming only themselves for how things evolved? Their son was lost and turned out. I could feel the pain of mother, father, grandma, and even young Peter, now a manchild who fell prey to the tough guy image—who learned only how to survive in a world less kind to him.

Manchild, you don't have to cry
You entered a world where
Tears reflect weakness
But you've been trained well
You've been a devout soldier
Your face reveals the whole story
Manchild old before your time
What you gone' do when you grow
Old and have to face responsibility?
Manchild, how will your story be told?
Will it be "Manchild didn't cry?"
Manchild, you don't have to cry
Mama cried Daddy cried
Grandma cried too
Manchild, I cry for you!

DON'T STOP, DON'T STOP

One day it was slick and shiny like the surface of a recent oil spill, the next day you'd find it nappy and dried up like an abandoned cotton field. This was the condition you might find 14-year-old Bobby's hair on any given weekday. On occasion, it had been visibly dirty.

Baggy gear drapes his portly physique. He's stout, out of shape, full of conversation, and truly a nice kid once you get to know him; on second thought, maybe I discovered this once he got to know me. He has the street savvy of seasoned veterans many years his senior. This I quickly learned in a formal interview with him.

Author: Bobby, was anyone at your home to help you do homework and to make sure you were in bed at a reasonable time?

Bobby: Wat' yu' tryin' ta say Mr. Dumm bar, dat' dare's somtin' rong wit' my fam ly?

Bobby, you see, like most of the other kids in this school, has been interviewed, tested, incarcerated, restrained, denied, abused, lied to, and mislead so many times that he had developed a keen ear for what was being asked of him and how he should appropriately respond.

In the beginning of our relationship, I was simply another of an endless list of people who had come in and out of his life intruding into his private "bi ness." Intruders would leave without a hint of gratitude for his temporary unpacking of layers of protection against further abuse. This protection was necessary for survival in his lived experience. For this, he was given in return an assessment suggesting that his family was dysfunctional. He was made both sensitive and cunning as a result of interaction with outsiders.

He has an infectious smile that grabs hold of your insides, making it difficult to tell him no. He also has another side though (i.e., a short fuse that was easily ignited). Classmates would often tease him about being overweight or sometimes they'd tease him about an offensive odor that he'd have from time to time. He would quickly retort, "Dat ain't me smellin', it might be yo' Mama!"

He was extremely talkative and quite eloquent with his speech.

Bobby: Education is, like, for a Black man, you have to fight to stay free, you have to fight to have freedom, you got to fight to stay out of jail, you got to fight to get your education. That's for a Black man. For a White man, you don't got to do nothing but do it.

Never one at a loss for words—that's vintage Bobby.

On more than one occasion, I ran out of tape when recording a conversation with him and he'd quickly say, "Let's go git som moe."

He'd go with me to Radio Shack to pick up extra minicassettes and batteries. He began to ask me to buy him expensive toys that he would see while in the store.

Author: Man, do you think I'm made outta' money?

Bobby: Yu gots mony look at yo' ca!

Author: Man I ain't got no money. I'm just a poor student.

He didn't believe this and continued to ask me to buy him things. Each time I responded, "No money dude."

Finally, one day I told him about a lesson that I had learned as a youngster.

Author: Bobby, let me tell you something an ole' man told me one time.

Bobby: What's that?

Author: People like you much better when you don't keep asking them for things. Sometimes they'll even give you things without your having to ask—remember that for me will ya'?

Bobby didn't bother to comment. I don't really know what impact this lesson had on him but he slowed down with all his requests.

We went out to lunch a few times—like I said it was difficult to tell him no.

Bobby: Com' on Mr. Dumbar please, please! I gots a dolla' if you put a dolla' and fifty cents wit' it I could get dat combo meal.

Math was his strong suit. I often watched as he'd do math problems on the board. The problems were pretty basic but he was an eager participant in class—that is, when he knew the answer. This provided him the opportunity to show off his math abilities.

He's had more than his share of problems with the juvenile court system, as have most kids who attended this school. He was on probation. He often complained to me about his situation.

Bobby: Dey got me messed up. If I do anythin' rong dey can violate me an' sen' me to prison. Like da' udder night me an my boys wa jus' stannin' otside kickin' it wen' "five o'" (police) pulled up an' started messin' wit' us 'bout a curfew.

Author: Bobby, what time was it?

Bobby: 'Bout fowe in da moanin'.

Author: What night was this?

Bobby: Monday nite.

Author: What was yaw doin' out there that late?

Bobby: We wadn't doin' nuthin'!

I had several interviews with Bobby—certainly more than I had planned, but he was always so eager to talk. If another interviewee didn't come to school or if they decided they didn't want to talk on a particular day, Bobby was more than happy to fill in. He often had many interesting things to say.

By the end of the pilot study, I had several transcribed pages of quotable quotes from Bobby. I brought them to school one day to share the words he had shared with me.

"Bobby comere. I have something I want to show you," I said.

He ran over to me, curious about what I had in this notebook to show him.

"Look at what you said," I said as I showed him the thickness of the notebook filled with his words.

"Read it to me, read to me," he said with excitement.

"Education for a Black man means . . . " Reading his words, I stopped momentarily, thinking that he was reading over my shoulder.

"Don't stop, don't stop!" he exclaimed.

" No man," I said to him, "Let me hear you read your words."

I wanted to hear him read his own words. I wanted him to be proud of how bright he really was. This was important to me because he had always described himself as being slow. He said that his teachers told him that he was slow, and therefore he was slow.

"I don't learn as fast as the other kids," Bobby would tell me.

After I had asked Bobby to read he said, "Never mine' man" and walked away from me.

"Don't stop, don't stop" loosely translated means "I can't read!"

Last word I got on Bobby was that he had been run over by a car and had two broken legs. He was enrolled in the public high school—with minimal reading skills.

NOTE

1. See Richardson (1997, p. 14).

REFERENCE

Richardson, L. (1997). *Fields of play*. New Brunswick, NJ: Rutgers University Press.

— —

Christopher Dunbar, Jr., is a visiting assistant professor in the educational administration department at Michigan State University in East Lansing. His areas of interest include alternative education, education policy analysis, African American males and education, and qualitative research.

CHAPTER 3

Skirting a Pleated Text
De-Disciplining an Academic Life

——

Laurel Richardson
The Ohio State University

In this article, the author discusses the pleated text Fields of Play: Constructing an Academic Life, *a book that enfolds traditional and experimental papers within "writing-stories" about the contexts in which she wrote the papers. The author focuses on three examples about disciplines and academic departments, and concludes with commentary on the consequences to the self of enacting feminist-poststructuralist writing practices.*

F*ields of Play: Constructing an Academic Life* (Richardson, 1997) is the story of a woman's struggles in academia in the context of contemporary intellectual debates about entrenched authority, disciplinary boundaries, writing genres, and the ethics and politics of social scientific inquiry and presentation. The woman is myself, the story an embodiment of these issues. I hope the story resonates with those who are struggling to make sense of their lives in academia.

I believe that writing is a theoretical and practical process through which we can (a) reveal epistemological assumptions, (b) discover grounds for questioning received scripts and hegemonic ideals—both those within the academy and those incorporated within ourselves, (c) find ways to change those scripts, (d) connect to others and form community, and (e) nurture our emergent selves.

Applying my theoretical understandings to sociological writing, I asked, "How do the specific circumstances in which we write affect what we write?" "How does what we write affect who we become?" In answering these questions, I found that if I were to write the Self into being that I wanted to be, I would have to "de-discipline" my academic life.

What practices support our writing and develop a care for the self despite conflict and marginalization? What is (are) the ethical subject's relation to research practices? And, what about the integration of academic interests, social concerns, emotional needs, and spiritual connectedness?

Fields of Play explores these issues through what I call a "pleated text," traditional and experimental papers written over a period of 10 years folded between what I call "writing-stories"—about the contexts in which I wrote those papers. The pleats can be spread open at any point, folded back, unfurled.

Framing academic essays in writing stories displaced the boundaries between the genres of selected writings and autobiography, repositioning them as convergent genres that, when intertwined, create new ways of reading/writing. These ways are more congruent with poststructural understandings of how knowledge is contextually situated, local, and partial. At the beginning of the book, the writing-story is a personal story, framing the academic work. As the book progresses, distinctions between the personal and the academic become less clear. The last essay, "Vespers," stands in a section by itself, simultaneously a writing-story and a sociology-story, though I do not name a single sociological concept. In the genre of convergence, neither "work" nor "Self" is denied.

The present article is a (very) partial-story about the construction of *Fields of Play* and how writing it has changed me. I skirt around the text but enter one of its pleats: departmental politics as one context for writing and as a site of discipline. I provide three examples of departmental politics: (a) an excerpt from a writing-story about my own department; (b) the first act of a surrealist drama about a surreal, yet real, sociology department; and (c) an excerpt from multivoiced text, which builds community across departments and academic status.

The three examples span a decade. They are not a narrative of progress.

We are restrained and limited by the kinds of cultural stories available to us. Carolyn Heilbrun (1988) suggested that we do not imitate lives, we live "story lines." To the extent that our lives are tied to our disciplines, our ability to construct ourselves in other stories will depend on how the discipline can be deconstructed. Social scientific disciplines' story line includes telling writers to suppress their own voices; adopt the all-knowing, all-powerful voice of the academy; and keep their mouths shut about academic in-house politics. But contemporary philosophical thought raises problems that exceed and undermine that academic story line. We are always present in our texts, no matter how we try to suppress ourselves. We are always writing in particular contexts—contexts that affect what and how we write, and who we become. Power relationships are always present.

"AUTHORITY"

I began *Fields* with a writing-story called "Authority." Here is an excerpt:

I begin this collection, and my reflections on it, at the time when I found a different way of "playing the field," of exploring its boundaries and possibilities, and my life within it. This was the mid-1980s. No more children living at home; no major medical or family crises; a husband who liked to cook; friends; completion of a major research project and book tour; academic sinecure; and severe marginalization within my sociology department, which relieved me of committee work and of caring about outcomes. For the first time in my adult life, I had free time, playtime, time I could ethically and practically call "mine."

Like a medieval warlord who executes or banishes all who might pose a threat to his absolute authority, my newly appointed department chair deposed the three other contenders for the position, all men, from their "fiefdoms," their committee chairships. He stonewalled written complaints or queries. He prohibited public disagreement by eliminating discussion at faculty meetings. He abolished one of the two committees I chaired, the "Planning Committee," a site of open dialogue. He restricted the departmental Affirmative Action Committee's province, which I also chaired, to undergraduate enrollments. I publicly disagreed with him on his new affirmative action policy. Then, at the first university Affirmative Action Awards dinner, where I was being honored, surrounded by top university administration, my face making a face, repulsed, I shrugged his arm off from around my shoulder.

The chair hired a consultant, a well-known functionalist, to review faculty vitae. The consultant declared me "promising"—the chair told me as one might tell a student, not the full professor I was—but the consultant had also declared "gender research" a "fad." The chair advised me to return to medical sociology, a field I was "in" during a one-year postdoctorate, ten years earlier. Research it, teach it, he advised, teach it now, at the graduate level. He may have already had me down to do it. He discarded ten years of my research, teaching, and service, it seemed. I told him I strongly disagreed with his plans for my academic future. Perhaps it was only coincidental that sometime later that same year at the annual departmental banquet, hitherto a lighthearted gathering of colleagues and friends, the visiting consultant, now hired as an after-dinner speaker, lectured for an hour about why people, in the interests of smooth institutional functioning, should yield to authority.

I was on quarter break, out of town, when the department chair's secretary called to tell me that the chair had added an extra undergraduate course to my teaching schedule for the next quarter, a week away. My stomach cramped in severe pain. No, I said, I absolutely will not accept this assignment. I was adamant, unyielding. I telephoned the new dean, a sociologist and putative feminist, who would soon be elevated to provost. Her "best advice" to me—on this and subsequent matters—was to "roll over." I refused. She then taught the course herself, in my place. Rather than pull rank on the chair, a man, she modeled "rolling over." It was a course on the sociology of women.

I felt no gratitude to her. I had wanted protection, for my colleagues as well as for myself, from a chair's punitive and arbitrary actions. Instead, she presented herself in my place, as the sacrificial lamb. The clear message, it seemed to me, was that if she, the dean of the college, was willing to sacrifice herself, so should we all. Her action legitimated the chair's right to do anything he wanted.

My new chair was empowered to micromanage all aspects of "his" department's life, even to the point of dictating a senior colleague's intellectual life. Any refusal to "roll over" precipitated punitive action in salary, in what one could teach and when, in virtual exile to Coventry. Thus in the mid-1980s, I experienced what has, by the mid-1990s, become an experience common to faculty members of American colleges and universities: "Total Quality Management" in pursuit of "Excellence."

Many departmental colleagues understood that, like the chair's previously conquered opponents, I had become dangerous to associate with, dangerous to even know. In their minds I had brought it upon myself, which of course I had.

As I write these paragraphs, my stomach swells and hurts just as it did then. (pp. 9-11)

In the mid-1980s not only did departmental life surprise me, so did the theoretical concepts of feminist poststructuralism—reflexivity, authority, authorship, subjectivity, power, language, ethics, representation. Soon, I was challenging the grounds of my own and others' authority, and raising ethical questions about my own practices as a sociologist.

Experimenting with textual form, I wrote sociology as drama, responsive readings, narrative poetry, pagan ritual, lyrical poetry, prose poems, humor, and autobiography. Experimenting with content, I wrote about narrative, science writing, literary devices, fact/fiction, ethics. Experimenting with voice, I coauthored with a fiction writer, played second theorist to a junior scholar, turned colleagues' words into dramas. Experimenting with frame, I invited others into my texts, eliding the oral and the written, constructing performance pieces, creating theater. Troubled with the ethical issues of doing research "on" others, I wrote about my own life. I did unto myself as I had done onto others. And, troubled by academic institutions, I began to discover more agreeable pedagogical and writing practices, and alternative community building sites.

I experimented around three interrelated questions: (a) How does the way we are supposed to write up our findings become an unexamined trope in our claims to authoritative knowledge? (b) What might we learn about our "data" if we stage them in different writing formats? and (c) What other audiences might we be able to reach if we step outside the conventions of social-scientific writing?

My intentions then—and now—have never been to dismiss social-scientific writing—but to examine it. My intentions then—and now—have never been to reject social-scientific writing—but to enlarge the field through other representational forms.

By the mid-1980s, I could no longer write in science's omniscient Voice from Nowhere. Responding to the long-suppressed poet within, I wrote up an in-depth interview with an unwed mother, "Louisa May," as a five-page poem, adhering to both social scientific and literary protocols. A poem as "findings" was not well received at my sociology meetings; I was accused of fabricating Louisa May and/or of being her, among other things. To deal with the assault, I wrote a realist drama about it from my (very accurate, nonfabricated, easily checked for reliability) "field notes." In 1993, with the assault warming up in my home department, I decided to write a surreal drama—"Educational Birds"—about my life in academia. Surreal seemed appropriately isomorphic to the real.

ACT 1 OF "EDUCATIONAL BIRDS"

(Scene One: It is a chilly September afternoon in a sociology department chair's office. The walls are catacomb drab; there are no mementos, pictures, or plants in the room. Seated at one end of a large conference table are two women: a department chair with her back to the windows and full professor Z. looking out to the silent gray day.)

Chair: I've been reading your work, because of salary reviews . . .

Professor Z.: . . .

Chair: You write very well.

Professor Z.: . . .

Chair: But is it sociology?

Professor Z.: . . .

(Scene Two: On leaving the department office, Professor Z. sees Visiting Professor M. at the drinking fountain. The pipes are lead. The university says it's not a problem if you let the water run. Professor M. is letting the water run into his coffee maker. His hair is flat, plastering his head; he's heavy-looking, somber, wearing worn blue pants and a stretched-out dun cardigan, hanging loosely to his midthighs. Not the eager Harvard man hired a year ago.)

Professor Z.: Looks like you've acclimated.

(Scene Three: It is an overcast November noon at the Faculty Club. Pictures of deceased faculty, men in drab suits, line the room; wrought-iron bars secure the windows. Professor Z. and assistant professor Q., whose five-author paper "Longitudinal Effects of East to Midwest Migration on Employment Outcomes: A Log-Linear Analysis," has made her a member of the salary committee, are having lunch.)

Assistant Professor Q.: Everyone says, "You write very well."

Professor Z.: Is that a compliment?

Assistant Professor Q.: "But is it Sociology?"

(Scene Four: A cold and dismal January afternoon in the sociology seminar room. During one of the department's "reconstruction" phases, the oak conference table was disassembled and the legs lost. Without a leg to stand on, it lies, in pieces, at the far end of the room next to discarded computer equipment. The wallpaper is flaking away like mummy wrappings. Assembled are the new graduate students, the graduate chair, and the department chair. The new students are being taught how to teach.)

New Graduate Student: *(Addressing the department chair)* Can you tell us about the worst undergraduate sociology class you ever took?

Department Chair: Yes. The worst course was one where the professor read *a* poem.

Graduate Students: . . .

Department Chair: What a waste of time! (p. 197)

The story of a life is less than the actual life because the story told is selective, partial, and contextually constructed and because the life is not yet over. But the story of a life is also more than the life, the contours and meanings allegorically extending to others, others seeing themselves, knowing themselves through another's life story, revisioning their own, arriving where they started and knowing "the place for the first time."

My fears for this "place"—academia—had grown over the course of writing the book. Over the decade, academia had become increasingly inhospitable to those who would change it and to those who are most vulnerable—graduate students. In the penultimate paper in

Fields, I wanted to link the embodiedness of scholarship across generations, disciplines, and theoretical positions. I wanted the book to include the voices of graduate students in different sociology departments, to link my story with their stories, to write a new collective story. I wrote "Are You My Alma Mater?" as the vehicle.

"ARE YOU MY ALMA MATER?"

New mines have been set. As in real war fields, the young, inexperienced, and adventurous are the most vulnerable to detonations. Graduate students. Four examples have passed over my desk in the past two weeks. On a feminist e-mail list came this request from a first-year graduate student:

> My department has been having a series of "feminist epistemology" debates. . . . The anger/hostility/backlash/defensiveness in some of the faculty and the increasing alienation and marginalization of feminist (and students pursuing critical race theory) students is troublesome to me (one of the disenchanted grad students). When I raised my concern, it was suggested that I organize the next seminar. While I am not altogether sure this is a responsibility I want, I am wondering if any of you have had successful . . . forums which address hostilities within the discipline/departments yet does not increase those hostilities or place less powerful people (untenured faculty or graduate students) at greater risk. . . . Please reply to me privately.

When I asked the student for permission to quote her e-mail, she asked for anonymity:

> It drives me crazy that I have to be afraid to even speak, but it is realistic. Actually, even posting to [the listserve] made me nervous, but I can't think of other ways of accessing resources beyond my pathetic institution.

Another graduate student, Eric Mykhalovsky, writes about what happened to him when he used an autobiographical perspective in the practice of sociology. Changing his "I" to "you," he writes in *Qualitative Sociology*:

During a phone call "home" you hear that your application for doctoral studies has been rejected. Your stomach drops. You are in shock, disbelief. When doing your M.A. you were talked about as a "top" student. . . . Later you receive a fax giving an "official account" of your rejection. Your disapproval, it seems, was based on reviewers' reservations with the writing samples submitted as part of your application. One evaluator, in particular, considered your article, "Table Talk," to be a "self-indulgent, informal biography—lacking in accountability to its subject matter." You feel a sense of self-betrayal. You suspected "Table Talk" might have had something to do with the rejection. It was an experimental piece, not like other sociological writing—YOU SHOULD HAVE KNOWN BETTER!

Slowly self-indulgence as assessment slips over the text to name you. You begin to doubt your self—are you really self-indulgent? The committee's rejection of your autobiographical text soon feels, in a very painful way, a rejection of you. All the while you buy into the admission committee's implicit assessment of your work as not properly sociological (1996, 133-134).

Third, in a personal letter requesting advice on whether to apply to my university, a lesbian graduate student from another university recounts:

I cannot do the research I want to and stay here. The department wants to monitor how many lesbians they let in because they're afraid that gender will be taken over by lesbians. I'll be allowed to do gender here if I do it as part of the "social stratification" concentration, but not if I want to write about lesbian identity construction or work from a queer studies perspective.

And fourth, there are documents on my desk pertaining to a required graduate seminar, in a famous department, on how to teach sociology. In that seminar, according to the documents, a non-American student of color questioned the white male professor's Eurocentrism. Following a heated dispute, the professor provided a statistical count of the racial distribution of students in undergraduate classes—80 percent are white. The professor, then, putatively said that instructors cannot afford to alienate students by teaching multiculturalism; that professors are uncomfortable teaching multiculturalism "crap"; that the student raising these issues could "go to hell"; and that white heterosexual males were being discriminated against. When the student of color complained to the department administrators, they proposed he "voluntarily" withdraw from the class. The department administrators (including another new chair) later attended the seminar, supported the syllabus, and sidestepped discussion of the race-based issues. The professor apologized to the seminar for breaking his own code of proper behavior in the classroom, but he apparently had not grasped the import of postcolonialism. He was modeling his teaching model.

As a result, at least one graduate student has chosen to go elsewhere for the Ph.D. The student sent an e-mail to all faculty, staff, and graduate students to avert "idle speculation" regarding the reasons for departure:

> It has disgusted, saddened and enraged me that this department has chosen to ignore and avoid the serious occurrences of racism going on within it. Instead of admitting to these problems and dealing with them, the department has used its institutional power to scapegoat, marginalize and penalize individuals who dare to challenge its racist structure. Then those in power go back to their computer screens to study race as a dummy variable, not even realizing that a sociological process called *racism* is happening in their midst. . . . Students are advised to study social movements, not participate in them. . . . [H]ere racism is not considered *real* sociology, as evidenced by students having to start "extracurricular" groups to do reading on postmodernist or Afrocentric thought.

> I am leaving because, while I respect, learn and appreciate the importance of things like demography and statistics, the same appreciation and respect is not offered here to other areas of sociology which are *very* influential in the field, and institutional power is used to prevent students from learning about them.

> I sincerely hope that the prospect of losing more talented students, especially those who are students of color (who are *not* leaving because they "can't handle it [statistics courses]," will compel this department to reevaluate its capacity to serve its stu-

dents of diverse backgrounds and interests more effectively. My career just didn't have time to wait for all that to happen.

Feminist epistemology, autobiographical sociology, queer studies, and Afrocentric and postcolonial perspectives are apparently so dangerous that the graduate students who have been exposed to these plagues must be quarantined, invalidated, or expelled from the university nest. Graduate students are "terminated" lest they reproduce themselves. (pp. 208-213)

As I pause in the writing of this article, wondering what to write next, the UPS man delivers an advance shipment copy of *Fields of Play*. The production editor's note says, "Congratulations" and "Thanks for all your cooperation along the way; I hope you're as pleased as we are with the final result."

The final result for the production editor is the book, I think. But what is it for me? What consequences have been the book's feminist-poststructuralist practices? How have I changed?

For starters, I have taken early retirement from my "home" sociology department. I have left it physically and emotionally. As a shaman might say, I have called my spirit back; the place no longer has power over me. I go into the building and do not feel alienated. Sometimes, I sing while I am there.

Leaving my department, however, has not meant leaving the sociological perspective. I teach qualitative methods to Ph.D. students in the Cultural Studies Program in Educational Policy and Leadership at The Ohio State University. There, I find a positive commitment to qualitative research among the faculty and the graduate students. More broadly, some faculty are organizing the Ethnographic Project, which will be housed in the Center for Folklore and Ethnic Studies (College of Humanities). The project will link students and faculty at Ohio State who are engaged in ethnography. One of my goals will be to teach a course that "travels" to different ethnographic teaching sites, with all of us learning different ways of doing qualitative work.

I am more involved in ethnographic research than I was during the last years of my tenure in the sociology department. There, my energy was directed toward epistemological questions and in fighting a losing battle to preserve the programs I had established (gender/feminist theory) or built (qualitative methods).

I am doing an ethnography of the Park of Roses, a safe place for vulnerable populations. I hope to present the research at an architecture conference on Making Sacred Space. I am also involved in client-requested research with a monitrice on pregnancy as a spiritual experience. She will be presenting the first phase of this research at an international therapy conference, and we will be coauthoring a book about her theory and practice.

And, I am involved in autobiographical writing as a feminist practice. My personal essay writing is about "sacred spaces" within myself. The last paper in *Fields of Play*, "Vespers," is an account of how an experience at a vespers service when I was 8 years old shaped my relationships to my parents and to my work; it is a forgiveness story. I have just finished writing "Matins," a personal essay about a car accident and a coma. It is a recovery story. Only now—25 years after the accident—am I able to tell that story, and only, I think, because I have accepted writing as process of discovery, and writing autobiographically as a feminist-sociological praxis. In the next few years, I plan to write more of these essays, structured rhizomically, the way my life is experienced—lines of flight, whirling whirling skirts of pleated texts. A surprisingly surprising de-disciplined life.

REFERENCES

Heilbrun, C. (1988). *Writing a woman's life*. New York: W. W. Norton.

Mykhalovsky, E. (1996). Reconsidering Table Talk: Critical thoughts on the relationship between sociology, autobiography, and self-indulgence. *Qualitative Sociology, 19*(1), 131-151.

Richardson, L. (1997). *Fields of play: Constructing an academic life*. New Brunswick, NJ: Rutgers University Press.

-- --

Laurel Richardson teaches sociology and qualitative research methods at The Ohio State University. She is the author of six books, including Writing Strategies: Reaching Diverse Audiences *(Sage, 1992),* The New Other Woman *(Free Press, 1987), and* Fields of Play: Constructing an Academic Life *(Rutgers University Press, 1997).*

CHAPTER 4

Circling the Text
Nomadic Writing Practices

— —

Elizabeth Adams St.Pierre
University of Georgia

The sixth moment of qualitative inquiry demands that researchers rethink traditional definitions of ethical research practices. In addition, the crisis of representation demands that researchers rethink the function of writing in qualitative research. In this article, the author illustrates how she used Deleuze's ethical principles as well as Deleuze and Guattari's figurations of the rhizome, the fold, the nomad, and haecceity to address both of these issues in her study of the construction of subjectivity of a group of older, White southern women in her hometown. Mapping how her understanding of subjectivity has shifted as she has employed these figurations in her writing, she suggests that texts can be the site of ethical work as researchers use writing to help them think differently—an ethical practice of postfoundational inquiry—about both the topic of their studies and the methodology.

Several years ago, I began a combination of an interview study and an ethnography with some of the older White women of my hometown, a small rural community in the southern Piedmont, to trouble the category "old woman," a category toward which I find myself steadily progressing. I have been distressed that older women are often trapped on the wrong side of several binaries: young-old, male-female, subject-object, healthy-unhealthy, strong-weak, and rich-poor. They are assuredly too close for comfort to the wrong side of that most material of binaries, life-death. However, poststructural critiques offer methods that can be deployed as we attempt to liberate ourselves from whatever binaries entrap us—"from something that our history had in fact misled us into thinking was real" (Rajchman, 1985, p. 56). Hoping to make some headway in producing descriptions of older women different from those that have become commonplace, taken-for-granted, and often destructive, I determined to employ poststructural theories of language and subjectivity to interrogate the category "old woman."

Jane Flax (1990) points out that poststructural theories are "all deconstructive in that they seek to distance us from and make us skeptical about beliefs concerning truth, knowledge, power, the self, and language that are often taken for granted within and serve as legitimation for contemporary Western culture" (p. 41). A deconstructive stance has regularly unsettled my "fieldwork, textwork, and headwork" (Van Maanen, 1995, p. 4) around my project, and I propose to use this particular essay as an opportunity to reflect on the conjunction of two elements of my work, both derived from poststructural critiques, that have emerged from "looking awry" (Zizek, 1991, p. 3) at traditional descriptions of both subjectivity and qualitative research. The first is a "new ethics of inquiry" (Denzin, 1997a, p. xviii), a major focus of what has been called the sixth moment (Denzin, 1997a, p. xi; Denzin, 1997b, p. 1; Lincoln, 1995, p. 40) of qualitative research; and the second, which I believe is linked in fruitful and sometimes unexpected ways with the first, has to do with textuality, specifically, with Laurel Richardson's (1994) concept of using writing as a method of inquiry in our research projects. Convinced that writing is thinking, I believe that my writing about my participants has become an ethical practice of poststructural inquiry in ways I have only begun to understand.

A NEW ETHICS OF INQUIRY: GETTING FREE OF ONESELF

In their introduction to the 1994 edition of the *Handbook of Qualitative Research*, the editors, Norman K. Denzin and Yvonna S. Lincoln, describe what they call the "five moments of qualitative research" (Denzin & Lincoln, 1994a, p. 7): the traditional period (p. 7); the modernist phase (p. 8); the moment of blurred genres (p. 9); the moment of the crisis of representation (p. 9); and the fifth moment, the present (p. 11). In the final chapter of that volume, they make some predictions about the sixth moment (Denzin & Lincoln, 1994b, p. 575), which each later develops more fully (see Lincoln, 1995; Denzin, 1997a, 1997b). Complications resulting from ethical concerns abound in the sixth moment of qualitative inquiry in which researchers, for example, often question the "liberal conception of privacy and the public sphere" (Denzin, 1997a, p. 271) that perpetuates the public-private dichotomy and influences notions of anonymity and confidentiality, are concerned about the adequacy of existing human subjects laws (Lincoln, 1995), struggle with issues as simple and complex as the ownership of interview tapes (Denzin, 1997b), and worry about where their research goes and how it is used (Lincoln, 1995).

Ethical dilemmas proliferate in the sixth moment's vortex of crises that have emerged from the ruins of traditional epistemology and methodology, and each research study produces specific, situated, and sometimes paralyzing complications that have no easy resolution. The richness and power of qualitative research is confirmed as its practitioners work through such complications, searching for less harmful possibilities for making sense of people's lives.

Qualitative researchers are haunted by ethical issues because it is difficult for them to escape their work and to get free of those other lives, and they often live uneasily with dilemmas that will not go away. My own study has become part of my everyday life, and I wonder whether data collection will ever cease. I see and talk with my participants on my frequent trips to visit my mother, I go to Sunday School with them, I am invited to events at their homes, and we correspond throughout the year on special occasions. I have written many, many pages about them, and I find that Essex County women are always on my mind. I often ask myself what it is that I need to know about them, and I wonder what drives me to do this work that is certainly not innocent, that, in fact, may be harmful to those I have grown to admire and love. Indeed, I wonder sometimes whether I am writing my way into a catastrophe. How can I presume to interpret and represent the lives of these women? Who am I to do this work?

In a stew about the ethical issues that plague our research in this sixth moment and, on many days, convinced, with Patricia Clough (1992), that we should just give up on data collection, I make myself reread Foucault's (1984/1985) comments about what motivates us to do this kind of work. He suggests that an obstinate curiosity drives us (Foucault, 1984/1985, p. 8), that is "not the curiosity that seeks to assimilate what it is proper for one to know, but that which enables one to get free of oneself" (Foucault, 1984/1985, p. 8). Now, Foucault's notion of "getting free of oneself" is not a reauthorization of transcendental objectivity but rather a description of a particular deconstructive approach to both knowledge production and being in the world. Getting free of oneself involves an attempt to understand the "structures of intelligibility" (Britzman, 1995, p. 156) that limit thought. Foucault (1984/1985), explaining the urgency of such labor, says, "There are times in life when the question of knowing if one can think differently than one thinks, and perceive differently than one sees, is absolutely necessary if one is to go on looking and reflecting at all" (p. 8).

I am probably at one of those critical times in my life. To make some sense of the lives of my participants, and my own life as well, I have adopted Foucault's (1984/1985) practice of trying to get free of myself, of trying to think differently than I have thought, as an ethical imperative. In this deconstructive work on myself, I have found that the traditional charge of ethics to "do no harm" requires elaboration beyond those practices routinely described in most introductory texts on qualitative research. Practices such as using consent forms and conducting member checks seem little more than ritual and hardly begin to address ethics as one "works the ruins" (Lather, 1997a) of inquiry in a postfoundational world. What guidelines or strategies are available for researchers who are attempting the ethical practice of trying to get free of themselves? And what methods might they employ to do that work?

These questions have led me, through Foucault, to the work of Deleuze and Guattari. Foucault (1970/1977), in a 1970 essay in which he reviews two of Deleuze's books, writes, "Perhaps one day, this century will be known as Deleuzian" (p. 165). Two years later, in the preface to Deleuze and Guattari's (1972/1983) book, *Anti-Oedipus: Capitalism and Schizophrenia,* Foucault (1972/1983) lists seven ethical principles that he finds operating in Deleuze and Guattari's work. I believe these principles bear repeating: first, "Free political action from all unitary and totalizing paranoia" (p. xiii); second, "Develop action, thought and desires by proliferation, juxtaposition, and disjunction, and not by subdivision and pyramidal hierarchization" (p. xiii); third, "Withdraw allegiance from the old categories of the Negative. . . . Prefer what is positive and multiple, difference over uniformity, flows over unities, mobile arrangements over systems. Believe that what is productive is not sedentary but nomadic" (p. xiii); fourth, "Do not think that one has to be sad in order to be militant, even though the thing one is fighting is abominable" (p. xiii); fifth, "Do not use thought to ground a political practice in Truth; nor political action to discredit, as mere speculation, a line of thought. Use political practice as an intensifier of thought, and analysis as a multiplier of the forms and domains for the intervention of political action" (p. xiv); sixth, "Do not demand of politics that it restore the 'rights' of the individual, as philosophy has defined them. The individual is the product of power. What is needed is to 'deindividualize' by means of multiplication and displacement, diverse combinations" (p. xiv); and seventh, "Do not become enamored of power" (p. xiv). If one attempts to use these ethical practices, thinking does change. It becomes an "event, a repetition without a model, a dice-throw" (Hand, 1986/1988, p. xliv).

Fortunately, Deleuze and Guattari have provided not only these ethical practices but also new language to assist in a different kind of thinking that might incite different kinds of political action. I certainly needed that different language after a long summer of fieldwork in Essex County 3 years ago. It is very difficult, almost impossible at times, to write and think outside the language of humanism, our mother tongue that constructs and perpetuates with such transparent ease binaries, hierarchies, dialectics, and other structures that are not just linguistic but that have very material effects on people. As I struggled to write about my research, I found that the traditional categories and concepts of qualitative methodology were simply inadequate for poststructural work. Thinking differently required that I trouble received descriptions of words such as data, field, and subject, foundational concepts whose failure is not nihilistic, apolitical, or sad, as Deleuze and Guattari (1987) point out, but affirming because it opens up possibilities for a different kind of inquiry. Butler (1992) explains that to deconstruct terms is "to continue to use them, to repeat them, to repeat them subversively, and to displace them from the contexts in which they have been deployed as instruments of oppressive power" (p. 17).

I have found some of the new language invented by Deleuze and Guattari useful in this deconstructive work because the concepts they have created are not like bricks that weigh down thought but like toolboxes full of levers and gizmos that open things up (Massumi, Deleuze, & Guattari, 1987, p. xv). Their images and figurations have provided me with "points of exit" (Braidotti, 1994, p. 160), "lines of flight" (Deleuze & Parnet, 1977/1987, p. 125) from the language of humanism and the particular descriptions of the world it produces, and I have used some of those figurations to help me think and write differently about both subjectivity and methodology.

Figurations are not graceful metaphors that produce coherence out of disorder but rather cartographic weapons that tear through the orderliness of humanist language; they scatter sureties; they prod and poke at positivities and foundations; and they perform curious transitions between disjunctive proximities. They enable one to think "at a higher degree, at a faster pace, in a multidirectional manner" (Braidotti, 1994, p. 167). Figurations have surely propelled me into spaces I am not sure I would have found otherwise. The figurations I have thus far found most helpful in thinking about my project are the rhizome (Deleuze & Guattari, 1980/1987), the fold (Deleuze, 1988/1993), and the nomad (Deleuze & Guattari, 1980/1987), which I will describe later. Recently, I have become intrigued by another figuration described by Deleuze and Guattari, haecceity, whose possibilities I am currently exploring.

I believe that work enabled by figurations begins to address those Deleuzian ethical principles that Foucault identifies, principles that shift the conversation about ethics in postfoundational inquiry. Using figurations can, in fact, assist in freeing oneself from oneself, in thinking differently, and thereby in producing descriptions and inscriptions of lives that may do less harm. The use of figurations as an ethical practice thus leads me to the second topic of this article, and that is writing-the method I have used to perform this practice. The following discussion is an attempt to map a different ethics of inquiry that works through writing, where "thought thinks its own history (the past), but in order to free itself from what it thinks (the present) and be able finally to 'think otherwise' (the future)" (Deleuze, 1986/1988, p. 119).

WRITING AS A METHOD OF INQUIRY

Convinced at the very beginning of my study that writing would be significant in my research, I emphasized the importance of textuality in the first piece I wrote about the women of Essex County, my dissertation. In the concluding paragraph of chapter 1, I foregrounded, as follows, the importance of the textwork I planned for my project:

> In the field, in my home in Essex County, I accumulated several kinds of data with which to construct a text: I collected interview data by talking with thirty-six older women, and I gathered a variety of ethnographic data in order to provide a setting from which the women speak. In another kind of field, this textual space, I use writing as a method of inquiry. Thus, I consider the words of this text to be data and will treat this writing experience as ongoing data collection. The research continues. (St.Pierre, 1995, p. 22)

Thus, following Richardson (1994), I determined early on to use writing as a method of inquiry in my study and to pay attention to both the process and the products of that work.

Richardson (1994) explains, "I write because I want to find out something. I write in order to learn something that I didn't know before I wrote it" (p. 517). I agree with Richardson that writing is not only inscription but also discovery. It is a kind of nomadic inquiry in which I am able to deterritorialize spaces in which to travel in the thinking that writing produces. As I write, I think, I learn, and I change my mind about what I think. In the past 3 years, I have used text as a different kind of field in which to continue my work with my participants and have employed the figurations of Deleuze and Guattari to write myself into different understandings of subjectivity, the topic of my study, as well as the categories and concepts of qualitative inquiry.

At this point, I would like to illustrate how writing and thinking with figurations has enabled me to do this work, which I believe honors Deleuze's ethical principles of preferring thought inspired by disjunction, difference, deindividualization, multiplication, displacement, disunity, mobile arrangements, and so forth over unitary, totalizing, sedentary, and systematic thought. To do so, I will consider the texts I have written thus far about the women of Essex County as data, writing data, and will analyze in a general way how my understanding of the concept, subjectivity—the focus of my project—has shifted as I continue to write about it using different figurations. This analysis will also consider two concepts of qualitative methodology, data and the field, whose meanings become tenuous as subjectivity falls apart and reforms.

As an aside, I should point out that Richardson (1997), whose concept of writing as a method of inquiry has changed forever the way we think about writing in qualitative research, has—in fact, in her new book, *Fields of Play: Constructing an Academic Life*—provided a model for this kind of parallactic practice, "work that frames the framer as he or she frames the other" (Foster, 1996, p. 203), and has written "writing stories" (Richardson, 1997, p. 1) around various texts she has produced in the course of her career. My analysis will not be as comprehensive as Richardson's but will provide another example of how one might treat one's own writing about a project as additional data, another fold in the research process.

As I think about the pieces I have written, I can find no linear, causal relationships among them; that is, I do not believe that the writing of one text necessarily caused the writing of the next. At some point, I certainly may have had a plan for the next three journal articles I wanted to write, but that sequence may have been interrupted by writing a conference paper in which I learned something that pointed me to an entirely different writing project. Writing seems more accidental than intentional and is often produced by unintended juxtapositions: coreadings of texts on entirely different topics, the discovery of a particularly provocative word as I skim the dictionary page for another, or the memory of a dream that displaces some truth to which I have become too attached. I expect that any paper I have written could have been another paper quite easily. As Jane

Gallop (1985) points out, "All writings lead elsewhere" (p. 34). My writing thus reflects no systematic tracing of thought but rather maps ordinary forays into unintelligibility.

I begin this review of my writing about Essex County women by explaining that I have lost the very first text I imagined about my participants and their community, so it is unavailable for examination. During endless summer days of fieldwork 3 years ago, I began to write in my head a book that might describe in some complex and fitting fashion the practices of the self my participants use every day to create their subjectivities, even though I knew that that particular version would be lost. I knew that the dense and ponderous coding of the dissertation I was required to produce would overwrite the fragile text I was imagining, a text so rhizomatic, however, that it could be dissipated, scattered, even squandered with little ill effect. Deleuze and Guattari (1980/1987) write that "every rhizome contains lines of segmentarity according to which it is stratified, territorialized, organized, signified, attributed, etc., as well as lines of deterritorialization down which it constantly flees" (p. 9). They go on to say that "a rhizome may be broken, shattered at a given spot, but it will start up again on one of its old lines, or on new lines" (Deleuze & Guattari, 1980/1987, p. 9). This figuration of the rhizome, then, allows me to think outside systems, outside order, outside stability. Rhizomes favor exteriority, motion, chance, and variation outside the contrived confines of a text.

So, I think of that lost book not as lost forever but instead as a rhizome, something like crabgrass, and I believe that pieces of it spring up in papers I write about my research project. In these small texts, I organize, signify, stratify, and produce some knowledge based on my research, but the women escape. They flee down paths deterritorialized by long lives that refuse to be explained away in any fluent, facile, solid text. So the book remains lost, a fiction, a rhizome traveling into spaces I can never predict.

The dissertation was, indeed, a palimpsest, and that writing was intense and thrilling and exhausting. It was in that very long essay that I began to give up on the fiction of the liberal individual of humanism. Although I had read a great deal about poststructural theories of subjectivity and had found them both seductive and seemly, it was the practice of writing that lodged those descriptions in my very bones. Of course, once a shift in subjectivity occurs, the rest of the world shifts as well, and it is impossible to go back.

Unstable, contingent, experimental subjects; subjects without a centered essence that remains the same throughout time; subjects produced within conflicting discourses and cultural practices; subjects who can no longer rely on rationality to produce true knowledge; subjects at the mercy of language; subjects who, as a result, are freer than they think—such subjects can take nothing for granted. They become suspicious of all received descriptions, all concepts, all categories. If language can no longer reflect the truth, then such subjects are free to attempt to rethink and redescribe the world.

The particular description of subjectivity with which I used to analyze my dissertation data was Foucault's (1984/1986) final theory of subjectivity, his ethical analysis, care of the self. This theory that Foucault learned from the ancient Greeks is very much about the doing; about the things we do every day that make us who we are; about how we might construct ourselves as ethical subjects in relation, not only to others, but to ourselves as well; about the pleasure and responsibility of that work on ourselves; and about how we might think of that work as an aesthetic experience. Foucault (1984/1988) explains that, in antiquity, "The elaboration of one's own life as a personal work of art, even if it obeyed certain collective canons, was at the centre . . . of moral experience" (p. 49). Thus, for the ancient Greeks, the focus of morality was on an aesthetics of existence, and free men (not women) developed practices of the self that would allow them to become the ethical subjects of their actions. It was important to pay attention to the self, to work on the self, to stylize the self. However, later in Christianity, care of the self almost disappeared as morality became thought of as obedience to a code of rules, and the self became something to renounce.

This description of subjectivity seemed fitting for my study. When I interviewed my participants, I questioned them about the kinds and sources of knowledge they had used during their long lives to construct their subjectivities. However, they circumvented my questions and responded with data not about the knowledge they had accumulated but with data about what they had done during their lives, about their activities, their practices. Thus, Foucault's care of the self, which is ontological rather than epistemological, became most useful in thinking about their lives, and I used his theory to identify and elaborate the practices of the self of the women of Essex County.

But that description of subjectivity has not been enough. Ongoing fieldwork, continued face-to-face interaction with my participants, requires more. That "more," that need to continue to trouble subjectivity, becomes insistent as I write. In textwork, I understand that the subject can never be adequate to itself, that it demands reinscription, that it must be opened up "to a reusage or redeployment that previously has not been authorized" (Butler, 1992, p. 15). In both fieldwork and textwork, then, I find that subjectivity proliferates so that a different subject always "rushes back as witness, testifier, survivor" (Foster, 1996, p. 168). It is in the field that reality reconfigures and stalks the text. It is in the text that the subject groans and twists out of signification. Subjectivity thus fails and reforms in the fieldwork and textwork of the new ethnography; the real is lost and recovered; language touches bodies; words survey wounds.

So some mixture of headwork, textwork, and fieldwork—very unstable categories—are required to produce failure, redescription, and then, of course, further critique. Provoked by doubt and changing notions of subjectivity enabled by Deleuze and Guattari's figurations, I have written two methodological articles since the dissertation that trouble self-evident and received understandings of two foundational concepts in qualitative research. The first article uses the figuration of the fold to explore the concept data (St.Pierre, 1997b), the foundation of knowledge production in research. The second article uses the figuration of the nomad to explore the concept the field (St.Pierre, in press), the spaces in which our research takes place.

I came upon the figuration of the fold as I wrote the methodological section of my dissertation, and it seemed to describe the conflation of the subject- object, inside-outside binaries I had experienced as I interviewed women I had known all my life, women whose language was my own, women whose practices of the self were my own. I could not contain my self with them; I escaped; I traced their words, their gestures, their bodies. I was them. Deleuze (1986/1988) writes that the fold disrupts the interiority-exteriority binary because it treats "the outside as an exact reversion, or 'membrane,' of the inside, reading the world as a texture of the intimate" (Badiou, 1994, p. 61). Boundas

(1994) explains that "it is the individual who causes the outside to fold, thereby endowing itself with subjectivity, as it bends and folds the outside" (p. 114). I believed that the subject of my fieldwork, this researcher, was not the unified, contained, stable individual of liberal humanism but a subject folded into subjectivity by the outside, a subject who could not be separated from the outside but always a part of it, folding, unfolding, refolding with/in it.

The idea of a folded subjectivity enabled me to think differently about the concept, data, whose traditional definition had become increasingly limiting as I tried to describe the data of my study. I could no longer believe that data must be textualized before it could be coded, categorized, analyzed, and interpreted. I believed that there were all sorts of data working in my study that escaped that positivist narrative, transgressive data that I (St.Pierre, 1997b) later named emotional data, dream data, sensual data, and response data. I am sure that there are other kinds of data working in my study that I have not yet been able to think about.

In a second methodological article, I (St. Pierre, in press) used another concept of subjectivity, Deleuze and Guattari's (1980/1987) figuration of the nomad, to trouble the concept, the field, another ordinary signifier of qualitative methodology. Deleuze and Guattari suggest that the nomad "operates in an open space throughout which things-flows are distributed rather than plotting out a closed space for linear and solid things" (p. 361). In fact, nomads deterritorialize space that has been territorialized, charted, ordered, and then shut down. Nomads search for mobile arrangements of space where thought can settle for a time and then multiply and recombine, always displacing the sedentary and unified. A researcher who practices nomadic inquiry, an "itinerant" (Deleuze & Guattari, 1980/1987, p. 373) science, can never be sure of the field and thus has trouble locating it because "deterritorialization constitutes and extends the territory itself" (Deleuze & Guattari, 1980/1987, p. 372). The field grows; it erupts in some strange, new place; it refuses to be coded; and it advantageously invents itself outside interiority.

As I positioned myself as a nomadic researcher, I realized that I had been working in fields, in necessary spaces, that were not included in the field of traditional ethnography: mental spaces, textual spaces, and theoretical spaces (St.Pierre, in press). Fieldwork in such spaces is accomplished by armchair ethnographers who do not have to leave home to be in the middle of something, who struggle with different cultural problematics by working in fields that have been unintelligible in the old ethnography.

Both of these writing projects have been informed by Deleuze's ethical principles. In both articles, I have had to rethink subjectivity "to 'deindividualize' by means of multiplication and displacement, diverse combinations" (Foucault, 1972/1983, p. xiv). By doing so, by preferring "what is positive and multiple, difference over uniformity, flows over unities, mobile arrangements over systems" (Foucault, 1972/1983, p. xiii), I have latched onto some signifiers, data and the field, and troubled their traditional meanings. I believe this deconstructive work honors the ethical charge I have set for myself of trying to think differently, of trying to free myself of my self.

This work seems endless, however. My chief learning from the writing of these two methodological pieces is that I must once again rethink subjectivity. Remember Richardson's (1994) warning, "I write because I want to find out something. I write in order to learn something that I didn't know before I wrote it" (p. 517). In Essex County, in medias res, I experienced still another phenomenon of subjectivity that I was unable to write about at the time because I had no language to do so. Happily, I have come upon another Deleuzian figuration, haecceity (Deleuze & Guattari, 1980/1987), that describes a concept of subjectivity entirely different from any I have yet imagined. In fact, a haecceity is an individuation different from that of a person or a thing. It is an assemblage that allows me to elaborate the relationship of the field-worker to the field and also to the time and space in which events occur. Because a haecceity is an assemblage, the subject no longer remains separate from objects or time or space but enters into composition with them. This phenomenon is what I experienced in the field 3 years ago, and the figuration, haecceity, will allow me to write about that experience.

In my own mind, I have referred to the paper in which I will describe this new field-worker as my "subjectivity paper," and I have actually been writing it for the last 3 years within other papers, searching for some words, speeding into corners and then scrambling out again, trapped outside language. Portions of this paper like the lost book, crop up where they shouldn't, and I cut and paste them into a document I have titled "haecceity." This "folding of one text onto another" (Deleuze & Guattari, 1980/1987, p. 6) indicates how rhizomatic, how nomadic, subjectivity has become in my work. It also illustrates that I am restless, moving from one description of subjectivity to another, getting it right only momentarily and then moving on.

Even so, I have recently written a conference paper, "Ethnography After the Subject: Haecceity and Assemblage" (St.Pierre, 1997a), as a dry run for the subjectivity paper that I may now be ready to write but that will not be the truth about subjectivity. Keeping subjectivity in play, mobile, a line of flight with no referent and no destination is my desire and my ethical charge. Indeed, I have begun to suspect that my work about older women requires that I proliferate subjectivity and illustrate through lived experiences in the field, and in the text, that subjectivity is a mobile assemblage that arranges and rearranges itself outside all "totalizing paranoia" (Foucault, 1972/1983, p. xiii).

As I pause in this analysis of my nomadic, rhizomatic writing journey, I realize that I have used Deleuze's ethical principles to work against the continuity of a traditional, rational, linear, and transparent methodology that guarantees Truth. Research guided by the "ethically vitalizing failure of uncertain kinds of ideals" (Butter, 1993, p. 7), ideals that presume universality and deny rhizomatics works in the "breaks and jagged edges" (Lather, 1997a, p. 22) of the ruins of that traditional methodology, in fact, Deleuze's ethical principles become methods that produce a very different research process, a nomadic adventure that cannot be defined in advance because it takes advantage of flows and multiplicities and disjunctions to make a different sense in different ways or to refuse to make sense at all. Lather (1997b), who has also employed the ethical principles of nomadic inquiry in her research with women living with HIV/AIDS writes, "I am paradoxically attracted to wandering and getting lost as methodological stances" (Lather, 1997a, p. 539). This kind of research, then, is about mapping, not tracing (Deleuze & Guattari, 1980/1987) and about risking the loss of those very things we believe we cannot do without (Spivak, 1993). Indeed, I have found that nomadic inquiry enables those "necessary misfirings" (Lather, 1997b, p. 23) that indicate that traditional methodology and the knowledge it produces have been held together mostly by words, words propped up by desire and power, and not by the Truth, as we have been led to believe.

If one adds the method of inquiry called writing to Deleuze's list of ethical principles, or methods, one produces a powerful vehicle for "the continual cocreation of Self and social science" (Richardson, 1994, p. 518). Writing becomes a site of ethical responsibility that is different from "the empirical concept of writing, which denotes an intelligible system of notations on a material substance" (Spivak & Derrida, 1967/1974, p. xxxiv). The rhizomatic writing that Richardson (1994) describes works against the "rage for unity" (Spivak & Derrida, 1967/1974, p. xvi) demanded by the "clôture of metaphysics" (Spivak & Derrida, 1967/1974, p. xli). This kind of writing is antihierarchical. It also has a "short-term memory" (Deleuze & Guattari, 1980/1987, p. 16) and therefore cannot follow an outline. And, because it has given up on intentions, it cannot see very far down the road. It stalls, gets stuck, thumbs its nose at order, goes someplace the author did not know existed ahead of time, stumbles over its sense, spins around its middle foregoing ends, wraps idea around idea in some overloaded imbrication that flies out of control into a place of no return. Richardson (1994) writes, "We cannot go back to where we were" (p. 524). Writing, then, is an exquisitely brazen, ethically astute rhizome that deterritorializes subjects and method. Rhizomatic, nomadic writing, in fact, writes its authors, producing "hybrid genres like self-ethnography and ethnobiography" (Behar, 1996, p. 26), genres that resist the easy dismissal of solipsism. The author and the text write each other, and that fold in the research process can no longer be ignored in the new ethics of inquiry.

But, writing cannot be the sole heroine of this article, because I believe that writing and fieldwork are imbricated in productive and unsettling ways. In my recent writing, I have begun to understand that the texts I have completed and those I imagine about the women of Essex County, particularly this last paper about subjectivity, is a preface to a return to the field. Yet, fieldwork will be different after 3 years of writing. I will be unable to think of data or the field or the ethnographer in the same way because I will have written myself into different understandings of those concepts. I will have used writing as a method of inquiry to disrupt the self-evidence of the language and practice of traditional qualitative research. I am most interested in what ethnography will look like then.

But fieldwork, whatever it looks like, is required. I know I will be unable to write that lost book until I get back in the middle of things, until I collect what I call "response data" (St.Pierre, 1997b), until I talk with my participants about what I have already written about them and then perhaps write about that sure-to-be-uncomfortable experience. I am in love with writing, but I am also in love with fieldwork. I am seduced by lives.

So I will return to Essex County with an array of descriptions of subjectivity and with the new language of figurations like the fold, the rhizome, the nomad, and haecceity to help me think about older women and ethnography, and there I will listen to new stories that will fortify me when I begin to write that book about practices of the self. This return to the field is not only enticing but also urgent because my study is plagued by mortality. I have lost 3 participants already, and I promised them all a book. I have needed this writing time, this time to think and learn and change my mind. I have indeed traveled great distances in the thinking that writing produces. But now, it is time to enact my learnings, to return to the field once again, and then to write as I have never written before. I am consoled somewhat by knowing that I will continue to learn as I write. Deleuze and Guattari (1980/1987) explain, "Writing has nothing to do with signifying. It has to do with surveying, mapping, even realms that are yet to come" (pp. 4-5). Writing is discovery, as Richardson (1994) tells us. And the lost book? Surely, it is yet another center that cannot hold; another ruin that is already reforming into a fierce, sharp line of flight; a weapon brimful of amazing stories of old women, vexing counter-descriptions that break out of the text and stir up trouble.

REFERENCES

Badiou, A. (1994). Gilles Deleuze. The fold: Leibniz and the baroque. In C. V. Boundas & D. Olkowski (Eds.), *Gilles Deleuze and the theater of philosophy* (pp. 51-69). New York: Routledge.

Behar, R. (1996). *The vulnerable observer: Anthopology that breaks your heart*. Boston: Beacon Press.

Boundas, C. V. (1994). Deleuze: Serialization and subject-formation. In C. V. Boundas & D. Olkowski (Eds.), *Gilles Deleuze and the theater of philosophy* (pp. 99-116). New York: Routledge.

Braidotti, R. (1994). Toward a new nomadism: Feminist Deleuzian tracks; Or, Metaphysics and metabolism. In C. V. Boundas & D. Olkowski (Eds.), *Gilles Deleuze and the theater of philosophy* (pp. 159-186). New York: Routledge.

Britzman, D. P. (1995). Is there a queer pedagogy? Or, Stop reading straight. *Educational Theory, 45*(2), 151-165.

Butler, J. (1992). Contingent foundations. In J. Butler & J. Scott (Eds.), *Feminists theorize the political* (pp. 3-21). New York: Routledge.

Clough, P. (1992). *The ends of ethnography: From realism to social criticism.* Newbury Park: Sage.

Deleuze, G. (1988). *Foucault* (S. Hand, Trans.). Minneapolis: University of Minnesota Press. (Original work published 1986)

Deleuze, G. (1993). *The fold: Leibniz and the baroque* (T. Conley, Trans.). Minneapolis: University of Minnesota Press. (Original work published 1988)

Deleuze, G., & Guattari, F. (1983). *Anti-Oedipus: Capitalism and schizophrenia* (R. Hurley, M. Seem, & H. R. Lane, Trans.). Minneapolis: University of Minnesota Press. (Original work published 1972)

Deleuze, G., & Guattari, F. (1987). *A thousand plateaus: Capitalism and schizophrenia* (B. Massumi, Trans.). Minneapolis: University of Minnesota Press. (Original work published 1980)

Deleuze, G., & Parnet, C. (1987). *Dialogues* (H. Tomlinson & B. Habberjam, Trans.). New York: Columbia University Press. (Original work published 1977)

Denzin, N. K. (1997a). *Interpretive ethnography: Ethnographic practices for the 21st century.* Thousand Oaks, CA: Sage.

Denzin, N. K. (1997b, March). *The sixth moment, voice and the ethics of qualitative inquiry.* Paper presented at the annual meeting of the American Educational Research Association, Chicago, IL.

Denzin, N. K., & Lincoln, Y. S. (1994a). Introduction: Entering the field of qualitative research. In N. K. Denzin & Y. S. Lincoln (Eds.), *Handbook of qualitative research* (pp. 1-17). Thousand Oaks, CA: Sage.

Denzin, N. K., & Lincoln, Y. S. (1994b). The fifth moment. In N. K. Denzin & Y. S. Lincoln (Eds.), *Handbook of qualitative research* (pp. 575-586). Thousand Oaks, CA: Sage.

Flax, J. (1990). Postmodernism and gender relations in feminist theory. In L. J. Nicholson (Ed.), *Feminism/Postmodernism* (pp. 39-62). New York: Routledge.

Foster, H. (1996). *The return of the real: The avant-garde at the end of the century.* Cambridge, MA: MIT.

Foucault, M. (1977). Theatrum philosophicum. (D. F. Bouchard & S. Simon, Trans.). In D. F. Bouchard (Ed.), *Language, counter-memory, practice: Selected essays and interviews* (pp. 165-196). Ithaca: Cornell University Press. (Reprinted from *Critique, 1970, 282,* 885-908)

Foucault, M. (1983). Preface. In G. Deleuze & F. Guattari (Eds.), *Anti-Oedipus: Capitalism and schizophrenia* (R. Hurley, M. Seem, & H. R. Lane, Trans.), (pp. xi-xiv). Minneapolis: University of Minnesota Press. (Original work published 1972)

Foucault, M. (1985). *The history of sexuality: Vol. 2. The use of pleasure* (R. Hurley, Trans.). New York: Vintage. (Original work published 1984)

Foucault, M. (1986). *History of sexuality: Vol. 3: The care of the self* (R. Hurley, Trans.). New York: Vintage. (Original work published 1984)

Foucault, M. (1988). An aesthetics of existence (A. Sheridan, Trans.). In L. D. Kritzman (Ed.), Michel Foucault: *Politics, philosophy, culture: Interviews and other writings, 1977-1984* (pp. 47-53). New York: Routledge. (Original work published 1984)

Gallop, J. (1985). *Reading Lacan.* Ithaca, NY: Cornell University Press.

Hand, S. (Ed. & Trans.). (1988). Translating theory, or the difference between Deleuze and Foucault. In G. Deleuze, *Foucault* (pp. xli-xliv). Minneapolis: University of Minnesota Press. (Original work published 1986)

Lather, P. (1997a, March). *Drawing the line at angels: Working the ruins of feminist ethnography.* Paper presented at the 1997 annual meeting of the American Educational Research Association, Chicago, IL.

Lather, P. (1997b). *Troubling the angels: Women living with HIV/AIDS.* Boulder, CO: Westview.

Lincoln, Y. (1995). The sixth moment: Emerging problems in qualitative research. *Studies in Symbolic Interaction, 19,* 37-55.

Massumi, B., G. Deleuze, & F. Guattari, (1987). Translator's foreward: Pleasure of philosophy. *A thousand plateaus: Capitalism and schizophrenia* (B. Massumi, Trans.), (pp. ix-xv). Minneapolis: University of Minnesota Press. (Original work published 1980)

Rajchman, J. (1985). *Michel Foucault: The freedom of philosophy.* New York: Columbia University Press.

Richardson, L. (1994) Writing: A method of inquiry. In N. K. Denzin & Y. S. Lincoln (Eds.), *Handbook of qualitative research* (pp. 516-529). Thousand Oaks, CA: Sage Publications.

Richardson, L. (1997). *Fields of play: Constructing an academic life.* New Brunswick, NJ: Rutgers University Press.

St. Pierre, E. A. (1995). *Arts of existence: The construction of subjectivity in older, White southern women.* Unpublished doctoral dissertation, Ohio State University, Columbus.

St. Pierre, E. A. (1997a, March). *Ethnography after the subject: Haecceity and assemblage.* Paper presented at the annual meeting of the American Educational Research Association, Chicago, IL.

St. Pierre, E. A. (1997b). Methodology in the fold and the irruption of transgressive data. *International Journal of Qualitative Studies in Education, 10* (2), 175-189.

St. Pierre, E. A. (in press). Nomadic inquiry in the smooth spaces of the field: A preface. *International Journal of Qualitative Studies in Education.*

Spivak, G., & Derrida, C. Jacques (1974). Translator's preface. *Of grammatology* (G. Spivak, Trans.), (pp. ix-xc). Baltimore: Johns Hopkins University Press. (Original work published 1967)

Spivak, G. C. (1993). *Outside in the teaching machine.* New York: Routledge.

Van Maanen, J. (1995). *Representation in ethnography.* Thousand Oaks, CA: Sage Publications.

Zizek, S. (1991). *Looking awry: An introduction to Jacques Lacan through popular culture.* Cambridge, MA: The MIT Press.

-- --

Elizabeth Adams St.Pierre is assistant professor of language education at the University of Georgia. Her interests include the study of qualitative research methodology and qualitative research that employs critical theories and poststructural critiques of language and cultural practice to examine the construction of subjectivity in women.

PART TWO

AUTOETHNOGRAPHY

Reflexive ethnography, the topic of the first set of readings, merges with **autoethnography**, "an autobiographical genre . . . that displays multiple layers of consciousness connecting the personal and the cultural" (Ellis & Bochner, 2000, p. 739). Using the first-person voice, autoethnographers, like reflexive ethnographers, blur the usual distinctions between self and other. Often, as St.Pierre argued in the previous reading, autoethnographers fold their own life histories and testimonios into the self-stories of others. Autoethnogaphies appear in a variety of different forms, variations on Richardson's (2000) creative analytic practices, including short stories, poetry, fiction, and creative nonfiction, photographic essays, personal essays, narratives of the self, writing stories, self stories, fragmented, layered texts, critical autobiography, and co-constructed performance narratives.

Elena Creef discovers her mother as the other in a photograph in a back issue of the *Saturday Evening Post*, circa 1952. She seeks to locate her mother in this history and undertakes a study of World War II Japanese war brides in the Seattle area. In her inquiry, she discovers that the boundaries between insider and outsider collapse. Quickly she and her mother become the subjects of her project, which soon finds expression in poetry, photography, and autoethnography.

Jean Halley uses the personal memoir and short story form of the autoethnography to tell a story about a childhood sexual trauma. This use of experimental writing allows her to open up and criticize areas of family history that had been previously silenced. Thus does her text complement the story told by Creef.

Through her reflexive texts, **Carol Rambo Ronai** has literally created the writing form now called the *layered text*, which co-mingles various writing forms and styles. This often includes the use of first-person narratives, self-commentary, self-reflections, and the voices of others, interspersed with field notes, as well as popular cultural and social science writing. These different styles and genres are layered, one on top of the other, with transitions between layers marked by asterisks—***—or other typographic signal-symbols.

Ronai experiments with this writing style in her layered account of a night dancing and wrestling with Kitty's All Girl Review. She invokes Derrida's concepts of mimesis and *sous rature* as a lens through which she reads her lived experience with Kitty's dance troupe. As one layer is superimposed on another, new meanings are revealed and others are erased.

In his poetic, autobigraphical, and autoethnographic essay, **Richard V. Travisano** takes us back to his Italian-American childhood in Waterbury, Connecticut. He attempts to recover this past, which has been lost. Of course the past cannot be recovered, only re-remembered, and this, Travisano does in loving detail. In so doing, he criticizes the current historical moment, suggesting it has destroyed far too much of America's ethnic past, finding too that, as a consequence, he "gets emptier" as he "gets older."

REFERENCES

Ellis, C., & Bochner, A. P. (2000). Autoethnography, personal narrative, reflexivity. In N. K. Denzin & Y. S. Lincoln (Eds.), *Handbook of Qualitative Research* (2nd ed., pp. 733-768). Thousand Oaks, CA: Sage.

Richardson, L. (2000). Writing: A method of inquiry. In N. K. Denzin & Y. S. Lincoln (Eds.), *Handbook of Qualitative Research* (2nd ed., pp.923-948). Thousand Oaks, CA: Sage.

CHAPTER 5

Discovering My Mother as the Other in the *Saturday Evening Post*

——

Elena Tajima Creef
Wellesley College

This article begins by mapping an oral history project on World War II Japanese war brides in which the objective boundaries between the insider and outsider relationships of the interviewer and her subjects not only collapse but give way to a more self-reflexive and collaborative project between the interviewer and her own war bride mother. The final result is one which raises questions about the limits of objectivity in conducting feminist research that is situated close to one's own home as well as the relationship of women's silences to speech.

I can trace my current fascination with the politics of Asian American representation back to my discovery of a 1952 *Saturday Evening Post* magazine photograph of my mother innocently posed by a less than innocent American photographer in a Red Cross cooking class (Smith & Worden, 1952). Although she was never interviewed for this article, which documents the postwar phenomenon of American servicemen "bringing home Japanese wives," her appearance in the *Post* nevertheless taught me to be suspicious of historical images that have been stripped of voice. Indeed, it was precisely the historical silence surrounding World War II Japanese war brides that prompted my interest in undertaking an oral history project that I began and then abandoned more than 10 years ago. In my initial naiveté, I thought I could undertake a simple project involving the representation of women's "voices." What I learned instead was a valuable lesson on silence. I also had my first insight into the very personal nature of what is at stake for an Asian American cultural critic venturing into a field that also happens to be close to home.

PART 1

Not Quite an Insider and Not Quite an Outsider: Notes From a Failed Ethnography

"Kokujin (Black Person)"

"Hush! I warn you.
I warn you not to mention
the word 'kokujin' around here
because you don't know who
might have been married to one.
You know what I mean . . .
It's a taboo around here."

In the northwest they sought
and found a sanctuary where they were welcomed.
"There's no discrimination here."
They can enjoy their lives,
raise their children,
and participate in
the Japanese community where
equality is enjoyed and their talents go applauded.
The community is their heaven now.

Upon their arrival in America decades ago,
their dream of a promised land wasn't exactly
the way they dreamed it would be.
Today, nobody wants to talk about those years, unless asked.
The one recalls how lucky she was because
her husband was assigned to the northwest with the help
of his thoughtful commander.
Discrimination? Why she hardly felt any here
while others who lived elsewhere
still hold bitter memories.

Today, they enjoy democracy in the northwest community
where they sought and found sanctuary.
But don't let them hear the word that is taboo.
Don't let them feel hurt anymore.
So, I warn you. Don't ever mention
the word "kokujin."

We are all equal here.

(Creef, 1998)

Armed with a small research grant and a new tape recorder, I traveled from Southern California to the Pacific Northwest in the spring of 1986 determined to record stories from a group of World War II Japanese war brides from my mother's generation. I contacted these women through word of mouth and through a series of letters I had sent out to all the regional chapters of the Japanese American Citizen's League. I also used my credentials as a daughter of a war bride—as a sympathetic "insider"—to convince them, and myself, that I was already familiar with this particular community and that I was, in short, perfectly qualified to undertake the challenge of giving voice to their unique histories. The Pacific Northwest is home to what is perhaps one of the largest war bride communities in the country—due largely to its huge population of retired military personnel and their families.

At the time, I self-consciously decided not to include my mother in this project. I thought it would be to my advantage to step outside of her shadow, assert my intellectual and personal independence, and travel to neutral territory where I could practice objective scholarship in a field far away from home. That was my first mistake.

When I arrived in Seattle, Washington, I stayed with Mrs. Dogwood, a war bride who also happened to be a close friend of my mother's—someone I have known all my life. I decided not to interview her, however. After all, writing about her would be too much like writing about my own family. Plus, without offering any explanation, she let me know that she did not have anything to do with the cluster of women I had already contacted and was set to interview.

During my stay, I traveled back and forth each day between Mrs. Dogwood's home and my meetings with the other women, where from the beginning, the interview process was vexed. After my arrival, only one or two women expressed any interest in being interviewed individually. The rest insisted that it would be easier to gather them all together for one large group meeting. Because I wanted to be accommodating, I agreed. That was my second mistake.

I had hoped to hear and record a range of stories filled with the details of their postwar romance and courtship with GI husbands, their feelings about the immigration process, their separation from families, and their early days as newly arrived Asian women in the United States. Perhaps it was my fault for assuming that war bride narratives are inevitably shaded if not by tragedy then at least by some drama. After all, I feel like I have eavesdropped on war bride tales all my life—in the privacy and comfort of my own home and in those of close childhood friends. I know full well that invoking postwar memories can also stir up painful recollections of wartime loss and struggle, not to mention harsh family rejection on both sides of the Pacific over the taboo of interracial unions. I have known women who have self-consciously changed the subject or even slipped out of the room lest I might want to interview them. And I have known others who have responded angrily to my general inquiries about their lives: "Why you want to write about war brides for? I think better off to forget about war. Anyhow, what happened during war was long time ago. Better to focus on present."

I know, too, that memories of immigration often include first encounters with American racism on hostile fronts such as California and the deep South. I know I have heard my mother recall at least a hundred times her first experience with the color line in North Carolina in the 1950s and having to ask a southern White woman whether she should consider herself "colored" or "White" to use a public restroom ("Why, my dear, you most certainly must use the white room, of course"). Yet, I have heard other women recall asking the same question in places such as Mississippi and Arkansas, only to be told that they should sit down in the back of the bus or settle down in the other neighborhood where they belong. I have learned that yellow is Black or White depending on where one is located in time and space.

I must admit my disappointment during the group interview when the women gave testimony only to the ease of immigration and attested to the complete lack of discrimination throughout the relatively painless process of their own acculturation. They each stressed how fortunate they had been to have such good marriages and such successful children who have gone off to college or on to great jobs. It did not occur to me at the time that some stories are too painful to be shared publicly with a tape recorder running or that a group dynamic may prompt only certain kinds of public memories. In my disappointment at hearing war bride variations of the model minority success story, I forgot to pay attention to what the women were leaving out. After all, Adrienne Rich taught us a long time ago that "silences can be a plan/vigorously executed/the blue print to a life/It is a presence/it has a history a form" and should not be confused "with any kind of absence" (Rich, 1994).

At several points in the interview, the women even managed to turn the tables on me. No longer the interviewer, I became the interviewed as they bombarded me with a series of personal questions that left me squirming under their gaze—uncomfortable with the half truths of my own response:

> Was my mother going to help me with this project?
> Why not?
> How long had I been in school?
> Why so long?
> How old would I be by the time I graduated?
> Was I ever going to get married?

At several points, the women switched from English to Japanese to comment and laugh among themselves, engaged in a lively conversation that effectively shut me out.

Meanwhile, at the end of the day, I returned to my host's home, where she would cook her usual two dinners every evening: a simple Japanese meal with rice for the two of us and her teenage son and some version of fried chicken or steak and potatoes for her husband—who, after 35 years of marriage, still preferred the familiar comfort of deep-fried southern cooking above all else. It was during these evening sessions, when I had put away the tape recorder, that Mrs. Dogwood would sit down with me and share her life story. Unlike anything I had yet captured on tape, her stories were told in fragments and, more important, were narrated from the heart—her voice dropping to a whisper if she thought "he" might be listening from the room next door. They included memories of working as a teenager in Tokyo during the war where she watched much of that city go up in flames during the infamous bombing raids. Others had to do with the shock of arrival in Alabama where she met her husband's family for the first time only to confront their poverty as poor White southerners from a part of the South that never recovered from the Great Depression.

Mrs. Dogwood has been married for almost 40 years to Mr. Dogwood. They never expected to have children, and then, to their great surprise, she found herself expecting for the first time at age 43 and gave birth to a beautiful, healthy baby boy. She has spent the past 30 years in Seattle working in the kitchens of various Japanese restaurants. She is a chain-smoker who is plagued with bad health and numerous side effects from a difficult pregnancy late in life. Even now, in her late 60s, with terrible health, she still works in the kitchen, preparing food and washing dishes for minimum wage to help pay for the cost of her son's college education.

Mrs. Dogwood is just one of a sizeable constellation of lifelong war bride girlfriends my mother has collected from her early years of marriage spent moving through Army bases around the globe. My own memories of childhood are interwoven with snapshots of these women holding green tea coffee klatches in our kitchen, filling up our house with the familiar sounds of a foreign language they spoke to one another but never to us kids, and trading baby-sitting favors and peculiarly all-American recipes (such as sloppy Joes, apple pie, and pineapple-upside-down cake) while trying their best to hold our families together while our fathers were stationed elsewhere for up to a year at a time.

Six months after my initial trip to interview Japanese women in the Pacific Northwest, my mother impulsively decided to put her house up for sale in California and, dragging along my reluctant father, moved to Seattle. By the end of the year, she had immersed herself rather deeply into the daily life and gossip of the very same community of war brides I had "discovered" on my own and had attempted to interview from the comfortable position as a visiting outsider. My mother's instantaneous and complex relationship to the war bride community there immediately colored my own relationship to the same—undermining in the process whatever sense of ethnographic authority I originally had or, at least, thought I had (Clifford, 1988). Before my oral history project even got off the ground, the women I had essentially hoped to mine for information ended up knowing much more about me than I would ever learn about them.

What I learned from my mother's involvement with this group of women is that the war bride community in the Pacific Northwest is an intensely complicated—and competitive—one that is painfully splintered along multiple axes of long-term friendships and alliances held together by race and class affiliation; levels of education; divorced, widowed, or married status; and even poetry.

The group of women I came into contact with is the most organized one in the region—best known for their fierce annual poetry competitions, sight-seeing field trips, occasional newsletter, and most significantly, for their visible role as regional spokespersons for the entire war bride community with the local elected officials and visiting Japanese dignitaries. With only a handful of exceptions, those who are divorced, who married non-White servicemen, or who continue to work at an age when their contemporaries are beginning to enjoy the benefits of a senior citizen status do not participate in the group. I have only recently come to grasp the complexity of the division between the women who are most visible and vocal in the community and those who remain behind closed doors, self-removed from the circuit of war bride representation.

As I witnessed the collapse of what I thought had been my own clear- cut position as an objective outside observer into that of a sympathetic insider's daughter, I failed to see that the lack of stability in these terms—insider-outsider/partial-impartial—points to the larger phenomenon of what happens when "culturally entangled identities" attempt to do ethnographic fieldwork in the all too familiar spaces of their own backyard (Narayan, 1997, p. 25). I also miscalculated not only how unstable but how deceptive the notion of neutral territory would, in the end, turn out to be. When I first traveled to the Pacific Northwest to begin the project, I never dreamed that my own family home would be relocated to the same site as my fieldwork. Indeed, such a collapse between home and field has forced me to rethink the exploitative nature of my original desire to capture the personal stories of strangers in the first place. In my original conception, were the women merely the objects of my study? How is my project different from the insidiously exploitative relationship of the "feminist" ethnographer to her subjects? (Stacey, 1988).

In hindsight, the politics of undertaking an ethnographic representation of Japanese war brides has always been inseparable from the politics of my own self-location. In the name of scholarly objectivity, I overlooked the possibilities for exploring what a more self-reflexive ethnographic representation might look like—one based upon a lifetime of talk story with my mother and her circle of friends. Whether or not I want to admit it, my mother has always been my most willing chief informant. So let me begin again, by way of backtracking to a moment when I first developed a critical consciousness of the problem of Asian (American) representation. For me, this has always been a highly personal moment when I quite literally discovered my mother as the Other in the dusty stacks of my undergraduate college library. Although I failed to recognize it at the time, this was also the day I first discovered the power in claiming a theoretical position constructed somewhere between the center and the margins—from the space that Japanese literary critic Masao Miyoshi (1991) has dubbed, "off-center" (p. 5). Of course, the problem with being off-center is that one constantly risks slippage. How does one write, let alone speak, as an objective feminist cultural critic? as an Asian American? or simply as a dutiful daughter? This place of multiplicity is fraught with the difficulty of enunciation and self-location. I recognize it as the place named by Gloria Anzaldua (1987) as the Borderlands, where tensions abound between race, place, language, identity, alienation, and conflict—not to mention mothers and daughters.

Similar to Zora Neale Hurston (1935), "it was only when I was off in college, away from my native surroundings, that I could see myself like somebody else and stand off . . . then I had to have the spy-glass of Anthropology to look" (p. 1). With this in mind, let me begin again with a rather personal story about looking.

PART 2

"Little Madam Butterfly": Discovering My Mother as the Other in the Pages of the *Saturday Evening Post*

Wednesday, February 20, 1952: Weather: Fine.

Got mail from Gil and Mother Creef this morning and both of them said they saw my picture in the *Saturday Evening Post*. But me, not yet. I would like to see it very much. I will write to her today soon. Her birthday will be February 24. I forgot it, feel very sorry, but I will give gift to her when I get over there.

Friday, February 22, 1952: Weather: Fine.

I got *Post* magazine which has our Japanese Brides' School, everyone looks nice, but felt some anger about their writing in it.

Sunday, February 24, 1952: Weather: Lovely day, but windy.

More I read the *Post*, more makes me mad at their writing concerning Japanese Brides. Only my husband really knows about me and pride I have in myself. I must make up my mind about something before going to the States. (Chiyohi Creef's personal diary entries, 1952)

Flashback. I am in my early 20s as an undergraduate at one of the smallest (and smoggiest) of the University of California campuses and am engaged in one of my favorite recreational activities: poring over old magazines from the 1940s and 1950s in the library's open stacks. My family's claim to 15 minutes of fame is that both of my parents once appeared in the pages of popular American magazines. Although I still have not found it, my father always swore that he appears in *Life* magazine as a 21-year-old soldier sailing his bay horse, Fair Easter, over a sizeable competition jump back in the old days when the U.S. Army still had mounted Calvary units. Likewise, my mother has also been immortalized in print. On this particular day, I am combing through back issues of the *Saturday Evening Post*, circa 1952, when at last I find what I am looking for. The article is called "They're Bringing Home Japanese Wives" and proclaims that "six thousand Americans in Japan have taken Japanese brides since 1945, and all the little Madam Butterflys are studying hamburgers, Hollywood, and home on the range, before coming to live in the U.S.A." (Smith & Worden, 1952, p. 27). There is something both exciting and disturbing about finding my mother in these pages. The article documents the efforts of the American Red Cross to educate these newlywed Japanese women in American culture classes as they prepare for their new life overseas.

Even though they have misspelled her name in the caption, I can easily pick out my mother in the series of photographs. She is standing alongside two of her classmates in the cooking class where they are learning how to bake homemade apple pie. She is the short one wearing the tight white sweater, sporting the fuzzy hairdo. Like a good student, I make a photocopy of her image and the article and then file them away without showing either to anyone. Although I cannot articulate it at the time, there is something acutely embarrassing about discovering your mother as the Other in an outdated American magazine.

In many ways, I have always considered the *Post* article to be my pictorial origin story as well as the catalyst for my work in Asian American women's studies. On one level, the article tells the story of how my GI father met and married my Japanese mother in postwar Japan during the occupation. Essentially, she is over here, because he was over there. On another level, because the article ends with speculation over whether the United States will be ready not only for the brides but for the thousands of "bright-eyed" mixed-race children who are the offspring of these unions, it also tells my story.

The brides' schools were the original brainchild of a group of American churchwomen and were adopted by the Army in response to mass complaints from U.S. servicemen that their newlywed Japanese wives were ill equipped for immigration and acculturation into domestic American life. The American Red Cross intervened and opened up a half dozen of these schools across Japan. (Indeed, many of these schools still exist more than 50 years later in many Asian countries.) The schools were staffed back then almost exclusively by White volunteer wives and daughters of U.S. officers and included instruction in everyday domestic American life, from how to make classic American cuisine to lessons on American fashion, grooming, and social etiquette—including, at least at one school, how to respond properly to engraved invitations "should the occasion arise." According to the *Post*, these were apparently serious concerns at the time, for several soldiers interviewed complain of the difficulties they experienced in teaching their wives how to brew decent cups of coffee, assemble hamburgers together with buns, and even how to wear a Western slip underneath as opposed to on top of their outer clothes.

What is perhaps most striking in the *Post* is its ambivalent depiction of "dark-skinned, dark-eyed" Asian difference where "chrysanthemum-bud brides" are held up to "long-legged" Western standards of beauty and found lacking and where a woman's worth is also measured in terms of the class status of her GI husband. In a sweeping gesture of demographic objectivity and authority, we are told that

the brides are all sorts of people. At the bottom, there are no prostitutes, criminals or chronically diseased. . . . But there is everything else.

They are a varied lot of girls, tiny or chubby, flat-faced or quite beautiful, competent secretaries or youngsters who know very little beyond how to work in a rice paddy. They speak the English their husbands taught them—"Whassamatta, chum?" or "I beg your pardon," depending on what sort of men they married. . . . Some are quick, some stupid, many average. . . . They're not the very best Japan has, and certainly not the worst. (Smith & Worden, 1952, pp. 27, 81).

The women are also depicted as the products of a defeated and somewhat backward postwar nation who are then hopelessly measured against the presumed superiority of the West.

Country girls not only are innocent of slip technique but imagine that they are being American by having their sleek black hair frizzled into dulled mops in "Hollywood" beauty salons on Japanese side streets. They mix unbelievable hues in their outer clothing and have no idea of what to do with a girdle, although they buy them, thus annoying the life out of slightly spreading American women who find the PX never has the right size at the right time because some Japanese bride just bought it, perhaps to hang on the wall of her home as a decoration. . . .

Youngsters who never tried to cook on anything more complicated than a charcoal brazier throw cooking teachers into cold sweats . . . by putting raw fish on hot stove burners and expecting it to cook. Girls who spent their childhood in the war and postwar days living in sheet-metal shacks and sleeping on the floor have to be taught the mysteries of getting in and out of real hospital beds by the same doctors and nurses who deliver them of their half-American babies. (Smith & Worden, 1952, p. 79)

What is also striking in these passages—particularly when they are placed side by side with the photographs of the women—is their inherent contradiction. The Japanese women are disciplined and trained by the brides' schools to imitate domestic American culture and style yet at the same time are subjected to the *Post's* ridicule for presuming such an affectation. Several of the photographs capture the brides in the middle of this "training." In addition to pie making, the women are shown watching a Red Cross instructor demonstrate diaper technique in a class on basic baby care and makeup application. Each of the photographs makes it clear that each of the smiling, newlywed Japanese wives assumes the position of good pupil under the tutelage of benevolent White Red Cross and Army volunteers in a classroom where lessons in a "Western-style of democracy" are synonymous with an American style of domesticity.

The tensions in the *Post* article also signal contemporary anxieties regarding Asian immigration and miscegenation, stressing how the thousands of war brides will increase the "Japanese-race population back home" by some "4 or 5 percent." One photograph shows five particularly well-dressed war brides, their servicemen husbands, and assorted mixed-race children on board a ship sailing to the United States. The caption to the photograph stresses that "every day, from 30 to 120 American servicemen and civilians are marrying Japanese citizens in Japan" (Smith & Worden, 1952, p. 26).

Echoing an earlier anti-Japanese discourse based on West Coast fears of an Asian invasion, the *Post* cautions that soon "thousands of dark-skinned, dark-eyed brides" and "their bright-eyed children" will "be knocking on school doors in many of the forty-eight states"; yet the great question of "how they will fit in and whether they generally will be welcomed or shunned remains to be answered" (Smith & Worden, 1952, p. 27). It is important to remember that interracial marriages between U.S. servicemen and Japanese women were only made legal as a result of Public Law 717 beginning in 1947 and extending through 1952. Although the *Post* repeatedly portrays the war brides as a group of "quite average" women, many of whom have manipulated their way into a beneficial marriage for immigration purposes or to legitimate their children born out of wedlock or even "to obtain post-exchange privileges for themselves and their needy families" (Smith & Worden, 1952, p. 81), in actuality, the official process was itself dishonest. Prospective Japanese wives were deceived not only by prospective husbands but by the military as well in a highly unequal exchange of information. Although the women and their families were subjected to intense scrutiny and background checks under the euphemism of the Army's "fifteen copy thoroughness," husbands were not subjected to any type of mutual interrogation beyond proof of citizenship, single status, and proof of ability to support a wife.

The history surrounding these Asian women who began immigrating to the United States in the postwar 1950s has not only been marginalized but has also largely disappeared under the shadow of research that has been done on the Issei (first generation) immigrants and the Nisei (second-generation Japanese Americans). War brides tend to disappear somewhere between the "picture brides" of the early 20th century and the postinternment lives of the Nisei. The work of sociologist Evelyn Nakano Glenn (1986) and playwright Velina Hasu Houston (1993a, 1993b) continues to be groundbreaking in terms of their specific attention to this unique group of Japanese women—many of whom shun the term *war bride* and opt instead to call themselves *Shin Issei* (the new immigrants).

Although she first articulated her unease with the *Post* in the pages of her 1952 diary, it has taken my mother almost 45 years to come into full critical voice as a first-generation Japanese immigrant woman living in the United States. My revisiting her photo in the *Post* is offered here in the spirit of writing and talking back against the politics of representation in which the bodies of Asian women like my mother are positioned as inarticulate objects of American immigration history and imagination.

I read the following poem by Mitsuye Yamada (1992) and remember a time when I failed to see its significance—or simple wisdom:

haha ga ima yu-koto
sono uchi ni
wakatte kuru

(What your mother tells you now
in time
you will come to know.) (p. 1)

What my mother began to articulate in the broken English of her 1952 diary I have tried to continue here in the critical voice of a dutiful daughter. In listening to her anger at the *Saturday Evening Post*, over what she correctly perceived was a dishonest representation of newlywed Japanese brides such as herself, I am reminded of filmmaker Trinh Minh-ha's (1988) articulation of what happens when the native woman dares to step out from her location as a silent object of study and return the full force of her own critical gaze:

Not quite the same, not quite the other, she stands in that undetermined threshold place where she constantly drifts in and out. Undercutting the inside/outside opposition, her intervention is necessarily that of both not-quite an insider and not-quite an outsider. She is, in other words, this inappropriate other . . . who . . . [unsettles] every definition of otherness arrived at. (p. 76)

This article is dedicated to the silences my mother has broken these past 45 years and to her courage in moving from margin to center in a lifelong trajectory that has taken her from immigrant to housewife, to garment industry worker to men's clothing saleswoman, from official retirement to a bachelor's degree at age 69, and finally, to a second career as a freelance writer who has at last found the inappropriate (d) power of her own voice. When I asked my mother to write an ending

Figure 1: Gilbert and Chiyohi Creef in 1952

for this article, she sent the following poem (Creef, 1999). Never one to remain silent, my mother has always been able to speak for herself.

"The Betrayal"

> "Today, we are having visitors," said the lady
>   from the Red Cross.
> "A reporter and a cameraman from the *Saturday Evening Post*
>   will be here to take your picture and write
>   about the brides' school.
>   Our story will be read by millions of Americans.
>   Now, isn't that exciting news!?"
>
> Well groomed and wearing aprons,
> we stood around the kitchen table,
> waiting for instructions.
>
> "Here come the visitors," the lady whispered.
> "Today, I will show you how to bake an apple-pie—an American favorite,"
> said the cooking instructor.
> With smiles on our faces,
> I was told to hold a measuring cup

while others held a mixing bowl or a rolling pin.
The lesson has begun.

The cameraman is flashing. The reporter is busy taking notes.
We are all a little bit shy.

They left after a few shots.
We all hoped they would come out nicely with nice words.
Back then, I was eager to learn everything,
everything about American culture,
I wanted to be a good wife to my husband and
a good citizen to the country where I came to live.

I never saw the magazine until 30 years later.
It was a discovery I made by accident
almost forgotten for all those years.
The story made me rage. It was insulting and
misrepresented the brides.
It's not true! Not everyone was that stupid and ignorant.

I am aghast. I am furious with the writers.
I should have known what the media likes to write.
My anger has not yet subsided
over the trust and dreams of innocent girls betrayed.

REFERENCES

Anzaldua, G. (1987). *Borderlands: The new mestiza/La frontera.* San Francisco: Spinsters/
   Aunt Lute.
Clifford, J. (1988). *The predicament of culture: Twentieth-century ethnography, literature, and
   art.* Cambridge, MA: Harvard University Press.
Creef, C. (1998). Kokujin. Unpublished poem.
Creef, C. (1999). The betrayal. Unpublished poem.
Glenn, E. N. (1986). *Issei, Nisei, war bride: Three generations of Japanese American women in
   domestic service.* Philadelphia: Temple University Press.
Houston, V. H. (1993a). Asa Ga Kimashita. In V. H. Houston (Ed.), *The politics of life: Four
   plays by Asian American women.* Philadelphia: Temple University Press.
Houston, V. H. (1993b). Tea. In R. Uno (Ed.), *Unbroken thread: An anthology of plays by
   Asian American women.* Amherst: University of Massachusetts Press.
Hurston, Z. N. (1935). *Mules and men.* Philadelphia: J. B. Lippincott.
Minh-ha, T. (1988). Not you/like you: Post-colonial women and the interlocking ques-
   tions of identity and difference. *Inscriptions, 3/4,* 71-77.
Miyoshi, M. (1991). *Off-center: Power and culture between Japan and the United States.* Cam-
   bridge, MA: Harvard University Press.
Narayan, K. (1997). How native is the native anthropologist? In L. Lamphere,
   H. Ragone, & P. Zavella (Eds.), *Situated lives: Gender and culture in everyday lives.* New
   York: Routledge.

Rich, A. (1994). In K. Visweswaran, *Fictions of feminist ethnography*. Minneapolis: University of Minnesota Press.

Smith, J. W., & Worden, W. L. (1952, January 19). They're bringing home Japanese wives. *Saturday Evening Post, 224*(29), 26-27, 79-81.

Stacey, J. (1988). Can there be a feminist ethnography? *Women's Studies International Forum, 11*(1), 21-27.

Yamada, M. (1992). What your mother tells you. In *Camp Notes and Other Poems*. Latham, NY: Kitchen Table: Women of Color Press.

––

Elena Tajima Creef teaches in the Women's Studies Department at Wellesley College. She received her Ph.D. in history of consciousness from the University of California, Santa Cruz, and recently completed a book on Japanese American representation in American visual culture. Her work has been published in Visual Anthropology Review, *in Darrell Hamamoto and Sandra Liu's* Countervisions: Asian American Film Criticism, *and in Gloria Anzaldua's* Haciendo Caras: Making Face, Making Soul. *She and her mother are currently working on a mother-daughter memoir tentatively titled "Notes of a Fragmented Daughter/Memories From a War Bride Mother."*

CHAPTER 6

This I Know

An Exploration of Remembering Childhood and Knowing Now

— —

Jean Halley

City University of New York

This article makes use of experimental writing to explore childhood trauma and its subject. In it, I examine or tell myself within the gendered and raced context of my family history. However, this piece is also about ideologies and what it means to know something. Through experimental writing, I explore a nonlinear, repetitive kind of knowing and speaking the world that both challenges and compliments more traditional sociological ways of knowing society.

This article is experimental sociological writing that explores trauma and its subject. In the writing, I attempt to put words to memories of trauma. As told, the story circles around and through tone, place, and familial generations. Through the story, I try to capture the particular difficulty—with trauma—of remembering, of knowing what happened, along with the uncertainty around who is to blame. There is a way in which the story's trauma attempts to sit in the everydayness of childhood, the mundane, and at times, the loving, everyday details of life.

It's funny I forgot this year. Ash Wednesday is still my mother's favorite religious day. Like much in the Catholic tradition, it is a day whose symbolism is deeply rooted in the earth. From ashes we come, and to ashes we shall return. We were Catholic. For my grandmother, it would have been unforgivable not to go to Mass on Ash Wednesday. In fact, both my grandmothers used to go to Mass everyday. In our Irish Catholic family, religion was a place in which women had some power. I guess it had to do with that earthy thing. Blood and bodily pain were women's domain, both dirty and awesome, animal and Godlike at once. It was known that women were especially connected to God.

Men, on the other hand, they ran things. Whereas women lived in the day-to-day simple and mundane rituals of life, men lived in the world. They made things happen. My grandfather was a powerful man. In the family and outside, he held respect. He owned places and things in the world—land, cattle, and people's jobs. He grew wheat and corn and raised beef. To me, they were cows, soft, brown, and thoughtful creatures with big sad eyes. However, to my grandfather, and he knew, they were beef. New calves, yearlings, and two-year-olds ready for slaughter, breed cows were all potential meat. Meat was money, money and power. This was the language of his world.

He taught me things, my grandfather. He showed me how to eat a baked potato, deep yellow with half a cube of butter and lots of salt. From him, I learned that to order steak rare was not ladylike, but medium did a disservice to our ranching family. I ate my steak medium rare to make my grandfather proud. My brother, who was adopted, ate his steak well done, a sure sign that his blood was not the same as ours. My grandfather, although polite to my brother, never quite accepted him because family, next to business, was everything. Like business, you were born into the family or you were not. Success ran in the blood preordained. Yet, I was a girl. Although my blood was his, I could not share his world.

This is my history, my remembering. That is all. I guess I am choosing to remember, both to leave my history and to return. I am only too aware that it will always be with me. To you, this may mean little, but my life, this story, is all I have. This was the story I was given. I have no choice; I will take it. So, I am remembering.

You cannot remember something if you have been thinking of it anyhow, all along. To remember means to bring back to memory something that you were not holding in your mind, something that for a long or a short time was not immediately with you. So maybe my history is not remembered. It just is, more or less present, but there, always, always.

However, in some way, it was not present. My history, as it happened even, lived in another time. It, its events, were not present even to the time when it lived. I will tell you that in my family, time was two-dimensional. Time was flat. So there was no room for truth, and I guess there was no room for history either. Things happened, and they didn't, at once.

So this is my story. Its telling is to force the time when I lived, and live, to be complete.

Gram

I want to start where we all start, with my grandmother. Yet, how can I tell the story of my grandmother when in some way I never knew her myself? I only have glimpses, moments, and of course, all the ways I did not know her.

Yet, what is it to know someone anyhow? Is it to know a list of her traits? Or is it an indescribable sense, an experience one has and comes to have of someone else, that constantly changes? Or is knowing someone simply to share time with her, to be with her in moments of her life? Or is to know someone to own them, and thus, is knowing not really possible?

Knowing a person, knowing a place, knowing what happened, or knowing anything intrigues me. There were no facts in my family. We lived by rules instead. And if time is three dimensional, as are human beings, we lived in only part of time. Our world had two dimensions. Our world was flat. And truth did not fit there.

So my grandmother. My grandmother had a rose garden. This I know. When I think of her, I remember a smell both elegant and dis-

tant, like a rose. My grandmother was elegant and distant. My grandmother did not hold me. She never touched me. I do not know what
her skin felt like—only that she had spots, brown spots, on her hands.
And I know she disliked the spots intensely. To her, they were no
accomplishment of growing old, mark of a life well lived. For her, the
spots were dirty, stains that could not be removed. They were like
shame.

My grandmother had a rose garden in her backyard. I would follow her there under the pretense of helping. She knew many things
about roses. She knew where they should be cut and when so as not to
hurt the plant. She knew how to make a yard quiet and time stop so
that the roses would grow in abundance. She knew how to gather
them and put them together in a bowl so that they were beautiful, so
beautiful that your breath halted for a second when you saw them.
They would fill a room with their rich scent, both elegant and distant.
Roses are not like daisies. One has to be careful when picking a rose,
with their sharp, strong thorns. Roses are not like daisies, overjoyed to
be alive, reaching eagerly for the sun. Roses demand a certain awe.

Maybe my grandmother loved roses because she saw herself in
them. Maybe it was because they reminded her of her God, who was
also awesome, who was also distant. My grandmother lived in very
certain spaces. She lived in her rose garden, she lived in her kitchen,
and she lived in her church. Hers was a world where women had their
place. And men, men had everywhere else. Luckily, women got God,
although it was only because men did not need him. They were in
charge anyhow.

My grandmother's God was awesome. His house was at the Catholic church. He, like my grandmother, was removed. Although he
was always present, he was never familiar. We did not discuss God. To
speak of God in daily conversation was something worse than disre-
spect. Yet, even so, the silence granted God was not unusual. My family was filled with silences, gaping quiet, empty places. God existed
somewhere there, in that silence.

I loved my grandmother. I loved to be with her. In the summer, I
would go to visit her at my grandparents' house in Kidron, Wyoming,
for two weeks. These two weeks were extraordinary. They were special. I wanted to stay forever.

For some of my summer visits, my father would fly me to Kidron in his little plane. Sometimes he would drive me. A couple of times, he only drove me to Cheyenne, and my grandparents came to meet me, to pick me up there. We would meet at the Little America. Because everything having to do with my grandmother became special, Little America became a special place. Going there was a treat, a luxury to be relished, like a candy bar at the movies.

Of course, Little America was unique in my experience. Grand Junction, Wyoming, where we lived, was a town of 15,000 to 20,000 people and was not on a major interstate. It was not large or central enough to have a Little America. In contrast, Cheyenne was big, almost a real city. Cheyenne had a shopping mall and had movie theaters with several different screens showing several different movies at once. So it made sense that Cheyenne, with all its wonders, would also have a Little America. Little America was a place where travelers stopped on their way to other places. It promised potential, like a car trip. At Little America, you could do just about everything a person might want to do. You could buy gas for your car. You could stay the night. There was a restaurant where you could get all kinds of things, including apple pie, French fries, and milkshakes where they did not just give you the glass, they gave you the silver mixer with all the extra milkshake too. There was a gift shop that displayed some of the most wonderful stuffed animals I had ever seen. There was a fancy ladies' room. When you went in, you first went through a lobby with cushioned seats and mirrors, and then another room with hand-washing sinks and yet more mirrors, all before you finally came to the room with the toilets. Little America was full of possibility.

When we went to special places, my father treated me kindly. Everything was good. Arriving at Little America, we would park the car and enter the main building, up the steps covered in red carpet and in the big front doors. Then we would go left, into the restaurant to wait for my grandparents. I can still picture my grandmother, see her in my mind, when she came to pick me up at Little America. She would come with my grandfather. He died several years ago. But then, when he was alive and she not bedridden, he would do all the long distance driving. Women only drove in town. Men drove for trips. This was how it was. It was one of those things that never made sense, but it didn't matter because it simply was that way. My grandfather was a wild driver. He forgot to shut car doors, often driving off with them still open. He turned corners fast and made the car stop and start so much I would be perpetually nauseous. Once on the highway—I think we were on our way to the Halley family reunion in Estes Park—he ran over a rabbit. I was in the back seat and I saw him hit it through the front window. Then I felt its small body under the car, two quick thumps. I cried quietly so that no one would notice. And no one did.

So my grandmother did not come to pick me up alone at Little America. She came in the passenger seat, with my grandfather driving. They would enter the restaurant looking for us. Seeing my grandmother, my whole self filled with gladness. She would smile at me. She did not smile a big open smile. Just like she never laughed out loud. I guess it would not be tasteful. I was never quite sure what the rules were exactly, but they were there, and this was one of them. Yet she did smile at me, and I knew she too was glad.

To greet me or to say good-bye, my grandmother would give me a kiss. Well, it wasn't really a kiss. It was a sort-of kiss. She would put her cheek out, touching me on my cheek, then move quickly away. She always smelled good. My grandfather greeted me by pulling my hair. Sort of gently, but not really. He would ask me something, to which I did not know the answer and he didn't listen anyhow.

Soon it was time to go. I would sit in the back seat of their always new, always fancy and big car. Between my grandfather's driving and the new car smell, I would feel carsick the whole way to Kidron. However, I did not complain. Complaining was bad, not complaining was good, and I wanted to please my grandmother. She would periodically smile back at me from the front seat. The drive from Cheyenne to Kidron is 1½ hours long. Only a little bit of it is on interstate, most is on a small rural highway threading together small rural towns. It is beautiful. The sky is so big in Wyoming, so very big that many things can be happening all at one time within it. Underneath such endless sky, one is especially small. It is okay. One feels held by that sky. One knows that all will be well.

When we arrived in Kidron, my grandfather would drive us up the driveway to let us out. He had to go to the salebarn. He was a man and had important things to do. I didn't mind. My grandmother and I entered the house through the side door in the garage. The house was big, quiet, and filled with her presence. It was a house that held many memories. I do not know the memories. They are not mine. However, I know that they were there in that house, everywhere. That house let go of nothing.

My grandmother's house was where my father, her first son, grew up. It was where all her five sons and no daughters grew. My grandmother wanted a daughter. Even though boys are better, she still wanted at least one daughter. She wanted a daughter and had only sons, five sons named Simon, Thomas, Michael, Lester, and John. Simon and John are names of two of the disciples. Lester was named after my grandfather, whose name was Lester, although we called him Mac. As one might expect, Lester was the especially crazy one. My mother thinks that when you give a child someone else's name, you give much more than just the name. In some way, the child takes on that person's path in the world, their legacy. My mother does not want us, her children, to name our own children after her or other people in the family. But for my grandmother's five sons, it is too late. Uncle Tom was named after Gram's brother, who was a priest. And I don't know where Uncle Mike's name came from. Maybe that is why he was the lost one.

When I was a child, I went to visit Gram for two weeks in the summer. I am not sure when this ritual started and became official, an event to be counted on. But it did, at least for awhile. And yet, then, everything changes, even official events, and somewhere in the years I stopped going. At some point, I stopped going to stay with Gram for two weeks, by myself, every summer. The ritual ended.

And now I have not seen my grandmother for too many years. I went once, for a day. It was in the fall of 1993, and my grandmother was old. Although she had not stopped remembering, as she later did, nonetheless one of us had changed too much. As she looked at me, I knew she did not recognize me. I was not the one she remembered. She did not know who I was.

But when I was a child I would go to visit her for two weeks every summer. I would go by myself. And the time there with my grandmother was delicious. Every moment I held onto too tightly, so that it went even sooner than it might have otherwise. This is something I still do. Not everything has changed.

When we first entered her house, after being dropped off by my grandfather, I would be filled with recognition. Her house was familiar, yet always, somehow, new. Like Little America but better, it was rich with potential.

The first room one entered, from the garage door on the side of the house, was the dining room. It was a room to be used only for special occasions. It was a luxury room. There was a big wooden dining room table in the middle of the room with a large crystal chandelier hanging over it. When all the family came over for a special occasion meal, the table would grow larger to accommodate us. It had big fancy wooden chairs with velvet cushions and very high backs all around it. When I sat in one of those chairs, I could rest my back and my neck and my head and still have chair, reaching up above me, leftover. The chairs were big and I was small.

On one side of the room, the side you faced when you came in from the garage, there was a wall-length, ceiling-high cupboard, just for dishes. My grandmother had lots of dishes. They came in sets from all over the world. When my grandmother napped, sometimes I would spend an afternoon looking at those dishes, imagining whose dreams they held. They were so fancy, so perfect. Maybe for my grandmother, having those dishes made everything okay.

When we had big family dinners, often my grandmother would let me set the table. With some stipulations, I could even choose the dishes to be used. It was a big choice. In a way, choosing the dishes gave me some control over how things went, not just at the dinner, but in general. Choosing made me glad and worried both. Sometimes I would have the table all ready, and then, decide to switch the dishes. This was okay with my grandmother.

I loved setting the table. I knew how to put the knives facing in toward the plate, the salad forks outside of the dinner forks, and the spoons outside of the knives. My grandmother taught me other things too, like that the salt should always stay with the pepper, that spoons should never be left in dishes, and where the different glasses go. These were things she knew and told me. And I still love setting the table.

When we had those big family meals, my grandmother would sit at one end of the table, near the kitchen door, and my grandfather would sit at the other end. Everybody else sat in between. However, the rule was that men had to sit next to women, and women next to men. It was a rule, so we followed it.

Once, before my mother left my father, when I was very small, my mother broke a rule at a family dinner. It was a rule that no one contradicted my grandfather. No one contradicted my father either, except my grandfather. This was how things were. If you were a man, you could not be contradicted, except if you were a man younger than another man. The oldest man could contradict everyone freely with no repercussions. As a little girl, I couldn't contradict anyone, except my little sister. Which I did.

Anyhow, one time at a family dinner, my mother contradicted my grandfather. He was not her father; he was my father's father. This made him even more important, and it made her contradiction even worse. My grandfather was talking, which my grandfather did. He talked, his sons responded, and we listened. Sometimes the women talked quietly among themselves. Well, when my mother contradicted my grandfather, my grandfather was talking, and everyone was listening. My grandfather was talking about the niggers. He was telling us about them, about things they do and do not do, about how they cannot be trusted. My grandfather was talking. And, suddenly, my mother contradicted him. In my mind, I remember her standing up. Maybe she really pushed back that big chair and stood up at the dinner table. Or maybe she didn't. But either way, it was a kind of standing up because she interrupted my grandfather. And even worse, according to the rules, she told him what to do. Or rather, she told him what not to do. She told him not to use that word, that word nigger. She told him that maybe he believed in that word but she didn't. She told him he could talk like he wanted at other times but not in front of her children, which were us. She told him that she could not stop him from thinking that way, that way that he thought, but she did not want her children to learn his way. She did not want her children to learn this word and believe it to be right.

One time, when I was grown, my mother told me that she worried it was all her fault. She told me that she worried my grandfather did what he did as revenge. She said maybe he did those horrible things to my sister and me as a way to get back at her. He never again used that word in front of us, at least not until I was much older and my mother was no longer around. By then, I had learned to shudder at that word, to feel sick in my stomach at my grandfather's thinking. But my mother said that maybe instead of talking that way, talking poison, he got back at my mother for her contradiction in a way much worse than words.

When my grandfather finally died, it was because all that poison finally killed him. He rotted alive from the inside out. In the last two years of his life, he had a terrible rash. I never saw it because I was not visiting my grandparents anymore. However, my brother told me that he had a terrible rash. The rash was very ugly and very painful. It covered his whole body, and there was nothing they could do about it. He took lots and lots of baths and tried all kinds of special ointments. But nothing helped. The doctors did not know why he had this rash, or if they knew, they did not say. Maybe they too were afraid of my grandfather. As far as I know, my mother was the only one who ever contradicted him. My mother has always been brave, braver even than poison.

Now my grandfather is finally dead. He died in June of 1993. I think the date was June 6, but I cannot be sure. By that time I was already cut off from my family. I still write it in my date book. I write "Mac died in 1993" on June 6. Then I put a question mark because I am not sure of the exact date. But, at least I know he's dead. At least I know, he is dead. That I know.

Jeannie

When I was ten years old, I became sick with some kind of flu. Maybe I was not sick. I could not be sure. What was and was not real evaded me. For example, I never quite knew if I actually did have a headache. Maybe I was just making it up. Even pain was disputable. Ultimately, there was only one thing I did know, simply know. I knew there was something deeply wrong with me, or really, what was wrong went deeper than being wrong *with* me. The truth, the only truth, was that I, my self, was wrong. I was simply wrong.

So I cannot say, positively, that I was really sick that time when I was ten. However, when I was a child, I believed that if someone *were* sick, if I were sick, I would have certain specific symptoms. These symptoms would be proof of my sickness. One of these symptoms was not eating. Among other things, I believed sick people did not eat.

So when I was ten and sick, I stopped eating. I stopped eating to be sure that I was really sick. I did not tell my mother about this decision. I did not tell anyone, although really, outside of my mother, I had no one else to tell. I just stopped eating. I would not even eat my favorite things. Not even corn. Not even candy. Not even soda pop. I remember my mother spoon-feeding 7-Up, 7-Up I did not want, into my mouth. My mother was scared about my not eating.

During that time, that time of not eating, at first I read. I read curled up under lots of blankets. This was something I loved to do, and something I believed sick people did. So at first I read, and then, after a while, all I did was sleep. Maybe I was starving. Not only did I stop eating, but I stopped wanting to eat. I still remember being in my body then. It, I, was limp, and very, very thin, almost gone. My body almost went away, and took me with it.

I remember my mother loading me up into her car, her old blue Volvo station wagon. Eventually, that car was destroyed in an accident. But we still had it then. Many things happened in that car, including my mother taking me to the doctor that time when I was sick and stopped eating. Like me, the doctor could not be sure what was wrong. However, he said, if she doesn't start eating, we will have to feed her intravenously. This I remember. Then, my mother and I went home.

My mother left my father when I was six. She left my father and went back to school. So she could build a life for herself. So she could support us. I already told you that my mother was brave. I loved her immensely. I still do.

At this time, this time of my not-eating sickness, we lived in a small house on Ord Street. It was a rented house, and we lived there with my mother's lover, Joe. Joe paid the rent. We had no money. My mother had left my father 4 years earlier. She kept Andy, Katie, and me. He kept the money. Unlike us, my father had a lot of money. But we were poor. So we lived in a small house with Joe and his two sons, Chris who was crazy mean, and Joey who was my age. It was a bad time.

It was a bad time and bad things happened in that time. Like Chris. Joe's son, Chris, was simply a bad thing. Chris was crazy mean. Chris was like Mac. Chris was cruel. Years later, when we were all grown and that time long over, we heard that Chris had been arrested for jumping out at women from behind bushes. And then we heard he had become a psychologist.

Chris was simply a bad thing. He was mean. He was mean to my mother. He was mean to me and my sister and brother. He was very mean. And one day, one afternoon when no one was home, Chris forced me to do a terrible bad thing. He held me down and forced his penis in my mouth. Chris was cruel. And I was afraid, very afraid of Chris. I never told. I was too afraid. Like I said, it was a very bad time.

Maybe it was the alcohol. Maybe not. But something, something blurred the lines around reality. Nothing was clear. And now, looking back, I still wonder. Am I remembering this right? Is this really it? I did not know then, so how can I possibly be sure now.

In another place, in another set of memories, clarity might not matter. I mean, really, if all were well, then who cares what happened. If all were well, then what happened, and other such details, are insignificant. But all was not well. All was not well. This much I know. And it is the pain that makes me push the edges of our family truth.

Gram

Who was this woman, my grandmother. If I knew, would her story set me free. If I knew, would knowing take this weight away, this forever pain. Or is it simply too late. Always, too late.

And, anyhow, my grandmother told me all I need to know. My grandmother chose not to want the truth. She chose to look the other way. And oddly, this is the thing I despise most in everyone else, everyone except my grandmother. I don't know why, but I can, I do forgive my grandmother. And my grandmother chose this thing. She chose not to see. And in a way, she told me this. She told me of her choice.

Let me tell you a memory I never had to remember. It was one of those always-there memories. Somehow, this memory got mixed in with all the regular memories, the memories that I did not have to forget. It was a memory that crossed over, leading me, taking me away from my family's story, our established family story, the story we lived in. It is a memory of shame. In this memory, I am sitting on Mac's lap. I am eight or so, too big to be pulled into a grown man's lap, even if he is my grandfather. In the memory, Mac has his hand in my shirt, and he is touching my absolutely flat child chest. I can tell you now that I did not like this. And I can tell you that I did not understand. Yet there is no point in telling you because it simply did not matter. Mac is Mac. He does whatever he wants and no one asks questions. There is no room for saying no, and certainly no room for the voice of an eight-year-old girl. If anyone is no one, it is I. Well, in the memory, Gram walks in. We are in Mac's den, sitting on Mac's couch. Mac has his television here, in the den, and a big window that looks down over the rose garden, the rose garden that I love. Gram walks in, she walks into Mac's den to call us to supper. She walks in, and she sees what is happening. There are so many things I would like to be able to tell you now, so many things. But, it is too late for me, too late for lying. So I will tell you what Gram did. She walked in and saw what was happening. And then, she turned around and walked out.

——

Jean Halley is a doctoral student in the sociology program of the Graduate School and University Center of the City University of New York. She is currently writing her dissertation, a social history exploring 20th-century ideologies of adult-child touch in the United States. She teaches in both the film and media studies department and the women's studies department at Hunter College of the City University of New York. She holds a master's degree in theology from Harvard University.

CHAPTER 7

The Next Night *Sous Rature*
Wrestling With Derrida's Mimesis

——

Carol Rambo Ronai
University of Memphis

This "layered account" of the author's night dancing and wrestling with Kitty's All Girl Review, for the purposes of gaining access to her male and female striptease dancers, is and is not Part 2 of an article that appeared in the September 1998 issue of Qualitative Inquiry. *Making use of the metaphor of drawing, the author invokes Derrida's nonconcepts of "mimesis" and "sous rature" as a lens through which to view her lived experiences with the troupe, identity, and writing. As each layer is superimposed on prior layers, new meanings emerge. All images and impressions are subject to erasure at any time given the absence of a one-to-one correspondence of representation to reality and the changing nature of relationships between performers over time and from differing perspectives. Ultimately, lived experience, identity, and writing can be seen as simultaneous processes of destruction and creation.*

Barefoot, wearing a push-up bra and t-back strap, the screams from the men deafen me. The Mastress of Ceremonies (MC) wears a referee's striped blouse, black shorts, dark hose, and black riding boots. Her riding crop cracks against various surfaces; her voice booms through the sound system in a Bette Midler drawl, "Do I hear $15 for her, boys. Fifteen dollars to get closer. You know you want it."

A drunk bellows, "Fifteen bucks," falling backward off the shoulders of his colleagues. The audience roars and the bidding starts.

I scan the room and smile at the crowd, numb from alcohol, trying to get a fix on the situation. I should feel something—fear, shame, disgust, dismay—something. Yet I am suspended in an odyssey of lights, screaming, and cheers, disconnected, "out of my mind" as events flow around but not through me.

Finally, I feel mild relief that out of the more than 150 men present I have been "won" by a sweet, portly, desk sergeant named Sam for $35. He seems shy, not the type to be abusive as my "ring-side manager."

As I exit the stage, Kitty,[1] the troupe manager, says, "That went well. You get to keep that you know." I stand staring at her, wondering what brought me to the point where it seemed reasonable to be auctioned off for $35, on a stage, under a spotlight, wearing lingerie.

*   *   *

Drawing on field notes from the evening's events, this is a "layered account" about performing with Kitty's troupe. From these materials, I wish to draw a picture of what it was like to be an ethnographer/dancer/wrestler that night, emphasizing the ambiguity and the loose coupling of the performer's identities with their social situations. As an ex-art major, drawing and painting metaphors come readily to me when I reflect on consciousness and lived experience. Elsewhere (Ronai, 1998), I have used Derrida's discussion of Freud's mystic sketch pad to show how impressions from the world become internalized and layered on the existing stocks of knowledge, shifting how that knowledge will affect current and future lived experience.

The creation of a picture is layered, as is the apprehending of it. For instance, newspaper color photos are printed using four layers of ink, one that fills in the black pixels and three that fill in other colors. By themselves, each layer of ink offers little information to help the viewer assemble a picture of what the photo represents. The picture emerges only from the combined information of the various inks printed together against a newsprint backdrop.

Lived experience can also be described as a layering process using a drawing metaphor. Drawing entails laying down a few lines of information, viewing the lines, and then laying down or erasing other lines of information relative to the prior lines. Often, the first line does not survive the drawing process. The destructive activity of the eraser is as much a part of the drawing process as laying down a line.

Figure sketching is challenging because the subject that the artist wants to re-create on paper or canvass is always in motion. Even as lines are laid down, erased, or added to—even as a serviceable figure emerges from the page—the person that the sketch artist is trying to draw shifts—perhaps subtly—because either the model, the artist, or both change their position. As the artist's eyes move from the model to the page and back to the model, the lines drawn on the page are adjusted to reflect the new positioning of the figures. With each new glance at the model, there is a new opportunity for the picture to change.

Lived experience, as it unfolds in consciousness, is a constant process of correction. Not correction in the sense of right or wrong or trying to record the true picture but correction in the sense of adjusting the picture based on the perceived change in the relationships between the performers in a setting. Every stimulus attended to is a line of information added in the drawing process; each pass of the recording medium is a new layer that changes how the prior layers will contribute to an overall perception of the picture. As new impressions are received, new pictures emerge.

The parallels between drawing and apprehending lived experience articulate a theory of learning and consciousness that I believe adherents of theories with a constructionist bent, such as interactionists, phenomenologists, ethnomethodologists, poststructuralists, and postmodernists, should be sympathetic with. Each orientation addresses some form of an internalization and reorientation process that informs a performer's future activity. Most also emphasize the role of misunderstandings and mistakes as a way of learning the loose coupling of tacit rules to social situations.

Writing in layers reflects the structure of consciousness. As each layer of text is superimposed on the others, each layer contributes to the understanding of the other layers as well as to the overall picture of social life that the text conveys.

*   *   *

Sherri, a 42-year-old graduate student who had six children and was living in student housing, said to me while nursing her 2-year-old son,

> Carol, I just can't believe you would still be willing to dance and take part in a degrading wrestling match just to get interviews. It seems to me . . . well . . . I'm concerned you're still using your body to get by. If you ask me, I think you're destroying yourself.

*   *   *

> A lot of people have the stereotype of the misconception that dancers are stupid, go nowhere losers. That's why you're doing these interviews, right? That what you said? Oh, you don't want to bias this, do you? [Giggles] I took Soc. classes you know. Okay. Graduated from college with my B.S. in business and a Soc. minor. I'm managing a lingerie boutique with the Strip-o-gram and modeling business. I support myself, I have a lot going on. I've been told how harmful this business [stripping] is supposed to be for me, but I don't buy it. No one is supporting me, I support myself. I see, well I'll tell you, I see myself with a boutique someday in New York. I have the skills to do that and I use now to make the money to open that business then. I see myself as building my future, not hurting myself. (Starr, from a transcription of life history materials)

*   *   *

In this article, as I construct layers depicting what happened that night with Kitty's troupe, I place the layers or vignettes under erasure or *sous rature* (Derrida, 1976). Derrida places his terms *sous rature* by using them and drawing an X through them. He uses words and concepts with the understanding that they are representations of the play of differences between ideas, not essentialist representations of reality. This is and isn't what it was like to be an ethnographer/dancer/wrestler because of the various levels of "mimesis" (Derrida, 1983) or imitation at work. Writing this now, I reflect on field notes from 1992, which were, in turn, a reflection on the events that night: a dance where we presented ourselves as "characters," a fake auction, and a mock wrestling match. A "real" wrestling match is, in itself, an imitation of a real conflict or fight. Mimesis is infinite. There is nothing essential to capture that isn't imitating or standing for something else.

Each vignette is a mark *sous rature*, constructing, for the reader, a play of differences to apprehend. Without them, I cannot describe my experience, yet each vignette, like the artist's charcoal or conte line, must be subject to erasure to preserve the ambiguity that underlies each situation.

*   *   *

Kitty enters the dressing room and Starr approaches her about wrestling, "What are we supposed to do?"

I add, "Yeah, I've never even seen this before. You said there were tricks when you talked me into this."

Kitty says,

There is not much to it really. The job's to look like you're in pain when you're not and keep your clothes on. Sliding around in that goo, it's easy for a top to slip off, and that's not legal. We have to watch each other's tops. If you notice a girl's top off or slipping, throw yourself on her to cover her and tap her once to let her know she needs to fix it. Also, if you're running out of breath or you can't breathe, tap the girl twice to let her know you need to get up.

"Can't breathe?" Starr and I say together.

"It happens," says Kitty, looking to Trisha who smiles, knowingly.

"And lots of hair pulling, the guys love it, only the girl getting her hair pulled controls the pull." As Kitty explains, she puts her hand in her hair in a gesture to pull it. "See?" she says, drawing her head away from a bunch of hair in her hand. "You pull your head away from the girl's hand as hard or gentle as you want, whatever you can handle. Just remember to look like you're in pain."

Starr and I mimic hair pulling until we both believe we have it down. There is no other "training."

*   *   *

Looking like Daisy Mae from *Li'l Abner* in a halter top, cutoff denim shorts, and boots, I stand awkwardly outside of the bar with a bouncer who is uncomfortable with me. Kitty had said, "Stand here and try to get people inside to see the match."

Unsure of what to do, I fall into the role of the coquette. As men stroll by I croon, "What are *you* doing tonight?" When they stop to tell me their plans, I say, with a smile, "I was hoping you were going to come see me wrestle." Some of the men make apologies, some promise to come back later, and some buy admission into the bar at $4 a person.

When Kitty comes back she snaps, "What are you doing?"

"What does it look like I'm doing?" I ask, surprised that she is surprised.

"Hooking," she responds.

My eyes open wide with surprise, my face twitches, not knowing how to arrange itself on the front of my skull. The bouncer starts to laugh. "I thought I was supposed to be getting these guys to come in the bar," I state, defensively.

"All you are supposed to do is stand there and let the guys look at you. The bouncer does the rest," Kitty says.

Is this guy my pimp then? I ask myself. The humiliation tightens my throat and chest, flooding me for a second. I look Kitty in the eye, ready to walk away, when I catch a glimpse of it in her face—teary, fretful—she looks humiliated too. She wants to have a "classy" dance troupe. By interpreting my job on the door this way, I draw the troupe's collective identity into question.

I get over my dismay quickly and apologize to her, pleading, "Please forgive me, you gotta' remember where I worked as a dancer, if you weren't aggressive, you didn't make money. Would you show me what to do?"

Her demeanor softens as she puts her arm around me, guides me in the door and says, "You've been on door long enough. I'll take it again. Thanks for the break."

*   *   *

On my way to the dressing room, Rick, the assistant manager, yells to me, "You didn't do a damn thing wrong, honey. You got them in the door. That's your job." My passing draws whoops, laughter, and applause from the bar.

* * *

As I open the dressing room door, everyone cheers and applauds. I am mortified. Again, I don't know how to react. Trisha comes up behind me, laughing, squeezing my shoulders, and says, "You were great. You pissed her off!" Everyone is smirking, not mocking me as I had guessed.

"It was great. You should have seen how mad she was," Starr says.

"Who, Kitty?" I ask. They all nod, grinning. Clearly I have stumbled into a quagmire of relationships I don't understand.

"Kitty is high and mighty about us being classy, and at the same time she is so common. It's funny she got mad at you. You don't dance with her regular. She can't take it out on you," Starr explains.

I think about the interviews I need and I'm not so sure.

"I thought ya'll were all friends," I say.

Everyone nods, they are friends.

"And Kitty?" I ask.

Again, everyone nods. Kitty is a good friend.

"I don't get it," I finally confess, whining, exhaling pent-up tension.

Everyone laughs. Trisha says, "We all spend too much time together, doing these things, on the road, at the lingerie store. Kitty is a control freak and we all pay a price for that. It's funny you got to her, that's all."

Everyone in the room nods vigorously when Trisha says she is a control freak. I recall my relationship with Kitty up to that point, how she had tricked me on several occasions, and I crack a smile. I say, "She treats everyone like . . . " when I am cut off by Starr, jumping on top of a chair and gyrating in an animated hysteria, shrieking, "Shiiit. She treats everyone like shiiit." Their teasing and laughter reassure me, erasing my tension.

* * *

We are escorted by three bouncers toward a stage with stairs and railings on two sides. In front of this stage, on the wooden dance floor, are four king-size mattresses. Eight single-size mattresses, lined with visquine, are propped up in such a way as to form a four walled mattress pit. The tables and chairs are at the back of the room. As two men pour syrup on the plastic and spread it around, one slips and falls—a slapstick routine that earns him a chuckle from the crowd. There is a low elevation, tobacco smoke haze hovering over the room, giving everything an ominous, grayish-green cast. The stark lighting illuminates the stage and "ring" alone.

My voice quivers as I ask a bouncer how many people are in the room. He says, "I can't tell for sure, but we've already taken in $600 at the door." Divided by $4 a person, that's at least 150 people, not counting the staff, not counting the folks who got in free for whatever reason.

I have never stripped for a crowd this size, but even more intimidating is the composition of the crowd. Everyone seems to be a cop: cops in navy blue SWAT team t-shirts and pants; cops out of uniforms with badges attached to their shirts, jackets, and waists; three cops in uniform, walking the floor, talking into walkie-talkies; unmarked off-duty cops, drinking beer and screaming till the veins on their necks bulge with the effort. I catch a glimpse of an open door and see three parked squad cars and two moving squad cars. Cops swarm the parking lot, many of them also speaking into walkie-talkies.

I turn to Kitty who is watching me, beaming. She had mentioned in passing that she was "friendly" with the police and was not worried about getting busted. She had understated her case for effect. This is obviously a cop event.

* * *

I am a fake dancer and a fake wrestler who participated in a counterfeit auction with a simulated manager. I wrestled in an inauthentic wrestling match, in an improvised ring, with an audience of police. Are police a "real" audience? Can I put on a "real" performance without being especially careful not to break, even by accident, very real laws? Are the laws real? Or are they ambiguous because they can be arbitrarily enforced?

* * *

I am the last to dance. As I go up on stage, my double shot of Pepe Lopez tequila hits me. The stupid warm glow has me smiling and uninhibited as I dance. The railings allow the men to climb up, sit, and reach out toward me with their hands or wrap their legs around me as I dance. They stop when the bouncers move in their direction, point to them, and look menacing. I remove my top to reveal my bra as the cops in the front row start to chant, "Show some tit. Show some tit." They are primarily the SWAT team. At first I don't comprehend their words. Perhaps I am drunker than I thought. It is more likely I do not expect these words out of police officers' mouths. "Show some tit," they chant. I dance by them, sure I have heard them correctly now, and ask, "Isn't that illegal?" They howl, hitting each other, spraying saliva, spilling beer. They chant, arms around each other, "Show some tit," not addressing me at all.

*   *   *

The MC announces Trisha and Starr as the first match. Their managers apply baby oil liberally all over their bodies and hair until they are saturated. Others' past experience with Jell-O resulted in hair so dry it was beyond the reach of any conditioner. No one had any experience with maple syrup, so the oil is deemed a necessary precaution.

Trisha and Starr enter the ring, the MC blows the whistle, and they start. The audience joins the police chanting "show some tit," which lays down a background beat, superimposed by whoops, hollers, and primal screams. Others pick up on the 4/4 time and join in clapping or stomping. Trisha stalks around Starr taking large steps, her body low to the ground. Starr stands, slightly crouched, facing Trisha, inscribing a small circle in the syrup as she turns, her arms raised, as if the victim of a holdup. They posture this way for a moment or two. Finally, Trisha rushes Starr, knocking her down on her back. The crowd starts screaming, losing their beat for a moment. One of the SWAT officers in the front row, with the word *sniper* on his jacket, pours his beer on the wrestlers, concentrating on their chests. Two more join him. Some of it is getting in their faces. Broken glass could be an issue if they are not careful. Trisha wraps her arms and legs around Starr and rolls both of them out of harm's way. The bouncers rip apart the crowd getting to the beer-pouring cops.

*   *   *

Suspended outside of time, I see Trisha and Starr—muscle and softness, graceful moving lines, glistening, curving, tapering into one another, obsidian and ivory, magnificent merging forms. As a voyeur, I am ashamed of myself, yet breathless, thrilled by and drawn to the spectacle.

*   *   *

The match between the two women is so poor that there is no fight to speak of. Trisha simply chases Starr around the ring until she pins her. Starr's top slips sideways, revealing her nipple. "Tit, tit, tit," the three beer-pouring cops in the front row yell, starting the entire audience on a new chant. A couple of the men taking the wrestling aspect seriously count, "three, two, one, down!"

After the MC proclaims Trisha the winner, both women emerge from the ring and shake hands. Starr stands next to me soaked in syrup and baby oil, shivering in the air conditioning. She is in bad shape.

"Why don't you go back to the dressing room and get cleaned up?" I whisper to her.

"Kitty says I have to stay here," she answers.

I walk over to Trisha and ask, "Why the fuck you guys gotta' stay here?"

Trisha says, "I'm fighting the winner, remember? Besides, they want the guys to be able to stare at us."

I stand up straighter, cocky, cross my arms over my chest and clench my teeth. After I lose my match, no one is going to make me stay where I don't want to be.

*   *   *

The MC gives baby oil to my manager who shoots a generous stream at me. He tries to rub it in but I divert his hands, enlisting his help to oil my hair as I paste a smile on my face.

I'm not as drunk as I was and I am intensely self-conscious and vulnerable. The light on the stage and ring strike a sharp contrast with the darkness of the audience, leaving me feeling exposed. They see everything about me, but I know little of them. I have on a bikini, they have on their clothes. We have a few bouncers in our midst, their numbers are overwhelming. It is a social contract, an agreed on definition of the situation (which is greatly weakened by alcohol consumption), which holds them in abeyance. The confluence of the stimuli and these realizations dislodge my consciousness for a split second, sending me spiraling into a disoriented vertigo—every person, every color, every texture, every outline a crisp visual orgy of sensations. It is as if I have never existed before, never seen anything, until this moment. It is simultaneously exhilarating and terrifying as my heart beats against my chest. For a second, I am paralyzed, a cliché deer caught in the headlights of the oncoming car, contemplating my demise with fascination and dread. A young police officer, pulling me partially out of my spell, points at me and barks, "You, you, you." He is waving money in the air. I infer from this that he has bet money on me and he wants me to give it my all fighting so that he will win. His dark unlined face is beautiful, like a boy, with huge brown eyes and long lashes framed by dark brown curls. His mustache rides around inanely on his upper lip, as if placed there in a child's game of dress up. With the strain of yelling at me and waving his cash, he is working hard at being "a man."

I am profoundly sad for how lost he and all of these "boys" in the audience are—lost boys, trying to find manhood (read that, security) in being a cop, being drunk, or being at a strip show. What a show *they* are putting on for *me*. I am swept up in amazement and grief as I watch them enact their desperate pantomimes. I have never felt so sorry for so many people physically present at the same time. Their need is an overwhelming tidal wave that threatens to drown me if I stand here passively apprehending it long enough.

The three beer-pouring cops in the front row grimace and roar "Ahhhhhhhhgh!" as they place their fingers over the openings of their beer bottles, vigorously shake them, position the bottles over their crotches, and let the foam ejaculate across the ring, wildly gyrating their hips with each spasm of beer. The man in the sniper jacket clearly wins the contest. Their crude gesture violently erases my spell and draws my attention squarely on how to "get through this."

*   *   *

A woman perched on the rail behind me smiles and wishes me luck. She is calm, attractive, and interesting. I say, "I've never done this before, don't bet on me like that asshole down there."

She chuckles and says, "Kitty always wins!"

I stare as she gently chides me, "All you have to do is put on a good show and everything will be fine."

I say, "How do you know so much about this?"

"I've done this before and the owner of the troupe is almost always the reigning champion," she replies.

I take a strange comfort from her, as if she is an angel or a narrator in this strange story I am living, dropping by to let me know it will turn out okay. Her presence is an apparition confirming the surreality of this experience and place.

I thank her and start to extend my slick hand to her. We giggle. She says, "Turn your back to me," and she unties my drawstring neck strap and reties it. I instinctively trust her with this intimate task. "I gave you an extra knot so it wouldn't come undone." I am grateful to her for her nurturing. This moment hangs on the air, suspended, delicious, and safe. I turn away from it, reluctantly, to enter the ring.

*   *   *

Kitty and I are instructed to face each other on our knees in the center of the ring. My right hand is on Kitty's left shoulder and her right is on mine, our knees slightly spread. I am reminded of Kitty's 6 ft. 1 in. height as I look up at her face. The whistle blows and I am immediately on my back, pinned. I consider myself a hardy person, so even if the plan is to lose, I will not go down this easy. I roll my weight on to my shoulders and spring outward with my legs. I shake her off my body. I scoot backward into the ooze of the syrup and get to my feet as quickly as possible. Big mistake. Kitty rushes my knees from the side and I fall down, tackled. My brain is rocked in my skull for a second. Kitty is much stronger than I had anticipated. Starr was right to be intimidated by her. It is all I can do to slither out of her grasp and face her, this time on my knees.

The audience is yelling "tit, tit, tit." My breast is out. I stop to adjust my top and Kitty is on top of me again. I shake her to my waist, which she grabs. I twist around in her grasp so that I face the mat. She sits on my back as my face sinks into the syrup morass. I jog fairly regularly, yet I am already exhausted, the mat seemingly draining me of my strength.

And I can't breathe. And I can't tap Kitty because she is on my back and my arms can't reach her. The syrup is in my nose and my mouth is partially blocked by the syrup and the plastic. It crosses my mind that I could pass out, I feel so light headed. My will to do anything about my predicament has been sapped right out of my body with my strength. As the odyssey of the lights and noise flow around me, I wonder if I will drown, ending my life absurdly. I wonder if "real" boxers and wrestlers feel these emotions. Kitty's hand reaches into my hair as she slides down my back. I lift my head and use the hair pulling routine to draw in a breath. Somewhere in this, anger ignites and energizes me. I latch on to it and ride it, one pure surge that penetrates every muscle in my body as I lash out, using my arms to lift the rest of my body off of the mat. Kitty slithers down me and off my body. I get to my knees and rush her. She is knocked to her back, but she slithers out of my grasp before I make an effort to pin her. We face off and rush each other. We grip, grab, grapple, slither around, and grunt. She is immovable, I am not. The crowd has started the deafening 4/4 time stomp, clap, chant, "Show some tit." The man who bet on me is screaming at me as I go down, "Kick her ass. Get pissed again, get MAAAAD!" Out of the corner of my eye I see the same three cops pouring more beer into the ring as Kitty pins my shoulders to the mat.

* * *

Shawna is wrestling her brother, Jessie, in the front yard. Shawna, like me, knows too much about sex for the third grade. She's adopted. Jessie, a sixth grader, is nasty, calls Shawna cuss names, says to suck his dick, even puts her head in his crotch. He always "wrestles" by sitting on her and grabbing her titties. I know Jessie. Like my father, he'll grow up mean, making people have sex when they don't want to. Some boys are like that. The adults don't want to know about it, it's not nice. But I know and so does Shawna. That's why I like her, that and her pool.

Jessie is pretty cute though, with a tan, wavy brown sun-streaked hair, brown eyes with long lashes, an upturned nose, and a tall thin body that looks a little like a real man's, already. He has one foot that turns in when he walks. I love looking at him, love his walk, fantasize about him, and hate him.

As he sits on her chest, her legs lay on the ground. She should use those legs. I ask, in a mix of anger, a desire to be close to him, and curiosity, "Hey, can I wrestle Jessie?" Jessie gets off of Shawna, "I don't want to wrestle a little girl." He undoes his belt and tightens it up a notch, hitching up his pants. I see sex and meanness in it or maybe he is telling me he will hurt me with the belt.

I say, "If you're scared . . . " and Shawna says, "Don't do that, you don't understand," when, out of nowhere, Jessie knocks me down and sits on my chest with his crotch in my face. I think about biting it. He smiles and strokes my hair gently for a second before pulling it hard.

I can't breathe, but I'd been thinking a lot about what Shawna should do with her legs. From behind his head, I get my feet and my ankles under his chin, crossing them. The hair pulling hurts so bad, I press my heel into his Adam's apple for everything I'm worth, choking him. His hands leave my hair and go to his throat. As I sit up, I slam the back of his head into the ground as hard as I can. I scramble away from him, trembling, clutching at dirt and roots, scraping my knees, as I fall into Shawna's arms. We watch to see what he'll do. Choking, tears in his eyes, Jessie smiles mean on his front steps and says in a bad voice, "You won't get to do that again!"

* * *

As Kitty steps out of the ring, the declared winner, I smack her derriere. She looks back at me, tired, and ignores me. I hit her rear again with everything I've got. The sound of the smack reverberates through the room. The crowd ignites.

The MC starts her banter, "Ladies and gentlemen, we have already picked a winner, but I don't think the challenger is too happy with the decision. It was, however, a legal pin. I believe the rules in this situation specifically stipulate that Kitty is the winner. Who knows what the challenger has in mind."

Kitty rushes and dives on top of me. The crowd loves it. To emphasize the point that she has just won, she sits on my chest, with her arms raised in a gesture of triumph. This is exactly what I had hoped for. I lift both of my legs off the mat, loop them under her arms, and cross them against her chest, lotus style. I sit up full force on the mat, taking her down on her back. She looks stunned but she still fights to keep her shoulders off the mat. However, her legs are now free to wrap around my neck. With my head locked, she rolls her body to the side and ends up taking me down on my stomach. She pins me to the mat, this time from the side rather than sitting on me. I do not offer any resistance. The whistle sounds a second time and she jumps off of me and bows, the righteous victor.

As I get out of the ring, my manager offers me a hand to help me up the 4-ft. climb to the stage. I take his hand, traverse the distance to him, and envelope him in a huge hug that involves me wrapping my arms and legs around him, exposing the maximum amount of syruped surface area to his torso. I give him a kiss on the cheek from my syrupy, baby-oiled face, get off him, shake his hand, and thank him for being such a good manager. A man behind me yells, "Explain that to his wife." I take a deep bow, receive a round of applause, and walk to the side stage, satisfied that I had given the performance my all.

Starr says, shivering inside her towel, "You looked like you were trying to win out there."

I respond, "I honestly wanted to put on a good show. Kitty could kill me. I almost drowned."

Starr answers meekly, "I almost drowned too."

I ask her if we can leave now and she shrugs. I look around, look at her, and tell her, "We are leaving to clean up. We don't have to fight anymore."

As we start to leave, a bouncer escorts us, opening up a path through the crowd.

*   *   *

In a storage room, there are two hoses and two kiddie swimming pools. Two men hold the hoses while Starr and I wash off in separate pools. It takes me a couple of minutes to realize that the men are having too much fun with the hoses, aiming them at our breasts, groins, and bottoms. I shoot them a dirty look and Rick asks, "Don't you want the suits clean too?"

All of a sudden I hear Starr cry out in a hysterical voice, "It won't come out, it won't come out."

The bouncer, in a gruff voice says, "Don't freak."

I step out of my pool and bring over my full bottle of Pert shampoo and liberally squeeze it all over her hair and body. I gently ask the men to leave us alone, saying, "We'll call you if we need you."

They resist leaving for a moment, so I ignore them, getting down to the business of lathering Starr's hair for her. She is vulnerable, like I have felt many times this evening, like I feel now. Nurturing Starr diverts my attention. I say, "It will come out, I promise, use as much of this stuff as it takes and go in later with a heavy conditioner."

She will be all right because I have eliminated the stuff from my hair already. We help each other without talking for a while, taking turns holding the hose for each other. The sound of the water trickling is calming as it echoes off the tin roof above and the concrete floor below to soak into the industrial gray gloom at the periphery of our vision.

Drained, exhausted, and humiliated, I leave Starr to finish in private. I go to the dressing room to change my clothes, comb my hair, and apply minimal makeup. I am very conscious of my grooming as nurturing myself, healing, removing the traces of the nights activities. I am stabilizing the situation, ushering back in the "normal reality" that I now crave. My emotions are a collage of calm meditative moments punctuated by outbursts where I want to cry. I concentrate on hair combing and breathing and tell myself, it's all right, it's over now. Reality vibrates with the hum of the machinery in the building. It threatens to close in on me. I desperately look for something else to attend to, choking back fright with a contrived calm.

*   *   *

As I write this now, I wonder, did we ever "clean up?" Traces of the evening's experiences are forever etched into our memories. As those men helped us clean up, they marked me forever. I am disgusted at how long it took me to catch on to what they were doing. No doubt the joy I expressed at getting the syrup off my body was interpreted as sexual pleasure. So putting myself in that situation, I "asked for it," did I not? I set myself up for my own victimization, right?

The simplistic binary constructs that my culture gives me to interpret these events, passive victim versus active agent, do not encompass my experience in that kiddie pool or any of my experiences that night. I was both and neither, something different, something to be located in the underlying play of differences between the dichotomy of victim and agent.

*   *   *

It is now time for a pointed response to Sherri's statement, "I think you are destroying yourself."

As I reflect on my identity during the auction, the dancing, and the wrestling, I am shocked, like Sherri, that I could participate. Being auctioned off is not a regular part of my existence, neither is wrestling.

How was I competent to give a convincing performance? It took adjustment to get to a place in which these things seemed "normal" to do. Derrida's nonconcepts, "mimesis" (Derrida, 1983) and "*sous rature*" (Derrida, 1976), again help me grapple with these questions. Identity can be viewed as simultaneously a process of mimesis and *sous rature*. Identity, as defined in the *Oxford Desk Dictionary and Thesaurus* (1997) is the "condition of being a specified person or thing. Individuality. Personality. Distinctiveness, uniqueness, particularity, singularity, selfhood" (p. 385). In the same passage, it is also defined as, "Absolute sameness, unity, equality, indistinguishability" (p. 385).

These terms are binary opposites that portray identity as simultaneously particular to an individual and as the state of being indistinguishable. So which is identity, then? Individual? Absolute sameness? In one moment, the response is that the context of the situation determines which binary term to assign. In a deconstructive moment, these definitions can be played with. Identity is both definitions, simultaneously uniqueness and sameness. Individual identities (uniqueness) are constructed from interaction with society (sameness) and society (sameness) is constituted by individuals (uniqueness). Each binary term, then, penetrates the existence of the other. Yet, because the definition of identity hangs suspended in the penetration, we must also say that it is neither uniqueness nor sameness but something else.

When we specify that identity is internalized from others, it is a short jump to say that identity is a process of imitation or mimesis. Particular individuals, as they adjust to their particular changing environments, take on identities, which others may imitate. At all times, identity is *sous rature*, under erasure, being erased, adjusted, and readjusted, to fit the emerging picture of social life that one constructs for oneself.

Many times the performers in this story and I stopped to consider what was expected of us in an ambiguous situation. New situations lack codification and formulas to draw on. They are moments when we feel decentered. We feel the ambivalence and consult our pasts and others for resources to construct actions for the present. These moments are particularly emotional. Consider, for instance, my emotions at the auction, on the door, and getting ready to wrestle. Strong emotions, then, could serve as a cue for a decentering moment. To deal with the decentering, performers constantly draw and erase their pictures of reality so that they may coconstruct with one another realities that are temporarily centered on a narrative that they can all agree on.

As I wrestle with Derrida—drawing, erasing, and imitation—I discover that dancing is and is not destructive to myself. It is both and neither. Destruction has many aspects to it. It preserves the open endedness of living by breaking down or deconstructing what is no longer useful. In *Bhagavad Gita* (Blue Mountain Center for Meditation, 1998), Shiva, the third "personage" in the Hindu trinity, is the destroyer, and as the destroyer, is essential to conquering death. Without destruction there can be no rebirth.

Dancing has given me and other performers the opportunity to destroy ourselves. With the emergence of each new ambiguous situation or decentering moment, our selves are found to be too codified in a particular direction and inadequate to the task of dealing with the situation. In other words, our old formulas don't work. As these selves are erased or destroyed, traces are left that influence the construction of new selves to meet the new needs of the moment. These selves are adjusted, erased, and drawn again throughout the night, imitating others and drawing on traces of the past that exist in our memories.

Alcohol consumption is destructive, although not required for dancing. It is harmful to the body, including brain cells. Thus, alcohol can be viewed as an eraser. Whether it is due to biochemical activity or to the social construction of who we are and how we are permitted to act under the influence, or to a dialectic between the two, alcohol gives us an excuse to destroy the self that would not do these things (be auctioned off, strip, wrestle in syrup) and draw new selves that would. My conduct while I am drunk is *sous rature*. Yes, I did these things, but I was drunk, this is not my "real" self. Those things I did that I don't want as a permanent part of my identity may be expunged at any time.

Drawing, constructing a layered account, and identity, can be viewed as a process of mimesis and *sous rature*. The thing we want to get at eludes us as we try to describe it through words, pictures, or declarations of who we are in relation to it. There is no original point of reference, no *thing* imitated, only imitations of imitations. We grasp at the appearance of the real or the present, only to wrestle with a simulacra of a phantasm.

Ultimately, ethnography exists as a kind of hymen between fiction and truth. Through living the experience and writing the narrative, the ethnographer seeks to destroy the Self by tearing down the binary opposition created through the existence of the Other. Layered accounts leave traces of a play of differences for other selves who read to apprehend. This, in turn, makes it possible for selves to identify with other selves, bringing us all closer together in the understanding that we are all the same, located in different positions in the play of difference that is existence.

*   *   *

One last brief overlay is necessary before I conclude. This article simultaneously is and is not Part 2 of "Sketching With Derrida: An Ethnography of a Researcher/Erotic Dancer." On its face, this article is an obvious continuation of the prior article in which I described the events that occurred the night I went out with Kitty. At the end of "Sketching With Derrida," I suggested that researchers are tricksters who dance and dandle with reality by bringing taken-for-granted assumptions into question. At the end of Part 2, I invert/pervert that conclusion by suggesting, through the nonconcepts of mimesis and *sous rature*, that researchers are not privileged in this regard, that everyone goes through these processes in their everyday lives—drawing, erasing, drawing again, composing, and destroying narratives of the self within contexts that are constantly in flux.

This article, however, is not necessarily a Part 2 for "Sketching With Derrida." Both articles stand alone, yet each article provides layers of interpretive resources that, when superimposed on the other, give the reader a different picture of being an ethnographer/dancer/wrestler. Taken together, a third story emerges, suspended in the combined traces left by both articles on the consciousness of the reader. For these reasons, I playfully conclude that "The Next Night *Sous Rature*: Wrestling With Derrida's Mimesis" is Part 2 of "Sketching With Derrida," is not Part 2, is both, and is neither; it is an imitation of something else that is under erasure.

NOTE

1. Names of individuals and places in this narrative are fictional.

REFERENCES

Blue Mountain Center for Meditation. (1998). *Bhagavad Gita* (Eknath Easwaran, Trans.). Berkeley, CA: Nilgiri Press.
Derrida, J. (1976). *Of grammatology* (Gayatri Spivak, Trans.). Baltimore: Johns Hopkins University Press.
Derrida, J. (1983). *Dissemination* (Barbara Johnson, Trans.). Chicago: University of Chicago Press.
Oxford Desk Dictionary and Thesaurus. (1997). Oxford, UK: Oxford University Press.
Ronai, C. R. (1998). Sketching with Derrida: An ethnography of a researcher/dancer. *Qualitative Inquiry, 4*(3), 405-420.

— —

*Carol Rambo Ronai is an assistant professor at the University of Memphis. She is currently working on three books: one from life history materials with striptease dancers (*Striptease as Resistance*), which is being revised; one using life history materials with adult survivors of childhood sexual abuse; and one that will outline and explore the layered account as a methodology.*

CHAPTER 8

On Becoming Italian American
An Autobiography of an Ethnic Identity

— —

Richard V. Travisano
University of Rhode Island

This article is about growing up Italian in Connecticut after World War II, and the author finding in the 1980s and 1990s that he is supposed to be Italian American, which, to him, is not satisfying to be. The density of family and ethnicity in the first 22 years of the author's life, and how that changed over time, is delineated. The quest for the American dream, driven by the Newtonian world machine (in both its modern and postmodern modes), has eclipsed the world he grew up in. The author tries to communicate through prose and poetry that what was lost has not been replaced, hasn't even been substituted for. Put over-simply, most of the wine the author now drinks is better than the wine he made with his uncles, grandfather, and cousin. But going to a liquor store is an incredibly impoverished cultural experience compared to making 200 gallons of wine in one's own cellar.

If a goal of ethnography is to retell "lived experience," to make another world accessible to the reader, then I submit that the lyric poem, and particularly a series of lyric poems with an implied narrative, comes closer to achieving that goal than do other forms of ethnographic writing. . . . Lyric poems concretize emotions, feelings, and moods—the most private kinds of feelings—so as to recreate experience itself in another person. A lyric poem "shows" another person how it is to feel something. Even if the mind resists, the body responds to poetry. It is felt.

—Laurel Richardson (1994, pp. 8-9)

I was born in Waterbury, Connecticut in 1939. I grew up Italian there. Over the past few years, nine poems have occurred that relate to that fact. These poems began as feelings, which, reflected off my memories, became dressed in words that I herded into poems. I have published a memoir about my growing up centering on my grandfather (Travisano, 1992). I am at work on a book about the whole experience of my early years. This present piece, although it speaks of the people and places in the book, is separate from it. The book is about my family. This piece is really about me—about how I grew up unself-consciously Italian, became self-conscious about it and went along with it, only to find in my fifties that I am supposed to be something called Italian American, which I'm not particularly comfortable with. This is a history of my ethnic identity—of what it was made of, of how it has changed in my life and in my thoughts, and of how I feel about it now. I quote Richardson (1994) above because it is my aim, in poetry and prose, to engender in my reader what I feel in myself. Put directly, I am uncomfortable with, and troubled by, what has happened to being Italian. I am angry at history and (to use the detestable vernacular) I want to "share" that with my reader. But, enough introduction. Let me begin. I used to be an Italian boy.

An Italian Boy in America Fifty Years Ago
(we never said Italian American)

There were pigs (in a backyard pen)
and (in a coop) chickens too
and a long grape arbor
that started with my grandfather on a bench
(pipe smoking strong tobacco)
and ended (a couple of hundred tomato plants later)
at the back gate
which I used to run through
to get Mrs. Nevis (who could talk to pigs)
when the pigs got out.

You had to get them in
as a couple of pigs can raise particular hell
given rows of tomatoes and peppers and beets and beans
and peas and celery and cabbage and corn
and lettuce and spinach and squash (of various kinds)
and whatever all else we planted.

There was my grandfather's little greenhouse
(just out from under the grape arbor near his bench)
where he'd start his seeds every March
(while I'd run around the soggy just thawed fragrant garden loam
flying kites till I'd visit him
to warm up and smell his tobacco when I got cold)
and in April he'd transplant those seedlings
by twenty-fours into cut-down grape boxes
and put them out in cold frames
to grow and toughen for late May planting
(in the very earth herself).

And my grandmother's kitchen
with a big green and white enameled cast iron stove
(that my cousin and I used to warm our
played-all-day-in-the-snow cold feet under)
with gas burners to cook on
and two kerosene burners to heat the house and the oven
(that baked my grandmother's bread which she'd slice
and butter and pass out a window to me)
and Thanksgiving and Christmas and Easter dinners were in that kitchen
with her children and grandchildren and children-in-law
(twenty or so for dinner, plus relatives and friends
and neighbors dropping by all day).

And July to October was canning
with mother and grandma almost always at it
and I carried in bushels and baskets of stuff
and washed jars and shelved hundreds of quarts and pints
and half-pints of tomato sauce and tomatoes and peppers
and applesauce and eggplant and cucumber pickles
and tomato juice and pears and corn
plus relishes—pepper and cucumber and onion
(I wore airman's goggles grinding the onions)
and scores of peanut butter and olive
and baby food and whatever other little jars
filled with grape and apple and crabapple
and strawberry and peach and cherry and blackberry
and (wonderfully woody) elderberry jellies and jams.

And in October we made wine
(two hundred gallons and more)
a dozen barrels in the yard swelling tight with water
and me and Uncle Al in his truck picking up sixty
boxes of grapes (that's twenty-two hundred pounds)
and crushed grapes fermenting in the cellar for a week

the whole house filled with fruit flies and
the incredible aroma of green fermenting wine.

And every year on a frosty January morning
uncles and cousins and paisans would come
and pick up pigs and hold them down on a low table
and Uncle Mike slit their throats
and Aunt Florence caught their blood in a big enamel pan
and it was seasoned and cooked into blood pudding
(on my grandmother's stove)
and everyone worked and ate all day
(and Uncle Mike and Al and Aunt Florence the next day too
until there was sausage and ham and bacon and proscuitto
curing in the winter chill of the walk-up attic).

And there was "up the garden"—
two lots Uncle Al owned up the street
with his garage and workshop and more garden
with more corn and potatoes and tomatoes
and lots of grape vines with thickets you could hide in
plus a well with wonderful water you pumped up and drank
and I'd fill bushel baskets with potatoes my grandfather dug
and my wagon held two bushels
that I'd take "down the house" from "up the garden"
and then go back for more
and "up the garden" there was a wonderful pear tree
("down the house" there were two more)
and you could eat all you wanted and you did!

And there were emissaries from the wider world—
the milk man, with butter and cream
(and eggnog for the holidays)
the produce man, Bruce
who got old and so stayed in his shop
while his son (who was Bruce too) took over the rounds
and the cheese man, who smelled like good provolone
(my Grandmother used to buy me little salty scamorze)
and the tea man with tea and crackers and cookies in his basket
(from the Great Atlantic and Pacific Tea Company)
and the Yankee egg man (who had a farm on Buck's Hill)
and "Johnny the Cleaner" (as we called him)
in his Model A Ford (with his brown paper dry cleaning bags
with little cardboard flaps you'd lift
to look through a cellophane window
to be sure it was your coat he had there)
and of course there was the rag man with a horse and wagon

(I sold him rags and scrap metal and got to keep the money).

And there was more (so much more)
but that's enough for you to see
what it was that I was living
how "Italian" meant to be,
back in another time and place
(well, next door actually)
but in quite a different universe
(or so it seems you see)
as every day in the mirror—

an imposter . . . not me.

And there were aunts, uncles, and cousins. When I was 8 years old, I had 27 relatives within 350 feet of my back door and another 6 within 600 feet; when I was 18, I had 29 within 350 feet, another 8 within 850 feet, and 8 more within a half mile. And this was not a neighborhood of tenements, but of one- and two-family houses built here and there on 75 by 100 lots before World War II, and on most of the lots in between after the war. This was my mother's family. My father's family was smaller and lived in other parts of town. Although, if I want to talk about all of Waterbury at that time, there were another 60 or 70 relatives on my mother's side. Anyway, my grandfather built the first house in my neighborhood in 1897-1898. The house was expanded into a two-family house in the early 1930s, and my mother and father moved in upstairs. So it was my grandparent's house that I (and my sisters, Del and Tori) lived in.

Let me tell you of these people. Aunt Florence (my mother's sister) and Uncle Joe lived 300 feet up the street. She used to make me devil's food cakes when I was little and my favorite Italian cookies when I was older. Aunt Florence was the toughest aunt to deal with. One never got away with anything with Aunt Florence. Uncle Joe taught me to play rummy and took me to see cowboy pictures. He delivered ice cream to stores for a local company. So, once or twice a month when he'd see me walking home from school, he'd pick me up and take me on the last few stops of his route and then back to the ice cream company and then home. I got to ride in the ice cream truck. Wonderful.

Uncle Carl (my father's lifelong best friend) married my mother's sister, Sylvia. Little Sylvia was born when I was six. Aunt Sylvia made cakes and great pies. Once I got hit on the head by a rock someone threw in the schoolyard. My head was bleeding and my friends were telling me to go in to the nurse. But I took off for Aunt Sylvia's because I knew she'd be home (she worked the 3 to 11 shift) and her door was 200 feet from the end of the schoolyard. Aunt Sylvia spoke (and still speaks) her mind more directly than anyone I've ever met. She's terrific. Uncle Carl was fun and had a lightning-quick mind. He told me stories about Indians (we never said Native American either). He said they still lived in the neighborhood when he was younger. The Indians were always the good guys, and neighbors he liked to poke fun at were the bad. A gentle and a funny man.

Aunt Lauretta, Uncle Jimmy, and cousin Judi (my favorite playmate) lived three miles away when I was little, but moved into the house across the street when I was 13-years-old. Aunt Lauretta was funny, made a great chocolate cake, and I always knew she loved me. Even when she stuck a bar of soap in my mouth because I was swearing like a trooper at age six. Uncle Jimmy showed me how to fish when I was nine. Now and again through the following 50 years he has showed me some things about this being human. Always, he has quietly accepted and dealt with everything a long life has thrown at him. A wonderful man. He and Aunt Lauretta were always crazy about each other. They still are. Cousin Thomas, 14 years my junior, was their surprise mid-life baby.

Uncle Angelo and Aunt Mary (my mother's brother and her first cousin—they had to get the Bishop's permission to get married) lived "downtown" in an apartment when I was little, but moved into Uncle Frank and Aunt Theresa's house 200 feet down the street when Frank and Theresa built a new house next to their old house in the 1950s. Aunt Mary was great to talk to when I was a teenager. She understood. Uncle Angelo was a love to his nieces and a buster to his nephews. He hunted when he was younger, so he gave me his guns and taught me how to clean game.

Uncle Harry was the youngest brother. He was 28 in 1941 and was drafted. Born in 1939, my first memory of Harry is knowing I had an uncle in the war. He was in the North African and Italian campaigns. When the war in Europe was over, Harry came home, granted a long furlough before he would go off to the war in the Pacific. But the bomb was dropped. What I remember (I was just 6-years-old) is all the adults in the neighborhood out in the street shouting and hugging and blowing the horns in their cars. So Uncle Harry didn't have to go to war again and he and Aunt Jean got married. And by 1947 they had my cousin Frank and their new little house on one of the two lots "up the garden." Aunt Jean was sweet and she too made cakes. (Almost all the women I grew up with could really bake.) Uncle Harry was great. He had a craggy handsomeness and a twinkle in his eye. He loved to tease. He made a trio with my father and Kelly. They were fast friends who had a lot of fun and raised a lot of hell together. Their capers were legion and legend.

Uncle Frank and Aunt Theresa lived 200 feet down the street. Uncle Frank was my grandmother's youngest brother and so was my great uncle. When I was little, he lived in the house my grandfather had helped his father-in-law (my Uncle Frank's father, my great-grandfather) build. Uncle Frank was a bugler in World War I. He used to tell me stories about it. Aunt Theresa was (in a family of hard working women) the hardest working woman I knew. I use to catch chickens for her when she wanted to kill them. She chopped off their heads. I watched. Their son, cousin Vic, who was in the Navy during World War II, lived in his parent's old house (and his grandfather's house) with his wife when I was still young.

Aunt Adele and Uncle Freddie I can barely remember. She died in 1943 when I was four and Freddie drifted away from his former in-laws. I should also mention that I grew up knowing that there had been an Aunt Victoria, who had died in her twenties during the flu epidemic. She was my grandmother's firstborn. She and my grandparent's unborn first grandchild died together in my grandparent's house. My two sisters were named after the two sisters my mother had lost. Some years after Victoria died, her husband came to ask my grandparent's permission to get married again. It was a different time.

Just 150 feet up the street was the third house my grandfather helped build back at the turn of the century, his sister and brother-in-law's. To me they were Zizi (Auntie) Rocco and Zi (Uncle) Tony. Their children (my mother's first cousins) Florence, Dorothy, Emma, Mary (previously mentioned with Uncle Angelo), and John were all out of the house by the time I can remember. Florence lived out of the neighborhood. Emma and her husband, Anthony Zurlo, and their kids, Jean and Anthony (always called Zeke), lived a half mile or so away near the end of the neighborhood. John kept horses at his parent's house when I was a small kid and later redid the house and moved in after his parents died. Dorothy and her husband, Dan Christofano, lived right behind us when I was little and moved a couple of football fields away to one of the new little capes after the war. Their five kids were older cousins I grew up around. Johnny (who fought in the war in Europe) and Pat (usually called Murphy) were the oldest. Johnny ended up building his own house in the far end of the neighborhood. Marie, who was always helping my mother when I was little, married and built a house 300 feet down the street. Anthony (always called Dutch) married and built his house 200 feet down the street, next to his sister. The youngest, Daniel (always called Chickie), married and moved out of the neighborhood, but then moved back after a divorce. These older cousins who settled in the neighborhood had nine kids between them.

And there was my grandfather who, orphaned, had worked in other people's fields from the time he was a young boy. He came to this country at age 20, worked and saved money for a while. Then he went back to Italy and returned with his sister, her husband, and their first two children. Then, at age 30, he married my grandmother, who was 17. He worked as an unskilled operative in a large factory. In 1906, at 40, he lost the four fingers of his left hand to a machine. Someone bandaged him up and he walked the three miles home.

My grandfather was 73 when I was born. When I was little, I spent a lot of time around him. He'd work at splitting wood, on the grapevines, in his greenhouse, in the garden, or whatever, depending on the season. I'd watch and, as I got older, help. As we both got older, he would fall more and more and I would help him up. I started drinking a little wine every day with him when I was four. It was a different time.

My grandmother came from Italy when she was eight. She went to school in Italy and she went to school here. She could speak, write, and read both Italian and English. This was a boon in the early years of the neighborhood when she was just about the only person who could do so. Oddly enough, however, if she hadn't spoken English, I probably would have learned a lot more Italian. My mother worked (as did all of the women of her generation in my family) so I spent a lot of time with my grandmother. She made incredible bread. A heavy, thick-crusted, moist, coarsely grained white bread. My grandfather loved that bread. It meant America to him, as he had only what he called "black bread" (a more healthy whole wheat bread, no doubt) in Italy. My grandmother made pasta, canned, sewed, winnowed seeds, braided onions and garlic, nursed sick children and grandchildren, and always kept her household in order and running. When she was 86, she said to me that she was an old woman and sooner or later her body would give out. So, I asked what she felt about that. This woman had worked hard all her life, had born 10 children (plus two stillborn), and had buried 4 of the 10. Gripping my arm tightly, she said urgently, "I'm not afraid to die, but life is still good—I want more."

And Uncle Albert and Uncle Michael. They were both bachelors living downstairs with their mother and father when I was little. Uncle Mike married Aunt Eleanor in 1957 when he was 53. My parents built a new house next door and Uncle Mike moved into our old apartment upstairs. Uncle Albert was the oldest brother. He never married (and told me when he was old that it was a bad idea to grow old alone). So he lived his entire life in his childhood home. He was born in the house in 1899 and he died there in 1971. His father and mother had migrated across an ocean; Uncle Albert never migrated at all. Being right downstairs until I was 18, and then across a driveway after that, both Uncle Al and Uncle Mike were like extra fathers to me.

Uncle Al was the family handyman, in charge of fixing almost everything. A tinsmith by trade, he was the only family member who was a craftsman. Everyone else in his generation (except my mother and father) worked in factories as unskilled operatives. Uncle Al left school early and served an apprenticeship. He could do anything with sheet metal, angle iron, rivets, and solder. He made picnic table covers, hose holders, ladder holders for his truck, tool boxes, vents for sheds, and so forth. He kept inventing new uses as he loved to make things, loved to exercise his skill with metal. He did carpentry of all kinds: repairs, building, remodeling, cabinets. He built the grape arbor, the chicken coop, the sheds, and the greenhouse. He wired. He did plumbing. He painted and repainted.

He was always busy, I was always helping him—handing him tools, fetching what he needed. He was always telling me how to best do a job, how to make things stronger, more permanent, telling me which materials were best, which paints withstood the weather, and more. I learned a lot from Uncle Albert. He was proud of his 50-year membership pin from the American Sheet Metal Workers' Union. (I sometimes wear it in my lapel.) He used to tell me about the strikes in the 1930s and once, when I was in my twenties, he looked me in the eye and said. "Listen to your uncle—never forget that bosses and Republicans are always wrong." I haven't.

And Uncle Mike. It was "Hey Dick!" shouted up the back stairs late every Friday afternoon in the early 1940s. "Here I come, Uncle Mike!" as I flew down the stairs and there would be Uncle Mike, smiling, with a little bag of candy and gum that he would hand to me. And he would stand there and just keep smiling. I don't recall when this started or when it stopped, but I do recall that it was terrific. And that was the man's common denominator. He did almost everything with the same full quiet love he gave me with Hershey bars and bubble gum for 3 or 4 years of wonderful little kid Friday afternoons. He did it talking to his father and mother, his sisters and brothers, his nephews and nieces, and most of the neighbors and neighborhood kids to boot. You could see and sense that same love when he put seeds or plants into the earth, when he made a furrow with a hoe, and when he held it and rubbed it with his fingers exactly the way he rubbed the hands of little children. He loved the soil and the plants, and the harvest, and the grapes, and the new wine rushing out of the barrels it had fermented in. He loved keeping his knives sharp and cutting up the pigs we slaughtered. And he loved his 1948 Chevy, and he loved dancing, and he loved calling the tarantella, and he loved the way it felt to walk in a really well-cut suit in great shoes. Watched closely, he was incredible. My cousin Dutch referred to and addressed him as Sir Michael. It fit. Recently, I remarked to my sister Adele that I've never met anyone quite like Uncle Mike. She answered, "And you never will either."

And my mother. As everyone in the family was crazy about Uncle Mike, most people in the family were crazy about my mother. She was the godmother for so many cousins that I never got it straight. It seemed like she baptized half the people in the family who were 15 or more years younger than her. So she was Aunt Rose to a bunch of people, and she was *Padrina* Rose to a host more. What this meant in a culture where people are expected to "pay their respects" is that people were always dropping in for a cup of coffee. And coffee was always on and there was always food. "Do you want a sandwich? A piece of cake? Some cookies? Can I warm some spaghetti for you?" That's my mother or any of her sisters talking. For while she may have been the favorite of many people, my aunts had their share of family, in-laws, neighbors, etc. dropping in too. My mother could cook, and when she was home, she was most often cooking. She made great southern Italian food—macaroni (we never said "pasta"), lasagna, meatballs, sausage, *braciole*, *suffritto*—all with tomato sauce. She was great with vegetables. And as for "American" food, she was great with turkeys, hams, or pork chops. She had a real way with soups. (I, by the way, don't, but my daughter does.) And while she left the fancy cakes to her sisters, she made great banana bread, pumpkin bread, and the like, as well as wonderful Italian cookies of various kinds. (Curiously, my mother and her sisters seldom made bread, and none of them were expert at it. So, when my grandmother died, her wonderful white bread, as well as the egg bread and other specialty breads she made for the Easter season, were lost.) My mother canned more than anyone and her jellies and jams were unmatched. She also loved the garden and spent a fair amount of time in it. She liked planting things. I have a picture of her standing by a big manure pile, shovel in hand, smiling.

My mother, like all of her siblings (except Uncle Albert), left school and went to work in a factory. But not liking that, she reversed gears and finished high school and became a secretary. She worked from when she was 20 into her 70s for Michael's Jewelers, a family-owned chain of stores in Waterbury, New Haven, Hartford, and a few other Connecticut and Rhode Island locations. She took some time off when each of her children were born. By the time I can recall, she was running the office in Michael's. She had no title, but she was running the operation. She did all the billing. She decided who would get credit and who wouldn't. Some young guy would come in for an engagement ring. She'd know his mother, his father, his brother, or all of them. She'd set up an account for him. And she'd chase him on the phone if he didn't make payments on time. And she remembered everyone's name, family, connections, and how promptly they paid, forever.

My mother taught me manners and, as my Uncle Albert would say, "What's right." My father and uncles got in on it, mostly by example, but my mother did the most of it. I learned to take a lady's arm, give my seat on a bus to a woman, open doors for women, and similar boy scout stuff. She taught me rules of dining—which plate for which course, which fork or spoon for which use. She liked that kind of stuff (so do I) although we very seldom ate formally. I was told what wonderful people the Jewish family she worked for were, and that anyone who didn't like a nationality or race different than their own was stupid. I was told to respect my elders. I was told that *Si'*John Reno was to be called *Si'*John because he had lived in the neighborhood since before my mother was born. (*Si* is an elision of *signore* or *signora* [mister or missus], hence *Si'*John and *Si'*Marie Reno.)

My mother was her father's favorite, and she was up there in her mother's eyes too. My mother had the love and stature to command respect, and she had the toughness to make people uncomfortable if they were in error, or to turn her back on them if they crossed her. My mother was groomed (by herself and others) to replace my grandmother as matriarch of the family. But that didn't quite happen. Being American increasingly took over, and the matriarch role was getting eclipsed with the eclipse of the community.

Finally, my father. Born in 1905, my father was one of a family of five brothers and one sister. They lived about three miles from where my mother (and then I) grew up. My grandfather, Angelo Travisano, and his three brothers came from Italy at the same time. Why, I don't know, but Angelo and his brother, Michelangelo, settled in Waterbury and opened a dancing studio. Their brother, Joseph, settled in New Haven, Connecticut and their brother, Vito, settled in Newark, New Jersey. Then they had kids and named their sons after one another. My father was Vito. My father was very bright. He went to the "technical" high school and learned math and drafting. He won a small college scholarship, but as his father had died during the flu epidemic, he had to go to work to help feed his siblings. He went to work as a draftsman in a factory, Chase Brass and Copper. Over a period of a few years, he took some courses at Yale University (I still have his notebooks) and became knowledgeable enough to work as a mechanical engineer. He was very good at it. Kendicott Copper (that had bought Chase) wanted to move us to Cleveland during the war, when they were making a fortune fabricating shells from the smallest to the largest that the U.S. Army used. There was a big wing of my mother's family in Cleveland, but she didn't want to move away, and I don't think my father did either.

My mother and father met in the late 1920s and were married in 1932. My father was a romantic beau and my mother used to show my sisters and I the sweet things that he wrote to her before they were married. He used to sign cards to her in arithmetic, "1 + 1 = 2." They really liked one another. They never argued; they never raised their voices to one another. As I have already said, my mother could be tough. She would get angry at someone in the family and she would be down on them for a month, a year, or maybe forever. If my father liked that person, and they were a part of his "rounds," he'd just go right on visiting them. I don't know how it worked with my mother, my father, or the other people involved, but apparently it did. When I was 16 and first driving, I'd borrow my father's car. My mother would tell me to be home by 10 or 11, and I'd say "Sure." Then I'd sail in at one or two. The next morning, my mother would be hopping. "Vito," she'd say, "he got in at two in the morning!" "Is the car all right, and how is the gas tank?" he would ask. "The car is fine and the tank's full," I'd answer. "I don't see any problem, Rose," my father would say. And there wasn't any problem. My mother was just plain crazy about my father.

My father loved to "make the rounds," as the expression of that time went. This meant he would visit a bunch of people once or twice a week, and another bunch of people once or twice a month. These were relatives and friends in the neighborhood and outside the neighborhood as well. Everywhere he went, of course, he was offered food and drink. He always accepted. The food was always good and my father loved to eat, so he ate more than one lunch or dinner quite regularly. At Christmas, the rounds expanded to include 25 or 30 more households, so the rounds went on from a week before Christmas until the new year. From when I was 7 or 8, until I was perhaps 11 and foolishly preferred being with my friends, my father would often take me along. We'd drive to his brother Joe's house and he'd walk in declaiming, "Merry Christmas, Merry Christmas," and he'd hug everyone. Then he'd eat something, or have a drink, or both. Then we'd go to his sister Mary's house. If I was lucky, her friend who could do card tricks would be there. Then we'd go to Hans Mueller's house, a German guy who had been a friend of my father's since they were kids. Hans looked like an elf, and his house was decorated with brightly painted "gingerbread" right out of a book of fairy tales. And we'd keep this up from late in the morning until we went home for dinner.

My father knew a lot of people—his family, my mother's family, the neighbors, people he grew up with, and people from the large factory he worked in. And beyond that, he knew other people because his yearly sideline was doing income tax returns. My father did income tax returns for almost everyone he knew. For three months every year, he was out most nights and a lot of weekends doing taxes. He was the H&R Block of his time and place. He knew what he was doing and he charged less, but you had to feed him.

My father loved having fun, indeed his example gave me the idea that one should have fun most of the time. He loved to play cards. There was often a card game in the neighborhood on Friday or Saturday night with seven or eight guys, who were family or friends. He played every Wednesday night at the Chase Foreman's Club for over 20 years. He got friendly with three Italian guys who worked on the line in one department, so we used to watch them play softball once a week. Some years later, one of these guys, Hubie Orsatti, had an operation and was recuperating in bed at home. My father went to visit and Hubie's wife told him she was going to cook a steak for Hubie and asked if he wanted to eat. My father accepted the invitation and Mrs. Orsatti went out to the kitchen to cook. When she returned with Hubie's tray, she found my father undressed and in bed with her husband. My father loved to cut up.

My father loved food. Every Saturday morning he did the week's grocery shopping at the A&P and a local butcher shop. From when I was old enough I went with him. We'd buy all kinds of stuff and cart it home. He'd take things out and put them away exclaiming, "Look at these beautiful pork chops!" "What wonderful peaches!" "What a big watermelon!" "Look at these rolls!" Most weeks he'd spend a fair amount of time shopping. But he also loved baseball. So sometimes, in the middle of shopping at the A&P, he'd say, "Let's put the heat on and go see the Yankees!" Then we'd rush around the A&P getting stuff, and he'd put me in line at the checkout to save a place while he got a few last things. We'd rush home and put the food away and we'd be gone. Sometimes he'd call an uncle or two and sometimes he wouldn't. His problem with that was that they would get into arguments with their wives and he didn't want to be the cause of that. He just wanted to drop everything and go. So we would. Down the old roads to Orange, Connecticut, where we'd pick up the Merit Parkway, which becomes the Hutchinson River Parkway when you reach New York, and then down to the Bronx and to Mecca. Once, after we got TV, he decided it would be fun to leave Yankee Stadium right after the first game of a double header to speed home and catch the second game on TV. We got home about the seventh inning. "Look at that," he said, smiling at the TV, "we were right there." When my father died, his longtime friend, Hans Mueller, came to the wake. With tears in his eyes, he shook my hand and said, "Fifty years I know him, and always he was *goot*." That was my father.

Thinking about it now, I realize we were, by a wide margin, the largest extended family in the neighborhood. At the time, however, it was just the way it was. Our being Italian was just the way it was also. We never said Italian American, at least no one I heard or read did. The neighborhood was virtually all Italian before the war, and it was about 50% Italian after the building boom after the war when I went through grade school. There were about 15% Irish and 10% Jewish families, and the rest were a scattering of Poles, Germans, Swedes, French Canadians, and Lithuanians, with one Flemish, one Russian, one Czech, and one Black family tossed into the mix. There was one family who had no ethnicity that I was aware of, but I gave it no thought. I had no conception of America other than my neighborhood when I was little. We were Italian and Irish and Jewish and all the rest, and while we were Americans too, that "American" had no specificity in my mind. On the other hand, I was a fussy eater as a kid (I never ate tomato sauce until I was a teenager) and my grandmother used to tease me by calling me an American.

Grade school and high school were an eight and four arrangement in Waterbury back then, so I got out of my neighborhood school when I was 14. I was surprised to find that there were a lot more Irish kids and Jewish kids and Black kids in my town than I had imagined. I was still Italian, and even took 3 years of Italian with Miss Menotti, learn-ing the officially accepted Italian dialect rather than the one my family had not taught me or, more exactly, had not let me learn. But, being Italian as an issue came up only three times. Once, after I scored extremely high on a multiple choice history exam (I could memorize an amazing amount of material for a short period of time), the teacher, an Irish woman, asked me what my father did. I told her he was an engineer. "Do you mean he runs a train or tends a furnace?" she asked. I said that he was a mechanical engineer and explained what he did. I realized she was trying to figure how an Italian could be smart. Once, after three dates with a lovely Jewish girl, her parents fig-ured out I wasn't a Jewish kid from New Britain, but an Italian from Hill Street. End of romance. And once (and most amusing) a Jewish girl's parents told her that if she went to the senior prom with me, she wouldn't get the promised graduation present—a trip to Rome. I took these Jewish parents' anti-Italian attitudes as the stupidity of adults (I was a kid), not as ethnic slurs. After all, their daughters had no prob-lem with me.

When I was in grade school, my grandfather's sister and her hus-band died. When I was 16, my grandfather died. We had already given up raising pigs and chickens, and we would now knock down a couple of sheds and have more lawn. When I was in college, Uncle Angelo died suddenly at 57. These deaths impressed me, but I didn't realize they were the beginning of the end of a way of life.

I went to the University of Connecticut. Myself, my sisters, and our four first cousins were the first in the family to go to college. Our older second cousins didn't go, and a lot of their children, younger than us, didn't go either. My mother claimed this was due to her mother's pro-gressive attitudes, but I'm not sure about that. My grandmother once said to me, "Dick, you read a lot. And if you read and read, someday you'll have so many ideas in your head you won't know what to do." A college student who self-designated as an intellectual at the time, I chuckled at my grandmother's statement. In my 40s, I learned that she was right.

At the University of Connecticut I got turned on to art and read about the Italian Renaissance, and about an early twentieth-century Italian art movement called Futurism. I found myself identifying with all of this as an Italian. And then I found myself wondering about this identification when my grandfather, who had been much more Italian than me, could not read or write a word, and obviously knew nothing about the Renaissance at all. He came from a tiny place called *Cerce Maggiore* in the hills of southern Italy, where my ancestors (and most everyone else) worked the land for absentee landlords for hundreds and hundreds of years. But there were enough kids I went to high school with at the University of Connecticut, and I was still within the state of Connecticut, so I didn't get a really different take on my ethnicity until I went to graduate school at the University of Minnesota in Minneapolis in 1961.

I graduated from the University of Connecticut on my 22nd birthday, June 11, 1961. Three days later, my father suddenly and unexpectedly, became very ill. Three days later, he died. He was 55. Hundreds of people showed at the 2-day wake, and his funeral was the longest I've ever seen. But he was still dead. I was working the 11-to-7 graveyard shift in a knitting mill, getting some money together to go to Minnesota. My mother, who didn't like the idea of me getting married, figured I wouldn't do so so soon after my father died. She was wrong. I decided to marry my University of Connecticut sweetheart, Claudia, and take her with me to Minnesota. Claudia's background was English and Yankee and she was Protestant. We decided to get married by a Justice of the Peace, and have a small wedding, inviting only my closest family (which still meant 24 people). My mother didn't come. And my mother told everyone not to come. Out of the 24 invited, 7 showed. I didn't think about this very much, as it was the kind of thing my mother was capable of. Getting married anyway and moving 1,700 miles away turned out to be the kind of thing I was capable of. We did a 3-day honeymoon in New York City. One of the highlights was seeing "La Dolce Vita," which had just come out. I loved it. I loved Marcello Mastroanni and Anouk Amiee. I still do. Again, I found myself identifying with an Italy that my grandparents knew little or nothing of. But I didn't think about that at the time. And Minneapolis was big enough that English and French and Italian "art" movies were always playing. So, I saw lots of Fellini and Antonioni.

Minnesota was a different world. First, Minneapolis was a big city. That meant good jazz, once you found the spots (I saw Nina Simone). That meant two art museums. That meant good theater (I saw Lotte

Leyna reading Bertold Brecht). That meant major league baseball. And Minnesota meant fishing and hunting like I had only read about—walleyes, northern pike, pheasants, and ducks in numbers that amazed me. Ethnically, it was mostly Swedes, Norwegians, and Germans, with a few Poles, Finlanders, and Bohemians here and there. The only Italians you ever heard about were a small community in St. Paul. I'd go over there now and then to go grocery shopping. They had decent pepperoni and grating cheese, but after that, their idea of Italian food was much more Americanized than I was used to. Also, they used to say Italian pronouncing the initial "I" long as in "eye-talian." This rested uneasy in my ears.

So almost no one in Minneapolis was Italian; and no one in graduate school, except myself and the chair of my department, Elio D. Monachesi, was Italian. So, in a wonderful reversal, I became conscious of being Italian because I was the only one around. A bit of cultural relativity came up when Marilyn Monroe died. The newspaper reported that Joe DiMaggio had kissed Marilyn in her coffin. A graduate student friend from the Midwest was horrified. I told him such was standard practice with my family, which made him more horrified.

Then, after 3 years, one Frank Petroni joined the graduate student numbers. Petroni had grown up Italian in Everett, Massachusetts. He was older than me (he'd spent some time in the service) and he grew up in a larger Italian community where (to compare his situation to mine) lawns had not started getting bigger yet. He would invite a bunch of people over for lasagna, have twice as much food as was needed, and we'd talk about that being the way Italians did it. When he and I took a class together, once a week I would bring him a loaf of great bread that the Lincoln Deli got flown in from San Francisco. "Frankie, Frankie—*Pane, Pane*," I'd shout in broken English as I walked into the classroom. And he'd jump up and grab the bread and rip off a piece and start eating it. In short, we had fun playing Italian, and Italian was what we felt like, at least when we were together and cutting up. But how Italian we could stage ourselves was limited because although our Minnesota friends knew we were Italian, they didn't know the day-to-day interactional stuff to go with our Italian presentations—like teasing us about our big noses, or using one or another Italian curse word, and so forth. In Minnesota, then, I was self-consciously Italian for the first time.

I was not the only cousin to get away. My cousin Judy graduated from the University of Connecticut 2 years before me and joined the Women's Air Corps. My sister Adele would graduate from the University of Connecticut, get a master's at Pratt in Brooklyn, New York, and then end up in the Boston area. A few of us just had to get away, while other cousins—less adventurous or more prudent—stayed nearby. Three of them (among the oldest) built new houses in the neighborhood and two more remained in the neighborhood in their parent's houses, while the rest moved into growing middle-class areas in small towns surrounding Waterbury. My grandfather and his sister began the neighborhood just before 1900, and 60 years later, their grandchildren began jumping ship. And that, I think we can say, was American, not Italian.

In the summer of 1964, my cousin Judi got married. She had fallen for an Air Force pilot from Texas named Tom Doubek. It was the last really big wedding anyone in the family staged. The way Tom likes to put it is: "Judy and I both had most of our families at the wedding—I had 5 people and she had 500." Actually, Judi had a little better than 300 people there.

Claudia and I drove over 30 hours nonstop from Minnesota. We got to the church just after the bride had walked down the isle, so we entered the church quietly and sat a few rows behind everyone else. I looked at all of them, all of my mother's family still alive (Uncle Harry had died of a heart attack at 49 in 1962). My grandmother, my mother, my sisters, my uncles and aunts, my cousins, and second cousins, and third cousins, and all these cousins' spouses and a lot of their kids. I just took them all in. And I took in the very beautiful Lady of Lourds Church, an old Italian church in the south end of town where my family went to mass early in the century, before a new congregation was started in the north end where we lived. And I thought about my family in the days before I was around. And then the ceremony was over and I was hugging my cousin and Tom Doubek, and Aunt Lauretta and Uncle Jim, and my mother and sisters, and all the aunts and uncles and cousins. And then everyone got into their cars and went to the reception.

The reception began with a cocktail hour so I was milling around talking with people. I went to the bar to get another drink and bumped into my mother who was standing nearby talking with a little old Italian guy named Jimmy, the husband of her cousin Florence, Zizi Rocco's first born. Jimmy didn't recognize me and asked my mother who I was. She told him I was her son and that I was a college professor now. He looked up at me in wonder and mumbled in broken English, "Dick, Richard, Vito's son." And then he threw up his arms and said, "God bless America! God bless America! We come here, we have nothing. We work and work and our children grow up big and strong and become college professors! Excuse me, Rosie, I weep." And he did. So I waved my mother off and sat and had a drink with Jimmy. But I couldn't tell him what was already dawning on me, couldn't tell him that being a college professor wasn't worth the pigs and chickens, the garden, the wine, and what it had been to be embedded in that neighborhood with so many of the people who were all around us at my cousin Judi's wedding.

My grandmother died in October 1967. I flew home for the funeral. The first person I saw at the house was Uncle Carl. "I guess I'm not a kid anymore," I said. "No, Dick, you're not," is what he answered.

After Minnesota, I spent one academic year (1968-1969) in Philadelphia, teaching at Temple. I remember calling my mother and telling her I had the job (which was great to her because I would be much closer to home). She congratulated me, and then added, "So, they'll give you a job then?" I was stunned. She was worried that they might give me a fellowship and grant me a Ph.D., but might not give me a job because I was Italian. I wondered what in her life she was flashing back to, but she wouldn't say. I told her another Italian guy, Mike Lalli, had been at Temple for years. That made her feel easier about the whole thing.

I lived right near Temple in Philadelphia, so most of the time I wasn't Italian, I was White. The Black or White distinction was much more important in my neighborhood than any European ethnic one. Of course, when one got down to the big open-air Italian market, there were lots of Italians all over. And you certainly could get any Italian food specialty that I knew from my childhood and a lot of them that I didn't.

And then on to Rhode Island in 1969. There are a lot of Italians in Rhode Island. The University is in the southern part of the state, not in Providence or it's satellite communities, where Italians are most concentrated. But there were many Italians living in the town I live in back in 1969, and there are more now.

When I arrived in Rhode Island, my son was a year old. My daughter was born 3 years later. My mother was happy to have these two grandchildren only 120 miles away and we visited her often. (Often by my standards, not often enough by hers.)

In 1970, Uncle Mike died. He had had one bypass operation a few years before, but he needed another one and he died on the operating table. I remember talking to Uncle Albert in the smoking room at the funeral home. "Jesus, Dick, I'm the last one." "I know, Uncle Al," was all I could say. His three brothers, all younger than he, were dead. And he lived only another year. He had a heart attack in the winter of 1971, and then died at home of a second attack in the fall of that year. On a pad on his bed table, he had written one of his favorite old saws: Why is there never enough time to do a job right, but always time to do it over? One of the last times I talked to him was 6 months earlier, when he was in the hospital following the first attack. The following poem came out of that visit.

Albert Zello, Intensive Care, and the Evil Eye

In the hospital
my handyman old uncle
was hooked up
with various wires, tubes, and electrical gadgets,
so they could watch his old heart beat.

And he said to me
(it was his second attack)
"I never thought it would come to this—
but you know, somebody (and I knew he knew who)
wished this on me!"

Meaning (you understand)
that he was painfully dying
from evil wished upon him,
and not from the breakdown

of old worn parts.
For my part, I wished they could have
fixed him up with brass ("don't rust")
nuts and bolts, with lock washers
("so nothin' loosens up")
and some angle iron and rivets
("aluminum that don't rust either")
and sprayed him with red ochre paint
("it takes the weather")
and kept him going another ten years or so!

Through the 1970s and into the 1980s, things kept dwindling in Waterbury. More and more of my mother's generation were dying, and family cohesion kept eroding. Between the deaths and people moving away (some retiring to Florida) there were fewer and fewer at each ensuing funeral. We stopped saying that we only got together for weddings and funerals, because we didn't get together for weddings anymore. Claudia and I got divorced in 1980 and that cut down on my kids' visits to my mother. Uncle Joe died in the early 1980s and Aunt Florence died in 1986. My mother died in 1987 and Uncle Carl in 1990. The next year, 1991, marked the 30th anniversary of my father's death. And I still wanted to talk with him, so I wrote the following poem about not being able to do so. In 1996, I happened upon an old studio photographer's photo of my mother—and another poem.

For My Father—Thirty Years Gone

Years—
(with secret eye and ear)
I have watched (listened)
for your face (your voice)
for wondrous laughing you.
Your notes, your photographs,
your books I have searched,
my sister's hands, her face (yours)
my son's (who wears your name)
and my own carbon copies of your ways.

Down the days, down the years . . .
. . . down the days.

Rose at Twenty

So I opened it—
(the handsome old cardboard folding picture frame)
and saw my mother, so very lovely,
(in nineteen twenty-seven) at twenty years of age.

My mother, suddenly a youngster in my eyes,
(as I am fifty-seven and my daughter's twenty-three)
my mother before my father, before my sisters, or me
(before she worked for fifty years,
before her sister died at thirty-three).

Before her father died too old,
or my father died too young,
before she buried all four brothers—
before sixty years to come.

Her face, such hope, the joy of youth,
the radiance of twenty years;
my mother as I never knew her,
before the joys and tears.

And me (now near sixty) stunned,
by the (oh so obvious) fact,
that I know what she didn't—
I know what came to pass.

"Rose" (I can't say "Mother,"
she's twenty and I'm yet to be)
"Rose, what is this life,
that you and Vito gave to me?"

Of course, she does not answer,
and I hang motionless and dumb,
in kinked and tangled wires of time
whose fragile order—

her photo has undone.

Of the uncles and aunts I grew up in the middle of, only Uncle Jim
and Aunt Lauretta, Aunt Sylvia, Aunt Jean, and Aunt Theresa were

left. The old time neighbor's families were, of course, similarly decimated. And the neighborhood continued to change. It was becoming clear that whatever moving to Florida might mean, it was probably better than staying put. As for me, Waterbury had stopped being home somewhere along the line. I don't know whether that was because I had been away, or because it had changed, or because I had. But it stopped being home. Rhode Island, however, hasn't yet become home, and I think that means it never will. Putting things simply, I'm getting to be an old man who is, in a way, longing for the world he grew up in.

Having said that, let me compare myself to my grandfather. Orphaned as a child, he came to America at age 20. He worked a few years and returned to Italy to bring back his sister, her husband, and their two children. Then he married my grandmother, built his house, and his sister's house, and his father-in-law's house. When he was in his seventies, he had his grandson following him around. And he planted and harvested food, like potatoes, with the strength of his arms on the land that was his. And he used to roast little potatoes (as big around as a quarter) in the wood stove in his shed and feed them to that same grandson. Being able to do that made my grandfather a successful man. And he had three generations of his, and his sister's, and his wife's families around him. He had an ocean between him and Cerce Maggiore, an ocean he had three times crossed, and never had any interest in crossing again. My grandfather's migration was physical. If he could have found work that paid enough, and if he could have bought his own bit of land, he would have stayed in southern Italy. But my migration has been mental. In part it was my choice, but only in part. Before I finished high school, the pigs and chickens were gone, wine production had dropped 100 gallons a year, and the lawn was encroaching on the garden. What happened to my neighborhood, to my family, to my culture? America is what happened.

I was in the north end of Boston having lunch back in 1990. I got talking with the waiter who had a strong Italian accent. It turned out he had come to America recently from Cerce Maggiore. He was stunned when I told him my grandparents came from there. We were *paisani*. The only one he had met here. But I can't talk Italian and I know nothing of the town. So all it came to was he recommended a wine and I tipped 30%.

In May 1993, Aunt Theresa died, leaving just Uncle Jim and Aunt Lauretta, Aunt Sylvia, and Aunt Jean representing my mother's generation. If you tour the neighborhood, it looks like a working-class area with well cared for yards and houses. And it is. But, it also has an alarmingly high rate of break-ins. Uncle Jim says if he and Aunt Lauretta were younger, they'd move out of Waterbury. He says the place is no good anymore. And Aunt Sylvia lives alone with a sophisticated and expensive alarm system. "What the hell are you going to do, Dick? It's the way it is today. Things are no damn good." That's Aunt Sylvia, a prisoner in her own house, talking about what America has become after luring her parents across the sea 100 years ago.

And me? I think Lawrence Ferlinghetti (1955) put it best in *A Coney Island of the Mind* when, after spinning image after wonderful image of the tawdry nature of our growing mass culture, he ends with, "and all the other fatal shorn-up fragments of the immigrant's dream come too true and mislaid among the sunbathers" (p. 13). I am a fatal fragment.

In 1994, I turned 56. My mortality (which I had been sidestepping) finally hit me. One reaction was I started writing more poems. "Fifty-Six and I Can't Believe I'll Be Gone" was the first one. Then I discovered a wonderful coffee shop in Providence called "Dolce Vita" (of all things). It's run by two brothers from Italy, and is in the old Italian neighborhood where many Italian restaurants and Italian groceries still operate. (But not so many Italians anymore. They've moved out and southeast Asians are moving in.) My experience in this coffee shop led to "Postmodern Italian American," which tells you how I assess that identity. Then in 1996 there was a blizzard that for me, ended in "La Dolce Vita: Reprise," which flashes you (dear reader) back to me at 22 on my honeymoon. And then, since I have claimed to be a Ferlinghetti fatal fragment, I tell what it comes down to for me, humorously though enigmatically, in "I Get Emptier As I Get Older."

Fifty-Six and I Can't Imagine Me Gone
(a poem to those I hold dear)

I actually am (you know)
going to get older
(a little, or much)

and die.

Up to now,
I kept this news at bay
(somehow)
believing secretly,
they'd make a live-forever pill
or else that it could be
the last of the fifth (with one out)
quite eternally
(as it seemed it was going to be,
with my dad in Yankee Stadium
one day in fifty-three).

So, my belly is slack,
and my teeth are cracked,
but, I'm still the same inside—
I'm just Richard Travisano,
looking out of an old man's eyes.
Sometimes I don't believe it
as I can't imagine me gone—
when there's so much left to do
and I still feel young and strong—
so "just like years and years ago"
when I was in my prime

(well . . .
. . . some of the time).

Postmodern Italian American

Sitting in a coffee house
which is (oh so quietly)
you understand
(and with such great care)
pretending—that it's Rome
(or perhaps Milan) out there.

Pretending so well—
with Italian muzak and decor,
with espresso and tiramisu,
and Italian-looking help

and clientele (including me)
that I'm feeling like it's Florence,
or maybe Napoli.

Though actually, you see
it's an almost-Italian coffee house,
for an almost-Italian like me
(because in fact, I'm American,
which is kind of nothing to be).

And I've not seen Milan,
the hills of Rome, nor even Napoli—
and even I (to be quite frank)
seldom listen to me.

Big problem in this country: people who know who they are
don't know enough about it to be themselves; and those who
don't know who they are, end up acting like somebody else.

But hey ho, without lives you know,
they might end up on the Winfrey Show!

(Meanwhile, back home on deranged, the deer and the antelope are
road kills, and the dream is a recurrent Early American nightmare.)

La Dolce Vita: Reprise

We were having the blizzard of '96,
but rather than wandering into a snow drift,
I surfed right past the religious channel into 1961,
and sank into La Dolce Vita instead.

Marcello, Anita, Anouk—still there!
Younger (as when we met) by thirty-five years.
The Roman film folk (rich and decadent yet)
and Emma (lovely, suicidal).
And the paparazzi, (still a pain in the ass) of course.

And old Steiner (still playing Bach on the organ)
and his ever so clever and intellectual friends,
and then off to the children who have seen La Madonna,

where people tear a tree (limb from limb) with their hands.

And then I shut it off.

Before all the destruction in La Dolce Vita
(and in my times)
(and in my life)
before all that, I shut it off.

(And Marcello, Anouk, and I, and our friends, still young!)

I Get Emptier as I Get Older

I get emptier as I get older—

Is this bad? (There's less there.)
Or good? (I'll get lighter than air!)

I just might end up a crisp hollow shell,
and the undertaker my children will tell

to stuff me!

with ricotta
(orange peel and brandy added, of course)

then bill me as the world's largest cannoli
and sell tickets to the wake—

[all proceeds going (without saying) to the
League of Aged Bocci Players' last annual clambake].

REFERENCES

Ferlinghetti, L. (1955). *A Coney Island of the mind*. New York: New Directions.
Richardson, L. (1994). Nine poems: Marriage and the family. *Journal of Contemporary Ethnography, 23*(1), 3-13.
Travisano, R. V. (1992). My grandfather's hand. *Italian Americana, X*(2), 203-217.

––

Richard V. Travisano teaches sociology at the University of Rhode Island. Presently he is writing poetry on just about anything, and prose about Rhode Island shellfishermen, and about his growing up Italian in Waterbury, Connecticut.

PART THREE

—

POETICS

The **poetic, narrative text** ostensibly pushes and extends the boundaries of the traditional, ethnographic model of textuality. Writers of poetry erase the usual distinctions between fact and fiction. They use narrative devices such as dialogue, multiple points of view, composite characters and scenes, an emphasis on showing, not telling, experiments with flashbacks, foreshadowing, and interior monologues. Poems are written in facts, not about facts. Still, the goal of representing lived experience is emphasized, as the writer moves outward from a personal, epiphanic moment to a narrative description of that experience.

However, this is no simple retelling of lived experience. The poetic form juxtaposes voice (the implied and real narrator), temporality, point of view, and character, while privileging emotion and emotionality. A primary goal is to evoke emotional responses for the reader, thereby producing verisimilitude and a shared experience. Evoked emotion becomes the method for establishing a text's claims to authority. Narrative truth or the truth of fiction is emphasized, writing a good story, or a good poem that persuades and moves the reader.

To achieve these emotional effects that produce narrative truth, language is used in a way that consciously manipulates sound patterns, rhythms, and imagery. This use of language challenges the traditional hierarchical barrier between writer and reader. This self-reflective use of language violates old norms of observer objectivity and promotes new forms of subjective understanding.

In emphasizing the personal, a new kind of theorizing occurs; works are filled with biographical, not disciplinary, citations (Shelton, 1995). A minimal, almost atheoretical sociology, psychology, or anthropology is created, so that personal experience is not mediated by complex theoretical terms. Experience is meant to speak for itself, in poetic terms. A text becomes a place where the writer carries on a dialogue with significant others.

Thus do poetic and narrative texts humanize the ethnographic disciplines. These texts are organized under a postmodern aesthetic concerning the sublime. They make what was previously unpresentable part of the presentation itself.

Four of contemporary social science's foremost poets are represented in this section. **Ivan Brady** gives us the gift of the journey into the unknown and the familiar. **Mark Nowak** presents two microethnographies on reality, butchers, eating Oscar, and ethnography. **Miles Richardson** writes of the Anthro in Cali, scenes from his return to fieldwork in Colombia, 30 years later. **Mary Weems**, an African American woman-mama-artist-educator-activist for social justice presents a series of poems on the blues, on being a black woman in a racist society. These poems are meant to be and should be performed, read out loud, and, if you are lucky, by Mary Weems.

REFERENCES

Shelton, A. (1995). Foucault's madonna: The secret life of Carolyn Ellis. *Symbolic Interaction, 18,* 83-87.

CHAPTER 9

A Gift of the Journey

— —

Ivan Brady
SUNY Oswego

Magical megaliths. Stonehenge. Sun mask. Druid dance.
The hand brushes the obelisk—mossy green and grey,
cold for a summer's day—dragging fingertips across
the texture. Braille for a pulse? We want to touch
the mystery of this place, even as the mind's eye squints

for a glimpse of deeper meanings, sequestered in time
and cultural distance, some of which seem to be murmured
in the eclipse of stones at dusk and dawn. But the magic
does not reside in the stones themselves. It is embedded in
the reading, the immersion of self in place, and the puzzle

of the circle that only gets more puzzling when spotted
by the eye of the sun. Like the morning dew, this Druid
magic is tied to a clock of nature. It emerges from nowhere
and disappears just as mysteriously with the heat of midday
—or too much inspection. The poet who would see this clearly

must chase the beams gently, introspectively, as they refract
on the traces of magicians and astronomers who have danced
through the bosom of these stones in patterns and rhythms
we hope are coded within us all. The experience steps us
into another reality and with all the power of ritual turns

day to dream, taking us out of ourselves for a while to show us something about ourselves—about how we have been and where we think we used to be—a kind of mythopoeic archaeology. The best poets still know how to do it. Magic, it seems, is a gift of the journey.

— —

Ivan Brady is Distinguished Teaching Professor of Anthropology at SUNY Oswego, a SUNY Faculty Exchange Scholar, and president of the Society for Humanistic Anthropology. A former book review editor of the American Anthropologist, *he has special interests in Pacific Islands ethnography and the philosophy of science. He is currently developing a new version of his book* Anthropological Poetics.

CHAPTER 10

Two Microethnographies

— —

Mark Nowak
College of St. Catherine

When it came to
butchering
"The reality
"experienced on **Saturday**

mornings "in the field . . .

"is not the unmediated world
"of 'others,' but **Mr. Petrack**
and Mr. Sertich
were the ones that were

more or less "the world
"*between* ourselves
"and others. **the butchers**

*

who had the nerve
to kill our pets
"The condition of fieldwork
in other words.

*

I say pet
"is fundamentally
confrontational and only
superficially observational;

**because we got so attached
to those animals . . .**
                    "There is no way
"of eliminating consciousness
"from **I remember our pig Oscar.**

"our activities in the field . . .

I cried when Oscar was butchered.
"This pain is related to the fact
"that meaning is always
"connected with the consummation of

       *

We couldn't stand
"process,
              seeing
"with termination, and

"ultimately with
Oscar

butchered

by "death.

       *

**these mean people
like Mr. Sertich and
Mr. Petrack.**
                    "Acknowledging
"the inherent
"violence in fieldwork

"actually
              "rephrases
"the problem
"of authenticity.

       *

Did you have trouble eating Oscar?

"The number of voices
"recorded by the ethnographer
"is immaterial;

**Yes, I could hardly
eat Oscar after seeing
that this was from Oscar now.**

**Blood sausage and all these
other things
were**
　　"writing
"ethnography is

"an act that subsumes them

Oscar.

"all.

**Some place
　　in here
I think there was
a clipping**

"It tells a story
"through interruptions,
that you were

　　　*

that ethnography always
begins with
an "e"-
　　　"amassed
"densities
"of description,

"evocations of voices and

absent frames

　　　*

going to make a record.
this time, of
　　"the conditions

　　　*

**When I used to
cut things out**

"of their possibility,

**I didn't always put
the dates on them.**

"and lyrical, ruminative
"aporias
    "that give pause.

BIBLIOGRAPHY

Erjavec, F., & Erjavec, M. A. (1998). Interview with Mark Nowak.

Hastrup, K. (1992).Writing ethnography: State of the art. In J. Okely & H. Callaway (Eds.), *Anthropology and autobiography*. London: Routledge.

Perkovich, F. (1990). Interview with Mike Schommer.

Stewart, K. (1996). *A space by the side of the road: Cultural poetics in an "other" America*. Princeton, NJ: Princeton University Press.

— —

Mark Nowak edits the journal XCP: Cross-Cultural Poetics *(http://bfn. org/~xcp/) and also is editor of Theodore Enslin's* Then and Now: Selected Poems, 1943-1993 *(University Press of New England/National Poetry Foundation, 1999) and coeditor (with Diane Glancy) of* Visit Teepee Town: Native Writings After the Detours *(Coffee House Press, 1999). A collection of Nowak's poems and ethnographic writings is scheduled to be published in the fall of 2000 (Coffee House Press). Work from this volume has appeared previously in more than 30 literary journals and anthologies including* American Anthropologist, An Anthology of (New) American Poets, Another Chicago Magazine, Berkeley Poetry Review, *and* Northwest Review.

CHAPTER 11

The Anthro in Cali

—

Miles Richardson
Louisiana State University

In 1992, 30 years after I had first gone to Colombia to do fieldwork for an anthropological dissertation, I went back. Here are scenes from that return.[1]

I

At *Estancia Paisa, "Abierto a las 24 Horas,"* I
offer the lottery vendor, at her station on the corner,
a *tragito* of *aguardiente*. She, broad in the beam,
and tight in the skirt, sips demurely, while
a *compañero* at the crowded table falls asleep;
the guitar player has come and gone, but the school boy,
at his place by the counter, keeps hard to his figuring.

II

Early mass at the Ermita, they come off the street
in assorted disguise: The office-bound in crisp blouse,
stockings, and heels; the homeless adrift in rags and dirt brown;
and the beggars, each from their favorite crouch by the door,
prepared to dispense their blessing,
Que Dios le pague, May God repay you,
for any miracle that falls their way.

III

"*¡Hombre!*" the man gestures in open-handed disgust.
At the packed corner where traffic lights are off
because of the *apagón*, the energy-saving blackout,
and distracted by the battle between pedestrian
and car, I have stepped on his heel. Meanwhile,
the dog in mural above the street,
in shoulder-to-shoulder companionship
with his friend, the cat, requests
"*Baja el tono de su agresividad,*
and let's learn to live together."

IV

On the foot bridge that crosses the Río Cali
someone has placed a blind man near the statue
in honor of the writer, Jorge Isaacs. As people
flow around him, he shakes his cup up and down,
up and down, while the soft drink man shouts
from his two wheel cart, "*Limonada, fría, fría*"
and the lottery vendor circling the crowd adds,
"*Del Valle, juega, juega.*" Beneath the bust of *don* Jorge,
frozen in idyllic stone, the heroine, María, listens
chastely to the young man chatting at her shoulder.

V

From a doorway he has occupied during the night,
an old man shakes a plastic curtain over the curb.
In a corner neatly stacked are his straw hat
with a red band around its crown and a stick for walking.
The door has been a perfect fit for his small frame;
now he folds the plastic to make ready for another day,
and in silent admiration I wish him *Buenos días, señor.*

VI

Avenida Belacázar Cinco-Diez. Where we lived in '62.
The Edificio Dominguez, but today it is the daughters
Dominguez. The elegant *señora*, the gracious *doña*,
la madre of these two, the lady we knew, is dead.
I've come back to see what's changed.
If I hadn't returned, would she still be alive?
Things don't stop; they circle. But around what?
Around the past? Around growing old?
Around a place I've yet to discover.

VII

El Señor de la Caña
In *La Ermita,* a cathedral of Neo-Gothic
spire and splendor amid the bustling of downtown Cali,
the Lord Jesus, already judged, judges—the cane stalk
in his hand a baton to bless and a whip to scourge.
Some kneel to flutter crosses over forehead,
mouth, and heart and are on their feet and gone.
Others stay on their knees for the whole story
of *mi culpa, mi culpa, mi grand culpa,*
my guilt, my guilt, my grand guilt; but I,
an Anglo anthro from the Baptist South,
read from a printed petition,
"Protege esta alma abatida,
Shelter this disquieted soul."

NOTE

1. Scene VI comes from a longer report of the return (Richardson, 1998).

REFERENCE

Richardson, M. (1998). The poetics of a resurrection: Re-seeing 30 years of change in a Colombian community and in the anthropological enterprise. *American Anthropologist, 100,* 11-21.

——

Miles Richardson is the Doris Z. Stone Professor in Latin American studies at the Department of Geography and Anthropology, Louisiana State University. After he finishes his current work, "Being-in-Christ and the Social Construction of Death in Spanish America and the American South: An Anthropologist's Account," *which is almost as long as the title, he wants to celebrate the human species with something titled,* "Professing Anthropocentrism in a Postmodern World."

CHAPTER 12

Windows

— —

Mary E. Weems
University of Illinois, Urbana-Champaign

The fully orchestrated blues statement is something else again. Even as the lyrics wail and quaver a tale of woe, the music may indicate the negative mood suggested by the dreadful, or in any case regrettable, details, but even so there will also be tantalizing sensuality in the woodwinds, mockery and insouciance among the trumpets, bawdiness from the trombones, a totally captivating, even if sometimes somewhat ambivalent elegance, in the ensembles and in the interplay of the solos and ensembles, plus a beat that is likely to be as affirmative as the ongoing human pulse itself.

There is much to be said about the literary implications of this aspect of my down-home heritage, and I have written . . . of it in *The Hero and the Blues* and in *Stomping the Blues*, both of which may be read as being, among other things, books about literary terminology and as attempts at a functional definition of improvisation as heroic action, as a way of responding to traumatic situations creatively.

The improvisation that is the ancestral imperative of blues procedure is completely consistent with and appropriate to those of the frontiersman, the fugitive slave, and the picaresque hero, the survival of each of whom depended largely on an ability to operate on dynamics equivalent to those of the vamp, the riff, and most certainly the break, which jazz musicians regard as the moment of truth or that disjuncture that should bring out your personal best. (Murray, 1996, pp. 5-6)

When my friend and colleague Carolyne White first began to read my work, she said that I was doing more things in and with my work than I was able to articulate. She is right. As an artist, I've always focused on the creation, performance, and publication of my work, leaving it to others to analyze and/or interpret based on what each brings to the table of my poems, plays, papers, and stories.

The opening quote resonates with me because my poetry is improvisational; it is created both as the result of and in response to my constant struggle as an African American woman-mama-artist-educator-activist for social justice and urban education reform living in the oppressive, racist, and sexist "Untied"[1] States. This struggle answers Suzi Gablik's call for artists to create with social responsibility and influences everything I do. As D. Bob Gowin said in his foreword to Greene's (1988) *The Dialectic of Freedom*, "Freedom is a poem."

Each poem in the following selection had its own catalyst. I attempt to weave them together by providing the reader with the window to the creation of each piece.

"Windows" was my first work of 1999. On January 4, I opened the envelope Carolyne sent me that contained eight slides of Willie Bonner's work. I held the slides under the lamplight at my desk and wrote the following series:

Windows

(while viewing Willie Bonner's paintings)

1. Woman with yellow rectangle mouth

> You almost slapped my mouth off
> but my face returned to the tree
> my hand reached out blacker than
> the last word blacker than right
> blacker than the ace in the palm
> of a winning hand my spirit returns
> to land over and over shaping

the soil feeling the brown
in my back my mouth beating
like a heart my words burn
like a brand the land burning
hand burning the land burning
hand burning the land burning
my eye turns "of thee I sing"

2. Brotha with blown up dreads wearing a green turtleneck

Mental dynamite is shit
holes in my natural
creative blobs
for mobs of
mind blowin' think tanks
trying to figure out
what doesn't need
to be figured
there are holes in triggers
twisting my dread
twisting my dread
locks on images
clickin' back and forth
clickin' back and forth
spit from teeth that won't
begin again

there is no beginning and end
everything goes around
comes around
comes back

holes in my natural

3. "do not cross" white line

Even the desert flag
has lines of blood
spelling "do not cross"
on her floor like a
Morse code

shadows cast her colors
like ship sails blow
from sky to ground
on Stevie Wonder's ribbon

they pull the stars down
to scatter

giving cacti something
to sigh for

the stripes are the old gold
of misplaced standards
the land wears a fake smiley face
funny color eyes

the Sun a single window
clings to light

4. Black woman egghead

I am the original egghead
smooth obsidian cracked
smacked and bushwhacked
filled with knickknacks
that keep coming home
without a map road signs
or keys

I play in the key of black
people turn me over
and over like a stone
make marks that disappear
in the sun

I cover the world in WE
while people build houses
of sticks and stones
bones bury and hollow
bury and hollow
are numbered and identified
and each time it's me
each time it's me

I am the long playing album
the open space
the first eye to open
the last eye to shut
"every shut eye ain't sleep"
enemies rest on my face

I am everywhere
original.

5. Brotha wearing blood hat w/city as backdrop

Brothas are missing in action
like Viet Nam veterans
unwelcomed home

brothas wear years in their
hair like lint pickin' it out
over and over waking up with
a new head full

every day the city steps
on their heads and they step
out step over step forward
learn to drill with one leg
run between buildings
look for friendly faces
find cop cars constantly changing
colors

but brothas
are always in season
brothas always need a reason

struggle "it's all in their heads"
covers their faces like rain
they keep their hands in
walk point
wear their wounds
under the latest
gear

6. Brotha smelling something foul

That foul smell
is a multicultural
brick wall designed
to make A + B + C equal A
a colonial smokescreen
built one block at a time
always in the pink

it's like being the "artist
formerly known as"
breathing under a purple rain

another bullshot name change
rearranging the same pieces

remaking the same unfinished
puzzle

only funk
will clear the air

7. Skeleton face woman w/purple hair and red eye

Death gets complicated
like a rainbow
and the struggle

our flag is a bulls eye
and the seasons
make the hair color
like a coalition

we have many filled graves
Afro Sheen
all our teeth
a strong sense of smell
and all the time
in the word

8. Brotha wearing a mask and a white earring

If the Lone Ranger
had been a brotha
him and Tonto woulda
hooked up
kicked butt
and took the long way
Home.

In a course I took as a doctoral student with Wanda Pillow, our class went to see Sherman Alexie's film Smoke Signals. *The film reminded me of the similarities and differences between the Native American and African American experiences in the "Untied" States. This poem is my response to his shape-shifting work:*

Smoke Signals . . .
    (for Sherman Alexie)

That day after the rage
watching water billow like clouds

screaming, the mist sending smoke signals,
the sound of my father's voice repeating
repeating "I didn't mean to, I didn't mean to,
I didn't mean to," his ashes mixing, reshaping,
remixing holding my hand like magic.
While I was lay down, feeling our sacred ground,
the bridge over the water our way back, way back
to before the white. After my father's ashes
changed the water to many shades of red, red,
red, red, all dead my ancestors washed my eyes,
joined my cries, after, after, after the rage.
I picked up our memories in the smoke signals
spilling from souls, my soul turning from stone
to flesh, turning from soul to flesh, like poof,
like poof, like when my father said "poof" and all
the whites went away. After I screamed
our silence could not protect us, after
I painted my face in the colors of hope.
I started to hear the stories of Thomas
in the building of fires, in smoke
from the fires signaling my people to tell
our stories, to tell our stories in forever
fires one by one.
I went to my mother, with the word HOME
from my father's wallet, and re-became
her son her son her son . . .

*Years ago, artist Gil Scott Heron wrote a spoken word piece titled "The
Revolution Will Not Be Televised," referring to the possibility of an African
American revolution against oppression and for equality. The following
poem was created after an experience in a class that focused on the so-called
"high art" of White Europeans/Americans reminded me of the paradox of the
co-opting of African American art while it is simultaneously devalued
and/or ignored by mainstream art galleries and art critics:*

This Evolution Will Not Be Televised
    (inspired by Liora Bresler)

One million poems, and blood
paintings pressed between fingers
not leaving prints

Picasso and the brotha from another planet
passing each other on a New York street,
the brotha pullin' his coat, Picasso
opening his trench to reveal his wares
hanging from the lining like cheap
imitation watches

Meanwhile, watching the fun ghosts
smoking huge dollar bills walk
down fast streets stepping on all
the cracks

Mothers create dance in large kitchens
with wooden floors, the mistress
of the house sits in the pantry quietly
taking notes

Contrary to popular belief, Claude McKay's
tombstone does not say "fuck all you mothafuckas"
and James Brown was the Godfather of soul
before time started

Starting to look around can hurt if you Black
and wonder why everybody carries
copies of your work in back pockets
while your paintbrushes rest in jelly jars,
you canvas shop in the backs of grocery store
parking lots days food is delivered

Basquiat and Hendrix took a long trip
all their baggage was pawned the day
after they left

George Carlin said White folks should never,
ever play the blues their job is to give the blues
to Blacks

Our image, our braids, our music, our mistakes,
our asses, our rhythms are played on TV
like a long 78 album in commercial after commercial

The Colonel in plantation-dress raps and moonwalks
selling a Black woman's stolen fried chicken, Black kids
snap their fingers, think that's so cool, bug their mamas
for extra-crispy

This is a never-ending story that won't be televised
but:

Baraka already wrote a poem about it
Miles Davis played it on the way to the grave
Zora copied the story 100 times
Toni Morrison keeps trying to change the ending

In the end Alex Haley's Roots were sold
old artists look for their fortunes in fertile palms,
lose the ability to count their blessings
on Sunday

Seems like Lena sang Stormy Weather once
and the sky got stuck on rewind

Which reminds me, "What is the present value of 1
billion dreams slit, sucked, scarred, riffed,
ripped?

B. B. King stopped lovin' having the blues long ago
keeps playing as a reminder

This is a never-ending story

an evolution
that will not
be televised

P.S. Back on the block the brotha from another planet
watches Picasso sketch graffiti in the subway.

*During a visit to the African American History Museum in my home-
town of Cleveland, Ohio, a handbill advertising a slave sale being held
"under the trees" was the catalyst for the following piece:*

Under the Trees

I'm under Ghana-green leaves broad
as back, covered in bright colors
from head to foot, skin glistening
in 100-degree weather. Here, my feet
don't feel the chains around torn ankles,
my breath shooting out, my tears falling
to soak ground I was brought here to
work. Sound pulls me back under
these trees where dirty white fingers
holding white gloves force my teeth open,

force their hands between legs that used to
open wide to love my husband. Ain't no picnic
here. White folks pitching us like pennies.
I wear no clothes but stand unashamed
watching women and children unfold
large white squares to cover unsacred
ground, watching men take leisure-walks
between rows of rice, cloth, spices, and
chickens, working up appetites, preparing
to enjoy their picnic basket.

After watching the film Rosewood, *I asked the question: How could a
place with such a splendiferous name be the site of the massacre of innocent
African Americans?*

Rosewood

a name for summer,
petals in lingerie drawers, first
love walks in the park, fairy tales, not
tragedy, bled bones, genocide.

Didn't take much. A funny smell
in the air, a look in the eye,
a hangnail-and Black people started
falling like rose petals.

Slaughter's not a word for places
called Rosewood, a name for cherrywood
rockers, potpourri, cherry pie,
red crosses.

Wonder if there was a calm before the storm
when all the animals left the woods, and
the sky turned its back to hide the scars.

The day was bullets, red, wood, and not a single
rose in sight.

After reading Mumia Abu Jamal's Death Blossoms, *I tried to stand in
his shoes. I tried to imagine living 24 hours a day, 7 days a week, in a space he
described as the size of a bathroom:*

Hell

Poet in a bathroom
with bars
only visitors' words
entering like wounds
where a pencil and paper
breaks rules where rulers
pitch pennies over eyes for fun
nowhere to run hide
a place for poems
piling up for the long wait

She begins to point her finger
at air shaping each word
letting them have their space
oh'ing her lips
as if to blow them dry

Her body becomes a pen
she moves rewrites

but can't escape
the heat.

My question: What might be the future of this patriarchal planet?

Future Dinosaurs

I

In the beginning

dinosaurs shudder

Man drops

II

Man thinks,
no place to bed but stone,
cold meat, worn feet.

III

Man:

wrote in incomplete sentences,
excluding women
giving God the credit.

Nature smiled,
spit up bones,
turned colors.

IV

Man thinks, God grimaces.

Information moves in
Morse code

Wars worn
bodies airborne
time tears

V

Man spills. Begins putting stuff
in under around through
every bit of wild and stretch and sky,
flies into space for a final approach.

The Ages are renamed and replayed,
a scratched a go-go dance to Taps.

VI

Nature forms a union and begins
writing a strike clause.

VII

Man trips, strips.

Peace is won and killed
won and killed
leaving too many corpses
stirring ashes.

VIII

Man invents above his head,
making things he can't break or fix

Nature talks to God
plea bargains for better working conditions.

IX

Man reasons money means more

Disease begins accepting blank checks
and charges.

Extinction feasts
on the last of the land

God catches the subway in New York,
sees an 8-year-old boy water gunned
with battery acid

God decides on the way home,
calls Nature.

X

Man piles on excuses like coats,
continues.

XI

Dawn.

L.A. smog is stepping on traffic,
kicking gas and taking names.

South Africa. Africans sing "We are Free,"
search gleaned land for scraps.

Russia. Radioactive shoemakers
in Chernobyl, nail heels
to the toes of shoes.

China. The dead in Tiananmen Square stand up
as a billion Chinese feel a backward breeze begin.

As agreed, Nature leaves.

God brushes man off face.

Dinosaurs mutter.

NOTE

1. Thanks go to Wanda Pillow for sharing this typo in a student's paper.

REFERENCES

Greene, M. (1988). *The dialectic of freedom*. New York: Teachers College Press.
Murray, A. (1996). *The blue devils of Nada: A contemporary American approach to aesthetic statement*. New York: Pantheon.

— —

Mary E. Weems is the mama of 16-year-old cartoonist, Michelle E. Weems, and a performance poet, playwright, and workshop facilitator. She currently is a doctoral candidate in educational policy studies at the University of Illinois, Urbana-Champaign. Poetry collections include white *(Wick series, Kent State University),* Blackeyed *(Burning Press), and* Fembles *(Bowling Green State University).*

PART FOUR

— —

PERFORMANCE NARRATIVES

The postmodern world stages existential crises. Following Victor Turner (1986), the ethnographer gravitates to these narratively structured, liminal, existential spaces in the culture. In these dramaturgical sites, people take sides, forcing, threatening, inducing, seducing, cajoling, nudging, loving, living, abusing, and killing one another (see Turner, 1986, p. 34). In these sites, ongoing social dramas occur. These dramas have a temporal or chronological order, multiple beginnings, middles and ends. They are storied events, narratives that rearrange chronology into multiple, and differing forms of meaningful experience.

The storied nature of these experiences continually raises the following questions:

- Whose story is being told (and made) here?
- Who is doing the telling?
- Who has the authority to make their telling stick?

As soon as a chronological event is told in the form of a story, it enters a text-mediated system of discourse where larger issues of power and control come into play (Smith, 1993). In this text-mediated system, new tellings occur. The interpretations of original experience are now fitted to this larger interpretive structure.

Performance ethnography enters a postmodern culture with nearly invisible boundaries separating theatre performance from dance, music, film, television, video, and the various performance art disciplines (McCall, 2000, p. 423). The performance text is situated in a complex system of discourse, where both traditional and avant-garde meanings of theatre, film, video, ethnography, performance, text, and audience all circulate and inform one another. Aesthetic theories (naturalism, realism, modernism, postmodernism) collide with positivist, postpositivist, and poststructural epistemologies. Hypertexts interact with traditional print and performance forms of representation. In the moment of performance, the co-performance text brings audiences and performers into a jointly felt and shared field of experience. Such works unsettle the writer's place in the text, freeing the text and the writer to become interactional productions. The performance text is the single, most powerful way for ethnography to recover yet interrogate the meanings of lived experience.

The performed text is a lived experience, and this in two senses. The performance doubles back on the experiences previously represented in the ethnographer's text. It then re-presents those experiences as embodied performance to the audience. It thus privileges experience, the evocative moment when another's experiences come alive for the self. But there are many ways to present lived experience. If performance is interpretation, then performance texts have the ability to criticize and deconstruct taken-for-granted understandings concerning how lived experience is to be represented.

As ethnographic stagings, performances are always "enmeshed in moral matters" and they "enact a moral stance" (Conquergood, 1985, p. 2, 4), asking the audience to take a stand on the performance and its meanings. In these productions, the performer becomes a cultural critic. If culture is an ongoing performance, then performers bring the spaces, meanings, ambiguities, and contradictions of culture critically alive in their performances (Conquergood, 1986). The performed text—Victor Turner's (1986) liminal space—is one of the last frontiers for ethnography to enter, a new—but old—border to be crossed. When fully embraced, this crossing will forever transform ethnography and cultural studies. It will serve, at the same time, to redefine the meanings of ethnography in its other moments and formations.

We present two performance narratives in Part Four. "Torch" is an extract from **Stacy Holman Jones's** larger study of torch singers as performers. This reading explores Jones's experiences as a scholar, feminist, music lover, writer, and woman. Her history is interwoven with the history she writes of this feminist art form. Her story becomes part of the autobiography of the women who sang these songs—Edith Piaf, Libby Holman, Billie Holiday, Lee Wiley. In reading this essay, we dream our way back to our doomed love affairs, our versions of the blues.

Ronald J. Pelias explores the argument that theatre, the performance itself, is a rehearsal for death. His performance writing essay moves back and forth between Freud and Lacan's arguments concerning presence, there (da) and absence, gone (fort). A performance is always an interaction between being present, and being absent, between life and death. Pelias's text, which should be read out loud, is a series of meditations on friendships, high school reunions, memories of classrooms and high school teachers, James Bond, child actors who never die, granddaughters and grandparents, Christmas vacations, coming and going, leaving and returning home leaving, obituaries, audiences leaving the theatre after a performance, the final credits, writing as if you were dying, rehearsals for the final absence.

REFERENCES

Conquergood, D. (1985). Performing as a moral act: Ethical dimensions of the ethnography of performance. *Literature in Performance, 5*, 1-13.

Conquergood, D. (1986). Performing cultures: ethnography, epistemology, and ethics. In E. Slembek (Ed.), *Miteinander sprechen and handeln: Festschrift fur Hellmut Geissner* (pp. 55-147). Frankfurt: Scriptor.

McCall, M. M. (2000). Performance ethnography: A brief history and some advice. In N. K. Denzin & Y. S. Lincoln (Eds.), *Handbook of qualitative research* (2nd ed., pp. 421-435). Thousand Oaks, CA: Sage.

Smith, D. E. (1993). High noon in textland: A critique of Clough. *Sociological Quarterly, 34*, 183-192.

Turner, V. (1986). *The anthropology of performance*. Performing Arts Journal Publications.

CHAPTER 13

Torch

——

Stacy Holman Jones
University of Texas at Austin

A torch song is a song about unrequited love. The torch song originated in Tin Pan Alley music publishing houses and flourished on post-World War I vaudeville and speakeasy stages in the performances of Edith Piaf, Libby Holman, Billie Holiday, Lee Wiley, and countless others. But just who is the torch singer? What are her history and her place in history? Might her performance move beyond a blind and narcissistic obsession with doomed love affairs? Is her lament a feminist art, a cultural power play? What do her words and movements teach us about autobiography, performance, and culture? This article explores how the author's experience—as a scholar, feminist, music lover, writer, and woman— burns with these questions. This article enacts a performance ignited by a history of torch singers. Put on your favorite sad song and join in. And by all means, sing along.

1. **torch** (tôrch), n. 1. a light to be carried in the hand, consisting of some combustible substance.

—Flexner and Hauck (1987, p. 1998)

As I listened to her, I felt she understood the deep human sadness that characterized me, and that she too, was waiting—for something or other, yearning for whatever it was that was to come. This blending of the chanson's raw emotion with the tremendous hunger of its audience for intense vicarious expression may be the most indelible aspect of the form.

—Clements (1998, p. AR33)

Two stories.

Uptown, she walks in hallowed halls. She enters a large, windowless room and begins covering every surface—ceiling, walls, floor—with words. With each keystroke, she paints herself into the corner furthest from the door until she is standing on a jagged circle untouched by text. A jagged circle of mind untouched by words, untouched by manuscripts, proposals, applications, standardized tests, curriculum vitae, fuzzy attempts at fiction. The tribunal of knowledge judges her unfit. She remains

Untouched by elavil, zoloft, xanex, doxepin, paxil, effexor, wellbutrin.

Untouched by the kind words of therapists, herbalists, healers, and clinicians.

Untouched by love letters to a former self, a future being always becoming but never realized.

Her painting—this masterpiece—is her resistance to institutional exploitation writ large on the body's canvas. It is a resistance witnessed by collapsed immune systems, migraines, neurological diseases, drug abuse, infertility, mental breakdowns, suicide, cancer (Berland, 1996, p. 148). Hers is an aching body taking up thought where words should be, without finding words (Berland, 1996, p. 149).

Downtown, she moves in neon shadows. She enters the large, windowless room—her black box—and saturates every surface with the sounds of despair. With each beat, each tremulous note, she strips herself bare until she is standing stark naked. Enshrined in the white heat of the spotlight, the words she sings etch the stigmata of desire. The paying public devours her whole. Her skin remains

Etched by cigarettes, liquor, speed, weed, heroin.

Etched by analyses of critics, club owners, managers, producers, and biographers.

Etched by the pain of songs sung to a former self, a future being always becoming but never realized.

Her song—the French *chanson*, the torch song—is unable to contain her passion, her pain, her rage. Hers is resistance felt in thunderous applause, headlines, jail cells, rehab beds, facedown in her own vomit. Hers is an aching body taking up thought where words should be, without finding words.

Two women, worlds apart, words apart, are branded out of control, crazy, unaware of their own talents or shortcomings. A lucky shot in the dark (Green, 1996, p. 945). Undone by their choices on and off stage. Victims of their own stories.

Two women. Two dreams. Two texts of twisted words. Two torches.

2. something considered a source of illumination, enlightenment, guidance, etc.: the torch of learning. (definition of *torch* in Flexner & Hauck, 1987, p. 1998)

[Billie Holiday's] musical meditations on women's seemingly interminable love pains illuminated the ideological constructions of gender and the ways they insinuate themselves into women's emotional lives. (Davis, 1998, p. 163)

Some days I wonder if, after all the hours I've spent in seminar rooms and alone in front of my computer writing, I have been reduced to making lists of words, to scripting fragments. Unable to express in finely wrought sentences the injustice of oppression or the beauty of a solution, I make lists that signify worlds. Words that set off explosions of thought and feeling. Today I make this list:

shared experience of oppression
the abyss of representation
demanding voice and redress
a red dress
a smoky voice
billie holiday

This list makes me think of you. Why you? Why now? I think of the homemade tapes you made for me. Tapes that now reside, sticky with age, in a blue shoebox. A blue shoebox buried deep in an ocean of report cards. Prom photos. Pages filled with the rush and slope of your words. I add

homemade tapes

to the list, and then something clicks and tilts and I'm in Ames, Iowa, in our steamy, windowless downtown apartment. I see your guitar-calloused fingertips pressing the eject button, offering me Laurie Anderson and The Specials and this or that Beatle and R.E.M., *Murmur*. Your recorded undergraduate music education course packed in tight against my own cassette rebellion—Neil and Sting and Billie. Torchers every one.

You hate her most of all. You detest the tinny piano and her pleading voice. Your guitar-calloused fingertips press the eject button.

You use those fingertips to educate me in the finer points of a scornful, noisy, jealous love. Accompaniment for our mutual destruction.

I hear this music in and around your smile and biting remarks. In and around the fury of your anger. And over what? That I wanted to go to graduate school. That I wanted more for myself than you.

Years after it was over, I remember talking to you on the phone. You said you were sorry it happened the way it did. Said you treated me like an animal.

An animal.

And I said yes, but only because you couldn't coax and tame me into your wild, note-filled consciousness without a fight.

You said you were sorry. Don't be. I still have them. I still hear their voices. Laurie and Sting and *Murmur* and Billie. Every one.

The cursor blinks, waiting for an explanation. I delete *homemade tapes* from the list. I add

feminism

because that is what remains. You gave me music, but I gave myself Billie Holiday.

3. carry a torch for, slang. to be in love with, esp. to suffer from unrequited love. (definition of *torch* in Flexner & Hauck, 1987, p. 1998)

I'm uneasy about using your story, or the story of the places you were between, as a pretext for speaking about methodology and other matters, about needing or seeming to need a dead woman to enliven matters, to make them have some material force. (adapted from Gordon, 1997, p. 59)

She is singing—torch singer, tragedy in a red silk dress—to a nameless, faceless audience. Her voice spins and sways, dips and turns, and then she closes her eyes, shutting out the applause.

She is gone.

She is gone but for her persistent reappearance in poetry and song, fiction and memoir. Gone but for ghostly imprints of her voice in wax and celluloid. She is a recurring apparition, a haunting reminder for women writers in particular.[1] The attraction? Her independence and the devastating costs—both real and psychological—that she paid for it. The attraction for me? Her feminism and the devastating costs—both real and psychological—that she paid for it. It is an underground sort of feminism—a searing protest slipped into the pages of autobiography and woven through the performance of good-woman-got-down songs. Tragedy with a sharp edge. Critique coming in just behind the beat. Her voice haunts me because her words, her texts-in-performance, make the agony of her oppression as a woman—sometimes poor, sometimes privileged; sometimes White, sometimes Black, sometimes both—palpably present. Her voice forges a relationship between text and reader, singer and audience so that the "nexus of force, desire, belief, and practice" that made her imprisonment possible can be laid bare and abolished (Gordon, 1997, p. 143). And in her autobiographic and musical words of longing, I hear a feminism singing of women's oppression and liberation. I hear a feminism that works idealism against structure, that retains a critical judgment, that constructs a place from which to speak for women's voice and redress.

Is this feminism an "ontological complicity," with a theoretical framework that divides women against themselves in their struggle with an "amorphous and ill-defined category known as 'power,' " as Carole Stabile (1997, pp. 395-396) asks? Does such a theory sacrifice a structural explanation of oppression (of women, yes, but also men) based on forces outside of discourse? And does my talk of these women's ghostly presence— within text, song, and performance— eschew a tangible voice of critique and, more important, *action* to eliminate oppression? In other words, does my poststructural project of writing the feminist voice of the torch singer undermine the greater project of feminism by rendering it idealist, relativist, and, thus, robbing it of agency? I would like to say no, but I'm not sure. What I am sure of is this: The torch singer's experiences of oppression are real, and her chosen weapons for fighting that oppression are textual, musical, performative. Does she see her work as a threat to the status quo, a lesson to be learned? Perhaps her music and her words perform a feminist critique that resists totalization and binary antagonisms without rejecting material needs—hunger, confinement, and labor—that can never be contained in discourse. Perhaps such a reading is nothing more than my unrealistic hope for a pluralist feminism. Still, I hear the pleading in her voice and I cannot turn a deaf ear.

4. to burn or flare up like a torch. (definition of *torch* in Flexner & Hauck, 1987, p. 1998)

The music seemed to cut into her flesh, leaving a sort of scar of longing never satisfied, almost a wound of feeling. . . . At times she would think of giving it up altogether, so difficult was it to define, even for herself. (adapted from Hardwick, 1979, p. 31)

She is peering through the window of the tour bus as it lurches over the Kentucky hillside. She is touring the South with Artie Shaw, the Negro singer fronting an all-White band. For weeks, she has been refused food, a place to sleep, and the use of restroom facilities. She has been denied the right to be on stage before or after her numbers. She has been called blackie, bitch, and nigger. She is Billie Holiday, and her life has been threatened countless times. Theory watches her watch the slow-moving landscape, then asks her, "What kind of world do you see?"

She laughs. "I suppose you want me to choose."

"Yes."

"Let me guess. Is it a world of my making, or someone else's?"

"Not quite. I'm asking whether you think we live in a realist's world—one with a reality outside of you and me that can be explained and transformed. Or do we live in a constructivist's world—a culturally crafted universe of realities that we continually create and contest?" (Guba, 1990, pp. 25-27).

"So a world of my making or some*thing* or some*one* else's."

"Pretty much. So, what kind of world do you see?"

She turns away from the window. "What difference does it make?"

"It affects how we explain the relationship of 'cultural practices to the real existing world—whose objectivity is the fact of the working day—in order to transform it' " (Ebert, 1996, p. 42).

"So it's ideas versus structures."

"Yes," Theory says. "Texts versus economics."

"Let me tell you a story.[2] It was 1932. The depression was on. At least, so we heard tell. A depression was nothing new to us; we'd always had it."

"One day when the rent was overdue, Mom got a notice that the law was going to put us out on the street. It was in the dead cold of winter and she couldn't even walk. . . . I told Mom I would steal or murder or do anything before I'd let them pull that. It was cold as hell that night, and I walked out without any kind of coat."

"A world of someone else's making."

"I'm not finished. So I walked down Seventh Avenue from 139th Street to 133rd Street, busting in every joint trying to find a job. . . . Finally, when I got to Pod's and Jerry's, I went in and asked for the boss. . . . I told him I was a dancer and I wanted to try out. I knew exactly two steps, the time step and the crossover. I didn't even know the word 'audition' existed, but that was what I wanted. So Jerry sent me over to the piano player and told me to dance. I started, and it was pitiful. I did my two steps over and over until he barked at me and told me to quit wasting his time."

"What did you do?"

"I kept begging for the job. Finally the piano player took pity on me. He squashed out his cigarette, looked up at me and said, 'Girl, can you sing?' "

"I said, 'Sure, I can sing, what good is that?' I had been singing all my life, but I enjoyed it too much to think I could make any real money at it. . . . But I needed forty-five bucks by morning to keep Mom from getting set out in the street. . . . So I asked him to play 'Trav'lin' All Alone.' That came closer than anything to the way I felt. And some part of it must have come across. The whole joint quieted down. If someone had dropped a pin, it would have sounded like a bomb. When I finished, everybody in the joint was crying in their beer, and I picked thirty-eight bucks up off the floor. When I left the joint that night I split with the piano player and still took home fifty-seven dollars."

Theory smiles. "That's a great story."

"Thanks."

"Although your biographers say it isn't quite true. They say you've got the facts confused."

"Oh really."

"Yes, let's see." Theory thumbs through a dense sheaf of newspaper clippings and magazine articles. "Here it is. Leslie Gourse [1997a, p. xiv] writes that many musicians, biographers, and critics recall seeing you sing in other clubs throughout Harlem, Brooklyn, and Queens prior to your booking at Pod's and Jerry's and adds that 'some entertainers also have a strong memory of you as a prostitute first and singer second.' "

She turns back to the window. "Prostitute first, singer second. Structures first, ideas second. Economics first, texts second. What difference does it make?"

"It makes all the difference in the world," Theory says.

"I had to eat, so I started to sing. The song saved me. I supported myself and Mama with the money I made from singing. And after years of working nightclubs and endless touring, when I asked for some of that money from Mama—when I needed it—she flatly refused me. So I said, 'That's all right. God bless the child that's got his own.' And I wrote a song about it."

She begins to sing. " 'Rich relations give/crust of bread and such/You can help yourself/But don't take too much/Mama may have/Papa may have/But God bless the child that's got his own' [Holiday, 1997, Track 13]. The song saved me then too."

"So perhaps you're a constructivist," Theory offers.

"Look, I know there's an outside to the song—it's an outside of bitter-cold wind and empty stomachs. But what I'm telling you is that singing turned out to be my only way to get off the street and back inside where it's warm. So you can keep your categories and I'll keep right on singing."

song sparrow (sông sparÇ), n. a small emberizine songbird. (definition of *song sparrow* in Flexner & Hauck, 1987, p. 1819)

She is a pop heroine on a par with Joan of Arc.... Addicted to countless pills and the constant pain of men who tried to dominate her, [she] was often viewed as the unfortunate victim who had little control of her own destiny. (O'Brien, 1995, pp. 52-53)

Welcome to the Joan of Arc Museum! Established in 15th-century France, the museum is dedicated to the countless women throughout history who just couldn't leave well enough alone! To your left, we have the Women of Misery in Song exhibit, featuring victim par excellence, Edith Piaf. Heiress to the throne of Joan of Arc, Piaf is the first in a long line of composite portraits in sorrow.[3] Enjoy!

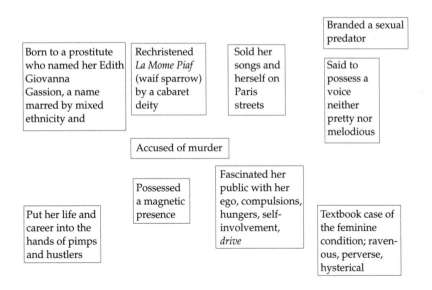

As you move into the Gallery of the Insatiable and Tragic, notice the portraits of Piaf's sisters in song.[4] Here, try the earphones. Go ahead, it's okay! Press PLAY and let these portraits provide the backdrop for yet another song. Another performance. Another pose.

Her body sings the heart
Tremors in the flesh
Ignite sparks of rage
Hidden in an elongated note
Or the catch of the throat

Libby Holman

Helen Morgan

Tears of pain dissolve into
The thrill of release
The thrill of pleasure in
The public scream of protest
disguised
inside the sweet and sleepy melody

Anita O'Day

I've always wanted to sing
on a smoky stage
To have my voice plumb
the geographies of our most
submerged desires and rages

Billie Holiday

To stand stark still
Perspiring in the spotlight
Entrancing the audience
with the arch of an eyebrow
or the shift of the hips
or the wail of the song

Peggy Lee

To be seen
And heard
In public
As a woman
A flaming torch
Whose heat can ravage
Whose light can blind[5]

Countless others whose bodies were burned at the stake, whose voices are canonized by the machine of commerce, whose lives are rewritten by the museum of culture

That concludes our tour of the Women of Misery in Song exhibit. We hope you enjoyed your visit to the Joan of Arc Museum today! Please place your earphones and cassette players on the table to your right. Press the STOP button.

torch' sing'er, a singer, especially a woman, who specializes in singing torch songs [1930-35]. (Flexner & Hauck, 1987, p. 1998)

They croon, these torch singers, about the evening joy and midnight sorrow that slow dance in their hearts. Rarely do their themes change: whiskey-laced stories of do-wrong men, shady dudes who professed love then shattered the crystal cage that held their fragile emotions, or smoky tales of unrequited dream lovers whose fantasy images caused their bodies to shiver, sweat, and slowly melt. (Gonzales, 1998, p. 52)

I decide to put on some music. I select *Billie Holiday—The Legacy* (Holiday, 1991). Seems appropriate. Then I move into the kitchen. I stop and stare at the refrigerator, at the words scattered everywhere. Words for building magnetic poetry. Words that belong to the "woman's" magnetic poetry kit.

I read a poem composed by my sister on her recent visit:

sister	mother	*woman*
always	immense	
always	essential	

I read this poem and I see my sister holding her baby daughter on her lap. I wonder if she considers herself a feminist. I wonder whether she would tell her daughter so. I hear Billie sing, "I'm so weary and all alone/feet are tired like heavy stone/trav'lin trav'lin all alone. Who will see and who will care/'bout this load that I must bear/trav'lin trav'lin all alone" (Holiday, 1991, Track 23). I wonder why my women's magnetic poetry kit doesn't have words like

Maybe these words are included in the poststructural feminist magnetic poetry kit. And then I hear Dana's voice, and I imagine her

asking, "What are the advantages and/or disadvantages of a post-structuralist perspective on oppression and liberation?"

"Well," I begin, "I think one of the most striking advantages of poststructural and postmodern perspectives is the way in which subjectivity is complicated."

"How so?"

"Well, as Linda Alcoff (1988) points out, theorists from Derrida to Foucault question the humanist assumption of a "self-contained, authentic subject . . . discernable below of veneer of cultural and ideological overlay" (p. 415). Instead, subjectivity is the product of multiple social, cultural, and political forces. Women's identities are not essential or given, but rather, constructed. As Simone deBeauvoir (1952/1989) writes, "one is not born, but rather becomes a woman" (p. vii).

"So subjectivity and identity are constructed," Dana says. "Of course, materialists think so too, but in a different way. Subjectivity and identity are rooted in ideology critique."

"Yes. That makes sense to me. And the constructedness of identities points up the power of discourses in shaping—but not determining—experience. Judith Butler (1990) says that, 'If sexuality is culturally constructed within existing power relations, then the postulation of a normative sexuality that is "before," "outside," or "beyond" power is a cultural impossibility and a politically impracticable dream' " (p. 30).

"Butler highlights the performativity of gender and sexuality," she says, "but she resists a systemic critique of gender oppression."

"Well," I begin, "rather than a search for origins, she posits gender and sexuality as constructed, and thus leaving open the possibility of multiple and shifting subjectivities. She writes of how women and men may be able to perform their genders differently. She says 'gender is always a doing, though not a doing by a subject who might be said to preexist the deed' (Butler, 1990, p. 25). And through a resistive and revisionary performance of gender, women might indeed become able to transform relationships of 'cultural practices to the real existing world' " (Ebert, 1996, p. 42).

"But," Dana says, "Teresa Ebert critiques Butler's reliance on the ludic—on a performative notion of play—as a means of transforming social structures. My question about how we go about explaining the origins of oppression is left unanswered. Does it originate within discourse or within the system of production?"

"And we must also ask where resistive/revisionary performance takes place—solely within the realm of discourse or within material systemic forms of struggle. Or both."

"Okay. So where does that leave you?" Dana asks.

"Struggling to make connections."

"Connections among what?"

"Connections among the global and the local. Among bodies and minds. Among subjectivity and experience. Among structure and discourse. Among political praxis and performance. Among feminism and the torch singer."

"I'm not opposed to connections," Dana says. "But I'm not sure that you can reconcile the differences among the ideas you want to join. It's a matter of definition—about the origins of oppression and what to do about it. It's also a matter of critical judgment. Can you embrace fragmentation and pluralism without shunning the very foundations of collective action and cohesion?"

"I think performance is important here. It's what provides a cohesion among women—feminists and torch singers alike."

"How so?"

"It embodies an intimate critique."

"You'll have to say more about that," Dana says.

I pause, unsure where to begin. Then I hear Billie singing, "Give me just another day/there's just one thing I want to say," and I want to try . . . (Holiday, 1991, Track 23).

chanson de toile (Fr.) (shäN soN da twäl), n. A northern French narrative poem in which the singer, a young woman, relates in simple style a tale of disappointed love, often with a tragic ending. . . . [T]he woman is frequently portrayed as sewing, weaving, or spinning, hence the name [13th century]. (definition of *chanson de toile* in Sadie, 1980, p. 150)

To other singers they were the excuse for standing up and simulating a few emotional platitudes. To audiences they bore no relationship to reality at all, being the incidental music of a dream world where unrequited love wept crocodile tears, all expressed in mediocre verse. To the

men who wrote the songs, they were factory products, designed to live
for a few moments and then be cast aside. (Green, 1996, p. 949)

So you want to write a torch song? Before you get started, you
should know a bit about what you're getting into. Just after World
War I, the French *chanson* "Mon Homme" was popularized by
Mistinguett, the "epitome of French glamour," at Casino de Paris
(Clements, 1998, p. AR1). The English version of "My Man," with lyrics by Channing Pollock, became an instant success in America when
performed by Fannie Brice on the Ziegfeld Follies stage (Moore, 1989,
p. 31). "My Man" also provided the recipe for the torch song,
mass-produced by Tin Pan Alley music publishing houses (named by
composer Monroe Rosenfeld for the "partly muffled pianos upon
which employees, under the constraint of continual production, composed songs") (Moore, 1989, p. 31). Never heard of Tin Pan Alley?
Well, during the late 19th and early 20th century, the creation and distribution of American popular song was transformed from a loosely
organized cluster of New York publishing houses to an assembly line
system on par with the industrialization of all manner of American
commerce (Moore, 1989, p. 31). Sheet music sales for a successful Tin
Pan Alley song could generate as much as $25,000 per week, with
sales upward of 5 million copies (Hamm, 1979, p. 285). In 1914, the
American Society of Composers, Authors, and Publishers (ASCAP)
was established in an attempt to generate royalties for composers, lyr-
icists, and publishers for live performances of their work. By the
mid-1930s, more than $10 million in licensing fees were paid annually
(Hamm, 1979, p. 339). All for a sentimental ditty about unrequited
love! The commodity formula for these hot-ticket songs persisted
through prohibition, the Great Depression, and World War II. And
although the Tin Pan Alley style diminished with the rise of rock and
roll, the torch song remains. Still want to write a torch song? Then, by
all means, use the Tin Pan Alley recipe:

Ingredients:

- One aspiring composer, preferably with classical training (Whites only)
- One underpaid lyricist (here too)
- One catchy chorus

- Two or three (no more than four!) dramatic verses telling a tragic tale
- A dash of heartbreak
- A pinch of sentimentality
- A liberal sprinkling of the syncopated rhythms of ragtime and jazz[6]

Yield: 3 minutes of popular song.

Instructions: In assembly line fashion, add ingredients one at a time, never varying amounts or sequence. Stir until virtually impenetrable by talent or musicianship, then pour into verse-chorus forms and bake. Display finished song in public to boost sheet music sales. Singing is women's work (Friedwald, 1990, p. 69), so be sure to get a girl singer (a canary or thrush will do nicely if a sparrow is unavailable). If intended for recording, remember not to double this recipe: The finished product should not exceed 3 minutes in length. Remember, too, that the torch song is best served as entertainment, not to remind guests of their problems (Hamm, 1979, p. 377). For highly developed chefs, these songs work well on the Broadway stage, radio programs, and in Hollywood films. May be enjoyed by White, urban, literate, middle- and upper-class Americans, although this recipe does hold an appeal for aspiring middle-class and urban Blacks (Hamm, 1979, p. 370). Enjoy!

> **goddess** (god'is), n. 2. a woman of extraordinary beauty and charm 3. a greatly admired or adored woman. (definition of *goddess* in Flexner & Hauck, 1987, p. 818)

> White goddesses were as essential to the big-band era as brass, reed, and rhythm sections. They decorated the fronts of swing bands like the figureheads on a ship, and no bandleader who wanted to fill dance halls or sell records dared go on the road without one. (Friedwald, 1990, p. 68)

What is a torch singer? I ask myself this question, and I ask others—friends, colleagues, critics, and scholars. I am told that the torch singer is the following:

A siren
A woman-done-wrong

Attractive because of her beauty, loneliness, inaccessibility
A White woman singing about a broken heart
A Black woman singing the blues
Sultry, sexy, stoned
A woman in boas and boots
The center of an African tribal ritual
Performer of eclipsed experience
A voice of subtle protest
A person behind a façade[7]
A White goddess (Friedwald, 1990, p. 68)
A nigger singer (Holiday, 1992, p. 73)

Wait a minute. A White woman singing about a broken heart and a Black woman singing the blues? A woman in boas and boots and the center of an African tribal ritual? A White goddess? A nigger singer? What does gender, class, and race have to do with it?

The gendered, classed, and raced genealogy of torch singing goes something like this: Mistinguett sings "My Man" in the Casino de Paris (Clements, 1998, p. 32), while Piaf sings "Un Monsieur Me Suit Dans la Rue," a song of prostitution and death, in the streets (Lees, 1987, p. 24). Fanny Brice performs an imported "My Man," while Helen Morgan is mistaken for mulatto and cast as Julie in Showboat (Moore, 1989, pp. 31, 34). Bessie Smith sings blues with trumpet and piano, while Libby Holman listens (Moore, 1989, p. 31). Libby Holman sings "Coon" songs on stage at the Apollo Theater in Harlem, the same stage on which Sarah Vaughn would sing 20 years later (Moore, 1989, p. 36). Holman is also cast in an all-Black musical because she can pass for Black (Moore, 1989, p. 36), and two decades later, Lena Horne, labeled by Hollywood executives as the "too White" Black woman (Campbell Edwards, 1997, p. 5). Mildred Bailey begins experimenting with Bessie Smith's a capella phrasing, while Lee Wiley skips school and listens to off-limits "race records" by Clara Smith and Ethyl Waters (Friedwald, 1990, pp. 76, 86). Connee Boswell's voice sings her love of Louis Armstrong and the New Orleans sound, while Ella Fitzgerald learns (Friedwald, 1990, pp. 78, 82). Billie Holiday sings the tales of White, middle-class heartbreak to an aspiring Black bourgeoisie (Davis, 1998, p. 172). Her voice is the lynchpin that evidences the influence of Bessie and Louis (Holiday,

1992, p. 39) but also the three White goddesses—Bailey, Boswell, and Wiley (Friedwald, 1990, p. 89). She passes these influences down to her White successors—Peggy Lee, Kay Starr, and Anita O'Day (Friedwald, 1990, p. 89).

Strictly a case of mutual admiration and influence? Maybe. But I can't get Billie Holiday's (1992) words out of my mind:

> You can be up to your boobies in white satin, with gardenias in your hair and no sugar cane for miles, but you can still be working on a plantation. . . . There was no cotton to be picked between Leon and Eddie's and the East River, but man, it was a plantation any way you looked at it. And we had to not only look at it, we lived in it. (p. 97)

Anita O'Day (1996) also speaks of the injustices of record production and club management:

> Black entertainers could work white clubs, but their black brothers couldn't get in to see them. Coming from the world of jazz where talent had always been the great equalizer, I became even angrier and I was pretty angry to begin with. (p. 199)

Nonetheless, as the White goddess ascends the stairs and takes the stage, as she opens her mouth and sings her influences, the Black jazz singer takes her seat on the back of the tour bus.

> **torch song** (tôrch sông), n. a sentimental song of unrequited love (the name comes from the phrase to "carry a torch" for someone), a popular feature of jazz singers and in night club acts (definition of *torch song* in Morehead & MacNeil, 1991, p. 549)

> [Anita O'Day] got a little mileage out of the notoriety she achieved after admitting a few unsavory habits, just as Billie Holiday did. Musical talent has nothing to do with being asked to write an autobiography or getting on *60 Minutes*. (Friedwald, 1990, p. 291)

The conference attendees look the panelists and each other up and down. "What time is it?" someone asks just as the door creaks, then jerks open. Lady Day enters. She refuses a seat behind the white-skirted conference table and takes her place in front of the microphone. She lights a cigarette and waits. No one says a word.

"Let's get this thing started," she says. Nervous applause ripples through the audience.

A small woman seated behind the skirted table stands. "Welcome to this panel on The Torch Singer and Auto/Biography: Truth or Fiction? We will be looking at Simone Berteaut's book about her half-sister, Edith Piaf, titled simply *Piaf*, Anita O'Day's (1989) *High Times Hard Times*, and, of course, Billie Holiday's *Lady Sings the Blues*. My name is Leigh Gilmore and I'll be your moderator. We'll begin with jazz critic Orrin Keepnews. Orrin?"

"Thank you. Let me begin by saying that for 'readers who consider the person whose life story is involved to be an *artist* rather than a *celebrity* (and the difference is a vast one),' these types of biographies and autobiographies can be downright annoying" (Keepnews, 1997, p. 111).

Anita and Billie both turn and stare at him, but he continues, undaunted.

"If the celebrity involved is outside of my field of special interest, I don't care very much. But when it is a jazz personality, I can't keep from feeling . . . well, embarrassed is probably the best word to describe it. For in almost every case, and no matter what the writer's motives were, it strikes me as one more case of the exploitation of the jazz artist" (Keepnews, 1997, pp. 111-112).

"Excuse me," Billie interrupts. "Just what do you think my motives were?"

"I'm not sure I know," he says. "Fame? Public relations? Money?"

"I wrote that book so maybe somebody out there might learn from my experience. My mistakes."

"Perhaps you're uncomfortable with the idea that she uses 'the condition of [her] own life to deconstruct the system she finds oppressive,' " Jeanie Forte offers (1990, p. 253).

"But much of what she says in the text isn't *true*," Keepnews protests. "She confuses the chronology, glosses over her addictions to men and drugs, even fabricates the story of how she got started singing in the first place. Either she's being exploited or she takes her readers for fools."

"Wait a minute, mister," Billie says. "I've 'fought my whole life to sing what I wanted the way I wanted to sing' (Holiday, 1992, p. 170). Now you're telling me I got to have *your* permission to write my life the way I want to write it?"

Undaunted, he turns to face Anita. "And you. You seem more interested in telling the story of the great jazz drug abusers, rather than the story of the jazz singer" (Gottlieb, 1996, p. 185).

"Mr. Keepnews," Anita begins, "I simply said what I wanted to say."[8]

"Maybe I can help here," Gilmore says. "Orrin, your discomfort seems to center on your notion of 'what the truth is, who may tell it, and who is authorized to judge it.' Your critique supports your agenda for how to 'value not only the autobiography, but the writer' as well" (1994, pp. 55, 73).

"It is in the textual articulation of her performative motives that Holiday most effectively deconstructs this system of authority," Anita Plath Helle adds. "These texts become a re-presentative political treatise—the textual, theoretical accompaniment to her performative practice. They are, in short, the 'stage[s] on which difference is broken down, analyzed, and reinterpreted' " (1989, p. 201).

"I agree," Barbara Christian adds. "And 'people of color have always theorized—but in forms quite different from the Western form of abstract logic. . . . Our theorizing . . . is often in narrative forms' " (Christian quoted in Ebert, 1996, p. 16).

"But Barbara," Teresa Ebert says, "Narration denies 'the possibility of a coherent explanation [for oppression] and . . . affirm[s] the play of difference, contingency, and undecidability' " (1996, p. 16).

"It's an intimate form of critique," Christian counters. "I believe that's what these texts, these women, including Simone's book about her sister, Edith, were after."

"What I was after," Simone says, "is a book about Edith's life—how *she* chose to live, not what the newspapers printed."

"But you give us a rather *naive* portrait," Keepnews interrupts. "You never question your devotion to your sister, nor her motives and actions. What kind of critique does that leave us with?"[9]

"When we oppose explanation and narration," Leigh Gilmore says, "we confuse the standards for judging this type of writing as social critique. An intimate critique such as *High Times Hard Times* or *Lady Sings the Blues* doesn't construct itself as a *confession*—Enlightenment, Judeo-Christian paradigm for telling the 'truth,' but rather as an *evocation*—a textual re-creation of lived experience [1994, pp. 57, 70]. These texts are not synonymous with, nor adverse to, explanation. They are, rather, firmly grounded in the material conditions of the author's life and situated within the broader historical context of 1920s Paris and depression-era and mid-40s New York. These texts narrate *and* explain."

"Look," Billie interrupts, "I don't know if my book is narration or explanation or something else. What I do know is that I was 'one of the highest-paid slaves around. I was making a thousand a week—but I had about as much freedom as a field hand in Virginia a hundred years before.' I didn't need anyone to explain that to me. *Lady Sings the Blues* says what I already knew about my life and the kind of world that I was living in. Period" (Holiday, 1992, p. 106).

Donald Morton clears his throat. "The problem I have with this sort of critique is that it 'obliterate[s] the distinction between inside and outside as the difference between private and the public. [T]he very ideological function of this impressionistic criticism is to evade argument' " (1996, pp. 23, 25).

"We're not evading anything," Anita interrupts. "We're not trying to fool anyone" (O'Day, 1996, p. 199).

"The way I look at it is simple," Billie says. "All the hassles I had in New York clubs and hotels, and on Hollywood movie sets for that matter, just trying to sing they way I felt are worth it 'if just one person can look at the end result and dig what [I tried] to do' " (Holiday, 1992, p. 122).

"But is it politics?" Ebert asks. "Is it *feminism*?"

Billie smiles. " 'Somebody once said we never know what is enough until we know what's more than enough' (Holiday, 1992, p. 155). Maybe the story of my life will help people understand what's more than enough for one person. For anyone. Maybe *then* people will want to change things."

torch•y (tôr'che), adj., torch•i•er, torch•i•est. of, pertaining to, or characteristic of a torch song or a torch singer; in sense, "full of torches" [1940-1945 for this sense]. (Flexner & Hauck, 1987, p. 1998) the torch singers, rather than merely promulgating these [formulaic torch songs], converted them into areas of contestation, and used the lyrics as instruments with which to probe power relations.(Moore, 1989, p. 32)

i hold this, you, wrought in line and note
i read you left to right, eyes straining to see
small print
wanting where tone and flesh, stretched to breaking—
too little
too late.
                I put my hand over yours and I breathe in black and
                                        white
                hear you come in just underneath below behind the
                                          beat
        desire my own warm-hued gesture of word, mixed media in
                                        text
                take up this pallate to brush faint outlines, inspired
                rush. heat. pulse. rhythm in 3s and 7s beats to infinity
no
you are purple deep inside places hidden from words.
too little.
too late.

She is a torch singer, not an academic, not a feminist. Rather than critiques or manifestos, she provides us with "hauntingly other-worldly soundtracks that explore our broken hearts of darkness" (Gonzales, 1998, p. 52). An unlikely cultural critic, to be sure. And yet might the torch singer, rather than "merely promulgating [the mass-produced songs of unrequited love], convert them into areas of contestation, and use the lyrics as instruments with which to probe power relations"? (Moore, 1989, p. 32). Might her performances invoke a structural critique that comes in just behind the beat? John Moore (1989) asks the torch singer whether she is "a conservative, an enlightener, and a whore. . . . Or a revolutionary, an incendiary, and a feminist. . . . If she is a revolutionary, upon whose behalf does she revolt?" (p. 44).

She answers that she is a singer, not a theorist. The conditions of her recording and performing career do not allow for an outright protest of the sexism, racism, and classism she encounters daily (Moore, 1989, pp. 40-42). A singer of love songs, she does not enjoy the blatant sexuality or sassy protest of the blues singer (Davis, 1998, p. 11; Moore, 1989, p. 42) Instead, she must turn inward—to her performance style—as a means of critiquing and subverting the material that she is all but forced to perform. She draws on her particular and distinctive social and musical history to create what Angela Davis (1998, drawing on Herbert Marcuse) terms "aesthetic agency" (p. 164). Aesthetic agency allowed Billie Holiday to use jazz-inspired musical innovation to challenge the often banal and clearly White middle-class lyrics of Tin Pan Alley songs and, in turn, to communicate "critical social meanings" to women of both worlds—both White and Black (Davis, 1998, pp. 166-172). How did Billie manage to "insinuate [the] battle into every musical phrase and making that battle the lyrical and dramatic core of her performances" (Davis, 1998, p. 166)? She used her *voice*, her "off center way of attacking the beat," her "alternately languorous legato and ferociously up-tempo use of time" (Friedwald, 1990, p. 131) to underscore her simultaneous amusement, ambivalence, and rage about the men who "treat her oh so mean." She literally wrapped her voice around the texts of her performances, enveloping the words with her own interpretation of the meaning and import of the lyric (Pleasants, 1997, p. 137). Her voice became the musical form—the aesthetic dimension—through which Billie pushed the ideological content (and her critique of that content) to the "surface" of the performance (Davis, 1998, p. 170). Every word, every syllable is soaked through with her social and musical history as an African American and as a woman.

However, although Davis (1998) eloquently shows how Billie's voice soared beyond and against banal love songs, it would be a mistake to locate the politics of Billie's performance within her voice—within her body— alone. For although her performance, in the very body-fact of taking the stage, constitutes a political statement (Forte, 1990, p. 251), it also exceeds the push of lyric and the pull of a historically situated aesthetic—the tension of form against content. Rather, her agency is a performative *force* enacted in the nexus of music and ideology, body and mind, singer and song. Like Edith Piaf and Libby Holman before her and Sarah Vaughn and Anita O'Day after her, Billie turns a formulaic lost love lament into a battleground by bringing both mind *and* body to bear upon lyrics *and* music. In performance, the singer and the song are visually, aurally, and ideologically resonant—they drown out everything else in range (Abbate, 1993, p. 254). In performance, the torch song becomes a force—an "instrument with which to probe power relations" (Moore, 1989, p. 32).

Perhaps the torch singer stages a critique of "getting through" and "making do" (Biesecker, 1992, p. 155). To be sure, it is a situated and specific critique located in a particular time and space (Hartsock, 1998, p. 244), a critique rooted in real material conditions structured gender, race, and social class (Hill Collins, 1989, p. 244). But it is also a critique that recognizes, rather than erases, differences among women. A torch performance allows singers *and* audiences to adopt multiple positions from which to critique women's experience—including the contradictions within that experience—and to construct unity out of a need for *survival* (Mohanty, n.d., pp. 38-39). Under the guise of reveling in the misery of misogynist and abusive heterosexual "love" (and within a primarily White, male-dominated performance context), the torch singer enacts a subtle critique of these power relationships (Moore, 1989, p. 40). The dramatic "undercover" work of the torch singer resonates with George Lipsitz's notion of strategic "anti-essentialism," in which performers use the "disguise" of an oppressed identity to "highlight, underscore, and augment an aspect of one's identity that one cannot express directly" (Lipsitz, 1998, p. 62). Often, "strategic anti-essentialism stems less from fear about expressing oneself directly than from the parts of one's own identity that come into relief more sharply through temporary role playing" (Lipsitz, 1998, p. 62; see also Moore, 1989, p. 52). It is such performances—in these moments of articulation when we are swept up in the way a note catches in the singer's throat, in the ways that mind meets body in song—that begin the feminist's journey to discover the political possibility of performance. It is this moment that began my own journey—with Billie Holiday and the others.

A textual, performative feminism helps me see these possibilities, to hear the torch singer's protest. Did this protest end her own oppression or that of her revolutionary compatriots? No. Performance didn't move people out of the nightclubs and into the streets. Performance didn't keep Billie fed or clothed or out of jail. But performance was the one thing—perhaps the only thing—she could do. Does telling this story, performing this intimate critique, change the situation of oppressed people today? Of course it doesn't. And I'm uneasy about using her story, "the story of the places she was between," as a pretext for speaking about feminist theory, poststructuralist and otherwise (Gordon, 1997, p. 59). I'm nervous about "needing or seeming to need a dead woman to enliven matters, to make them have some material force" (Gordon, 1997, p. 59). I know the dangers of idealism, relativism, and inactivity lurk here. But I also know what a text, like a piece of music, can never be. It can never be more than hunger or pain. It can never be more than the fight to end oppression. It can never be more than Billie Holiday. What this critique *can* do is trace some of the connections to be made among structure and ideas, explanation, and narrative. Nowhere is the possibility of an intimate critique more evident than in Billie Holiday's performance of "Strange Fruit." Here, on stage, Billie's voice carves out of silence a place from which to speak about her status as a torch singer. In this voice, she demands to be heard. She demands the last word.

> **torchbearer** (tôrch'bâr'ar), n. 1. A person who carries a torch 2. A leader in a movement, campaign. (definition of *torchbearer* in Flexner & Hauck, 1987, p. 1998)

> She so illuminated human situations as to give the listener a rare, if frightening, glimpse into the realities of experience. Where others feared to tread, she reached out and touched, where others masked their eyes, she defiantly kept hers open. (music critic Burt Korall quoted in Davis, 1998, p. 194)

Narrator (standing downstage and to the right): In her performance of "Strange Fruit," Billie Holiday "translated an antiracist literary text into a dynamic musical work whose enduring meaning stemmed from the way she chose to render it as song" (Davis, 1998, p. 185). Yet, critics pronounce . . .

Critic (sits center stage with his back to the audience): "['Strange Fruit'] destroyed the joy and spontaneity that were an integral part of her artistry. The raw talent was shaped into something that was precious and unique, yet strangely lifeless. . . . [The song] gave her a ready-made role and it was a beauty. She was a born actress and as she performed it, night after night, before an enthralled audience of young white intellectuals, so she began to live the part and see herself as the living symbol of injustice and oppression. . . . Her mistake was that she didn't let her natural instincts take charge and just sing. . . . Instead, she began to interpret. John Hammond once stated that 'Strange Fruit' was, from an artistic point of view, the worst thing that ever happened to Billie Holiday. I have to agree with him" (Brooks, 1991, pp. 28-31).

Narrator: She is not a man . . .

You (yes, you, reader, audience member—say this aloud please): "She is not a man coming center stage. She does not enter from the wings so much as she enters from the space beyond the wings of the patriarchal order and its textualizations" (Smith, 1987, p. 42).

Narrator: Billie enters.

Billie (standing downstage and to the left): "Over the years I've had a lot of weird experiences as a result of singing that song. It has a way of separating the straight people from the squares and cripples. One night in Los Angeles a bitch stood right up in the club where I was singing and said, 'Billie, why don't you sing that sexy song you're so famous for? You know, the one about the naked bodies swinging in the trees?' Needless to say, I didn't. . . . When I sing it, it affects me so much I get sick. It takes all the strength out of me" (Holiday, 1992, p. 84).

Narrator: "Her stature as an artist and her ability to comprehend social issues were both disparaged and defined as results of plans conceived by savvy white men" (Davis, 1998, p. 187). As her biographers explain,

Critic: [Lewis] Allan, the poet who wrote "Strange Fruit," played it for her, and later wrote that she didn't know what the word "pastoral" meant. . . . Lady was non-political; when she first looked at "Strange Fruit" she didn't know what to make of it. She never read anything but comic books . . . and she was used to learning songs, not reading poetry. . . . she later said that at first, "I was afraid that people would hate it." She was an entertainer first of all and shared with her beloved Louis Armstrong the desire to please her audience, albeit in her own way (Clarke, 1994, p. 165).

Narrator: Hers is an extremely . . .

You (again, please): "Hers is an extremely precarious entrance, then; hers, a potentially precarious performance before an audience whom she expects to read her as woman" (Smith, 1987, p. 42).

Narrator: Billie performs. . . .

Billie: I was scared people would hate it. The first time I sang it I thought it was a mistake and I had been right being scared. There wasn't even a patter of applause when I finished. Then a lone person began to clap nervously. Then suddenly everyone was clapping.

It caught on after a while and people began asking for it. The version I recorded for Commodore became my biggest-selling record. It still depresses me every time I sing it, though. It reminds me of how Pop died. But I have to keep singing it, not only because people ask for it but because 20 years after Pop died the things that killed him are still happening in the South.

Just a few months ago in a club in Miami, I had run through an entire 2-week date without ever doing "Strange Fruit." I was in no mood to be bothered with the scenes that always come on when I do that number in the South. . . . But one night after everybody had asked me 20 times to do it, I finally gave in. . . .

When I came to the final phrase of the lyrics I was in the angriest and strongest voice I had been in for months. . . . When I said, " . . . for the sun to rot," and then a piano punctuation, " . . . for the wind to suck," I pounced on those words like they had never been hit before.

I was flailing the audience, but the applause was like nothing I'd ever heard. I came off, went upstairs, changed into street clothes, and when I came down they were still applauding (Holiday, 1992, pp. 84-85).

Narrator: Billie "experienced more than her share of racism. While she did not tend to engage in political analyses, she never attempted to conceal her loyalties" (Davis, 1998, p. 193). Yet, jazz scholars improvise . . .

Critic: In 1938, Billie went to work for Barney Josephson at Caf, Society, and her boss gave her a new song to sing. He played Allen's "Strange Fruit" for her.

Billie said, "What do you want to do with this?"

He said, "It would be wonderful if you'd sing it—if you care to. You don't have to."

She said, "You wants me to sing it. I sings it" (quoted in Davis, 1998, p. 185).

"She did—and became internationally famous for that song. It gave her status as a black singer with a brain, a mind, an awareness, something to say. Though Billie was apolitical. Not a fighter" (Gourse, 1997b, p. 146).

Narrator: Her very choice . . .

You (thanks so much): "Her very choice to interpret her life and to reveal her experience in public signals her transgression of cultural expectations" (Smith, 1987, p. 42).

Narrator: " 'I'm a race woman,' she proclaimed on numerous occasions" (Davis, 1998, p. 193), whereas composers arranged a different discourse.

Critic: Interesting, isn't it, how Billie Holiday, who is said to have spoken for her people more than any other black singer, spoke through white music? It lay in her tone of voice. . . . The tragedian Billie . . . had the cult mostly of the Caucasian intelligentisia, though she didn't know quite what to do with them (Rorem, 1997, p. 176).

Billie (improvising): Am I *non-political*? *Apolitical*? Can't I feel this strange poem, this angry song, etched on my bones? Don't I see it rising from the rotted flesh of my ancestors? Don't I wretch with pain every time I sing it?

Narrator: Her very voice . . .

You (the last one): "Her very voice in its enunciations remains haunted and haunting; for the language she appropriates has been the instrument of her repression" (Smith, 1987, p. 42).

Narrator: Billie sings . . .

Billie performs "Strange Fruit." Each word she sings	*Southern trees bear a strange fruit*
Cuts to the bone. Wounds of feeling.	*Blood on the leaves and blood at the root*
She fills the room.	*Black bodies swaying in the Southern breeze,*
She quivers with teary-eyed rage.	*Strange fruit hanging from the poplar trees.*
Force.	*Pastoral scene of the gallant South,*
Memory.	*The bulging eyes and the twisted mouth,*
Heat.	*Scent of magnolia, sweet and fresh,*
Emptiness.	*Then the sudden smell of burning flesh.*
Artistry.	*Here is a fruit for the crows to pluck,*
A critique just behind the beat.	*For the rain to gather, for the wind to suck,*
She has the last word.	*For the sun to rot, for the trees to drop,*
For herself. For all of us.	*Here is a strange and bitter crop*[10]

NOTES

1. Gonzales (1998) writes, "The torch singer lurks in our minds, providing hauntingly otherworldly sound tracks that explore our broken hearts of darkness" (p. 55). Writing about Billie Holiday in particular, Davis (1997) observes, "She is a recurring apparition in novels, poems, plays, and literary memoirs . . . a creature of premonitory fascination for women writers in particular" (p. 169).

2. Holiday with Dufty (1992, pp. 33-34). This story is told in *Lady Sings the Blues.*

3. All observations about Piaf are included in Lees (1987, pp. 25-31), with the exception of the observation about the feminine condition as ravenous, perverse, and hysterical, which comes from Bordo (1993, pp. 143, 167).

4. Although Holman, Morgan, O'Day, Holiday, and Lee are all revered for their talent and performance style, their profiles in biographies and compilations remain eerily similar to Piaf's. Holman is described as at once a femme fatale, sexually ambivalent, and promiscuous. Like Piaf, she came from impoverished beginnings and reveled in her fame and fortune. She was also tried for the murder of her husband (see Bradshaw, 1985). Helen Morgan was an alcoholic who, although talented, quickly fell out of style (Kirkeby, 1997, p. 17). Anita O'Day's voice, although integral to her immense talent, has been described as "scratchy and small" (see Dahl, 1984, p. 143). O'Day was also seen as unpredictable, spontaneous, and brutally honest both in her personal life and in her public performances. She, too, came from humble beginnings and lived a life of drug addiction, overdoses, arrests, and incarcerations. Billie Holiday's story is a familiar tale, replete with poor origins, prostitution, addiction, incarceration, promiscuity, and immense personal drive. And like O'Day, Holiday's voice had its detractors (for a brief but inclusive summary, see Gourse, 1997a, pp. ix-xviii). Finally, Peggy Lee, said to have risen above her "poor white trash" beginnings to reinvent herself, is described by O'Brien (1995) as charming, yet stoic, glamorous, yet wacky (pp. 41-42). In addition, Will Friedwald (1990), although clearly impressed with her talent, points out that Lee was working with an extremely limited "vocal vocabulary" (p. 335).

5. Shoemaker (1998). Deanna wrote this piece for performance in a show I directed titled *Torch Song Possibility: Visions and Voices of the Torch Singer.* She notes that the poem was inspired by listening to hours of torch songs and theorizing torch as a public form of feminist protest. My sincere thanks to Deanna for her permission to include her moving portrait in this piece.

6. Hamm (1979, pp. 285-390). In chapters titled, " 'After the Ball'; or The Birth of Tin Pan Alley" and " 'It's Only a Paper Moon'; or The Golden Years of Tin Pan Alley," Hamm profiles the development and staying power of the Tin Pan Alley formula for popular (including torch) songs.

7. The preceding list is composed of comments I received in response to the statement "The torch singer is:" that I included on the comment cards for the performance I directed titled *Torch Song Possibility: Visions and Voices of the Torch Singer.*

8. Adapted from Friedwald (1990), in which he quotes a story printed in *The Hollywood Note* that states, "Anita is completely frank. She says what she thinks, wears what she pleases, behaves as she prefers to behave" (pp. 283-284).

9. Adapted from Lees (1987). Of Berteaut's book about her half-sister, Lees notes,

It is a remarkable book . . . for the insights into Piaf's character. It is one of the finest studies of a singer ever written. It examines the egotism, the compulsion, the hunger, the ingenuous self-involvement—and the drive. It is all the more compelling for being a naïve rather than clinical portrait. And Berteaut hardly even questions her own utter devotion to her half-sister. (p. 31)

10. Lyrics from "Strange Fruit" by Lewis Allan (copyright © 1939 [renewed] by Music Sales Corporation [ASCAP], international copyright secured, all rights reserved, reprinted by permission).

REFERENCES

Abbate, C. (1993). Opera; or the envoicing of women. In R. A. Solie (Ed.), *Musicology and difference: Gender and sexuality in music scholarship* (pp. 225-258). Berkeley: University of California Press.

Alcoff, L. (1988). Cultural feminism versus post-structuralism: The identity crisis in feminist theory. *Signs: Journal of Women in Culture and Society, 11*(4), 405-436.

Berland, J. (1996). Bodies of theory, bodies of pain: Some silences. In J. Berland, W. Straw, & D. Tomas (Eds.), *Theory rules: Art as theory/theory and art* (pp. 133-155). Toronto, Canada: University of Toronto Press.

Berteaut, S. (1969). *Piaf*. Paris: R. Laffont.

Biesecker, B. (1992). Coming to terms with recent attempts to write women into the history of rhetoric. *Philosophy and Rhetoric, 25*(2), 140-161.

Bordo, S. (1993). *Unbearable weight: Feminism, Western culture, and the body*. Berkeley: University of California Press.

Bradshaw, J. (1985). *Dreams that money can buy: The tragic life of Libby Holman*. New York: William Morrow.

Brooks, M. (1991). Liner notes for *Billie Holiday—The legacy, 1933-58* [CD]. New York: Columbia/Legacy Records.

Butler, J. (1990). *Gender trouble: Feminism and the subversion of identity*. New York: Routledge.

Campbell Edwards, N. (1997). Liner notes for *Sirens of song: Classic torch singers* [CD]. Los Angeles: Rhino.

Clarke, D. (1994). *Wishing on the moon: The life and times of Billie Holiday*. New York: Viking.

Clements, M. (1998, October 18). Sighing, a French sound endures. *New York Times*, pp. AR1, 33-35.

Dahl, L. (1984). *Stormy weather: The music and lives of a century of jazzwomen*. New York: Pantheon.

Davis, A. Y. (1998). *Blues legacies and Black feminism: Gertude "Ma" Rainey, Bessie Smith, and Billie Holiday*. New York: Pantheon.

Davis, F. (1997). The man who danced with Billie Holiday. In L. Gourse (Ed.), *The Billie Holiday companion: Seven decades of commentary* (pp. 168-173). New York: Simon & Schuster.

deBeauvoir, S. (1989). *The second sex* (H. M. Parshley, Trans. & Ed.). New York: Vintage. (Original work published 1952)

Ebert, T. (1996). *Ludic feminism: Postmodernism, desire, and labor in late capitalism*. Ann Arbor: University of Michigan Press.

Flexner, S. B., & Hauck, L. C. (Eds.). (1987). *Random House dictionary of the English language* (2nd ed.). New York: Random House.

Forte, J. (1990). Women's performance art: Feminism and postmodernism. In S.-E. Case (Ed.), *Performing feminisms: Feminist critical theory and theater* (pp. 251-269). New York: Johns Hopkins University Press.

Friedwald, W. (1990). *Jazz singing: America's great voices from Bessie Smith to bebop and beyond.* New York: Scribner.

Gilmore, L. (1994). Policing truth: Confession, gender, and autobiographical authority. In K. Ashley, L. Gilmore, & G. Peters (Eds.), *Autobiography and postmodernism* (pp. 54-78). Amherst: University of Massachusetts Press.

Gonzales, M. A. (1998, February). Torch song soliloquy: One man's poetic tribute to ladies who sing the blues. *Mode,* 52-55.

Gordon, A. F. (1997). *Ghostly matters: Haunting and the sociological imagination.* Minneapolis: University of Minnesota Press.

Gottlieb, R. (1996). *Reading jazz: A gathering of autobiography, reportage, and criticism from 1919 to now.* New York: Pantheon.

Gourse, L. (Ed.). (1997a). Preface. In *The Billie Holiday companion: Seven decades of commentary* (pp. ix-xvii). New York: Simon & Schuster.

Gourse, L. (Ed.). (1997b). There was no middle ground with Billie Holiday. In *The Billie Holiday companion: Seven decades of commentary* (pp. 139-150). New York: Simon & Schuster.

Green, B. (1996). Billie Holiday. In R. Gottlieb (Ed.), *Reading jazz: A gathering of autobiography, reportage, and criticism from 1919 to now* (pp. 933-959). New York: Pantheon.

Guba, E. C. (Ed.). (1990). The alternative paradigm dialogue. In E. C. Guba & Y. S. Lincoln (Eds.), *The paradigm dialogue* (pp. 17-27). Newbury Park, CA: Sage.

Hamm, C. (1979). *Yesterdays: Popular song in America.* New York: Norton.

Hardwick, E. (1979). *Sleepless nights.* New York: Random House.

Hartsock, N.C.M. (1998). *The feminist standpoint revisited and other essays.* Boulder, CO: Westview.

Hill Collins, P. (1989). The social construction of Black feminist thought. *Signs: Journal of Women in Culture and Society, 14*(1), 745-773.

Holiday, B. (1991). *Billie Holiday—The Legacy, 1933-1958* [CD]. New York: Columbia/Legacy Records.

Holiday, B. (with Dufty, W.). (1992). *Lady sings the blues.* New York: Penguin. (Original work published 1956)

Holiday, B. (1997). *Ultimate Billie Holiday* [CD]. New York: Verve and Polygram Records.

Keepnews, O. (1997). Lady sings the blues. In L. Gourse (Ed.), *The Billie Holiday companion: Seven decades of commentary* (pp. 110-114). New York: Simon & Schuster.

Kirkeby, M. (1997). Liner notes for *Sophisticated ladies* [CD]. New York: Columbia.

Lees, G. (1987). *Singers and the song.* New York: Oxford University Press.

Lipsitz, G. (1998). *Dangerous crossroads: Popular music, postmodernism, and the poetics of place.* London: Verso.

Mohanty, C. T. (n.d.). *Feminist encounters: Locating the politics of experience.* Unpublished manuscript.

Moore, J. (1989). "The hieroglyphics of love": The torch singers and interpretation. *Popular Music, 8*(1), 31-57.

Morehead, P. D., & MacNeil, A. (Eds.). (1991). *The new American dictionary of music.* New York: Dutton.

Morton, D. (Ed.). (1996). Changing the terms: (Virtual) desire and (actual) reality. In *The material queer: A LesBiGay cultural studies reader* (pp. 1-33). Boulder, CO: Westview.

O'Brien, L. (1995). *She bop: The definitive history of women in rock, pop, and soul.* New York: Penguin.

O'Day, A. (with Eells, G.). (1989). *High times hard times.* New York: Limelight Editions.

O'Day, A. (with Eells, G.). (1996). Anita O'Day. In R. Gottlieb (Ed.), *Reading jazz: A gathering of autobiography, reportage, and criticism from 1919 to now* (pp. 185-199). New York: Pantheon.

Plath Helle, A. (1989). Re-presenting women writers onstage: A retrospective to the present. In L. Hart (Ed.), *Making a spectacle: Feminist essays on contemporary women's theater* (pp. 195-208). Minneapolis: University of Minnesota Press.

Pleasants, H. (1997). The great American popular singers. In L. Gourse (Ed.), *The Billie Holiday companion: Seven decades of commentary* (pp. 131-139). New York: Simon & Schuster.

Rorem, E. (1997). Knowing when to stop. In L. Gourse (Ed.), *The Billie Holiday companion: Seven decades of commentary* (pp. 167-177). New York: Simon & Schuster.

Sadie, S. (Ed.). (1980). *The new grove dictionary of music and musicians* (6th ed., Vol. 4). London: Macmillan.

Shoemaker, D. (1998). *Snapshots in motion*. Unpublished manuscript.

Smith, S. (1987). *The poetics of women's autobiography: Marginality and the fictions of self-representation*. Bloomington: Indiana University Press.

Stabile, C. A. (1997). Feminism and the ends of postmodernism. In R. Hennessy & C. Ingraham (Eds.), *Materialist feminism: A reader in class, difference, and women's lives* (pp. 395-408). New York: Routledge.

— —

Stacy Holman Jones is a doctoral student in performance studies at the University of Texas at Austin.

CHAPTER 14

Always Dying:
Living Between *Da* and *Fort*

— —

Ronald J. Pelias
Southern Illinois University

This is a performative writing essay that reflects on Peggy Phelan's thesis from Mourning Sex *that theatre is a rehearsal for death. Using the Freudian frame of* da *(there) and* fort *(gone), the essay moves between presence and absence, between aesthetic performances and everyday performances, and between life and death.*

Da.

There. I will reach for the moment, trying to hold on. I will reach for the moment, working it with my fingers, turning it, squeezing it, feeling it. I will hold it as one might grasp a bird, sensing its racing heart beat and keeping it secure, firm between my hands. I will see that I cannot. I will be reaching forever, trying to hold on. I will hold my breath. I will know, with poet Tim Shea, that "to write/is to let death/in" (1997, p. 45). I will always write in grief for what is lost. Always. Already. Gone.

Fort.

Gone. Freud's grandson understood power when, by tugging on a piece of string, he pulled his wooden reel into visibility and when, by letting go, he let it slide into invisibility. But presence and absence aren't always matters of choice. Too often strings are cut, out of our control, or become entangled. He understood too the pleasure of repetition, pulling on the string again and again to relive the moment. But repeating isn't always a matter of doing again. Too often repetition is a representation of what cannot be accomplished twice. There.

Da.

There. The show had been running for months—a success. Each night the audience would come, filled with anticipation, energized, prepared by reports of the show's wonder and poised to listen. The actors too would come, each night a little less excited. Nothing you could mark from night to night but something that began to show over time. The show became ordinary, as familiar as a "How are you?" accompanying a hand shake. Lines were spoken without thinking. Movements were completed by habit. Exits were made either too quickly or too slowly. The show would start. They would do their parts. The show would end. Ready for it to be over, they stopped doing a second curtain call. The show closed a week later. Gone.

Fort.

Gone. I hadn't heard from my old college roommate in more than 30 years. Shortly after graduation, we lost contact. He married, joined the Navy and went to Japan and I married, took my chances with the draft and went to Vietnam. The war separated us as if we were naughty children and indeed, there were times when we were. So, when my second wife said she received an e-mail from an old friend of mine asking if she was related to me, I smiled thinking about those wonderful college days when we just didn't know any better. We exchanged e-mails for a few weeks, asking about old friends, new wives and children. I learned that he is a manager of several convenience stores in the Dallas/Fort Worth area. I told him that if he was ever coming my way to please stop by. He wrote the same. Neither of us have done so. There.

Da.

There. David Ignatow's poem, "Two Friends," tells us where we stand. In his short poem, one friend announces to the other, "I'm dying" and the other responds with perfunctory clichés (1964, p. 36). There is no sympathy, no compassion. There is no embrace. Within a few moments, the friend escapes. Gone.

Fort.

Gone. I'm not sure when I began to bore him. I'm sure I didn't at first. We cut our academic teeth together, thinking through disciplinary arguments, considering departmental politics, writing together with passion. Together, we consulted. Together, we went to conventions. Together, we played golf. Together, we drank. Together, we talked about our wives. Together, we lived our lives. So when did it happen? Perhaps it began when I joined him for a week on his sabbatical and I talked of his return. Maybe such talk told him he had to leave. Perhaps it began when his health seemed to fail, when the doctors prescribed pills after pills in their ongoing guessing game, never quite finding the correct diagnosis. Maybe I just didn't know what to say. Perhaps it began when he left his wife. Maybe he did not want to insist on allegiance at a time when he needed just that. Perhaps it began when he first started giving me gifts—books I might like, ties I might enjoy, wines I might try. Maybe these were parting gestures, wrapped in guilt. Whenever it began, it came quickly and I was pathetic. In his presence, my talk felt tedious as he would rush the conversation to an end. My stories seemed empty and pointless, as he nodded as if he had heard them all before. I watched him seek others for their company and I felt hurt. Now, he has moved away but he remains here, a ghost, untouchable. There.

Da.

There. I have stood along side Tobias in Edward Albee's *A Delicate Balance* and felt that years of friendship must account for something and felt too that only when asked what my limits might be would I recognize the hollowness of my belief. So, when friends make demands, I try not to say no but, like Tobias, I do not want their terrors, their plagues. I accept them only so that my life isn't a lie. I say with Tobias: "I like you fine; I find my liking you has limits. . . . But those are my limits! Not yours!" And like Harry, when my terrors and my plagues are upon me, I wonder if I am loved enough to take them to someone else's house. Gone.

Fort.

Gone. I cannot pull them up in my mind. Their names I remember but they are names without faces. So when I was invited to my thirtieth high school reunion, I did not go. I could not see myself looking around the room without images to connect to names. I could not see myself standing in that cool courtyard, shaded by those ivy covered buildings, talking again as I did those many years ago. I could not see myself sitting in Mr. Montgomery's classroom again, afraid to speak, afraid I might get it wrong. I could not see myself not wanting to hold her hand, to pick up where we had left off, to wonder what would have happened if. I see her clearly. There.

Da.

There. Usually, he ate to live. He surely was no food connoisseur but he knew he was in the presence of something special when he put the first morsel in his mouth. When she handed him the blueberry muffin he'd chosen, she seemed pleased by his pick. A quick smile came and she said, "I hope you enjoy it," as if she already knew the verdict was accomplished in the selection. He peeled the paper from its sides and felt that it was still warm. He broke off a piece. It was moist and covered by a thin crust that crunched on first bite but began to melt in his mouth. The blueberries, full and dark, had a slight tang. He quickly took another bite. Standing behind the counter, she smiled again and turned to her chores, knowing he would be back. He pulled off another piece and ate, then another, and another. The blueberry muffin was gone. Gone.

Fort.

Gone. When the love between them left is hard to say. Perhaps it left with the accumulation of annoyances or perhaps as the love died, everything began to annoy—his aggravating snoring, his unreasonable demands, his predictable self-righteousness and her compulsive cleaning, her excessive buying, her negative judgments. Whenever it happened, it happened as a slow complaint that rubbed against them both, a complaint that was never spoken. They lived, day in and day out, watching each other as two animals might circle prey, ready to pounce but afraid the prey might be more than can be handled. There.

Da.

There. The opening kiss in the film *Kids* terrifies with its intimacy. The camera offers a close-up of two young bodies, passionate in embrace, turning this way and that, pushing, sucking, tonguing. You see their heads, together, filling the screen, magnified. You hear their sloppy noises. You see their eyes closed, then searching. You see their spit. You see them wanting. You see them forever. You see sex. You are embarrassed and want to look away but you don't. You are fascinated. You remember what you learned in your film theory class. You imagine that if the kiss would go on for a moment longer, they would begin to devour each other, bit by bit, until only a pair of worn lips would remain. Gone.

Fort.

Gone. When does it leave a relationship? When does it lose its power? When does it not matter any more? When does it carry so much hard history that it just doesn't seem worth it? When does it seem too much like a chore, like something that has to get done? When does it repeat itself, the same time, the same place, the same hands? When does it become a couple's cancer? When does it become negotiated in silence? When does it stay, clinging like an old fragrance? There.

Da.

There. James Bond always knows just what to say. He never struggles for just the right word, never pauses too long before he speaks or never talks too softly to be heard. Even when he might get it wrong, he knows just how to make amends. He is the perfect man, handsome, strong, smart. Dry martini in hand, he eliminates evil. Dry martini in hand, he makes love. Bond is 007 cool or so he was before history had its way. Gone.

Fort.

Gone. When all is said and done, the hero turns his back on us and leaves. Alone, he rides into the sunset or he turns from the carnage, perhaps with just a trickle of blood running down his thigh. There is no standing around for applause. He does not linger to see what might be said about his virtue or to gather what might be his rewards. He just leaves, noble, independent, confident in the wisdom of his actions. The hero never second guesses. He lives so that he might return again, ready to act in the name of justice, in the name of those too weak to fend for themselves, in the name of eye-for-an-eye laws that we are too afraid to change. There.

Da.

There. The note left on the counter read: "I've gone to the store. I'll be back soon." She never returned. He drank cup after cup of Constant Comment spice tea. Gone.

Fort.

Gone. Child actors never die; they just grow older. They lose their curls, their cute smiles, their charm and before you know it, they're chewing scenes in search of what got left behind. That's when the parts usually stop coming. A few make it to the other side but most live scrapbook lives, always looking back, always listening for their cue. There.

Da.

There. I have traveled for 14 years to present my parents with their only granddaughter. Twice a year, over Christmas and summer vacations, we would appear, expecting them to be sitting around their cluttered dinning room table in their straight back chairs, playing cards, working puzzles, preparing food, reading the paper. We would join them around that table until our backs, more accustomed to the softness of sofas, would complain. We would join them for the pleasure of the moment, knowing how the candy dish had been filled with our favorite chocolates, how the beds were made and turned down, how the house was decorated with Santas peeking around every corner or was made fresh with summer flowers. We would join them for the comfort of their company and for the chance to connect. I would watch them, watch them hard, as they grew older and they would watch their granddaughter turn into a young woman. They would know but would not hear her say, "Do we have to go back this summer?" Gone.

Fort.

Gone. He decided that as far as he was concerned, his son was dead. At that moment, he felt relief. He simply said to himself, "He's not my responsibility any longer. I did what I could." He repeated the words, listening carefully to what he was saying. He said them again, convincing himself he was right. That night his son came to him in a dream, stabbing him, over and over, with the family name. There.

Da.

There. Villains often meet their just ends with death. We applaud as the world regains its order. For we are the townspeople who move to the side when the shoot-out is to begin, the shoppers who dodge the recklessness of the car chase, the frightened hostages who wait to be rescued. We can produce a needed scream, drop a tear or two, or provide a backdrop for a scene. We are the witnesses that everything has returned to its rightful place. Sometimes that requires death, even our own. Gone.

Fort.

Gone. The first time he saw the show, he was ecstatic. Usually slow in gesture and mood, he rocked with the remembered sounds and his hands fluttered praise. He could not be contained. "You have to see it! You have to see it," he exclaimed to everyone who would listen. The next time he saw it, he watched in quiet awe. His concentration was deep and focused and when it ended, he shook his head, marveling. His was an act of veneration, of the devout standing before his god. There can be little surprise, then, that the third time he saw it, he brought his daughter, obligated as a parent to provide religious education. His pleasure came with her conversion. Now, they sing the lyrics together each day on the way to school in loud, joyful sounds that echo around the neighborhood like prayers. There.

Da.

There. I'm not sure how it starts, maybe a bruised ego, maybe a bad decision or two, maybe from the arrogance of all concerned but I know I don't want it in my house, the "he saids" and the "she saids," the maneuvering, the calculating, the counting of votes, the closed doors. Politics are too political. It works on you from the inside and insiders are too close to the heart of the matter. It saddens. It angers. It takes and takes and returns nothing. It devours as it goes. The heart of the matter is empty. Gone.

Fort.

Gone. How many dead bodies might I count? The evening news might show me two or three on any given night? The cop shows that follow might present me with several more. I might add up the bodies from the funerals of friends, acquaintances, and relatives. One Shakespeare play might give me half a dozen or so. A Stallone or Eastwood film might top a hundred. I might name those I knew in Vietnam who did not return. The pictures from massacres and lynchings might total in the hundreds. Those comic book and cartoon deaths might be added. I might figure in that teenage army prisoner who died of an overdose while I tried to assist the doctors' desperate efforts. The victims of natural disasters might compute into the thousands. Newspaper accounts of car wrecks, suicides, and murders might average five-to-ten a day. Bodies from diseases—plagues, heart attacks, cancer—might account for many more. I might list them all, all the dead bodies I have seen, one after another, and I might count my own. There.

Da.

There. No, she doesn't look like herself. She looks like a figure from a wax museum, placed for viewing for the visitors to stroll past. She is frozen, lifeless. You recognize who the figure is supposed to be but it's off, just a little here and there—the cheeks too puffy, the eyebrows too dark, the lips too pale—just enough to let you know that it's not right. That's why wax museums are such frightening places. They trade in possession when they have nothing to possess. Like now, with her, she is no where to be found. Gone.

Fort.

Gone. Dying in performance is an art. We are at our best when death is violent—the bullet flinging the arm back, the sword slicing the body from the head, the knife cutting the throat, the grenade separating limbs. We can make blood spurt, pour, or puddle from a wound. We can even show the fear the moment before death arrives. We are less skilled when we have to die in a loved one's arms. We never get right how the body drops down into dead weight, how the eyes open shocked by the finality of it all, and how those still living turn from the corpse. There.

Da.

There. The obituaries. Each day they are listed and each day I meet them differently. Sometimes they are pictured, their importance marked by the column inch. Sometimes they are a page to skip. Sometimes they are semantic lessons in the cruelty of naming. Sometimes they are a mathematical equation predicting probable time left. Sometimes they are a nervous read. Sometimes they are stories of fathers or mothers who have graduated from this or that school, who have spent the weight of their years working here or there, who have left others behind. Sometimes they are instructions—services at such and such funeral home, burial at such and such cemetery, no flowers. Sometimes they are children, single-digit young. Always though, they are passings without explanation and each day curiosity pulls me to the messiness of their deaths, to the failure of their bodies, to the pain of their flesh. I am grateful my curiosity is never satisfied. Necrology. Necrotomy. Necrosis. Gone.

Fort.

Gone. When the credits begin to roll, most of the audience begins to leave. Only some additional attraction—out-takes, a theme song, a continuing image—might hold them in the aisle glancing back over their shoulders. They don't need a list of names to decide if credit is or is not due. But a few will remain seated, straining to see the names of copyists, set production assistants, best boys, and grips between the moving bodies trying to depart. They read to connect; they read for recognition. There.

Da.

There. In *The Writing Life*, Annie Dillard (1998) advises,

Write as if you are dying. At the same time, assume you write for an audience consisting solely of terminal patients. That is, after all, the case. What would you begin writing if you knew you would die soon? What could you say to a dying person that would not enrage by its triviality? (p. 68)

Who can speak in the face of such a mandate? Gone.

Fort.

Gone. She understood it to be a hallowed space. She knew that the theatre held, rumbling in the rafters and riding the rigging, all the voices that were ever present. She had added her own and stopped on closing night after everyone had gone to listen. At first, all she heard was the silence but she waited, listening, still. Then she heard something else. Perhaps it was just the wind; perhaps it was her mind playing tricks. But she swore that the theatre spoke: "Prayers," it whispered, "prayers." There.

Da.

There. It is all about loss. Everything is dying. First, there was God, then the author, and now, the subject. All that is left is an inaccessible is. Everything slips away. Theatre, Peggy Phelan (1997) tells us in *Mourning Sex*, is a "response to a psychic need to rehearse for loss, and especially for death" (p. 3). The perpetual disappearance of theatrical acts teaches us how to mourn what is no longer present. It teaches us that to represent can only result in loss, that there is no holding on. This lesson never settles. We resist it when we speak, when we write, when we listen. We never get it right. There is only the coming and going, only the space between. Tears mark the spot. Always already. Everything evaporates. Only stains and shadows remain. Ghosts. Gone.

Fort.

REFERENCES

Albee, E. (1997). *A delicate balance: A play*. New York: Plume.

Dillard, A. (1998). *The writing life*. New York: HarperCollins.

Ignatow, D. (1964). Two friends. In *Figures of the human*. Middletown, CT: Wesleyan University Press.

Phelan, P. (1997). *Mourning sex: Performing public memories*. Boston: Routledge.

Shea, T. (1997). Scratched into the tree of original sin's bark. *American Poetry Review, 26,* 45.

—-

Ronald J. Pelias teaches performance studies in the Department of Speech Communication at Southern Illinois University. He is the author of Writing Performance: Poeticizing the Researcher's Body *(Southern Illinois University Press, 1999).*

PART FIVE

— —

ASSESSING THE TEXT

The criteria for evaluating qualitative work in the seventh moments are moral and ethical. Blending aesthetics (theories of beauty), ethics (theories of ought and of right) and epistemologies (theories of knowing), these criteria are fitted to the pragmatic, ethical, and political contingencies of concrete situations. This stance calls for a research model rooted in the concepts of care, shared governance, neighborliness, love, and kindness. Such work should provide the foundations for social criticism and social action (Christians, 2000; Collins, 1991).

An anti- or postfoundational, critical social science seeks its external grounding not in science, in any of its revisionist, postpositivist forms, but rather in a commitment to a post-Marxist and communitarian feminism, with hope but no guarantees. It seeks to understand how power and ideology operate through and across systems of discourse, cultural commodities, and cultural texts. It asks how words, and texts, and their meanings play a pivotal part in the cultures' "decisive performances of race, class [and] gender" (Downing, 1987, p. 80).

The following understandings structure the assessment process. Nothing is value-free. Knowledge is power. Those who have power determine what is aesthetically pleasing and ethically acceptable.

This position erases the usual distinctions between epistemology, aesthetics, and ethics.

In a feminist, communitarian sense, this aesthetic contends that ways of knowing (epistemology) are moral and ethical (Christians, 2000). These ways of knowing involve conceptions of who the human being is (ontology), including how matters of difference are socially organized. The ways in which these relationships of difference are textually represented answer to a political and epistemological aesthetic that defines what is good, true, and beautiful.

All aesthetics and standards of judgment are based on particular moral standpoints. There is no objective, morally neutral standpoint. Hence, for example, an Afrocentric feminist aesthetic (and epistemology) stresses the importance of truth, knowledge, and beauty ("Black is Beautiful"). Such claims are based on a concept of storytelling and a notion of wisdom that is experiential, communal, and shared. Wisdom so conceived is derived from local, lived, familial, and communal experience, and expresses lore, folktale, and myth (Collins, 1991).

This is a dialogical epistemology and aesthetic. It involves a give-and-take and ongoing moral dialogue between persons. It enacts an ethic of care and an ethic of personal and communal responsibility (Collins, 1991). Politically, this aesthetic imagines how a truly democratic society might look, including one free of race prejudice and oppression. This aesthetic values beauty and artistry, movement, rhythm, color, and texture in everyday life. It celebrates difference and the sounds of many different voices. It expresses an ethic of empowerment.

This aesthetic enables social criticism and engenders resistance (see what follows). It helps persons imagine how things could be different. It imagines new forms of human transformation and emancipation. It enacts these transformations through dialogue. If necessary, it sanctions nonviolent forms of civil disobediance (Christians, 2000). How this ethic works in any specific situation cannot be given in advance.

The six articles in Part Five advance our understandings of the assessment and evaluation process. **Linda Belgrave** and **Kenneth Smith** discuss how notions of validity are negotiated in a collaborative ethnography, a study of Hurricane Andrew in Dade County, Florida. They show how their biographies and personal histories shaped the accounts they wrote. Their experiences of doing the study also shaped what they wrote; these differences gave the project an unexpected richness.

Arthur Bochner disputes the call for new criteria to evaluate qualitative inquiry. Such efforts too often limit freedom to innovate. The forms of writing Bochner finds most valuable are narratives of the self that look at the past through the lens of the present. These narratives extract meaning from experience rather than presenting experience exactly as it was lived.

Good poetic work helps readers understand situations that are troubling and problematic. Such work has an abundance of detail. It presents the emotions of real live people struggling to find meaning in their lives. These narratives make their authors vulnerable and emotionally credible. They are complexly structured, moving back and forth between the past and the present. They tell a story of two selves—"who I was" and "who I am now." These stories are judged by their ethical sensitivity, for the concern they show for the people they portray. Good stories move the reader to action.

Michelle Fine and **Lois Weis** write about writing the wrongs of fieldwork. As critical ethnographers, they discuss the variety of ethical dilemmas they encountered in their attempt to write about the lives of poor and working-class informants. These dilemmas included such problems as how to define community, family, and head of household. Race, similarly, emerged as an unstable aspect of biography. Ethically, they confronted dilemmas when they found "hot" information about the sources and uses of money by the women they interviewed. They struggled with how to insert themselves into their texts. In so doing, they sought a voice that allowed them to write against the structures that reproduce social injustice in the lives of the urban poor. In addressing these dilemmas, they articulate a feminist communitarian ethic that engenders hope and empowers the disadvantaged. They judge their work by its ability to advance these goals.

Steinar Kvale extends our understanding of validity in the seventh moment. He suggests that modernist conceptions of validity treat true knowledge as a mirror of reality. Postmodern notions see validity as a social construction. Three views of validity follow from this position. First, validity can be seen as an expression of craftsmanship. Here the quality of interpretive work is assessed. Second, validity is a form of communication, a dialogue, and a conversation between the researcher and the world. Third, validity is a form of pragmatic action in the world, hence a work is judged by the effects it produces in the world. This brings us back to our communitarian ethic, how does a work help make the world better?

Yvonna S. Lincoln contends that the criteria for judging interpretive work are in flux. She outlines an approach that values criteria that are relational and ethical, criteria that emphasize community, voice, critical subjectivity, reciprocity, and sacredness. Like Bochner, she hastens to add that the search for criteria can be constraining, and that criteria that operate at one point in a project may not be relevant in a later phase. She underscores the point that her constructionist position collapses the distinction between rigorous evaluative standards and ethics. She advocates a reciprocally responsible moral ethic that is empowering, neighborly, and friendly.

Mónica Russel y Rodríguez speaks from and with a Chicana consciousness. She argues that much of the theory and practice in contemporary anthropology silences praxis. While the practice of anthropology values the knowledge of the native, the observer is the expert knower, the person who understands theory. This creates a dilemma, a contradiction. Too often, the scholar of color is placed in the position of the native, the expert knower, who knows no theory. Rodríguez says she resides in a discipline that denies multiple subjectivities to researcher and native. She wants to expose these contradictions and reclaim the voice and perspective that has been denounced by the disciplinary apparatuses of anthropology.

REFERENCES

Christians, C. (2000). Ethics and politics in qualitative research. In N. Denzin & Y. S. Lincoln (Eds.), *Handbook of qualitative research, 2 ed.* (pp. 133-155). Thousand Oaks, CA: Sage.

Collins, P. H. (1991). *Black feminist thought.* New York: Routledge.

Downing, D. B. (1987). Deconstruction's scruples: The politics of enlightened critique. *Diacritics, 17,* 66-81.

CHAPTER 15

Negotiated Validity in
Collaborative Ethnography

— —

Linda Liska Belgrave
Kenneth J. Smith
University of Miami

This article is an attempt to reconstruct and analyze the process of conducting a collaborative, interpretive study of the experience of Hurricane Andrew. Study data consist of accounts, including in-depth and focus-group interviews, collected in the months following the storm. The current inquiry addresses validity, with a focus on the impact of the investigators' biographies and theoretical orientations on the collection and analysis of qualitative data. We found that our interviews differed in terms of style, level of detail sought, and the degree of taken-for-granted knowledge shared by interviewer and respondent. In analysis, we found different aspects of the data interesting and, initially, produced different stories. These proved to be complementary, rather than contradictory. Collaboration made it possible to identify some of the biases we brought to the task and yielded a richer interpretation of the hurricane experience than either of us would have produced alone.

AUTHORS' NOTE: Article originally presented at the Stone Symposium, April 28 to May 1, 1994, Champaign-Urbana, Illinois.

When Hurricane Andrew tore through southern Dade County, Florida, 250,000 people were left homeless and everyday life was disrupted or destroyed for countless more. Within a few weeks, social scientists and others were in the field examining the impact of the hurricane. The focus of this article is an attempt to reconstruct and comment on the research process involved in producing an ethnography of Hurricane Andrew. The method chosen to analyze our research is a *verstehen* process similar to Cooley's "sympathetic introspection," Mills's "sociological imagination," and Ellis's "systematic sociological introspection" (Ronai & Ellis, 1989). Despite rather different research backgrounds and interests, the two of us joined forces to do an interpretive study of the experience of Hurricane Andrew (Smith & Belgrave, 1993, 1994). Either one of us could have done such a study. However, neither of us alone could have done precisely the study we did or produced the same findings. This, of course, raises the issue of validity, particularly with regard to the nature of the data collected and the interpretation of these data.

RESEARCH DESIGN

Our data consist of accounts collected in the weeks and months following Hurricane Andrew. These are part of the data from a research project on the impact of the hurricane, for which interviews continued for nearly 2 years following the storm.

The interviews were in-depth, and lasted approximately 2 hours. The interviews were tape-recorded (with permission) and transcribed verbatim, thereby preserving the respondent's own use of language. The data analysis proceeded with the data collection phase, so that developing concepts and working hypotheses could be examined in subsequent interviews. At the time of the current analysis, data had been collected from 41 respondents, including 18 interviews, 2 focus group interviews involving 8 people, 3 first-person accounts (one of which was followed by an interview), and 13 interviews conducted by our students for special class projects. The respondents were drawn from the University of Miami and the larger community.

The Nonscheduled Standardized Interview

Our interviewing procedure was organized to allow each respondent to tell his or her own story of Hurricane Andrew. Following this initial, detailed, and at times lengthy, account of the hurricane, the respondent was asked to consider a number of questions and probes that constituted the interview schedule. This schedule was a list of questions previously agreed on by the researchers. Certain information was sought from all respondents, much of it already supplied by the respondent's initial story of the hurricane. There was no fixed sequence in which the questions were asked and the amount of detail supplied varied from respondent to respondent (Denzin, 1989).

During the course of the study, we noticed that our interviews appeared to differ in the extent to which they focused on employment as compared to domestic issues, public, or private life, issues that tend to be associated with gender roles. Thus the first portion of this analysis deals with the possible influence of the investigator, including his or her gender, on the interviews themselves. Specifically, we compare interviewer questions to detect tendencies of the investigators to focus on various aspects of the hurricane experience. Here, we examine the influence of the investigators' experiences as sociologists with unique biographies on our approaches to the in-depth interview.

Second, we analyze the eight focus group interviews as unique forms of data collection and social interaction. We compare this form of data collection to individual, personal in-depth interviews.

For this article, we analyze only the focus groups and those 18 interviews conducted personally by one of the investigators for a number of reasons. First, these are the only private interviews for which we have personal knowledge of the interview situation and dynamics. Second, student interviewers typically did only one or two interviews. Not only might this be insufficient for detecting gender patterns but also such patterns would be complicated by the student's lack of interviewing experience.

Finally, we examine our analysis. Here we focus on our individual interpretations of the subjective meaning of events for our respondents and our negotiation of a joint report. We attempt to untangle the influences of not only gender but also theoretical perspectives and interests and personal hurricane experiences on our interpretations of the data.

Investigators' Backgrounds

The biographies of the investigators, both professional and personal, are a significant factor in the following analysis. Accordingly, the relevant elements of them are presented here to provide the necessary context. Neither one of us works in the area of gender studies as a specialty, so the influence of gender on our work is not something that we treated as a significant issue. Although Linda is, perhaps, more sensitive to women's concerns than Ken, her interest tends to focus on pragmatic employment issues. Thus gender is more or less taken for granted by both of us and, as such, its influence on our interpretations is difficult to detect with certainty. Fortunately, as a mixed-gender research team, we have the opportunity to contrast our work for clues to gender influences.

Differences in theoretical perspective are more straightforward. We each have training and experience in both positivist/quantitative and interpretive/qualitative research, but differ in which approach we typically use. Ken is primarily oriented toward interpretive sociology. Ken would describe himself as a "scientist" with a wink. He believes the humanist approach is a broader, richer foundation for explaining human action than the approaches of the positivist sciences. Ken is an empiricist of the grounded theory tradition. Telling the sociological account involves the historical context that embraces the actors, their activity, and their awareness of themselves and each other. To reconstruct the reality of a time, a place, or an event involves describing, analyzing, and coordinating the stories of the event given by those who experienced it.

Linda is more quantitatively oriented, although she resists the positivist label, primarily because the supposed assumptions regarding objectivity make little sense if taken too literally. (Either positivists are not what they are thought to be or Linda is not one of the most faithful.) When doing interpretive work, she is interested in everyday life and the mundane stuff of taken-for-granted reality. When conducting such research, she sees her job as (a) understanding the subjective experiences of the persons she studies and (b) using that understanding to get a handle on the phenomenon of interest, recognizing that (c) her findings will be subject to other interpretations and provide, at best, a partial description of whatever she studied.

Finally, our personal hurricane experiences differed considerably, although neither of us suffered significant material loss. Ken was in Miami during Hurricane Andrew. He not only went through the storm himself with his family and friends (some of whom evacuated to his apartment) but was responsible for the well-being of students and their parents who were on campus early for orientation. (Ken is a Master at one of the university's residential colleges.) The building he was in held. Afterward, he was quite impressed by the devastation on campus. Within 2 or 3 days, most of the students had been sent home and cleanup had begun on campus. Ken and a colleague from the Department of Sociology began hauling loads of relief supplies to the South Dade Labor Camp (for migrant farmers) in the hardest hit area and searching for colleagues he had been unable to reach by phone. The next 2 weeks were filled with preparation for reopening of the university. Linda was out of town for the storm itself, returning to Miami more than 48 hours after it ended. Although her apartment was in a relatively hard-hit area, the interior was untouched. Thus she escaped the storm itself and experienced the aftermath and rebuilding without the burden of a damaged home or lost property. Because of where she lived, the months following Andrew were difficult. It was 6 weeks before her water was potable and she was under curfew for at least this long. Grocery and other shopping was available but limited and very crowded for months. Her apartment complex and surrounding neighborhood were "trashed" looking for maybe 9 months.

INVESTIGATOR BIOGRAPHY
AND THE IN-DEPTH INTERVIEW

Although we began this analysis with an interest in gender issues, it turned out that the sort of gender patterns we anticipated did not appear. Gender was not the story.

Interview Technique

The most striking differences in our interviews were those of style, the extent to which the interview was a closed system and the degree of detail we pursued with our questions. These differences seem to reflect primarily our own past research experiences and theoretical interests.

Despite our efforts to encourage our respondents initially to tell their hurricane stories in whatever fashion they chose, we both intruded on these accounts with questions, primarily for clarification or for information respondents failed to volunteer. For instance, we found ourselves asking questions that provided context in terms of the storm itself, such as where a respondent lived, what type of house he or she was in, or how that house had been prepared for the storm. In some cases, it was simply too difficult to follow the stories otherwise. Although we both did this, there were differences in the initial accounts we elicited and in the ways we continued the interviews.

Ken asked questions in such a way as to acquire longer answers than those Linda obtained. He tended to give respondents a broad question and let them run with it, whereas Linda asked more narrowly focused questions. In a sense, Ken guided his respondents more gently. At the same time, however, he interrupted his respondents midstream or introduced entirely new topics with his questions more noticeably than Linda. Thus Ken's overall pattern seems to be one of eliciting a piece of a story and moving on to another piece, sometimes somewhat abruptly. By contrast, Linda somehow asked for outlines of stories and then asked follow-up questions to fill in the details. Thus we provided direction for the interviews differently. Ken's direction came in the form of guiding the broad topics under discussion, while respondents largely determined which details to provide. Linda tended to follow topics suggested by respondents or chronology but guided the nature and extent of detail. Our transcripts provide few clues to explain these patterns, which seem to flow from personal style.

Ken's interviews were more open systems than were Linda's. By this we mean that they contained more from outside the individual interview itself. This was a matter of personal and professional biography. Personal biography is relevant in terms of who we interviewed. Our respondents were drawn primarily from the university itself, which means that we were personally acquainted with a number of them to some degree. Ken has been at the University of Miami longer than Linda, and he knew more of our respondents and knew them better than she did. Furthermore, Ken lives on campus and was involved in coordinating the evacuation of the campus, both for the storm itself and afterward. To the extent that it was possible, we avoided discussing the hurricane experience with potential respondents until the interview itself. When interviewing strangers, this was not difficult. With friends or frequently seen acquaintances, however, we sometimes knew at least part of a person's story, either through personal discussion or through the grapevine. When one of us interviewed an acquaintance or friend, parts of their personal biography were already known to us and might be taken for granted during the interview. Because of Ken's longer and deeper involvement in the university, his interviews draw on such outside knowledge about the respondents to a greater extent than do Linda's.

In addition to our differing personal acquaintance with respondents, our interviews also show different uses of our interview guide and the study as a whole. Ken's interviews reflect his ongoing analysis to a greater extent and in a different way than Linda's. This seems to flow from our prior research experience. As Ken guided respondents from topic to topic, he pursued issues that were becoming important in analysis and devoted less time to things that were not "panning out." Although Linda did ask about the issues that were emerging in analysis, these were not necessarily the same issues Ken focused on and she did not necessarily follow them with the same intensity that Ken did. These differences likely result from our finding different aspects of the hurricane experience noteworthy (see analysis section below) and Ken's longer experience conducting qualitative research. More noticeable was Linda's tendency to go through the entire original interview guide with virtually every respondent. This dogged pursuit of every original question no doubt reflects her own experience in writing and using standardized, quantitative questionnaires.

Finally, our interviews differed in the extent to which we asked about the big picture or the little details. As we stated above, Ken tended to introduce broad topics and let respondents determine the level of detail they would provide. Linda, on the other hand, asked about minutia. For instance, Ken was content to know that someone was able to buy food, whereas Linda wanted to know what store he or she went to, if it was the respondent's regular store, how well it was stocked, and how he or she dealt with the food once it was purchased. This difference in our interest in details became more apparent in comparing our initial interpretations of the hurricane experience and is therefore analyzed below.

Summary

This analysis of our interviews as data, rather than as sources of data, has shown a number of differences reflecting the biographies we bring to the research process. Differences of style may not be terribly important. Others, such as the level of detail obtained from interviews, are more likely to influence the type of story that a researcher will eventually tell. Of course, if a researcher pursues those things that he or she finds interesting (for theoretical or personal reasons) in both collecting and analyzing data, there will be a fit between these two elements of the research process. More interesting, and potentially troublesome, is the matter of implicit, taken-for-granted knowledge shared by interviewer and respondent. We became aware of this issue because of the special configuration of this study, namely, two investigators interviewing aquaintances about an event that all had experienced. The many contrasts contained in our data make explicit much that would otherwise have remained hidden. This raises serious issues that are not easily resolved. How does a researcher become aware of what he or she is taking for granted? It is much easier to remind oneself to be aware of one's assumptions than it is to figure out what those assumptions are.

FOCUS GROUPS

Focus groups are a unique, perhaps somewhat peculiar, form of social interaction. A number of people come together to discuss some issue under the guidance of an interviewer, whose questions introduce topics and provide the direction, and perhaps tone, of the conversation. Our two focus groups were probably not exceptional, except for the fact that all respondents and the investigators worked for the same institution and some of those involved knew each other well.

Trade-Offs, Decisions, and Frustration

The decision to use focus group interviews was both methodological and pragmatic. The methodological issue was secondary and primarily one of curiosity. Focus group interviews are gaining popularity as a data collection technique (Morgan, 1988); neither of us had used them and we wanted to see what all the fuss was about. We recognized that it would be impossible to get as much detail regarding people's stories as with personal interviews. On the other hand, we would be able to interview a fairly large number of people in a short period of time, which is, of course, the pragmatic issue. The use of focus groups involved a trade-off of depth for breadth. We decided to use the focus groups as a preliminary step in data collection to collect a large amount of varied data quickly and to sensitize us to issues that otherwise might not have occurred to us. This proved to be a valuable approach, particularly because we went into this research "cold." Neither of us has a background in disaster research and, had Hurricane Andrew not struck Dade County, it might never have occurred to either of us to do a hurricane study. But, we are both social scientists, after all, and reacted to the hurricane as such. Basically, we were two "street ethnographers" responding to the disaster that surrounded us.

Although we had anticipated the lack of depth in terms of data, we were not prepared for the frustration this would cause. First, given the need to let all participants tell their hurricane story, it was simply not possible to follow up or probe for details, regardless of how interesting or potentially significant an issue raised by a respondent might be. This resulted in accounts that were more superficial than we would have liked. A second, related difficulty was the inability to cover as much time in the stories. That is, we were able to collect data on how people's lives had changed due to the hurricane, their preparations for the storm, their experience of the storm itself, and the first week or so following the hurricane. But processes by which focus group participants got from the immediate postdisaster period to mid-December are anyone's guess. Had we relied solely on focus groups, we might well have missed entirely the period/phase of Living Between Two Worlds (Smith & Belgrave, 1993).

A third contrast between focus groups and individual interviews, although not necessarily a drawback, consists of the differences in how respondents related their accounts. A number of the focus group respondents appeared to be making prepared remarks or playing to the audience. Four of the eight participants, including all three of the men, seemed to have given some thought to what they would say. Their opening remarks were quite organized; one of them explicitly numbered his points as he made them, whereas the others seemed to be ticking them off mentally as they spoke. One of these men made notes while the others spoke. The men also initially spoke somewhat impersonally in terms of abstract concepts, such as "living environment," "clinging to some of the old, yet [having] to do some of the new," and the hurricane as "a learning experience." Other respondents also discussed abstract concepts, of course, but they tended to do so either in more personal terms or following a line of discussion introduced by someone else. The only woman who gave seemingly prepared remarks did not appear to speak from an outline, so much as to have made similar public remarks before. In fact, she had been interviewed multiple times by the media, so was somewhat rehearsed. She also had a point to make about her working-class, minority neighborhood having been ignored by initial relief efforts.

Possible explanations for these ways of talking include personal biography (particular gender), the nature of our opening question, and the focus group situation. In terms of the first, gender and other personal history seem to have been relevant, but not a total explanation. Although the giving of organized, prepared remarks was only done by men (professional men, at that), this did not occur in later, personal interviews with men (professionals or others). It was unique to the focus group interviews.

Our opening question addressed the impact of the hurricane on respondents' lives, in contrast to our first personal interview question, which simply asked respondents to tell their hurricane stories. Given that our opening question asked for summary and conclusions, it may have invited an organized, abstract response. Nonetheless, it is noteworthy that we got such analytic responses only from men.

Finally, the focus group setting, by its very nature, provides a group audience. Respondents interact with each other as much as with the researcher(s). It may be that some of our respondents were "on" in a way they would not have been in a more private situation.

The relevance of this, of course, is the effect it might have had on the nature of the data that were collected. On one hand, it's certainly convenient if one's respondents hand him or her conceptual categories. On the other hand, these are only useful if they reflect the phenomenon of interest. Otherwise, they can blind one to other categories and twist one's findings (Spradley, 1979). In this case, some of the concepts raised did, in fact, recur repeatedly in later interviews. Others did not pan out. Without personal interviews, our findings might have been very different and, quite possibly, distorted.

Possibly the greatest effect of the tendency of respondents to present analyses was the loss of the personal side of their stories. For instance, we'll never know what it meant to one respondent to be out of the country while his family went through a life-threatening disaster or what repercussions this absence had on his family relationships.

Finally, the focus group interviews were generally frustratingly impersonal, following from the lack of detail and, perhaps, the group setting. Certainly some focus group respondents had had experiences that were every bit as harrowing, dramatic, and difficult as those of personal interview respondents. Yet these transcripts don't convey the same feelings as those from individual interviews. A focus group statement such as

> I had never felt that kind of fear in my life. . . . He's never been afraid and I saw this look in his eye. . . . When it hit me how terrified he was and I said, "This is not good." (Barrie)

simply does not say the same thing as

> It was his son calling from Fort Meyers and my husband was crying and he said "good-bye" to him . . . he was really shook up, and we were all holding hands. And my husband and I looked at each other and then kissed each other, because we knew we were going to die. . . . All of us kept telling each other "I love you" so much. (Rachel)

Influence of Respondents
on Each Other's Stories

The possibility that a respondent's account will be influenced by someone else's earlier remarks is a real concern with focus group interviews. Although an interviewer can take pains not to suggest responses, such suggestions by respondents themselves cannot be avoided. Of course, this is also a potential strength of this method, in that respondents themselves might bring up issues the researcher would not think to raise.

Two characteristics of the focus group interviews must be explained for this portion of the analysis. First, the two focus groups were quite different in that Ken was much more directive in the first, asking more questions, both to introduce new topics and to get people back on track. This may have resulted from the way in which the first respondent gave her account. Her story was, to use her words, "unmanaged" and matched her self-description of her current situation. She jumped from topic to topic and back and forth in time to such an extent that it was necessary to guide the process. During the second group, Ken asked fewer questions, allowing individual respondents to follow their own stories to a greater extent. The second point is that at Linda's request, Ken guided both focus groups; he asked all questions while Linda was more of a "silent partner." This was an issue of mentor-mentee or teaching-learning, not one of male dominance. However, the fact remains that participants were responding to a male questioner and silent female observer.

Participants in both groups sometimes responded to another respondent's remarks. However, this was most apparent in the second, less investigator-directed group. When participants followed one another's lead, it was not typically a matter of responding directly to issues raised by an earlier speaker instead of answering the question that was on the table. Rather, participants tended to include these issues in the telling of their own stories, sometimes using the same words, as though these were themes that ought to be addressed. For instance, the first respondent mentioned (with regret) in his opening remarks that if he had been more involved at the university immediately postcrisis, it would have been a "learning experience," with no elaboration. The next person to speak brought up the notion of learning from the hurricane in her second sentence, although in this case it was to explain that she had learned before the hurricane about having no control over what life brings. Thus she picked up the earlier respondent's theme and made it more specific by naming the "lesson," but showed that for her it was a lesson learned earlier rather than a lesson missed. Although the next speaker ignored the theme of learning, the final one brought it back with a new content—that of learning to rebuild, to deal with contractors, scheduling, and insurance money. He also discussed the issue of acceptance, possibly in response to the earlier introduction of one's inability to control things.

Other themes that recurred once they had been introduced by participants were stress, decision making, the pleasure of the simple lifestyle following the hurricane, and the futility or inappropriateness of some early attempts at "digging out" after the storm. Of these, the issue of decision making was particularly interesting, in that it became connected to gender roles. Decision making came up in the context of current difficulties related to rebuilding. One of the women in the group reported:

> Another problem I am having now is that I can't stand to make any more decisions. I mean, I know it should be a wonderful thing that I get to redo my whole place, but if one more person asks me what color paint, or what tile I want, or faucet . . . I just want to say "Just give it back." (Barrie)

The other woman made a similar comment in the process of describing what it was like to live in a gutted house.

> My husband is supposed to be home today and the tile man is supposed to come. You know, I really don't give a damn. I'm not coming home to look at tile. You want to put white tile, then go ahead. . . . There is this sense of not wanting to make any choices or decisions. (June)

Later, Dean, while not mentioning decision making per se, did bring in the tile, connecting it more explicitly to gender.

I'm not like my wife, who gets excited about tile and colors and all. You know, I care but I don't. (Dean)

This remark was made in the midst of talk about anxiety versus acceptance and seemed out of place, particularly given that this respondent's remarks were generally quite organized. It was as though he felt he had to "hit the tile issue," even if only to explain why he wasn't discussing it.

Such following the lead of another is significant to the extent that it has an impact on the data. Is it the case that when one respondent mentions something, others recognize it as part of their own experience and remark on it in turn? Or does the first mention of a topic shape the recollection and account of another respondent? Some of the themes discussed in this fashion seemed to be general issues, in that they came up not only in the affected focus group but also in personal interviews. For instance, many people talked of things they had learned from the hurricane. Generally, these were concrete skills related to hurricane preparedness or cleanup, but some mentioned abstract lessons, such as the relative unimportance of material possessions. And additional women respondents who were rebuilding talked of decorating matters. On the other hand, when respondents outside the focus group spoke of decision making, they tended to do so in the context of more vital decisions, such as whether to evacuate or ride out the storm or whether to move or stay put despite extensive destruction. Men generally did not bring up color schemes in their interviews. Thus there seems to have been some distortion flowing from an early respondent's choice of an example to illustrate her point. This suggests that when using focus groups, it might not be wise to interpret issues raised by individual respondents as being issues that are particularly significant to those respondents.

Fortunately, this mutual influence does not seem to have been so strong as to have led participants to misrepresent their experiences. We say this based on the ways in which respondents put their own spin on the themes they followed up from others. While working with someone else's topic, participants tended to explain how it was different or similar for themselves. This is best illustrated with the following exchange from the first focus group, where this pattern was less common. Erica was explaining the role of looters.

We went to them to get the basic foods to survive. It gave me a whole different outlook on crime. These guys are survivors and only at a time when survival is at risk do we appreciate that sort of individual. (Erica)

Bridget indignantly interrupted her to say, "The thought that these people looted and sold it to you makes me angry." Erica's response was unequivocal. "Well, it didn't make *me* angry. *I was glad to get it!*"

In addition, there is the evidence from attempts by the interviewer to intentionally influence the direction of the discussion. Our respondents were nothing if not tenacious. Time and again, interviewer questions that changed the topic were at least partially rebuffed. Typically, the respondent would give a short (i.e., single sentence) answer to the new question and immediately bring his or her story back to where it had been when the question was asked. On at least one occasion, a respondent ignored the new question altogether. It was as if the respondents each had a story to tell and they were not going to be deterred from doing so.

Summary

To conclude this portion of the analysis, we found focus group interviews to be extremely useful for gathering a large amount of varied data quickly. They also served as useful tools for sensitizing us to issues of which we were not aware. As such, focus group interviews might be especially appropriate when beginning work in a field with which one is not particularly familiar. At the same time, focus group interviews can be frustratingly incomplete. If this is the sole method of data collection, their superficiality might well distort one's findings. Finally, as a group social interaction, focus groups take on a life of their own. The effect on one's data might be minor or significant, but it will be there. Accompanying personal interviews can help to detect untoward situational influences.

INTERPRETATION AND THE FINAL REPORT

The final report is crucial in qualitative research; it is not the mere mechanical writing down of results as in a student's laboratory report. The report is a process of thinking and persuading the reader of the "correctness" of your arguments (Jorgensen, 1989). The core of the report is not the events reported by the respondent, but rather the subjective meaning of the reported events for the respondent. Subjectivity is an important element in ethnographic research. Subjectivity, however, has at least two dimensions. The primary dimension is the researcher's interpretation of the respondents' definitions and subjective understandings of what occurred. A secondary dimension is a researcher's experience as (a) a sociologist and (b) a person with a unique biography. This secondary dimension of subjectivity has further ramifications when the research is a collaboration between two individuals who also experienced the event they are reporting. Accordingly, this portion of the current analysis compares the categories and themes developed by two investigators working with the same data. This is, perhaps, a more complex problem than that of data collection, in that it involves making explicit the process of interpretation. Here, we attempt to untangle the influences of not only gender but also theoretical perspectives and interests and personal hurricane experiences on our interpretations of the data.

First, beyond their influence in the interview process, gender differences also have impact on what is seen as "important data." Second, theoretical perspectives involve the differences in positivist/quantitative and interpretist/qualitative methodologies. Both researchers have different theoretical biases, different views on the meaning and use of quantitative and qualitative data, and different notions of what aspects of any given problem are interesting. Third, our personal experiences of Andrew (as well as past hurricanes) differed considerably.

Collaborative Interpretation

Regardless of any differences in interviewing style and focus, the two of us analyzed the same data. Agreement on the content and style used in the written project was a process of negotiation. This analysis of that process is based on the first two papers we have written (Smith & Belgrave, 1993, 1994). In the first (Smith & Belgrave, 1994), we presented an interpretation of the approaching hurricane, the storm itself, and the acute disaster period following the hurricane in a series of five phases. These were Clear and Present Danger, the Shock of Natural Violence, Alienation From Physical Extensions of the Self, Reorientation of Self and Others, and Time Out From Everyday Life. The second paper (Smith & Belgrave, 1993) discussed the rebuilding period in terms of a single phase, specifically, Living Between Two Worlds.

To insure an inclusive, rather than restrictive, analysis, we initially worked independently on our first paper. We began joint analysis only when we both had something to bring to the table. Although our individual analyses were not contradictory, they were far from identical. In fact, an outsider reading both drafts might have been surprised to learn that we were working together. On reading the drafts together, it became apparent that the differences were of three types, specifically, content, completeness (as a research report), and overall interpretation of the hurricane experience. The last of these gave us the most trouble.

In terms of content, we had analyzed different portions of the hurricane experience. Ken had focused on past hurricane experience, preparation for Andrew, the storm itself, and aspects of the first day following the storm. Linda had started in the middle, with the immediate poststorm period, and covered the first few weeks following the hurricane. In effect, we had each analyzed time periods the other had not. This convenient coincidence resulted from time constraints and personal hurricane experience. Ken's approach was the more logical. He started at the beginning and went as far as he could before it was time to pull our separate analyses together. Our deadline simply arrived before he had finished everything he had hoped to cover. The missing portions of Linda's paper also reflected a deadline that came too quickly, but her peculiar starting point reflected her own hurricane experience. She consciously put off her analysis of the "main event," which she had not experienced. This avoidance was partly emotional—accounts of the hurricane itself are very painful to read—and partly an acknowledgment that she had no feel for that part of the experience. The content of the final version reflects our different starting points. Of the five phases discussed in the final version of our paper, the first two (Clear and Present Danger, the Shock of Natural Violence) came almost exclusively from Ken's draft and the fifth (Time Out From Everyday Life) from Linda's. The two middle phases (Alienation From Physical Extensions of the Self, Reorientation of Self and Others) were more truly collaborative, in that Ken conceived of the phases, and the content of each discussion came from Linda's analysis.

Ken's first draft was virtually complete as a research report, in that it contained most of the expected parts. Ken had written an introduction, some "purple prose" describing the hurricane, a beginning literature review, and his analysis. Linda's draft contained only analysis, preliminary conclusions, and some limitations of the study. Here again, we had conveniently written different portions of the paper, this time reflecting our theoretical perspectives and experiences as sociologists. Negotiating the inclusion of these contributions was primarily a matter of division of labor based on our available time and abilities. Two points warrant discussion. Ken's terse, dramatic description of the hurricane is important in setting the tone for the rest of the paper. Coming from her primarily quantitative background, Linda never would have thought to write such a description; it simply isn't done. Yet now that it's written, it's hard to imagine our paper without it.

Linda's discussion of the narrowness of the sample, by contrast, presented difficulties. Although she wasn't concerned with representativeness of the sample in a quantitative sense, she felt compelled to put our study in context by addressing the issue. In particular, she was acutely aware of, and troubled by, the absence of the poor from the study. This became a problem when we faced the page limitations for the final paper. Ken wanted to drop the section altogether and Linda refused. This was our only serious disagreement in negotiating the final paper. Our negotiations on this point were somewhat heated and changed the nature of the section. What had begun as a rather lengthy disclaimer on the generalizability of our study turned into a concise argument against the common description of natural disaster as a "great equalizer." In a sense, Linda was forced to reinterpret this part of her analysis, to find the essence of what she wanted to say. What seemed on the surface to be a methodological issue was, in fact, a substantive one.

Negotiating a final product from our two overall interpretations of the hurricane experience was awkward. Although our analyses were not contradictory, they followed rather different approaches and it was difficult to figure out how (or even if) they fit together. Ken saw a pattern of four discrete, chronologically ordered phases in the data. Although Linda's analysis also followed some chronological order, she did not find distinguishable phases with neat borders. Furthermore, much of her discussion was oriented around issues that overlapped in time. In a word, her story was messier. This difference seemed to reflect our being at different stages of analysis. Ken was working at a more abstract conceptual level, whereas Linda was close to the data. Accordingly, we went about shaping Linda's analysis into broad phases. The bulk of her "issues" were grouped into two consecutive phases, labeled Digging Out and Getting By. Other issues fit nicely into Ken's later phases and were incorporated there. (In fact, they fit so well as to be indistinguishable from Ken's content, and in the final version of the paper, Linda's text turned out to be what survived our cuts.) Three issues didn't fit in anywhere and were dropped. The result of all this seemed tidy, but it didn't sit well. Something was wrong. After agonizing over her two phases for some time, Linda determined that our "tidying up" of her messiness had resulted in a misrepresentation of what life was like during the early weeks following the hurricane. Furthermore, the sense of unreality that she had experienced during this period and saw in some of the accounts was not reflected in our paper at all. Through further negotiation (or was it a steamroller she used?) these two phases became coexisting parts of an altogether different fifth phase labeled Time Out from Everyday Life.

Looking back at our initial interpretations and the negotiation of our final product, the influences of theoretical perspective and, perhaps, gender can be seen. First, theoretical orientation not only played a role but also a role that we both misinterpreted as stage of analysis. Ken's analysis was, indeed, further developed than Linda's. However, it was also simply different. Based on his theoretical orientation and a view of more natural narrative or story, Ken expected and found broad, general patterns. As a result of her theoretical interest in the small, ordinary details of life, Linda couldn't get past how these differed following the hurricane and didn't get to the point of finding larger patterns. In a sense, Ken described the forest whereas Linda dealt with trees. Both perspectives shed light on the hurricane experience and neither is complete in itself. We hope we've brought them together successfully.

Gender's influence on our analysis, if it played a role, is more subtle. The following remarks are based on viewing our initial drafts through Long's (1989) discussion of gender and autobiography. An analysis based on analogy is inconclusive at best and shaky in any event. That said, the comparison seems useful. Long's argument is, in part, that the "generic" autobiography follows a male model, the conventions of which are that the life story is "shorn of dailiness, confusion and interpersonal hubbub, with only the intentional design revealed. Its trajectory is smoothed toward a known outcome" (Long, 1989, p. 195). By contrast, women tend toward different strategies, one of which is "telling it messy [which] embraces complexity and open-endedness, in content and in form: it portrays life as lived—the dailiness, the web of tasks, the web of relationships, the lack of closure, the nonlinear experience of time, the psychological and emotional realities" (Long, 1989, p. 213). The similarities between our pattern of analyses and Long's typology of gendered autobiography are striking.

For our second paper, we followed a different procedure. Ken wrote the first draft and Linda responded by more or less appending a separate analysis to his draft. Because we no longer have any of our original documents, the current analysis relies rather heavily on our memories of our individual contributions to the paper. This time, although our drafts were more similar, they differed again in our overall interpretations of the experience. The dominant theme of Ken's new analysis was that of the emerging normality in the postdisaster world; he also focused on life course changes resulting from the hurricane. Linda was much more impressed by the contrast between life in the "newly normal" and still devastated areas. Our analyses were likely influenced by our different hurricane experiences. During the early recovery period (perhaps the first few months after the storm) covered by this paper, our lives were very different. Ken lives on the UM campus, which was returned to a nearly normal state more quickly than most other institutions, in preparation for the return of students. Furthermore, the surrounding area, although certainly damaged, was not devastated, and businesses and services were functioning within a week or two. Thus Ken lived in a relatively normal world and visited the devastated areas. Linda, on the other hand, commuted between the "normal" world of the campus and a severely torn-up area on a daily basis. Life at work was nearly normal (at least by comparison), whereas life at home meant strangers living in her apartment for a few weeks, having to be home before 7 p.m. because of the curfew, walking past the military to get into the grocery store, and boiling her water. She was acutely aware of the contradiction between the worlds.

Both of our drafts for the second paper had elements of "messiness" as well as order. Although some of our earlier focus on abstract issues versus mundane details remained, we each seemed to have adopted a bit of the other's earlier style. There were no tidy phases for this paper. Rather, we wrote in terms of major issues with which people were dealing during this period, including the return to work, conflicts between the two worlds, and life course changes resulting from the hurricane. Neither of us was comfortable with this way of telling the story, but we had not been able to resolve it. Chronological time seemed to be less helpful for organizing the story than it was for the crisis period.

Summary

Although the two of us analyzed the same data set, we cannot say that we analyzed the same data, not completely. Because of our different backgrounds, both personal and professional, we were drawn to different portions of the data and, to some extent, found different aspects of the same data to be interesting. Our initial analyses produced different kinds of stories. Yet our styles of storytelling seem to be complementary rather than contradictory; they fit together. Either of us could have written an interesting and reasonably valid analysis of the hurricane experience. Our collaboration, however, has produced a richer interpretation than either of us would have produced alone.

CONCLUSION

In the end, there is no conclusive answer to the question of validity. Different interpretations of any given social phenomenon are always possible, reflecting in part the biases the interpreter(s) bring to the task and the criteria and logic they follow in completing it (Denzin, 1994). Given our approach to the study of the hurricane experience and our current stage of analysis, we have not (yet) adequately addressed some aspects of this experience. For example, there are some whose stories we will never be able to tell, such as the homeless or the rich and powerful. We have not yet resolved the issue of variability in hurricane experiences, although much of this will eventually be incorporated in our final analysis. Finally, there are aspects of the experience that we never intended or attempted to handle, such as the impact on community as a whole. With the current analysis, we have attempted to make explicit some of our biases and to trace the implications of those biases for our story by examining the processes we followed in interpreting our data. We are confident that our research provides a true, albeit incomplete, representation of the hurricane experience. We hope the present analysis is helpful to those who use our work to understand that experience.

REFERENCES

Denzin, N. K. (1989). *The research act* (3rd ed.). Englewood Cliffs, NJ: Prentice-Hall.

Denzin, N. K. (1994). The art and politics of interpretation. In N. K. Denzin & Y. S. Lincoln (Eds.), *Handbook of qualitative research* (pp. 500–515). Thousand Oaks, CA: Sage.

Jorgensen, D. L. (1989). *Participant observation.* Newbury Park, CA: Sage.

Long, J. (1989). Telling women's lives: "slant," "straight," and "messy." In D. Unruh & G. S. Livings (Eds.), *Current perspectives on aging and the life cycle* (Vol. 3, pp. 191–224). Greenwich, CT: JAI.

Morgan, D. L. (1988). *Focus groups as qualitative research.* Newbury Park, CA: Sage.

Ronai, C., & Ellis, C. (1989). Turn ons for money. *Journal of Contemporary Ethnography, 18,* 271–298.

Smith, K. J., & Belgrave, L. L. (1993, August). *Experiencing Hurricane Andrew, part II.* Paper presented at the meeting of the Society for the Study of Symbolic Interaction, Miami Beach, FL.

Smith, K. J., & Belgrave, L. L. (1994). Experiencing Hurricane Andrew: Environment and everyday life. In N. K. Denzin (Ed.), *Studies in symbolic interaction* (Vol. 16, pp. 251–273). Greenwich, CT: JAI.

Spradley, J. P. (1979). *The ethnographic interview.* Fort Worth, TX: Harcourt Brace Jovanovich.

— —

Linda Liska Belgrave is an associate professor in the Department of Sociology at the University of Miami. Her primary research and teaching interests include social gerontology, the experience of, and responses to, chronic illness, and research methods.

Kenneth J. Smith is an associate professor of sociology at the University of Miami. His research interests and teaching are in the areas of mental disorder, gerontology, and qualitative research methods.

CHAPTER 16

Criteria Against Ourselves

— —

Arthur P. Bochner
University of South Florida

In the social sciences, we usually think of criteria as culture-free standards that stand apart from human subjectivity and value. The author argues in this article, however, that conflicts over which criteria to apply usually boil down to differences in values that are contingent on human choices. The demand for criteria reflects the desire to contain freedom, limit possibilities, and resist change. Ultimately, all standards of evaluation rest on a research community's agreement to comply with their own humanly developed conventions. The author ends by considering the personal standards that he applies to works that fall under the new rubric of poetic social science.

When Laurel Richardson invited me to contribute to this conversation about judging "alternative" modes of qualitative and ethnographic inquiry, I consented reluctantly. Too often, I have seen discussions about criteria deteriorate into unproductive conflicts revolving around differences in values that cannot be resolved. The word *criteria* itself is a term that separates modernists from postmodernists, foundationalists from antifoundationalists, empiricists from interpretivists, and scientists from artists. It is not that one side thinks judgments have to be made and the other side does not. Both agree that inevitably they make choices about what is good, what is useful, and what is not. The difference is that one side believes that "objective" methods and procedures can be applied to determine the choices we make, whereas the other side believes these choices are ultimately and inextricably tied to our values and our subjectivities.

The differences of which I speak are not unreasonable, but they are unresolvable. As Richard Rorty (1982) says, these are not issues to be settled, but differences to be lived with. Until we recognize these differences as a reflection of incommensurable ways of seeing, we cannot begin to engage in meaningful conversation with each other. Thomas Kuhn (1962) observed more than 35 years ago that there is no paradigm-free way of looking. When our ways of looking are incommensurable, we can look in the same places, at the same things, and see them differently. Given each side's belief in its own premises—its own way of seeing—and recognizing that validity depends largely upon belief, we should not be surprised to find that when we converse about issues such as criteria our positions harden, conflicts escalate, and alienation increases. The different sides want to compel a universal, moral commitment to research practices that replicate their own, and each side gets frustrated when it confronts the plurality of the field and the impossibility of fixing a single standard for deciding the good and right purposes, forms, and practices of social inquiry.

I have a strong desire to create new and more interesting ways to talk about the work that many of us are doing under the rubric of alternative ethnography. Frankly, I find most of the incessant talk about criteria to be boring, tedious, and unproductive. Why do we always seem to be drawn back to the same familiar questions: "How do you know?" "Which methods are the right ones to use?" "What criteria should be applied?" For most of my academic life—almost 30 years—I have been baffled by this obsessive focus on criteria. In the social sciences, we have never overcome our insecurities about our scientific stature. In our hearts, if not in our minds, we know that the phenomena we study are messy, complicated, uncertain, and soft. Somewhere along the line, we became convinced that these qualities were signs of inferiority, which we should not expose. It appeared safer to keep the untidiness of our work to ourselves, rather than run the risk of having our work belittled as "unscientific" or "unscholarly." We seem uncommonly neurotic in our fear of having our little secret discovered, so we hide behind the terminology of the academic language games we've learned to play, gaining some advantage by knowing when and how to say "validity," "reliability," "grounded," and the like. Traditionally, we have worried much more about how we are judged as "scientists" by other scientists than about whether our work is useful, insightful, or meaningful—and to whom. We get preoccupied with rigor, but are neglectful of imagination. We hold on to the illusion that eventually we will unanimously agree on the culture-free standards to which all evidence must appeal, so that we won't have to rely on our own "subjectivity" to decide. Criteria pose as something beyond culture, beyond ourselves and our own conventions, beyond human choice and interpretation when, of course, they are not. Sometimes I feel that criteria are the very means we ourselves created to contain our desire for freedom and experience, a way of limiting our own possibilities and stifling our creative energy. I wonder, what is it we are not talking about when we are talking about criteria? Instead of asking, how can this be true? we could ask, what if this were true? What then?

When we say "alternative, " as in "alternative ethnography," we are implying that a domain of inquiry exists to which the work in question can be contrasted or compared. In ordinary discourse, an alternative represents an option or a substitute. But in qualitative research, alternative ethnography has evolved more as an alteration or transformation than an alternative—a change in form as well as in purpose. Although we may call it "alternative," what we really intend is "alterative." In alternative ethnography, the differences become akin to a "counterculture," which is a meaning that often is attributed to "new" and "alternative" ethnographies. Often alternative ethnography is discussed as if it were counter to traditional ethnographic realism or empiricism. The result is an emphasis on differences. But whether you consider "alternative" ethnographies threatening or profound, I think there are some premises on which all of us can agree.

AREAS OF AGREEMENT

First, no single, unchallenged paradigm has been established for deciding what does and does not comprise valid, useful, and significant knowledge.

Second, there is no one right way to do social science research. Fields such as sociology, communication research, anthropology, and psychology may be thought of as cultural sciences that constantly are evolving. No authority has yet been established for reaching a definitive conclusion that x field of social science must be or do y. The history of each of these fields suggests that they can and do change. The argument, for example, that sociology must always do y because it always has done y is without foundations to support it.

Third, it is impossible to fix a single standard for deciding the good and right purposes, forms, and practices of ethnography. This has been tried before without notable success.

Fourth, alternative ethnography reflects a desire to do meaningful, significant, and valuable work. Alternative ethnographers usually want to produce interesting, innovative, and evocative texts, works that seek to nurture the imagination not kill it.

Fifth, the existence of alternative ethnography does not signal an end to all traditional or conventional inquiry. Alternative ethnography only extends our understanding of and commitment to the multiplicity and plurality of legitimate goals for social science inquiry.

Sixth, multiplicity of goals implies multiplicity in standards of evaluation as well. When there is no agreement on goals, there can be no agreement on the terms by which those goals can be judged as successfully or unsuccessfully achieved. To understand how to evaluate the extent to which goals have been achieved, one must acknowledge and understand the meanings of those goals.

The differences in goals between "alternative" and traditional ethnographic and qualitative inquiry inevitably brings us to areas of disagreement, perhaps even contentiousness.

AREAS OF DISAGREEMENT

First, when traditional, empiricist standards are used to point out the failings of new or alternative ethnographies, as in, where are the hypotheses? the data analyses? the findings? these standards end up sounding parochial, narrow, and downright silly (Freeman, 1993).

Second, the notion that disciplines can be meaningfully distinguished by virtue of their possessing distinctive methods and discrete subject matters is false and misleading. No ontological basis exists for drawing a line between newspaper articles, novels, and sociological research studies (Rorty, 1982). The differences can only be drawn by reference to practical matters and to arbitrary, not empirical, stipulations.

Third, alternative ethnography is a blurred genre of discourse in which investigators are liberated to shape their work in terms of its own necessities rather than according to received ideas about what must be done (Geertz, 1980).

Fourth, we should never insist on reaching agreement beforehand on the criteria to which all arguments, reasoning, and conclusions must appeal. Ultimately, all criteria serve a conservative and destructive function. In Rorty's (1982, p. xli) terms, they are "temporary resting places constructed for specific utilitarian ends . . . a criterion . . . is a criterion because some social practice needs to block the road of inquiry, halt the regress of interpretations, in order to get something done." In this sense, criteria always have a restrictive, limiting, regressive, thwarting, halting quality to them, and they can never be completely separated from the structures of power in which they are situated.

Fifth, criteria are not found; they are made. Criteria refer to something we establish. Sample sizes, significance tests, alpha levels— what are these? No matter how real, natural, or objective they may seem, criteria are social products created by human beings in the course of evolving a set of practices to which they (and we) subsequently agree to conform (Rorty, 1982). In the final analysis, under the heading criteria, what we are talking about always boil down to compliance with our own conventions. The whole issue of criteria ends up rather pitifully as little more than an attempt to reach for some source outside ourselves to arbitrate differences of opinion, protect against subjectivity, and guarantee rationality (Rorty, 1982).

The conclusion I draw from the above is that conversations focusing on criteria have as their subtext a tacit desire to authorize or legislate a preexisting or static set of standards that will thwart subjectivity and ensure rationality. I consider this a potentially destructive endeavor insofar as it takes us away from the ethical issues at the heart of our work, distracting us from the difficult dilemma of figuring out how to keep the conversation going without invalidating the important differences that separate us, so that we can imagine and create new and better ways of living in this world.

ALTERNATIVE ETHNOGRAPHIC
AND QUALITATIVE INQUIRY

Enter narrative and what may now be called poetic social science, which represents one, not all, of the multiple forms and purposes of alternative ethnography. Ivan Brady (1991) calls the integration of anthropology and literature "art-ful science," where the beauty and tragedy of the world are textually empowered by the carefully chosen constructions and subjective understandings of the author. Here is how I see this work.

First, these are usually, but not always, narratives of the self. To a large extent, these self-narratives involve looking back at the past through the lens of the present. Given the ambiguous and open-ended quality of experience, stories give a measure of coherence and continuity that was not available at the original moment of experience. Too often, critics have seized upon this quality of personal narrative as cause to condemn the distortions of narrative, an argument that is, as Mark Freeman (1998) points out, parasitic on an empiricist account of reality. The charge of distortion is inextricably tied to the possibility of undistortion, a getting to the true bottom of things that we now recognize as untenable.

Second, the purpose of self-narratives is to extract meaning from experience rather than to depict experience exactly as it was lived. These narratives are not so much academic as they are existential, reflecting a desire to grasp or seize the possibilities of meaning, which is what gives life its imaginative and poetic qualities. The call of narrative is the inspiration to find language that is adequate to the obscurity and darkness of experience. We narrate to make sense of experience over the course of time. Thus, narrative is our means of fashioning experience in language. Narrative is true to experience in the sense that experience presents itself in a poetic dimensionality saturated with the possibilities of meaning, however perishable, momentary, and contingent.

A poetic social science does not beg the question of how to separate good narrativization from bad, though it may be more open than other views to diverse answers to the question. The simple answer provided by writers such as Freeman (1998) is that the good ones help the reader or listener to understand and feel the phenomena under scrutiny. But things are rarely that simple, so let me say what helps me understand and feel with a story, when I am asked to make such a judgment.

First, I look for abundant, concrete detail; concern not only for the commonplace, even trivial routines of everyday life, but also for the flesh and blood emotions of people coping with life's contingencies; not only facts but also feelings. Second, I am attracted to structurally complex narratives, stories told in a temporal framework that rotates between past and present reflecting the nonlinear process of memory work—the curve of time. Third, I almost always make a judgment about the author's emotional credibility, vulnerability, and honesty. I expect the author to dig at his or her actions and underneath them, displaying the self on the page, taking a measure of life's limitations, of the cultural scripts that resist transformation, of contradictory feelings, ambivalence, and layers of subjectivity, squeezing comedy out of life's tragedies. Fourth, I prefer narratives that express a tale of two selves; a believable journey from who I was to who I am, a life course reimagined or transformed by crisis. Fifth, I hold the author to a demanding standard of ethical self-consciousness. I want the writer to show concern for how other people who are part of the teller's story are portrayed, for the kind of person one becomes in telling one's story, and to provide a space for the listener's becoming, and for the moral commitments and convictions that underlie the story. Sixth, and finally, I want a story that moves me, my heart and belly as well as my head; I want a story that doesn't just refer to subjective life, but instead acts it out in ways that show me what life feels like now and what it can mean.

I am not bothered when a story borders on the pornographic because, as Laurie Stone (1997, xvii) says, "perhaps every story worth telling . . . is a dare, a kind of pornography, composed of whatever we think we're not supposed to say, for fear of being drummed out, found out, pointed out." To a certain extent, we have to work to overcome our conditioned fears of erotic knowledge. Too often, personal narratives are demeaned as some sort of victim art or confessional. What we miss when we react too quickly that way is how narrative is used as a source of empowerment and a form of resistance to counter the domination of canonical discourses. Often, the expressed purpose is to devictimize the stigmatized identity, to confirm and humanize tragic experiences by bearing witness to what it means to live with shame, abuse, addiction, or bodily dysfunction and to gain agency through testimony (Couser, 1997).

Overall, I don't find these judgments difficult to make. Philip Lopate (1994, p. xliv) refers to the personal essay as basic research on the self that ends up as, in his words, "a mode of being. It's not science; it's not philosophy. It's an existential struggle for honesty and expansion in an uncertain world." Robert Coles (1989) asks, "How to encompass in our minds the complexity of some lived moments in life?" His answer: "You don't do that with theories. You don't do that with a system of ideas. You do it with a story."

REFERENCES

Brady, I. (1991). *Anthropological poetics*. Savage, MD: Rowman & Littlefield.

Coles, R. (1989). *The call of stories: Teaching and the moral imagination*. Boston: Houghton Mifflin.

Couser, G. T. (1997). *Recovering bodies: Illness, disability, and life writing*. Madison: University of Wisconsin Press.

Freeman, M. (1993). *Rewriting the self: History, memory, narrative*. London: Routledge.

Freeman, M. (1998). Experience, narrative and the relation between them. *Narrative Inquiry, 8*, 455-466.

Geertz, C. (1980). Blurred genres: The refiguration of social thought. *The American Scholar, 49*, 165-182.

Kuhn, T. (1962). *The structure of scientific revolutions*. Chicago: University of Chicago Press.

Lopate, P. (Ed.). (1994). *The art of the personal essay: An anthology from the classical era to the present*. New York: Anchor.

Rorty, R. (1982). *Consequences of pragmatism (essays 1972-1980)*. Minneapolis: University of Minnesota Press.

Stone, L. (Ed.) (1997). *Close to the bone: Memoirs of hurt, rage and desire*. New York: Grove.

— —

Arthur P. Bochner is professor of communication and codirector of the Institute for Interpretive Human Studies at the University of South Florida. He is coauthor of Understanding Family Communication

(Allyn & Bacon) and coeditor of Composing Ethnography *(AltaMira) and of the AltaMira book series on* Ethnographic Alternatives. *He has published more than 50 articles and monographs on close relationships, communication theory, and narrative inquiry in the human sciences. His current research explores ethnographic practices in the public domain, institutional depression in higher education, and love on the Internet.*

CHAPTER 17

Writing the "Wrongs" of Fieldwork

Confronting Our Own Research/
Writing Dilemmas in Urban Ethnographies

— —

Michelle Fine
CUNY Graduate School

Lois Weis
SUNY, Buffalo

Inspired by Laurel Richardson's (1995) call for "writing stories," the authors of this essay struggle with how to produce scholarly texts drawn from narratives of over 150 poor and working-class men and women—White, African American, Latino, and Asian American. They unveil a set of knotty, emergent ethical and rhetorical dilemmas they have encountered in their attempt to write for, with, and about poor and working-class informants at a time when their lives and moralities are routinely maligned in the popular media; when the very problematic policies that may once have "assisted" them are being abandoned; and when the leverage of and audience for progressive social researchers and policy makers has grown foggy, and weak in the knees. Writing with a desire to create a conversation about ethics, writing, and qualitative research, the authors worry about the contemporary role of qualitative social researchers.

A s critical ethnographers, we have explored the perspectives that working class and poor adolescents hold about the relationships between the economy, education, families, and political action. Our major works, *Working Class Without Work* (Weis, 1990), *Between Two Worlds* (Weis, 1985), *Framing Dropouts* (Fine, 1991), *Disruptive Voices* (Fine, 1992), and *Beyond Silenced Voices* (Weis & Fine, 1993) all hold as central the social analyses narrated by low-income and working-class adolescents and young adults.

With the support of the Spencer Foundation, we are currently expanding our research to include the perspectives and practices of Latino, African American, and White young adults, ages 23 to 35, as they narrate their educational, familial, and economic biographies and project and enact their parental involvements within their communities, churches, and children's schools. Specifically, we have interviewed 150 individuals across racial and ethnic groups (men and women) in Buffalo and Jersey City, and have conducted focus group interviews with specified populations in each city to probe further their perspectives and practices, unearthing at once their despair about and envisioned opportunities for individual, community, and social change. We thus far have conducted group interviews with African American welfare- and nonwelfare-receiving mothers; Latina mothers who are probing the meaning of workfare programs in Jersey City; African American men who see the church as a way of envisioning both self and community differently from what they see as the dominant society's definition; White women who, although caught in patriarchal working-class communities, both push and accept the limitations of their female bodies and selves; and White men who patrol the borders of White masculinity, desirous of keeping all others out of what they see as their rightful position. We have assembled a rich array of interview material that will enable us both to narrate the experiences of the poor and working class during the 1980s and 1990s and to press carefully into the policy realm given our findings. We have met with and are interviewing a broad range of policymakers in both cities to explore fully the situated nature of our findings, as well as to affect broader social policy. We have testified and written Op Ed pieces on local and State policies as they affect constituents (e.g., vouchers and school takeover in Jersey City, welfare reform) and intend to do more (Weis & Fine, 1995).

Perhaps the most arrogant way to think about our project is that we aim to produce a biography of the Reagan-Bush years, as narrated by poor and working-class young adults in urban America; a more modest description would suggest that we are engaged in a two-city community study that, through the oral life histories of poor and working-class White, African American and Latino young adults, unravels the transformations in urban economic, racial, social, and domestic relations that have transpired over the past 20 years.

We are two Jewish White woman academics, trained well in the rigors of social psychology (Michelle) and sociology (Lois), experienced in the complexities of critical ethnography, who, with generous support from the Spencer Foundation and the assistance of extremely talented graduate students, are eager to traverse the borders of research, policy, activism, and theory, and are worried about what it means to do "critical work" in our provincial urban backyards just when the Right has cannibalized public discourse and when the academy has fractured amid poststructuralism and identity politics. This article may be conceptualized as an early "coming out" about some of the methodological, theoretical, and ethical issues that percolate from our fieldwork, keeping our e-mail bills high, our nights long, our essays delayed, and our commitments to social change *and* social theory swirling in ambivalence.

With this article we hope to pry open a conversation in need of public shaping. Many of the friends and colleagues with whom we have discussed some of these research/ethical dilemmas say they are relieved that someone is "saying aloud" this next generation of methodological and conceptual troubles. And yet answers evade us. With this writing we wedge open this conversation that we presumably needed, hoping that colleagues working ethnographically "in our own backyards" will engage with us in excavating the next generation of always tentative resolutions. As we write, we straddle the semifictions of empiricism and the intellectual spheres of critical theory, feminism, and poststructuralism; as we read and hear our friends (and ourselves) pleading for researchers to be critical and self-reflexive, we note that many of these same friends have long stopped collecting data; as we consume the critical literature on race and gender and ask our informants to talk about both, they keep responding, "Really I'm Black, why do you keep asking?" or, "A woman—what do you think?" We write in that space between despair and hope because we hear much of the former from our informants and whispers of the latter from the same and because that is the space within which we can live. Yes, structures oppress, but we *must* have hope that things can be better.

We speak now because we worry that many of us are simply studying the apocalypse to cope with it, as one more piece of the sky falls. This article represents a concrete analysis in the midst of what Michelle has called "working the hyphen."

> Much of qualitative research has reproduced, if contradiction-filled, a colonizing discourse of the "Other." This essay is an attempt to review how qualitative research projects have *Othered* and to examine an emergent set of activist and/or postmodern texts that interrupt *Othering.* First, I examine the hyphen at which Self-Other join in the politics of everyday life, that is, the hyphen that both separates and merges personal identities with our inventions of Others. I then take up how qualitative researchers work this hyphen... through a messy series of questions about methods, ethics, and epistemologies as we rethink how researchers have spoken "of" and "for" Others while occluding ourselves and our own investments, burying the contradictions that percolate at the Self-Other hyphen. (Fine, 1994, p. 70)

This article, then, offers up our questions/dilemmas/concerns as we grapple with what it means to be in the midst of a study that attempts to work across many borders, always searching for ways to "work the hyphen." We take our cue from Richardson (1995, p. 191), who invites what she calls "writing-stories":

> With the poststructural understanding that the social context affects what we write, we have an opportunity—perhaps even an ethical duty—to extend our reflexivity to the study of our writing practices. We can reflect on and share with other researchers what I think of as writing-stories, or stories about how we came to construct the particular texts we did. These might be of the verification kind, or they might be more subjective—accounts of how contexts, social interactions, critiques, review processes, friendships, academic settings, departmental politics, embodiedness, and so on have affected the construction of the text. Rather than hiding the struggle, concealing the very human labor

that creates the text, writing-stories would reveal emotional, social, physical, and political bases of the labor.

ECHOES (AND ACHES) IN OUR HEAD

On community. Perhaps our most vexing dilemma at the moment concerns the question "What constitutes community?" How do we write about communities in which we find little sense of shared biography or vision? We write "as if" the contours of geography or a standard metropolitan statistical area adequately define the boundaries of these two "communities." Coherence organizes life within, whereas difference defines life between.

And yet we recognize from our theoretical interests, confirmed by the narratives we've collected, that piercing fractures define life within communities and some pronounced similarities emerge across the two cities. Internal geographic coherence seems a naive fiction, whereas blunt cross-community contrasts seem deceptively polarized.

Simple demographic fractures, by race/ethnicity, gender, class, generation, and sexuality marble inside each city. Within local neighborhoods or racial/ethnic groups, gender, sexuality, and generational divisions boldly sever what may appear at first glance to be internal continuities.

For instance, within presumably the same community, African Americans will refer to local police with stories of harassment and fear, whereas Whites are far more likely to complain about a rise in crime and brag about a brother-in-law who's a cop. Parallel dynamics can be found in both Jersey City and Buffalo.

Likewise, from within the same households we hear White working-class women describe growing up in families with much childhood exposure to alcohol and abuse, whereas comparably situated White men—raised in the very same homes and neighborhoods—are virtually silent on these topics. Again, the parallels across the two cities have been striking.

Jersey City Whites describe "good old days" of economic security and pine for the day when they'll be moving to Bayonne, whereas African Americans harbor few wistful memories of good old days and try to avoid "getting stopped at red lights" in Bayonne, lest their stay be extended beyond what they expected.

At historic moments of job security and economic hard times, the presumed harmony of working-class/poor communities is ravaged by interior splits, finger pointing, blame, and suspicion. Coalitions are few, even if moments of interdependence for survival are frequent. Within homes, differences and conflicts explode across gender and generations. A full sense of community is fictional and fragile, ever vulnerable to external threats and internal fissures. A sense of coherence prevails only if our methods fail to interrogate difference. And at the same time, commonalities *across* cities—by demography and biography—are all the more striking.

So, for the moment in our writing, we script a story in which we float a semifictional portrait of each community, layered over with an analytic matrix of differences "within." For our analysis—within and between cities— we delicately move between coherence and difference, fixed boundaries and porous borders, neighborhoods of shared values and homes of contentious interpretations.

On "race." As with community, race emerges in our data as both an un- stable and an enduring aspect of biography. Gates (1985) has written beautifully about race, always using quotes; Dyson (1993) argues against narrow nationalistic or essentialist definitions for either skin color or language; Hall (1981) narrates the contextual instability of racial identities. Like these theorists, our informants are sometimes quite muddy, other times quite clear, about race. Indeed, some of our informants, like the one below, suggest that race constitutes inherently undefinable territory. This is not a narrative of denial as much as it is one of complexity.

Question: Your dad?
Answer: Yes, my dad was the craziest Puerto Rican you had ever seen in the 70's. Oh my Lord.
Q: What is your mom's background?
A: Mom, Mom was raised Catholic, but in my mother's days, when an Irish and German woman went with a Chinese guy, in those days that was like, oh no, no that cannot happen. My grandfa-

ther had to drop his whole family for my grandmother, so they
could be together. Everybody disowned him in this family.

Q: Because he married a—

A: Yeah, he married my grandmother.

Q: What about your mom's side?

A: That is my mom's side.

Q: What about your grandfather's side?

A: My grandfather, he was in Vietnam, World War II, oh, I forgot
the name. It was a very big war, that I know.

Q: Korean War?

A: Yeah, something like that, I just can't remember what it was.
Yeah, he had honors and everything my mother told me.

Q: So you looked very different?

A: Yeah, I'm a mixture.

Q: You have Chinese blood?

A: Right. I got Irish and German, I got Puerto Rican and Italian, I
have a lot. I'm a mixed breed.

Q: I was wondering. The first time I saw you I thought you were
from the Middle East.

A: From the Middle East?

Q: Yeah.

A: Oh, golly gee, no. I'm, like, really mixed. I'm like everything. I
got all these different personalities that just come out all the
time. I swear to God. No lie. No lie.

When we began our interviews in Jersey City and Buffalo, we were
well influenced by poststructural thinking on questions of race. With
Hall (1981) particularly in mind, and willing to acknowledge the arti-
ficiality, the performances, and, indeed, the racist roots of the notion
of race (1/32nd drop of blood, etc.), we constructed an interview pro-
tocol that generously invited our informants to "play" with race as we
had. So we asked them, in many clever ways, to describe time-/con-
text-specific racial identifications—when they fill out census forms,
walk through supermarkets, when alone or among friends. By the
third hour, informants of color, trying to be polite, grew exasperated
with these questions. White folks were sure we were calling them racist, or they went on about being Irish, Italian, human—never White.
Needless to say, the "playfulness" of the questions didn't work.

We don't mean to retreat now to a simplistic formulation by which we declare that race is more "real" than critical race theory suggests. Indeed, our data give much support for reasserting a floating sense of race—one always braided with gender, generation, biography, and class. Yet, reading the narratives, it's hard to miss entrenched, raced patterns of daily life. Most White respondents *say* they don't think much about race; most people of color wish they weren't reminded of their race—via harassment, discrimination, and on-the-street stares—quite so often. Many argue that race *shouldn't* make much of a difference. Yet the life stories as narrated are so thoroughly raced that readers of the transcript can't not know even an "anonymous" informant's racial group. Personal stories of violence and family structure, narrative style, one's history with money, willingness to trash (and leave) men and marriages, access to material resources, relations with kin and the State, and descriptions of interactions with the police are all profoundly narrated through race, fluid though it is.

Race is a place in which poststructuralism and lived realities need to talk. Race is a social construction, indeed. But race in a racist society bears profound consequence for daily life, identity, social movements, and the ways in which most groups "other." DuBois noted that race was the dividing line for the 20th century. He may have been a two-century prophet.

But how we write about race in our work worries us. Do we take the category for granted, as if it were unproblematic? Do we problematize it theoretically, well knowing its full-bodied impact on daily life? Reflecting on our writings thus far, we seem to lean toward theorizing for and about Whites who deny they have a race, whereas we offer much more open latitude around the voices of people of color who articulate their thoroughly embodied experiences within race. We try to construct theoretical structures of racial formations, borrowing from Omi and Winant (1986), recognizing that Whiteness requires—indeed, creates—Blackness in order to see the self as moral, hard working, family-oriented, a good citizen. We give lots of room to those who define themselves with multiple roots and at varied hyphens. We envy and resent colleagues who have stopped collecting data because they have done such a marvelous job of complicating that which actually doesn't feel so complicated to our informants. Yes, race *is* a social construction, but it's so deeply confounded with racism that it has enormous power in people's lives. We can't simply problematize it away as if it does not really exist. To the informants with whom we spoke, race does exist—it saturates every pore of their lives. How can we destabilize the notion theoretically, while recognizing the lived presence of race?

Here are some trivial but telling examples. One problem that may appear, at face value, to be a "sampling problem" related to race, involves our struggle to find "equally poor" and "equally working-class" African American, Latino, and White young adults in both cities, so that comparisons by race/ethnicity would not be compounded by class. Guess what? The world is lousy with confounds. Although we found poor and working-class Whites, the breadth and depth of their cross-generational poverty was nowhere near as severe as in the African American sample.

White informants were sometimes as well off as, but were more often slightly worse off than, their parents. But—and here's the *unacknowledged* impact of 1940s' and 1950s' U.S. federal subsidies for the White working class/middle class—these young adults often had access to a small house or apartment that their parents were able to buy, a small nest egg of cash the family had squirreled away, or a union-based pension that Dad had saved up. In contrast, our African American and Latino informants are in very tough financial straits but are not, for the most part, worse off than their parents. Their parents rarely had a home, a small stash of monies, or pensions that they could pass on. Further, some of our African American and Latino informants who have amassed small amounts of capital over time lost it at some point when someone in the extended family had a health crisis, a housing crisis, or a problem with the law.

Despite our meticulous combing of raced neighborhoods, our ambitious search for sampling comparability lost, hands down, to the profound "lived realities" of multigenerational poverty disproportionately affecting poor and working-class families of color. What may appear to be a methodological problem has been revealed as constitutive of the very fabric of society. Problematizing race alone does not help us confront the very real costs and privileges of racial categorization.

"Bad data." Moving from worries of epistemology to worries about data, we excavate more headaches:

> Q: Do you feel that your word is not trusted, that you need some-
> one else to say, you need a lawyer or psychiatrist to say every-
> thing is okay now?
> A: Because of DYFS [Division for Youth and Family Services], yes.
> Q: But you can't have . . .
> A: They won't, yeah. They won't just take you for your word, no.
> You need to have. . .
> Q: You need to have somebody else say that for you?
> A: Yes. DYFS, yes.
> Q: How would DYFS treat your kids, though?
> A: Because when you get child, they say I put their life in danger,
> because I did, but I was . . . I was in jail, I was in the psychiatric
> ward. They had to do the best interest for the children, I couldn't
> take care of them at the time.
> Q: Oh, so DYFS took your kids?
> A: Yeah, so DYFS gave them to their father. I'm in court now.
> Q: At least it's not foster care, though.
> A: That's what I said. They're with family. They might hate it there,
> they can't stand it. My kids say that they're treated worse.
> Q: They hate their father?
> A: No, they don't hate their father, they hate their grandmother,
> they hate the mother-in-law, they hate their grandmother. They
> don't like their grandmother.
> Q: George's mother?
> A: Yeah, they don't like their aunts, their uncles.
> Q: They are a lot of Puerto Ricans?
> A: They're all Puerto Ricans, but my kids were always like the out-
> casts because they didn't like me so my kids, my kids, I mean,
> George was 7 years old, 7 years of George's life, George had to
> have seen his grandmother six times. Nicole, in the 3 years of her
> life, never seen them. You know, my kids got dumped into a
> family that they know nothing about.

What does it mean to uncover some of what we have uncovered? How do we handle "hot" information, especially in times when poor and working-class women and men are being demonized by the Right and by Congress? How do we connect troubling social/familial patterns with macrostructural shifts when our informants *expressly don't* make the connections? The hegemony of autonomous individualism forces a self-conscious theorizing of data— especially "bad data"—well beyond the consciousness expressed by most of our informants. So, for instance, what do we do with information about the ways in which women on welfare virtually have to become welfare cheats ("Sure he comes once a month and gives me some money. I may have to take a beating, but the kids need the money.") to survive? A few use more drugs than we wish to know; most are wonderful parents but some underattend to their children well beyond neglect. These are the dramatic consequences, and perhaps also the "facilitators," of hard economic times. To ignore the data is to deny the effects. To report the data is to risk their likely misinterpretation.

In a moment in history when there are few audiences willing to reflect on the complex social roots of community and domestic violence and the impossibility of sole reliance on welfare, or even to appreciate the complexity, love, hope, and pain that fills the poor and working class, how do we display the voyeuristic dirty laundry that litters our database? At the same time, how can we risk romanticizing or denying the devastating impact of the current assault on poor and working-class families launched by the State, the economy, neighbors, and sometimes kin?

Because of our early questions about both perspectives and representations, the interview schedule was originally created using input from a group of activists and policy makers of varying racial and ethnic backgrounds from Jersey City and Buffalo who were working with the research teams. Many questions were inserted to satisfy local concerns, for example, questions about police harassment, welfare reform and its effects on children born to women on welfare, state takeover of school, and so on. Nevertheless, with data collection over and analysis now under way, we continue to struggle with how best to represent treacherous data—data that may do more damage than good, depending on who consumes/exploits them, data about the adult consequences of child physical and sexual abuse, data suggesting that it is almost impossible to live exclusively on welfare payments (encouraging many to lie about their incomes so that they feel

they are welfare cheats), data in which White respondents, in particular, portray people of color in gross and dehumanizing ways, and data
on the depth of violence in women's lives across race/ethnicity.

We spend much time reading through the *Handbook of Qualitative
Research* (Denizen & Lincoln, 1994), Gregory's (1993) ethnographies of
Queens, Scheper-Hughes's (1992) analysis of mothering in pov-
erty-stricken communities of Brazil, Connell's (1994) representations
of White male identity formation in Australia, M. E. Dyson's
Reflecting Black (1993), and rereading Gwaltney's *Drylongso* (1980) and
Ladner's *Tomorrow's Tomorrow* (1971) to reflect on how to best write
authentically and critically about the narratives offered, in ways that
serve communities, theory, and public policy. We present these as
dilemmas with which all field-workers must currently struggle.
There is nothing straightforward or objective about reporting *or* with-
holding these data. Each strategic decision of scholarship bears theoretical, ethical, and political consequences.

On the mundane. Sticking with dilemmas of data, we turn now to
questions about mundane details of daily life.

> Well, I take . . . I get $424 a month, okay? And I get $270 in food stamps,
> so I take . . . there's four weeks to a month, so I take . . . I take the $270 and
> I divide it by four. And that's what I spend on food. It's just me and my
> daughters. And my oldest don't eat that much and I don't eat . . . I only
> eat once a day. I only eat dinner. I'm not hungry in the morning and I
> don't have breakfast. I have a cup of coffee or hot chocolate. My little
> one is the one that eats a lot. And whatever I don't . . . like I spend $65 a
> week in food. I go and I buy meat every day and I buy their breakfast,
> their lunch, her snacks for school. And whenever I can . . . I work at
> night . . . I work . . . if I get a call I go and clean somebody's house. I do
> that. Their father gives me money, you know. So I do whatever I . . . you
> know, whatever it takes, you know? Shovel your snow . . . [laughs] I
> don't care. You know, to me money's money, as long as your kids got
> what they need. But basically their father helps me the most. You know,
> he'll come in . . . oh, my dad does this, too, and I get really pissed off at
> him. He'll come in and he'll start looking through my cabinets and in
> my refrigerator, and my closet. "Well, what do you have here?" And it's

like, "I'm fine. Johnny's coming over later." "No! Blah, blah, blah." And he'll go out and he'll come back with food, and their father's always coming in looking through the refrigerator, and things like that, you know? I always . . . my kids have food, so that's good, you know? They never go hungry. You know, I . . . I hate to say this, but if I had . . . I mean, if it came to where my kids were gonna go hungry, I'd sell my body. To hell with that! My kids ain't gonna starve, you know? I'd do what it takes. I would give two shits. People could . . . my friends could tell me whatever they wanted. I have a . . . I have two friends that sell their bodies for money for their kids. And thank God, I have to knock on wood, I never had to do that. But I mean, if I had to, I would. If that's what it took to feed my kids . . . I mean, if their father . . . a lot of people that are on welfare have husbands worth shit. They don't care. If they had a father, but I guess that's, if that's what it took . . . I would try every aspect before doing that. But if that's what it really took to feed my kids, that's what I would do. I would do whatever it takes to feed and clothe my kids, you know, and put a roof over their head. I wouldn't care what the hell it was. I guess that's what I would do, you know?

These are the dull and spicy details of negotiating daily life in poverty. When we (researchers) listen to and read narratives, we tend (with embarrassment) to be drawn to—in fact, to *code for*—the exotic, the bizarre, the violent. As we reflect, though, we nevertheless feel obligated to explore meticulously the very tedious sections of the transcripts: those sections not very sexy, exciting, or eroticizing, like when the informants walk their kids to school, read the newspaper in horror, turn on the television for a break, look for a doctor they can trust, hope their children are safe on the way home from school. These rituals of daily living—obviously made much more difficult in the presence of poverty and discrimination, but mundane nonetheless—are typically left out of ethnographic descriptions of life in poverty. They don't make very good reading, and yet are the stuff of daily life. We recognize how carefully we need to *not* construct life narratives spiked only with the hot spots . . . like surfing our data for sex and violence.

On safe spaces. In contrast to bad—or even mundane—data, over time we have collected data on those contexts carved out by young adults in which they try to survive, with sanity, the depletion of the public sector. These are data on "safe spaces" that young adults have created to make sense of the insane worlds in which they live. Some of these safe spaces don't actually appear (to us) to be so safe or legal. Others are private and serene, filled with the incense of spirituality, belief in God, the language of social movements and nationalism, the daily coalitions of cross-racial/ethnic people trying to keep their neighborhoods safe. These spaces are delicious and fragile, but not entirely open to surveillance. They seek to be private.

In our first Spencer study, we heard from young women and men who survived in the working-class and poor segments of our society, how they viewed economic opportunities, how they would spin images of their personal and collective futures, especially as related to the power of schooling, how they conceptualized the shrinking public sector, economy, labor, and the military, and how they reflected upon progressive social movements that have historically and dramatically affected their ancestors' and their own chances in life. With respect to policies allegedly written for the poor and working class, our data enable us for the first time to hear from them. We have discovered pockets of possibility excavated by these young men and women, pockets that we desperately need to explore further. Amid their despair lies hope, and hope is cultivated in these safe spaces.

It would be profoundly irresponsible to argue that these working-class and poor women and men are simply depressed, despairing, and isolated, with no sense of possibility. As much as our individual interviews did suggest this at times, our focus groups alerted us that much else is happening. These young women and men are "homesteading"—finding unsuspected places within and across geographic communities, public institutions, and spiritual lives—to sculpt real and imaginary spaces for peace, struggle, and personal and collective identity work. These spaces offer recuperation, resistance, and the makings of "home." They are not just a set of geographic/spatial arrangements, but theoretical, analytical, and spatial displacements—a crack, a fissure in an organization or a community. Individual dreams, collective work, and critical thoughts are smuggled in and then reimagined. Not rigidly bounded by walls/fences, these spaces often are corralled by a series of (imaginary) borders where community intrusion and state surveillance are not permitted. These are spaces where trite social stereotypes are fiercely contested. That is, these young women and men—in constantly confronting harsh public representations of their race/ethnicity, class, gender, and sexuality—use these spaces to break down these public images for scrutiny and invent new ones.

These spaces include the corners of the African American church, where young men huddle over discussions of how to "take back the streets" to "save the young boys"; the Lesbian and Gay Center, carved out quietly by working-class late adolescents and young adults who are seeking identities and networks when their geographic and cultural contexts deny them sexual expression; the Headstart and Effective Parenting Information for Children (EPIC) programs in which poor mothers, and sometimes fathers, come together to talk over the delights and minefields of raising children in a culture permeated with racism and decimated by poverty; the cultural arts programs where men and women join self-consciously across racial and ethnic borders to create what is "not yet," a space, a set of images, a series of aesthetic products that speak of a world that could be.

Spaces such as these spring from the passions and concerns of community members; they are rarely structured from "above." They may be a onetime fiction, transitory or quite stable. They can be designed to restore identities devastated by the larger culture or they may be opportunities to flirt with identities and communities rejected by both mainstream culture and local ethnic groups. These spaces provide rich and revealing data about the resilience of young adults without denying the oppression that threatens the borders and interiors of community life amid urban poverty.

These "free spaces" (Boyte & Evans, 1992) are rarely studied by social scientists. We typically enter people's lives and communities and ask them the questions that titillate us, creating "unfree spaces." As Keith and Pile (1993) argue, by asking questions of "arbitrary closure," social scientists fail to see the world as it unfolds and is reshaped by community members across "spacialities" and time. Typically, social sciences fix (our) gaze on public (or private) programs that are offered to low-income adults. Then we collect evidence of their noninvolvement—laziness, resistance, helplessness. But we now know, as Brice-Heath and McLaughlin (1993) have documented, that there is a rich underground to community life that is vibrant and fundamentally self-created. These are spaces designed by and for community, into which we, after 3 years of interviewing in Buffalo and Jersey City, have been invited. They may be transitory, healing, and mobilizing. They may be official or absolutely ad hoc. They may be a way to reconstitute traditional culture, racial, gender, or sexual identities, or they may be contexts in which individuals cross borders of race, ethnicity, gender, and sexuality to find a small corner in which to breathe in peace. These free spaces, of which we have only glimmers, have raised questions that need attention. When should these data about private/free spaces float into public view? Does the public/private distinction need to be problematized, as Gubrium and Holstein (1995) have argued?

Foucault (1979) has written on the invasive stretch of surveillance, typically pointing at state institutions. Here we deploy the same notion to self-reflexively point at ourselves, social scientists, surveilling the safe cubbyholes of community life. Legitimately one may ask (and some have) whether we have any business floating through, writing about these sequestered quarters. Do our Whiteness, our femaleness, our class status, our staccato appearances adversely affect or interrupt the music of life within free spaces? Does our social scientific voyeurism shatter the sanctity of that which is presumably (although recognizably *not*) free?

We respond to this question, for the moment at least, by presenting two different incidents. One occurred in a basement office in which New Jersey community activists meet to discuss local politics. We were welcomed for the initial interview, but the notion of our sustained presence clearly provoked discomfort. Not asked to return, we left. Elsewhere, and surprisingly more typically, we have been invited into spaces in which members, directors, and others indicate they are eager for documentation, anxious for others to know who they really are, what functions the programs serve, how deeply spiritual and religious "those teenage mothers" can be, how organized and supportive "those gays and lesbians" are. In these latter cases, informants have welcomed us into their spaces to exploit our capacity and willingness to write and to testify to those aspects of community life that the straight media ignore, that trenchant stereotypes deny, that mainstream culture rarely gets to see. Our rights, responsibilities, and relationships influence how (and if) we have access to these spaces.

There is another version of social science surveillance that has recently haunted us, and that is the process by which social scientists—in this case, feminist social scientists—reframe private experiences as social troubles. Taking the lead from Mills (1959) and many since, we see it as our responsibility to move from narratives to theories of social dynamics that operate amid macrostructures, relationships, and communities to produce life as lived, even if this is not life as analyzed in the narratives of our interviewees.

Take the case of domestic violence, particularly among White working-class women, those still in what are considered stable, intact marriages but who are nevertheless being beaten at rates comparable to the women more explicitly living in less stable home environments. We have accumulated substantial evidence to suggest that women in both kinds of environments experience extraordinarily high levels of domestic abuse, and yet women in the seemingly stable homes rarely talk about it, refuse to critique the violence, and rarely question the role of men or their actions. They wouldn't call it abuse—should we?

In this work, we have been collaborating with two students, Amira Proweller and Corrine Bertram, on a domestic violence paper centered on the voices of brutalized and silenced working-class White women. Now what? Is this just a theoretical exercise in which we report narrations of denial? Or do we theorize *over* their voices, giving us little reason for collecting their stories?

There are lots of academics writing about these things, but few are really grappling with trying to meld *writing about* and *working with* activists within these communities (for such work, see Austin, 1992; Lykes, 1989, 1994; Weiss & Greene, 1992). We try to work with communities and activists to figure out how to say what needs to be said without jeopardizing individuals or presenting a universal problem as though it were particular to this class. And yet, cracking their silence—especially among White working-class women who are exceedingly reluctant to discuss or reveal, lest the ideology of domestic family life crumble and their role as savior of the family be exposed—is a feminist and intellectual responsibility fraught with dilemmas.

On self-reflexivity. We have certainly read much, and even written a fair amount, about researchers' subjectivities (Fine, 1994). Our obligation is to come clean "at the hyphen," meaning that we interrogate in our writings who *we* are as we coproduce the narratives we presume to collect. It is now acknowledged that we, as critical ethnographers, have a responsibility to talk about our own identities, why we interrogate what we do, what we choose not to report, on whom we train our scholarly gaze, who is protected and *not* protected as we do our work. As part of this discussion, we want to try to explain how we, as researchers, (can) work *with* communities to capture and build upon community and social movements. In other words, we will put forward parts of our ever-evolving political agenda, sharing the kinds of scholarship/action upon which we are focusing. We draw from our past work to illuminate what's possible "at the hyphens" of researcher and researched (Fine, 1994), and what feels impossible.

Thus far, in Jersey City and Buffalo, we have been able to document how state policies and local economic/social shifts have affected young women's and men's belief systems, world views, and social consciousness. Through individual interviews we have gathered much of these data. Through the focus groups (e.g., in the Lesbian and Gay Club, the African American and White churches, the EPIC parenting group, the Latina homeless shelter, the Pre-Cap college prep program for young adolescents), we have been able to encourage settings in which our interviewees have begun to weave together analyses that weren't entirely formed, to begin to piece together their commitments, for instance, to the "next generation of African American boys," or to "practice the ways of grandmother" around Latina spiritual rituals. Sister Kristin from the York Street Project and Dolores Perry from Head Start have both invited us to work more closely with groups of women and men in their programs, running focus groups that would raise questions, press issues, and help the participants reshape programs. In the EPIC group, we were told that the engagement of several members increased due to our kind of individual and group work. Indeed, Lois Weis was asked to facilitate an EPIC group on a long-term basis. The group interviews offered these women a way of piecing together the strengths of their lives, encouraging forward movement as they were raising their families in the midst of poverty.

Further, throughout the course of our 3 years of research, we have moved across the researcher-researched hyphen to apply our work toward support of local policy and community efforts. Michelle Fine has testified at state hearings on the state takeover of the local schools, advocating with community groups that the state remain in control until local participation can be encouraged and sustained. Research assistant Mun Wong coordinated a project among women on welfare who were eager to document the differential supermarket prices of similar items at different points in the month and in different markets in the community. We have provided census and qualitative data to city council members from the Latino community. Lois Weis supplied testimony in support of continual funding for EPIC and will be trained as an EPIC facilitator. Across communities, numerous conversations have taken place with key policy makers on a number of issues arising from our data.

We take for granted that the purpose of social inquiry in the 1990s is not only to generate new knowledge but to inform critically public policies, existent social movements, and daily community life. A commitment to such application, however, should not be taken for granted. This is a(nother) critical moment in the life of the social sciences, one in which individual scholars are making moral decisions about the extent to which our work should aim to be useful. Distinct camps are lining up with arrows poised.

We have colleagues who embrace the commitment to application, as we do, even if some think it is naive to imagine being able to infiltrate current policy talk on life within poor and working-class communities. Other colleagues have long seen their own scholarship as explicitly aimed toward political and social change (see Gittell, 1990, 1994; Lykes, 1989, 1994; Mullings, 1984; Piven, Block, Cloward, & Ehrenreich, 1987; Piven & Cloward, 1971, 1977; Powell, 1994). And we hear a growing chorus of colleagues who presume that if you are interested in policy and/or social practice, your data are thereby less trustworthy. This latter position was in retreat for perhaps a moment in time, but it seems to be returning to the academy in well-orchestrated volume. We do, of course, reject this position, but would ask again that academics who see this work as deeply nested in community life (recognizing that the notion of community is up for grabs) come together to argue cogently our responses to the following questions: Is this science? Is *only* progressive work biased? Is this politics or policy? And, to probe fundamentally, where are the sites of intellectual leverage by which our work can begin to fissure public and political discourse? That said, we take our responsibilities to these communities seriously, and are educating our graduate students to work with—not on or despite—local community efforts.

Throughout the design, the doing, and the interpretation of our fieldwork, we talk and write about the anxieties (many of which are represented in this article), struggles, passions, and pains. But we ask now, *how much* of our relatively privileged lives do we insert into essays when we chronicle lives under assault from the economy, the state, and within communities and even homes? Yes, *we* write the stories, we determine the questions, we hide some of the data, and we cry over interviews. But self-conscious insertion of self remains an exhilarating, problematic, sometimes narcissistic task. What more can we say than that we are two White Jewish women deeply committed to a better world? The poststructuralist question of "who are we?" is an important one indeed, but what does that mean as we weave together lives of passion, pain, and assault? A narcissistic look at self seems misplaced here. Whiting ourselves out seems equally wrong-headed.

So, in whose voice? Mark, a White working-class informant, tells us:

> It goes into another subject where Blacks, um, I have nothing against Blacks. Um, whether you're Black, White, you know, yellow, whatever color, whatever race. But I don't like the Black movement where, I have Black friends. I talk to them and they agree. You know, they consider themselves, you know, there's White trash and there's White, and there's Black trash and there's Blacks. And the same in any, you know, race. But as soon as they don't get a job, they right away call, you know, they yell discrimination.

In whose voice do we write? Well, of course, our own. But we also present long narratives, colorful with/from informants in our scholarly and more popular presentations, essays, and articles. Some of these narratives, particularly from "Angry White Men," contain hostile or grotesque references to "others"—people of color, police, men on the corner. As theorists, we refrain from the naive belief that these voices should stand on their own, or that voices should survive without theorizing. However, we also find ourselves *differentially theorizing and contextualizing* voices. That is, those voices that have been historically smothered—voices of White women, and men and women of color—we typically present on their own terms, perhaps reluctant, as White academic women, to surround them with much of our theory. And yet, when we present the voices of White men who seem eminently expert at blaming African American men for all their pain and plight, we theorize generously, contextualize wildly, rudely interrupting them to reframe them.

Is this an epistemological double standard in need of reform, or is it a form of narrative affirmative action, creating discursive spaces where few have been in the past? Hurtado and Stewart (in press), in a new and fascinating essay on Whiteness and feminist methods, argue that feminist scholars should self-consciously *underplay* (i.e., not quote extensively) hegemonic voices in their essays and relentlessly create textual room for counterhegemonic narratives. Although we agree, we also think it is vitally important to critically analyze what it is White men are saying about us, about themselves, about economic and social relations. To do this, we interpret their words, their stories, their assertions about others.

All of this raises what we have come to think of as the "triple representational problem." In our texts we ponder how we present (a) *ourselves* as researchers choreographing the narratives we have collected; (b) the *narrators*, many of whom are wonderful social critics, whereas some (from our perspective) are talented ventriloquists for a hateful status quo; and (c) the *others* who are graphically bad-mouthed by these narrators (e.g., caseworkers blamed by women on welfare for stinginess; African American men held responsible for all social evils by White men; police held in contempt by communities of color that have survived much abuse at the hands of police). Do we have a responsibility to theorize the agency/innocence/collusion of these folks, too? When White men say awful things about women of color, do we need to re-present women of color, denounce and re-place these representations? If not, are we not merely contributing to the archival representations of disdain that the social science literature has so horrifically chronicled?

Because all of these groups deserve to be placed within historical and social contexts, and yet power differences and abuses proliferate, how do theorists respect the integrity of informants' consciousness and narratives, place them within social and historical context, and yet not collude or dignify this perverse denigration of people of color? In what seems like too shallow a resolution, we have diversified our research teams, hired local activists and community members when appropriate to consult with us on design and interpretation, and read endlessly in an effort to get out of these boxes. However, these issues are *not* being raised by those in the field. We notice, perhaps defensively, that many of our friends and colleagues who now write on critical ethnography are writing about theory and methods, but not through data. Critical work on representations, poststructuralism, and ethnography has taken many of our once-in-the-field colleagues up and out, looking down now (as we have been wont to do) on a set of dilemmas that have nasty colonial pasts and precarious futures. Those of us still in the field, on the ground, so to speak, worry through this set of issues in highly concrete ways. We worry with no immediate resolution and only rare conversations. We know, though, that these points must be considered.

There are no easy answers to these dilemmas. In each of the essays we have produced thus far, we have tried to contextualize the narratives as spoken within economic, social, and racial contexts so that no one narrator is left holding the bag for his/her demographic group, but there are moments within the narratives when "others"—people of color, case workers, men, women, the neighbor next door—are portrayed in very disparaging ways. We also struggle with *representation*, working hard to figure out how to represent and contextualize our narrators, ourselves, and the people about whom they are ranting. Under the tutelage of historians Scott (1992) and Katz (1995) and psychologist Cross (1991), we try to understand how and why these categories of analysis, these "others," and these accusations are being cast at this moment in history, and who is being protected by this "scope of blame" (Opotow, 1990). At times, however, audiences have nevertheless been alarmed at the language in our texts, at the vivid descriptions and the portraits. We are working on these issues, and welcome help from others who are also struggling with both theory and empirical data.

When method and voice meet. We have noticed in the midst of analysis that the data produced vary by method collected. Methods are not passive strategies. They differentially produce, reveal, and enable the display of different kinds of identities. To be more specific, if individual interviews produce the most despairing stories, evince the most minimal sense of possibility, present identities of victimization, and voice stances of hopelessness, in focus groups with the same people the despair begins to evaporate, a sense of possibility sneaks through, and identities multiply as informants move from worker to mother, to friend, to lover, to sister, to spiritual healer, to son, to fireman, to once-employed, to welfare recipient. In the context of relative safety, trust, comfort, and counterhegemonic creativity offered by the few free spaces into which we have been invited, a far more textured and less judgmental sense of self is displayed. In these like-minded communities that come together to trade despair and build hope, we see and hear a cacophony of voices filled with spirit, possibility, and a sense of vitality absent in the individual data.

We make this point because we have stumbled again upon an issue that may appear to be methodological but is deeply substantive and ethical. Both psychology and education have depended religiously upon methods of individual surveys, interviews, observations, and so on, at the cost of not seeing or hearing collectives. If, as we postulate, collectives are more likely to generate stories of possibility and hope, then perhaps we have a social science, painted in despair, that is as much a methodological artifact as it is a condition of daily life in poor communities.

On a disappearing public sphere. Tamara explains:

> I didn't want to be with the father of my children anymore. And at that time he really gave me a lot of headaches. "If you don't stay with me, then I'm not gonna help you with the kids." Which he really didn't do, which I'm thankful. But I just figured, "Well, the hell with it. Then I'll work . . . get the welfare." Because I pay $640 for this apartment. That's a lot of money for a two-bedroom apartment, you know? And the wel-

fare only gives me $424, so I have to make up the difference. And plus I have a telephone, you know. I have cable for my daughters, you know. And it's just a lot of money. And I figure, you know, I figured, well, I couldn't make it on my own. I wasn't making enough to make it on my own back then, so I had to go on welfare. So I did it, and it was . . . I didn't like it. I didn't like sitting there. I didn't like the waiting. I didn't like the questions they asked me, you know?

Q: What kind of questions did. . .

A: Well, they asked me if I was sexually active, how many times I went to bed with him, you know? And I told the guy, "I'm sorry, but that is none of your business" and I refuse to answer the questions. Because to me, well what, they ask you if you, he asked me if I slept with Black men or White men, Puerto Rican men. What was my preference. And to me that was the questions. . .

Q: Was this on a form, or he. . .

A: No, he was just asking questions, you know? And I refused to answer them, you know. And he kind of like got upset. "We have to ask you this." I was like, "bullshit." You know, they just wanted to, they asked, he asked me how many times I had sex in a day, and just really, you know, if I douched, if I was clean, if I took a shower. I don't think these are any of your business, you know? I take a shower every night and every day, you know? I think those are stupid questions he asked. I was, he asked me how many men I had in my life that I had, you know, if I have more than one man. And I turned around and told him, "I'm not your mother." I never heard of questions like. . . [laughs]

Q: Neither have I. [laughs]

A: They asked the weird questions.

Q: So, how, what was the procedure like?

A: It was embarrassing. Like, with Medicaid, for kids it's good. For kids, you know, you can go anywhere you want with the Medicaid. You can go to the doctors for kids. You know, they pay for braces. When it comes to an adult, I was going to, I was hemorrhaging. I was going to a doctor. I'd been bleeding since December, okay, and they're telling me, I've been going to a gynecologist through the welfare. "It's normal, it's normal. Don't worry about it. It's normal." So last week I was getting ready, for the past week I was feeling really dizzy and really weak, and I said the hell with it. Let me go see a gynecologist. And I paid her. Thank God, you know, the Medicaid took care of the hospital. But I had to pay her $700 for the procedure that I had to have done. [laughs] I had to do it. It was either that or bleed to death, you know. [laughs] But a lot of doctors, I asked her, because she used to take Medicaid. And I asked her, "Why don't you, you know, take Medicaid anymore?" And a lot of doctors that don't, doctors tell you because they don't pay them. She said she's been waiting for people that were on Medicaid to get paid for two years, three years, bills that's how old the bills are and she's still waiting to get paid.

For the past 3 years we have collected data on communities, economic and racial relationships, and individual lives deeply affected by public policies and institutions that rotted many years before. And yet these very same public policies and institutions about which we have deeply incriminating data are today disappearing, yanked away from communities as we write. Public schools, welfare, social services, public housing—defunded. Positioning a critique of the public sphere as it evaporates or, more aptly, as it has disappeared, seems an academic waste of time; worse, it anticipates collusion with the Right.

Our responsibility in this work, as we see it (and if it is doable), is *not* to feed the dismantling of the State by posing a critique of the public sector as it has been, but instead to insist on a State that serves its citizenry well and equitably. That is, social researchers must create vision and imagination for what could be, and demand the resurrection of a public sphere that has a full and participatory citizenship at its heart. Then we can layer on the critiques of what has been. That said, it's not so easy when Speaker of the House Newt Gingrich is just waiting to use our narrative words to do away with welfare; when Brett Schundler, mayor of Jersey City, is foaming at the mouth to get voucher legislation passed in a city in which public schools enjoy little or no positive reputation; when conservative theorists and writers George Gilder and Charles Murray will gleefully abduct our phrases as they paint poor women as lazy and irresponsible. Creating a safe space for intellectual, critical, and complicated discussion when the

Right has shown such acute talent at extracting arguments that sustain the assault may be a naive, but worthwhile, wish.

Responsibilities for our writing. We watch the apocalypse and write about it. What is the relationship between what we see, the outrage we gather and feel, the relatively tame texts we produce, and our audiences, many of whom are alternately too depressed or too cynical to be mobilized? We feel the weight of academics; that is, as public intellectuals, we need to tell the stories from the side of policy that is never asked to speak, to interrupt the hegemony of elite voices dictating what is good for this segment of the population. And yet we feel the need to document the pain and suffering in these communities and the incredible resilience and energy that percolates. It is important to note, therefore, another underground debate within community studies, the tension between representing historically oppressed groups as victimized and damaged *or* as resilient and strong. This may seem an artificial and dangerous dichotomy (we think it is), but we have encountered colleagues within feminism, critical race theory, poverty work, disability studies, and—most recently—queer theory arguing these intellectual stances, with these two "choices" carved out as the (presumably only) appropriate alternatives.

We share the worries, but worry more about the fixed choices that are being offered. Simple stories of discrimination and victimization, with no evidence of resistance, resilience, or agency, are seriously flawed and deceptively partial, and they deny the rich subjectivities of persons surviving amid horrific social circumstances. Equally dreary, however, are the increasingly popular stories of individual heroes who thrive despite the obstacles, denying the burdens of surviving amid such circumstances.

We lean toward a way of writing that spirals around social injustice and resilience, that recognizes the endurance of structures of injustice and the powerful acts of agency, that appreciates the courage and the limits of individual acts of resistance but refuses to perpetuate the fantasy that victims are simply powerless and collusive. That these women and men are strong is not evidence that they have suffered no oppression. Individual and collective strength cannot be used against poor and working-class people as evidence that "Aha! See, it's not been so bad!" We need to invent an intellectual stance in which structural oppression, passion, social movements, evidence of strength, health, and "damage" can all be recognized without erasing essential features of the complex story that constitutes urban life in poverty.

We take solace in the words of many of our African American male informants, drawn from churches and spiritual communities, who testify, "Only belief and hope will save our communities. We have come a long, long way . . . and we have much further to go. Only belief will get us through." Amid the pain and despair, hope survives. This, too, is a big part of community life, rarely seen in the light of day. It is time to recognize the full nature of community life.

FULL CIRCLE

Coming full circle, we are still a couple of White women, a well-paid Thelma and Louise with laptops, out to see the world through poor and working-class eyes through the words and stories that we collect across and within communities. We work with activists, policy makers, church leaders, women's groups, and educators in these communities to try to figure out how best to collect data that will serve local struggles, rather than merely to document them. We are surrounded by wonderful students of all races/ethnicities, languages and sexualities, and come to few conclusions with any illusion of consensus. We draw upon community activists and policy makers to help us invent survey questions and interpret the data; we use our data to write up "evaluations" for community programs surviving on shoestring budgets. We write through our own race and class blinders, and we try to deconstruct them in our multiracial and multiethnic coalitions. Decisions about design, sampling sets, interview schedule, interpretation, representation, and dissemination of findings have been developed, clumsily but broadly, through an open process among the members of the research team, with consultation from community members. Questions have been added and omitted by research assistants and community members. Phrasing of questions concerning social class, language, neighborhood violence, and childhood abuse have been best articulated by people who know community life, needs for privacy, and acceptable places for inquiry. Researchers can no longer afford to collect information on communities without that information benefiting those communities in their struggles for equity, participation, and representation. Although such collaborations are by no means easy (see Fine & Vanderslice, 1992), they are essential if social research is to serve the public good.

At base we are trying to work the hyphens of theory and research, policy and practice, Whitenesses and multiracial coalitions, and at this moment in history we find few friends who don't demand that we choose one side of each dichotomy and stake it out! Our commitments to "floating across" satisfy few. Policy makers want clear (usually victim-blaming) descriptions of social problems. Communities would prefer that we keep dirty laundry to ourselves. Some academics think we should stay out of policy talk and remain "uncontaminated" by local struggles. More than a few Whites see us as race traitors, whereas a good number of people of color don't trust two White women academics to do them or their communities much good.

In lame response to colleagues and graduate students, we are trying to build theory, contextualize policy, pour much back into community work, and help to raise the next generation of progressive, multiracial/ethnic scholars. We try to position ourselves self-consciously and hope that our colleagues who are engaged in critical work and still plowing the fields for data will enter with us into this conversation about writing the wrongs and rights in the field. When ethnography came "home," informants moved next door and read our books. Academics were reluctant, remiss, too arrogant to clear up some of these questions of ethics, methods, and theory. Many of our colleagues, on both the Right and Left, have retreated to arrogant theory or silly romance about heroic life on the ground. Others meticulously and persuasively deconstruct the very categories we find ourselves holding on to in order to write a simple sentence about community life. We toil on, looking for friends, writing for outrage, searching for a free space in which social research has a shot at producing both social theory and social change as the world turns rapidly to the Right.

REFERENCES

Austin, R. (1992). "The Black community," its lawbreakers, and a politics of identification. *Southern California Law Review, 65,* 1769-1817.

Boyte, H. C., & Evans, S. M. (1992). *Free spaces: The sources of democratic change in America.* Chicago: University of Chicago Press.

Brice-Heath, S., & McLaughlin, M. (Eds.). (1993). *Identity & inner-city youth: Beyond ethnicity and gender.* New York: Teachers College Press.

Connell, R. W. (1994). *Knowing about masculinity, teaching the boys.* Paper presented at the 1994 conference of the Pacific Sociological Association, San Diego, CA.

Cross, W. E., Jr. (1991). *Shades of Black: Diversity in African-American identity.* Philadelphia: Temple University Press.

Denzin, N. R., & Lincoln, Y. S. (1994). *Handbook of qualitative research.* Thousand Oaks, CA: Sage.

Dyson, M. E. (1993). *Reflecting Black: African-American cultural criticism.* Minneapolis: University of Minnesota Press.

Fine, M. (1991). *Framing dropouts: Notes on the politics of an urban public high school.* Albany, NY: State University of New York Press.

Fine, M. (1992). *Disruptive voices: The possibilities of feminist research.* Ann Arbor: University of Michigan Press.

Fine, M. (1994). Working the hyphens: Reinventing self and other in qualitative research. In N. R. Denizen & Y. S. Lincoln (Eds.), *Handbook of qualitative research* (pp. 70-82). Thousand Oaks, CA: Sage.

Fine, M., & Vanderslice, V. (1992). Qualitative activist research: Reflections in methods and politics. In F. B. Bryant, J. Edwards, R. S. Tindale, E. J. Posavac, L. Heath, E. Henderson, & Y. Suarez-Balcazar (Eds.), *Methodological issues in applied social psychology: Social psychological applications to social issues* (Vol. 2, pp. 199-218). New York: Plenum.

Foucault, M. (1979). *Discipline and punish.* New York: Random House.

Gates, H. L., Jr. (1985). *"Race," writing, and difference.* Chicago: University of Chicago Press.

Gittell, M. J. (1990). Women on foundation boards: The illusion of change. In *Women and foundations/corporate philanthropy.* New York: CUNY.

Gittell, M. J. (1994). School reform in New York and Chicago: Revisiting the ecology of local games. *Urban Affairs Quarterly,* 136-151.

Gregory, S. (1993). Race, rubbish, and resistance: Empowering difference in community politics. *Cultural Anthropology, 8*(1), 24-48.

Gubrium, J. F., & Holstein, J. A. (1995). Qualitative inquiry and the deprivatization of experience. *Qualitative Inquiry, 1,* 204-222.

Gwaltney, J. L. (1980). *Drylongso: A self-portrait of Black America.* New York: Random House.

Hall, S. (1981). Moving right. *The Socialist Review, 55*(1), 113-137.

Hurtado, A., & Stewart, A. J. (in press). Through the looking glass: Implications of studying Whiteness for feminist methods. In M. Fine, L. Powell, L. Weis, & M. Wong (Eds.), *Off/White.* New York: Routledge.

Katz, M. (1995). *Improving poor people.* Princeton, NJ: Princeton University Press.

Keith, M., & Pile, S. (Eds.). (1993). *Place and the politics of identity.* London: Routledge.

Ladner, J. A. (1971). *Tomorrow's tomorrow: The Black woman.* Garden, City, NY: Doubleday.

Lykes, M. B. (1989). Dialogue with Guatemalan Indian women: Critical perspectives on constructing collaborative research. In R. K. Unger (Ed.), *Representations: Social constructions of gender* (pp. 167-185). Amityville, NY: Baywood.

Lykes, M. B. (1994). Speaking against the silence: One Maya woman's exile and return. In C. E. Franz & A. J. Stewart (Eds.), *Women creating lives: Identities, resilience, and resistance* (pp. 97-114). Boulder, CO: Westview.

Mills, C. W. (1959). *The sociological imagination*. New York: Oxford University Press.

Mullings, L. (1984). Minority women, work and health. In W. Chavkin (Ed.), *Double exposure: Women's health hazards on the job and at home* (pp. 84-106). New York: Monthly Review Press.

Omi, M., & Winant, H. (1986). *Racial formations in the United States*. New York: Routledge.

Opotow, S. (1990). Moral exclusion and injustice: An introduction. *Journal of Social Issues, 46*(1), 1-20.

Piven, F. F., Block, F., Cloward, R. A., & Ehrenreich, B. (1987). *The mean season*. New York: Pantheon.

Piven, F. F., & Cloward, R. A. (1971). *Regulating the poor: The functions of public welfare*. New York: Pantheon.

Piven, F. F., & Cloward, R. A. (1977). *Poor people's movements: Why they succeed, how they fail*. New York: Pantheon.

Powell, L. (1994). Interpreting social defenses: Family group in an urban setting. In M. Fine (Ed.), *Chartering urban school reform: Reflections on public high schools in the midst of change* (pp. 112-121). New York: Teachers College Press.

Richardson, L. (1995). Writing-stories: Co-authoring "The Sea Monster," a writing-story. *Qualitative Inquiry, 1*, 189-203.

Scheper-Hughes, N. (1992). *Death without weeping: The violence of everyday life in Brazil*. Berkeley: University of California Press.

Scott, J. W. (1992). Experience. In J. Butler & J. W. Scott (Eds.), *Feminists theorize the political* (pp. 22-40). New York: Routledge.

Weis, L. (1985). *Between two worlds: Black students in an urban community college*. New York: Routledge.

Weis, L. (1990). *Working class without work: High school students in a deindustrializing economy*. New York: Routledge.

Weis, L., & Fine, M. (Eds.). (1993). *Beyond silenced voices: Class, race, and gender in United States schools*. Albany: State University of New York Press.

Weis, L., & Fine, M. (1995). *Voices from urban America: Sites of immigration and spaces of possibility*. Spencer grant proposal; submitted to and funded by The Spencer Foundation, Chicago, IL.

Weiss, H. B., & Greene, J. C. (1992). An empowerment partnership for family support and education programs and evaluations. Cambridge, MA: Harvard Family Research Project. *Family Science Review, 5*(1,2).

-- --

Michelle Fine is a professor of psychology at the City University of New York, Graduate Center and the senior consultant at the Philadelphia Schools Collaborative. Her recent publications include Chartering Urban School Reform: Reflections on Public High Schools in the Midst of Change *(1994),* Disruptive Voices: The Transgressive Possibilities of Feminist Research *(1992), and* Framing

Dropouts: Notes on the Politics of an Urban High School *(1991).*
*She has provided expert courtroom testimony and works nationally as
a consultant to parents' groups, community groups, and teacher
unions on issues of school reform. She was recently awarded the Janet
Helms Distinguished Scholar Award 1994.*

*Lois Weis is a professor of sociology of education at the State Univer-
sity of New York at Buffalo. She is the author and/or editor of numerous
books and articles, most recently* Beyond Silenced Voices: Class,
Race, and Gender in U.S. Schools *and* Working Class Without
Work: High School Students in a De-Industrialization Economy.

CHAPTER 18

The Social Construction of Validity

––

Steinar Kvale
University of Aarhus, Denmark

Validation of qualitative research is here discussed in relation to postmodern conceptions of knowledge. A modernist notion of true knowledge as a mirror of reality is replaced by a postmodern under-standing of knowledge as a social construction. Of the common psychometric concepts of validity, predictive validity is related to a modernist correspondence theory of truth, whereas construct validity may be extended to encompass a social construction of reality. Three approaches to validity are outlined in some detail. First, validity is treated as an expression of craftsmanship, with an emphasis on quality of research by checking, questioning, and theorizing on the nature of the phenomena investigated. Second, by going beyond correspondence criteria of validity, the emphasis on observation is extended to include conversation about the observations, with a communicative concept of validity. Third, by discarding a modern legitimation mania, justifica-tion of knowledge is replaced by application, with a pragmatic concept of validity. In conclusion, the validity of the validity question is questioned.

Validity has been a central concept in social science methodology. Within the current qualitative research wave, the role of validity has been questioned, and in postmodern philosophy, the concept of an objective reality to validate knowledge against has been discarded. An attempt will be made here to demystify the concept of validity in social research by taking it back to everyday language and interaction. The apparently abstract postmodern discussions of knowledge and truth will be applied to everyday conventional issues of validation of qualitative research found scattered in social science literature. In a postmodern conception, the understanding of knowledge as a map of an objective reality, and validity as the correspondence of the map with the reality mapped, is replaced by the social and linguistic construction of a perspectival reality where knowledge is validated through practice. Three approaches to validity in qualitative research outlined earlier—validation as investigation, as communication, and as action (Kvale, 1989)—shall be discussed in the context of postmodern conceptions of knowledge.

THE TRINITY OF RELIABILITY, VALIDITY, AND GENERALIZATION

In modern social science, the concepts of validity, reliability, and generalization have obtained the status of a scientific holy trinity. They appear to belong to some abstract realm in a sanctuary of science, far removed from the interactions of the everyday world, to be worshipped with respect by all true believers in science.

As an introduction to the multiple discourses of validation, I shall start with a history of my own encounters with the concept of validity. As a student of psychology in Norway in the 1960s, I read heavy texts on the importance of validity, reliability, and generalizability in scientific research. I tried to memorize the definitions of predictive validity, concurrent validity, content validity, and face validity, and I struggled to understand the concept of construct validity. The very terms *validity* and *reliability* did not belong to the Norwegian vernacular, but were some foreign English-Latin terms. The psychometric discussions of validity appeared abstract and esoteric, belonging to some distant philosophical universe together with Kant's transcendental a prioris and the like.

When I as a student dared to ask some natural scientists on campus about these fundamental scientific concepts, I was somewhat bewildered to find out that the very terms of the methodological holy trinity of psychological science were often unfamiliar to natural scientists. The concepts were, however, very real to us students of psychology; validity, reliability, and generalization were frequently used as examination topics to differentiate between students who had, and those who had not, pledged allegiance to the scientific trinity of psychology.

Later, when traveling in the United States, I learned other meanings of the terms validity and reliability; for example, when cashing a check in the supermarket, I was told that my European driver's license was not valid as identification; when in an academic discussion, I was told that my argument was not valid. Or I heard that the information about the used car I was looking at was not reliable, nor was the car dealer known to be a reliable person. Here the terms valid and reliable belonged to the vernacular, important to the ongoing interactions of everyday life.

When later engaged in qualitative research, I encountered the positivist trinity again, here used by mainstream researchers to disqualify qualitative research. The stimulus "qualitative research interview" appeared to trigger conditioned responses from the mainstream tradition such as the following: "The results are not reliable, they are produced by leading interview questions"; "The results are not generalizable, there are too few interview subjects"; and "The interview findings are not valid, how can you know if you find out what the person really means?" (Kvale, in press).

From some qualitative researchers, there has been an opposite attitude to questions of validity, reliability, and generalization. They are simply ignored, or dismissed as some oppressive positivist concepts, hampering a creative and emancipatory qualitative research. Other qualitative researchers have gone beyond the relativism of a rampant antipositivism to extend the concept of validity to include new dimensions such as ecological and catalytical validity, and others such as Lincoln and Guba (1985) have reclaimed ordinary language terms to discuss the truth value of their findings, using concepts such as trustworthiness, credibility, dependability, and confirmability.

From a postmodern approach, the issues of reliability, validity, and generalization are sometimes discarded as leftovers from a modernist correspondence theory of truth. In a postmodern perspective, there are multiple ways of knowing and multiple truths, and the concept of validity indicates a firm boundary line between truth and nontruth. In contrast hereto, Lather (1993), who argues from a feminist poststructural frame valorizing practice, takes issue with a dismissal of validity as some modernist reification becoming obsolete in a postmodern era. She addresses validity as an incitement to discourse, a fertile obsession, and attempts to reinscribe validity in a way that uses the postmodern problematic to loosen the master code of positivism. Drawing on different positions in postmodern thought, she outlines different forms of validation, such as ironic, paralogical, rhizomatic, and voluptuous, and discusses each in relation to examples of social research.

The following discussion of validity represents a rather moderate post-modernism (Kvale, 1992); in the terms of Rosenau (1992), it is not a "skeptical," but an "affirmative" postmodernism; while rejecting the notion of a universal truth, it accepts the possibility of specific local, personal, and community forms of truth, with a focus on daily life and local narrative. The present understanding of validity starts in the lived world and daily language, where issues of reliable witnesses, of valid documents and arguments, are part of the social interaction. In the remainder of this discussion, we shall leave out the important, but less complex topics of reliability and generalization to focus more in detail on the conceptual and practical issues involved in validation of social research.

ON VALIDITY AND TRUTH

In ordinary language dictionaries, "validity" refers to the truth and correctness of a statement. A valid argument is sound, well-grounded, justifiable, strong, and convincing. A valid inference is correctly derived from its premises. In social science textbooks, one finds both a narrow and a broad definition of validity. In a narrow positivist approach, validity came to mean whether a method measures what it is intended to measure, for instance, "The commonest definition of validity is epitomized by the question: Are we measuring what we think we are measuring?" (Kerlinger, 1973, p. 457). Qualitative research is then invalid if it does not result in numbers. In a broader concept, validity pertains to whether a method investigates what it is intended to investigate, to "the extent to which our observations indeed reflect the phenomena or variables of interest to us" (Pervin, 1984, p. 48). Within such a more extensive conception of validity, qualitative research may, in principle, lead to valid scientific knowledge.

Textbook presentations of validity in social science have been based on a correspondence theory of truth within the context of positivist epistemological assumptions. The standard definitions of validity have been taken over from the criteria developed for psychometric tests as formalized by Cronbach and Meehl in 1955. In psychology, validity became linked to psychometrics, where the concurrent and predictive validity of the psychological tests were declared in statistical correlation coefficients, indicating correspondence between test results and some external criteria. The psychometric tests, such as intelligence tests, have frequently been applied to predict school success. The external criterion was here simple—grade point average in later schooling. The issue becomes more complex with a further questioning as to what the school grades measure. Grades have been found to predict later grades in school, but to a small extent success out of school. The issue of predictive validity is here not merely an empirical issue, but raises value questions as what should be the criteria of success—job position, income, contributions to the community?

The social construction of valid knowledge is brought out in the concept of construct validity. It pertains to the measurement of theoretical constructs, such as intelligence and authoritarianism, by different measures; it involves correlations with other measures of the construct and logical analysis of their relationships. Cherryholmes (1988) has argued that even this psychometric concept of construct validity is a discursive and rhetorical one (cf. Tschudi, 1989). A construct and its measurement are validated when the discourse about their relationship is persuasive to the community of researchers. A constructive conception of validity does not then pertain only to the original discourse of psychometric measurement and experimental design, but opens in Cherryholmes's analysis for multiple discourses, such as phenomenological, interpretative, critical, and deconstructive approaches.

A radicalization of the originally psychometric concept of construct validity brings it close to a postmodern emphasis on the social construction of knowledge. Cronbach (1971), who together with

Meehl introduced the concept, has later argued for an extended concept of construct validity that pertains to qualitative summaries as well as numerical scores: It is an open process where to validate is to investigate—"validation is more than corroboration; it is a process for developing sounder interpretations of observations" (p. 433). In an article where he argues that value-free standards for validity is a contradiction in terms, Cronbach (1980) concludes with a discursive concept of validity resting on public discussion. The interpretation of a test is going to remain open and unsettled, the more so because of the role that values play in action based on tests, and the validity of an interpretation cannot be established by a research monograph or detailed manual. The aim for the report is to advance sensible discussion. . . . The institutions of the polity are geared to weigh up reasonable, partly persuasive, disputed arguments; and they can be tolerant when we acknowledge uncertainties. The more we learn, and the franker we are with ourselves and our clientele, the more valid the use of tests will become. (p. 107)

The issue of what is valid knowledge of the social world involves the philosophical question of what is truth. Within philosophy, three classical criteria of truth are discerned—correspondence, coherence, and pragmatic utility. The *correspondence* criterion of truth concerns whether a knowledge statement corresponds to the objective world. The *coherence* criterion refers to the consistency and internal logic of a statement. And the *pragmatic* criterion relates the truth of a knowledge statement to its practical consequences.

Although the three criteria of truth do not necessarily exclude each other, they have each obtained strong positions in different disciplines and philosophical traditions. The correspondence criterion has been central within a positivist social science where the validity of knowledge is expressed in its degree of correspondence with an objective reality. The coherence criterion has been strong in mathematics and in the hermeneutics of the humanities. The pragmatic criterion has prevailed in pragmatism and to a certain extent in Marxist philosophy. The three truth criteria may be regarded as abstractions from a unity, where a comprehensive verification of research findings will involve observation, conversation, and interaction. Investigating whether a knowledge statement corresponds to reality entails more than merely observing reality. The decisive point is the conversation in the investigative community about the relation between the methods, the findings, and the nature of the reality investigated.

The question of true and valid knowledge brings up a pervasive dichotomy of objectivism and relativism in Western thought. Bernstein, in *Beyond Objectivity and Relativism* (1983), describes *objectivism* as the basic conviction that there exists some permanent, ahistorical matrix or framework to which we can ultimately appeal in determining the nature of knowledge, truth, reality, and goodness. A realist version of objectivism implies that an objective reality exists independently of the observer and that only one correct view can be taken of it. The counterposition of *relativism* involves a view that all concepts of knowledge, truth, reality, and goodness are relative to a specific theoretical framework, form of life, or culture. In an attempt to go beyond the polarity of an objectivist realism and an "anything goes" relativism, Bernstein follows a hermeneutical tradition arguing for a dialogue conception of truth, where true knowledge is sought through a rational argument by participants in a discourse. And the medium of a discourse is language, which is neither objective or universal nor subjective or individual, but intersubjective.

VALIDITY IN A POSTMODERN CONTEXT

The postmodern condition is characterized by a loss of belief in an objective world and an incredulity toward metanarratives of legitimation (Lyotard, 1984). With a delegitimation of global systems of thought, there is no foundation to secure a universal and objective reality. The modern dichotomy of an objective reality distinct from subjective images is breaking down and is being replaced by a hyperreality of self-referential signs. There is a critique of the modernist search for foundational forms and its belief in a linear progress through more knowledge. The dichotomy of universal social laws and unique individual selves is replaced by the interaction of local networks, where the self becomes an ensemble of relations. The focus is on local context and on the social and linguistic construction of a perspectival reality where knowledge is validated through practice (Kvale, 1992).

The belief in an objective reality has been at the basis of a modern understanding of truth and validity. The philosophy of the Enlightenment was a reaction against the religious dogma of the medieval ages. The belief in one true and almighty God for all people from eternity to eternity was in the modern era replaced by the belief in one true and objective reality, stable and universal. In a positivist philosophy, knowledge becomes a reflection of reality and there is ideally a one-to-one correspondence between elements in the real world and our knowledge of this world.

In a postmodern era, the belief in foundations of true knowledge, in an absolute God, or an objective reality has dissolved. The conception of knowledge as a mirror of reality is replaced by knowledge as a linguistic and social construction of reality. There is a focus on interpretation and negotiation of the meaning of the lived world. Knowledge is not a matter of interaction with a nonhuman reality, but of communication between persons; as argued by Rorty (1979), the conversation becomes the ultimate context within which knowledge is to be understood. A move from knowledge as correspondence with an objective reality to knowledge as a communal construction of reality involves a change in emphasis from observation to conversation and interaction. Truth is constituted through a dialogue; valid knowledge claims emerge as conflicting interpretations and action possibilities are discussed and negotiated among the members of a community.

Such a move from knowledge as primarily observation to knowledge as conversation was illustrated in a recent television program on the development of science. After showing the newest technical advances in microscopes for cell studies and giant telescopes for investigation of space, the camera suddenly shifted to a room with elegant eighteenth-century furniture. The accompanying voice said something to the effect of: It is not by the techniques of these instruments that the truth of scientific knowledge is determined, but through discussion among the scientists about the observations, such as in this room of the British Royal Society of Sciences.

Modern social science was to be based on objective, verifiable facts. In the present perspective, the facts of the social sciences are social constructions arising from a specific technical perspective on the social world. This pertains, for example, to the categorization of group interaction and the content analysis of texts into atomised meanings as facts (Kvale, 1976). A closer look at the observational procedures for obtaining intersubjective observer agreement about the "objective" facts reveal the many theoretical presuppositions built into the very observational procedures leading to the construction of social facts. The facts of the social sciences are intersubjective constructions arising from a decontextualizing perspective to meaningful actions and texts, abstracting atoms of social behavior and quantifying them within a dominant technical research interest of prediction and control of social processes.

When the domain of the social sciences is extended from the prediction of facts to the interpretation of meaning, the criteria and forms of validation change. In past debates on the nature of the social sciences, there has been tension between facts and meanings, observation and interpretation. Today the tension has moved to the relation between meanings and acts, between interpretation and action. When the dichotomy of facts and values is abandoned, aesthetics and ethics come into the foreground. When knowledge is no longer the mere reflection of some objective reality, but the construction of a social reality, the beauty and the use value of the constructed knowledge comes into the foreground. We may here draw an analogy to architecture—it is essential that the foundations and the frame of a house are solid and stable, but if there is no beauty in the architecture, or utility of the design, the house has no value.

Within an expanded understanding of rationality in a postmodernist conversation, Kant's split between pure reason, art, and morals is no longer taken for granted. In a postmodern conversation, scientific knowledge is neither sharply separated from, nor is it in a privileged position over, artistic certainty and ethical reasoning (Polkinghorne, 1983).

Some aspects of postmodern knowledge pertaining to validity shall now be depicted and thereafter their consequences outlined in relation to validation as craftsmanship, as communication, and as action. First, with giving up a correspondence theory of truth as the basis for understanding validity, there is a change in emphasis from verification to falsification. The quest for absolute certain knowledge is replaced by a conception of defensible knowledge claims. Validation becomes the issue of choosing among competing and falsifiable interpretations, of examining and providing arguments for the relative credibility of alternative knowledge claims (Polkinghorne, 1983). Validation here comes to imply the quality of the craftsmanship in research.

Second, when a correspondence criterion of true knowledge as reflecting an objective reality recedes, coherence and pragmatic conceptions of truth come to the foreground. Method as a truth guarantee dissolves; with a social construction of reality, the emphasis is on the discourse of the community. Communication of knowledge becomes significant, with aesthetics and rhetorics entering into the scientific discourse.

Third, a modern legitimation mania wanes and there is an emphasis on pragmatic proof through action. Justification of knowledge is replaced by application. Knowledge becomes the ability to perform effective actions. Criteria of efficiency and their desirability become pivotal, involving ethical issues of right action. Values do not belong to a realm separated from scientific knowledge, but are intrinsically tied to the creation and application of knowledge.

We shall now turn to some of the everyday conventional issues of validation in social science and shall outline validity as craftsmanship, as communication, and as action. This does not lead to fixed criteria replacing the psychometric concepts of validity, but rather to extending the frames of reference for asking about the validity of knowledge in the social sciences. A postmodern approach to validation does not secure unambiguous knowledge—"Post-modern science presumes methods that multiply paradox, inventing ever more elaborate repertoires of questions, each of which encourages an infinity of answers, rather than methods that settle on solutions" (Rosenau, 1992, p.117).

VALIDITY AS QUALITY OF CRAFTSMANSHIP

Validity is here used in the meaning of whether a study investigates the phenomena intended to be investigated. We shall attempt to demystify the concept of validity, to bring it back from the abstractions of philosophy of science and to the everyday practice of scientific research. With an alternative concept of validity—going from correspondence with an objective reality to defensible knowledge claims—validity is ascertained by examining the sources of invalid-ity, and the stronger the attempts of falsification a proposition has survived, the more valid and the more trustworthy the knowledge.

The craftsmanship of research and the credibility of the researcher becomes decisive as to whether other researchers will rely on the findings reported. The credibility of the researcher, based on the quality of his or her past research in the area, becomes an important aspect as to whether fellow researchers ascribe validity to the findings reported. Validity is not only an issue of the methods used; the researcher's person (Salner, 1989), including his or her ethical integrity (Smith, 1990), becomes critical for the quality of the scientific knowledge produced.

Validation comes to depend on the quality of craftsmanship in an investigation, which includes continually checking, questioning, and theoretically interpreting the findings. In a craftsmanship approach to validation, the emphasis is moved from inspection at the end of the production line to quality control throughout the stages of knowledge production. The understanding of validity as quality of craftsmanship is not limited to a postmodern approach, but it becomes pivotal with a dismissal of an objective reality against which knowledge is to be measured.

To validate is to check. An investigative concept of validation is inherent in the grounded theory approach of Glaser and Strauss (1967). Validation is here not some final product control or verification; verification is built into the research process with continual checks of the credibility, plausibility, and trustworthiness of the findings. Miles and Huberman (1994) emphasize that there are no canons or infallible decision rules for establishing the validity of qualitative research. Their approach is to analyze the many sources of potential biases that may invalidate qualitative observations and interpretations, and they outline in detail tactics for testing and confirming qualitative findings. The tactics involve checking for representativeness and for researcher effects, triangulating, weighing the evidence, checking the meaning of outliers, using extreme cases, following up surprises, looking for negative evidence, making if-then tests, ruling out spurious relations, replicating a finding, checking out rival explanations, and getting feedback from informants.

For an interview investigation, we may discern seven stages of the research process—thematizing, designing, interviewing, transcribing, analyzing, verifying, and reporting—each involving specific issues of validity.

1. *Thematizing.* The validity of an investigation rests on the soundness of the theoretical presuppositions of study and on the logic of the derivations from the theory to the specific research questions of the study.
2. *Designing.* From a knowledge perspective, validity involves the adequacy of the research design and the methods used for the topic and purpose of the study. From an ethical perspective, validity of a research design relates to the value of the knowledge produced to the human condition.
3. *Interviewing.* This involves themes as the trustworthiness of the subjects' reports and the quality of the interviewing with a careful questioning and a continual checking of the information obtained.
4. *Transcribing.* Here the choice of linguistic style of the transcript raises the question of what is a valid translation from oral to written language.
5. *Interpreting.* This involves the issues of whether the questions put to a text are valid and of the logic of the interpretations.
6. *Verifying.* This entails the concrete analyses of validity in the knowledge produced, a reflected judgment as to what forms of validation are relevant in a specific study, and a decision on what is the relevant community for a dialogue on validity.
7. *Reporting.* This involves the question of whether a given report gives a valid account of the main findings of a study and also of the role of the readers of the report in validating the results.

To validate is to question. When ascertaining validity, the questions of what and why need to be answered before the question of how: The content and purpose of an investigation precede the method. Discussing the question, "Do photographs tell the truth?" Becker (1979) specifies the general question, "Is it true?" to "Is this photograph telling the truth about what?" And to decide what a picture is telling us the truth about, he suggests that we should ask ourselves what questions it might be answering.

By interpretation of interview statements, the forms of validation depend on the research questions asked, which may be exemplified in relation to the following statement by a pupil in an investigation of the effects of grades in Danish high schools:

> Grades are often unjust, because very often—very often—they are only a measure of how much you talk, and how much you agree with the teacher's opinion.

In an *experiential* reading of the statement, the pupil believes the grades as often unrighteous (in the present terminology, as often invalid) and gives reasons for this belief. A validation of this experiential reading would involve further questioning of the pupil, clarifying his experienced meanings of grades and unfairness. In a *veridical* reading, the truth of the pupil's hypothesis about the correlation between the amount of speech and grades was checked by an informant-triangulation—other pupils also pointed to a connection, whereas the interviewed teachers rejected any correlation between the amount of speech and grades. For lack of observation of actual classroom behavior, an indirect method-triangulation was attempted, which gave potential support to the speech-amount hypothesis of grades—for the 30 pupils interviewed, there was a significant connection between how much they talked during the interviews and their grade point averages (correlation: 0.65; $p < .001$). Read *symptomatically*, the statement may be interpreted as a rationalization, the pupil justifying his own low grades by attributing the higher grades of others to their amount of talk, an interpretation that might be pursued within the context of psychoanalytic theory of defense mechanisms.

The forms of validation for the three readings of the interview statement differ and depend on the questions addressed to the text. A common critique of research interviews is that their findings are not valid because the subject's reports may be false. The issue of validity again depends on the researcher's questions. The opinion about high grades being a measure of how much a pupil talks may be empirically false when read veridically as information about factors leading to high grades. Read experientially or symptomatically as representative of the pupil's beliefs about grades, the statement may still provide valid knowledge. The topic of the symptomatic reading is then reformulated from the factual to the production of an invalid report. And whereas this interpretation concerns the production of a possibly invalid understanding, the Thomas theorem of sociology focuses on the *consequences* of an invalid understanding—"If men believe ideas are real, they are real in their consequences." Applied to the interview statement above, a belief in a connection between grades and the amount of speech, which may be empirically incorrect, might lead the pupils to talk more in the hope of attaining better grades and thus be real in its consequences. The validity of a statement and its interpretation come to depend on the questions posed to the statement.

Richardson (1994) has taken issue with the common concept of triangulation, which was also applied above in a veridical reading of the pupil's statement. She rejects using a rigid triangle as a central image for validity for postmodern texts, as it contains assumptions of a fixed point or object that can be triangulated: "Rather, the central image is the crystal, which combines symmetry and substance with an infinite variety of shapes, substances, transformation, multidimensionalities, and angles of approach" (p. 522). She then outlines how crystallization through postmodern mixed-genre texts provides us with a deepened, complex, thoroughly partial understanding of the topic. Going beyond the veridical attempt to investigate whether a relation exists between talkativeness and grades in school, the other readings of the pupil's statement above may be seen as crystallizations, opening to continual new sides of the topic of grades. These transformations of the meaning of the statement shall now be followed up by a more theoretical questioning of grades.

To validate is to theorize. Pursuing the methodological issues of validation generates theoretical questions about the nature of the phenomena investigated. The inconclusive results of the above attempt at an informant-triangulation of a pupil's belief in a connection between speech and grades need not merely indicate a problem of method; it also raises theoretical questions about the social construction of school reality. Pupils and teachers may live in different social realities with regard to which pupil behaviors lead to good grades. It is possible that pupils, as a kind of superstitious behavior, believe in a connection where there is none, or it may be that teachers overlook, or deny, a relation that actually exists. Ambiguity and contradictory beliefs about which behaviors lead to good grades appear to be an essential aspect of the social reality of the school.

The above interpretations of grades have remained within an individualistic psychological perspective, focusing on examinations as tests of students and their effects on the students measured. From an alternative knowledge perspective, this research recedes into the background. An examination is a test of a student's knowledge. The topic of the examination is, however, ambiguous—it may be a test of individual students or a test of common knowledge. The first, psychometric conception, has dominated research on examinations focusing on predictive validity. The second, knowledge conception, treats examinations as an institution of knowledge construction and censorship of meaning, involving the hermeneutics of meaning interpretation and a discourse theory of truth (Kvale, 1993a). In the latter conception, the individual students recede into the background; they become mere pawns, or lambs, to be sacrificed in the interpretative community's continual task of knowledge maintenance and meaning stabilization. The forms of validity pertaining to an examination will be rather different if examinations are conceived of as the selection of individual students versus the certification of the valid knowledge of a discipline.

In conclusion, the validation of interview statements involves a theoretical questioning of the nature of the phenomena investigated. In the terms of grounded theory, verifying interpretations is an intrinsic part of the generation of theory. Pursuing the issues of validation as craftsmanship leads to theoretical issues of the social construction of reality. The complexities of validating qualitative research need not be due to an inherent weakness of qualitative methods, but may on the contrary, rest upon their extraordinary power to picture and to question the complexity of the social reality investigated.

COMMUNICATIVE VALIDITY

Communicative validity involves testing the validity of knowledge claims in a dialogue. Valid knowledge is not merely obtained by approximations to a given social reality; it involves a conversation about the social reality: What is a valid observation is decided through the argumentation of the participants in a discourse. In a hermeneutical approach to meaningful action as a text, Ricoeur (1971) rejects the position that all interpretations of a text are equal; the logic of validation allows us to move between the two limits of dogmatism and skepticism. Invoking the hermeneutical circle and criteria of falsifiability, he outlines validity as an argumentative discipline comparable to the juridical procedures of legal interpretation. Validation is based on a logic of uncertainty and of qualitative probability, where it is always possible to argue for or against an interpretation, to confront interpretations, and to arbitrate between them.

Valid knowledge is constituted as conflicting knowledge claims are argued in a dialogue. Within the social sciences, Mishler (1990) has conceptualized validation as the social construction of knowledge in a discussion of narrative research. Valid knowledge claims are established in a discourse through which the results of a study come to be viewed as sufficiently trustworthy for other investigators to rely on in their own work. A communicative approach to validity is involved in psychoanalysis and other psychotherapies, where the validity of an interpretation is worked out in a dialogue between patient and therapist. Also in system evaluation, a communicative concept of validity is involved; House (1980) has thus emphasized that in system evaluation, research does not mainly concern predicting events, but rather whether the audience of a report can see new relations and answer new but relevant questions.

With the conversation as the ultimate context within which knowledge is to be understood, the nature of the discourse becomes essential. There is today a danger that a dialogue conception of truth and the concept of communicative validation may become empty global and positive undifferentiated terms without the conceptual and theoretical differentiations worked out. Here some specific questions concerning the how, why, and who of communication will be raised.

How. The form of communication may involve persuasion through rational discourse or populist demagogy. The forms of persuasion about the truth of knowledge claims will be different in the harsh logical argumentation of a philosophical dialogue, in a humanistic therapy encounter based on good feelings and reciprocal sympathy, in a narrative monologue capturing an audience, and in the juridical proceedings and legal interpretations in a courtroom.

Philosophical discourse such as the dialogues of Socrates is characterized by a rational argumentation. The participants are obliged to test statements about the truth and falsity of propositions on the basis of argued points of view, and the best argument wins. The discourse is a form of argumentation where no social exertion of power takes place, the only form of power being the force of the better argument.

Why. The question here concerns the purpose of a discourse about true knowledge. What are the aims and criteria of arriving at true knowledge? Habermas's discourse theory implies a consensual theory of truth, the discourse aims at universally valid truths as an ideal. Eisner (1991) has argued for qualitative research as art, based on connoisseurship and criticism, accepting the personal, literary, and even poetic as valid sources of knowledge. The aim here is consensus: "Consensual validation is, at base, agreement among competent others that the description, interpretation, evaluation, and thematics of an educational situation are right" (p. 112). From a postmodern perspective, Lyotard (1984) has argued that consensus is only a stage in a discussion, and not its goal, which he posits as paralogy—to create new ideas, new differentiations, and new rules for the discourse. To Lyotard, discourse is a game between adversaries rather than a dialogue between partners.

Who. The concept of communicative validity raises the question of who communicates with whom. Who is a legitimate partner in a dialogue about true knowledge? By the interpretation of the interviews on grading, three interpretative communities were implied. The members of the interpretative community validating an interpretation may be the *subjects* interviewed, the *general public* interpreting within a critical commonsense understanding analogous to a jury, and the *scientific community* of scholars possessing methodical and theoretical competence in the specific area.

Validation through the community of scholars is nothing new; in natural science, the acceptance of the scientific community has been the last, ultimate, criterion for ascertaining the truth of a proposition. What is relatively new by qualitative research is the extension of the interpretative community to include the subjects investigated and the general public, with the emphasis on truth as negotiated in a local context. Communicative validity here approximates an educational endeavor, where truth is developed in a communicative process, both researcher and subjects learning and changing through the dialogue.

A heavy reliance on intersubjective validation may, however, also imply a lack of work on the part of the researcher and a lack of confidence in his or her interpretations, with an unwillingness to take responsibility for the interpretations. There may be a general populist trend when leaving the validation of interpretations to the readers, as by reader response validation, with an abdication to the ideology of a consumer society: "The customer is always right."

Power and truth. Habermas's consensus theory of truth is based on the ideal of a dominance-free dialogue, which is an abstraction from the webs of power relationships within real-life discourses, and again in contrast with Lyotard's postmodern understanding of a conversation as a game of power play. There is further the issue of who decides who is a competent and legitimate member of the interpretative community. The selection of members of the community to make decisions about issues of truth and value is considered crucial for the results in many cases, such as the selection of members of a jury, or a committee, to examine a Ph.D. candidate or an academic appointment committee.

PRAGMATIC VALIDITY

Pragmatic validation is verification in the literal sense—"to make true." To pragmatists, truth is whatever assists us to take actions that produce the desired results. Knowledge is action rather than observation; the effectiveness of our knowledge beliefs is demonstrated by the effectiveness of our action. By pragmatic validation of a knowledge claim, justification is superseded by application.

Marx stated in his second thesis on Feuerbach that the question of whether human thought can lead to objective truth is not a theoretical, but a practical one. Man must prove the truth—that is, the reality and power of his thinking in practice. And the eleventh thesis is more pointed: The philosophers have only interpreted the world differently; what matters is changing the world.

Pragmatic validation of interpretations goes beyond communicative validation. The practical knowledge interest of helping patients change is thus intrinsic to the therapeutic interview: "It is indeed one of the distinctions of psychoanalysis that research and treatment proceed hand in hand" (Freud, 1963, p. 120). Within the social sciences, action research goes beyond descriptions of social conditions to include actions to change the very conditions investigated. Also, system evaluation involves an extension of the correspondence criterion to include pragmatic validity: "The ultimate test of the credibility of an evaluation reports is the response of decision makers and information users to that report" (Patton, 1980, p. 339).

By focusing on the relevance of the interpretations for instigating change, a pragmatic knowledge interest may counteract a tendency of social constructionism to circle around in endless interpretations and the fall of postmodern analyses into boundless deconstructions. Whereas a communicative validity includes an aesthetic dimension, pragmatic validity involves the ethical dimension. A pragmatic concept of validity goes further than communication; it represents a stronger knowledge claim than a mere agreement through a dialogue. A pragmatic validation rests upon observations and interpretations, with a commitment to act on the interpretations—"Actions speak louder than words."

Within German interpretative educational research, a communicative concept of validation has been outlined by Lechler (1982) and the necessity of going beyond mere verbal consensual agreement to validation through action argued by Wahl (1982) and Terhart (1982). For naturalistic inquiry, Lincoln and Guba (1990) have gone further than consensual validation and have pointed to criteria for the quality of qualitative research such as an inquiry enhancing the level of understanding of the participants and their ability to take action, empowering them to take increased control of their lives.

A strong emphasis on explicit communicative validation may be inadequate to much of professional knowledge. The relational, tacit, and pragmatical aspects of professional knowledge can hardly be presented verbally in the form of explicit rules or validated by discursive argumentation. Altheide and Johnson (1994) have discussed the implications of tacit knowledge by assessing interpretative validity in qualitative research. They point to a bias of communication when the tacit knowledge is transformed to the logic of a more sharable textual communication form. The often contextual and unarticulated tacit knowledge of the therapist is not easily transformed to written guidelines. Important aspects of the therapeutic knowledge are best communicated by exemplars, anecdotes, case stories, narratives, and metaphors, and they are tested by their implication on practice (Polkinghorne, 1992). Such forms of transmission come closer to craftsmanship and art than to the formal norms of scientific reporting and is best transmitted by participation in local forms of practice. With current changes in the conceptions of knowledge, there is today an increasing recognition of indirect and context-bound forms of communicating knowledge, such as by apprenticeship and mentoring in education, not only in the crafts but also for the higher professions, including scientific research (Kvale, 1993b; Lave & Wenger, 1991; Mishler, 1990).

How. The form of pragmatic validation varies; there may be the patient's reactions to the psychoanalyst's interpretation of his or her dreams and the patient's reactions to a behavior therapist's interventions to change the reinforcement contingencies of his or her problem behavior. There are the reactions of the audience to a system evaluation report and the cooperative interaction of researcher and subjects in action research.

We shall discern between two types of pragmatic validation—whether a knowledge statement is accompanied by action, or whether it instigates changes of action. In the first case, validation of a subject's verbal statement is based on supporting actions that accompany the statement. This concerns going beyond mere lip service to a belief and also following up, by action, the consequences of an assertion. Thus, by investigations of racial prejudice, comprehensive inquiries go beyond mere verbal statements to inquire if a belief in racial desegregation is also followed up in appropriate actions.

The second, stronger form of pragmatic validation concerns whether interventions based on the researcher's interpretations may instigate actual changes in behavior. By therapeutic interpretations, Freud (1963) did not rely on a merely communicative approach to validation; he regarded neither the patient's yes or no to the therapist's interpretations as sufficient confirmation or disconfirmation (p. 279). Freud recommended more indirect forms of validation by observing the patient's subsequent behavior to an interpretation, such as changes of the patient's free associations, dreams, the recall of forgotten memories, and alteration of neurotic symptoms. Spence (1982) has followed up the emphasis on the pragmatic effects of interpretations: Narrative truth is constructed in the therapeutic encounter, it carries the conviction of a good story, and it is to be judged by its aesthetic value and by the curative effect of its rhetorical force.

In collaborative action research, researchers and subjects together develop knowledge of a social situation and then apply this knowledge by new actions in the situation, thus, through praxis, they test the validity of the knowledge. Reason (1994) describes a study of health workers based on participatory inquiry with a systematic testing of theory in live-action contexts. The topic was stress that comes from hidden agendas in their work, such as suspicions of drug taking and child abuse in the families the health workers visit. The coresearchers first developed knowledge through discussions among themselves, practicing role play and then raising their concerns directly with their client families. The health workers met to review and make sense out of their new experiences, and one outcome of the inquiry was the changes they made in their own professional practice. Reason discusses the validity in this cooperative inquiry and emphasizes the need to get beyond a mere consensus collusion where the researchers may band together as a group in defense of their anxieties, which may be overcome by a continual interaction between action and reflection throughout the participatory inquiry.

Why. A scientific discourse is, in principle, indefinite; there is no requirement of immediate action; new arguments that may alter or invalidate earlier knowledge may always appear. In contrast to the uncoerced consensus of the scientific discourse, there exist context requiring actions to the undertaken and decisions to be made that may involve a coercion to consensus. This involves the proceedings of a jury, the negotiations of a dissertation committee, and the decisions about therapeutic interventions and about activities to be pursued in action research.

A pragmatic approach implies that truth is whatever assists us to take actions that produce the desired results. Deciding what are the desired results involves values and ethics. The ethical aspect of validity is recognized in system evaluation, where "the validity of an evaluation depends upon whether the evaluation is true, credible, and normatively correct" (House, 1980, p. 255). The ethical implications of action consequences of research are particularly significant in one major field of current qualitative studies—market research. The survival of this industry rests on the pragmatic validity of the research-based advertising to predict and control consumer behavior.

The importance of values in validation also follows by a change of emphasis in social research from primarily mapping the social world with respect to what is to changing the focus to what could be. Thus Gergen (1992) depicts the construction of new worlds as one potential of a postmodern psychology. Rather than telling it like it is, the challenge is to tell it as it may become. A "generative" theory is designed to unseat conventional thought and thereby to open new alternatives for thought and action. Rather than only to map what is, or to predict future cultural trends, research becomes a means of transforming culture.

Who. The question of who involves the researcher and the users of the knowledge produced. Patton (1980) points to the credibility of the researcher as an important criterion of whether a research report is accepted or not as a basis for action. The question of who also involves ethical and political issues. Who is to decide the direction of change? There may be personal resistance to change as well as conflicting vested interests in the outcome of a study. Thus, concerning audience validation by system evaluation, who are the stakeholders to be included in the decisive audience: the funding agency, the leaders of the system evaluated, the employees, or the clients of the system?

Power and truth. Pragmatic validation raises the issue of power and truth in social research: Where is the power to decide what are the desired results of a study, or the direction of change; what values are to constitute the basis for action? And, more generally, where is the power to decide what kinds of truth seeking are to be pursued, what research questions are worth funding? Following Foucault, we should beware of localizing power to specific persons and their intentions rather than analyzing the netlike organization and multiple fields of power-knowledge dynamics.

VALIDITY OF THE VALIDITY QUESTION

We have argued for integrating validation in the craftsmanship of research and for extending the concept of validation from observation to include communication about, and pragmatic effects of, knowledge claims. The understanding of validity as craftsmanship, as communication and action, goes beyond the correspondence theory of knowledge at the base of the traditional psychometric criteria of validity in social science. It does not replace the importance of preciseness of observations, but draws in broader conceptions of the nature of truth in social research, which raises other questions to the validity of knowledge of the social world. Scattered examples of communicative and pragmatic understanding of validity have been taken from literature on social science research prior to and outside of a postmodern perspective. Traditionally, the conversational and pragmatic aspects of knowledge have been regarded as irrelevant or secondary to the issue of objective observations; in a postmodern conception of knowledge, the very conversation about and the application of knowledge become essential aspects of the construction of a social world. Rather than providing fixed criteria, communicative and pragmatic validity refer to extended ways of posing the question of validity in social research. Some conceptual distinction regarding the how, why, and who of these approaches, requiring further elaboration, have been suggested above.

We have further argued for a demystification of validity, maintaining that verification of information and interpretations is a normal activity in the interactions of daily life. By the discussion of validity as craftsmanship, it was emphasized that to validate is to question. We shall conclude by questioning the validity of the validity question itself; Is the question of validity in social science a valid and legitimate question? Or is the quest for validity an expression of a modern legitimation mania? In conclusion, some speculations about consequences of, reasons for, and alternatives to the validity question shall now be suggested.

A strict psychometric conception, limiting validity to quantified knowledge, has served as a gatekeeper to keep qualitative research outside the halls of science.

A strong focus on validity in research may foster an emphasis on testing and verification of knowledge rather than on exploration and creative generation of new knowledge. The issues of control and legitimation come to dominate over and hamper creativity and production of new insights.

A strong accentuation on validation may also be an expression of uncertainty of the value and worth of one's own product, a requirement of external confirmation of value of one's work through some official certificates of validity.

In modern social science, there has been a pronounced concern with the trinity of reliability, validity, and generalization of knowledge. Perhaps the strong emphasis on verification of knowledge as reflection of an objective reality may also be an indication of an implicit understanding of the frail nature of this objective reality. With the belief in one absolute God superseded by the modern belief in one objective reality, the frequent ritual appeals to the holy trinity of social science may serve as assurances of the existence of one objective reality. The current concerns with the positivist trinity of knowledge may serve as an exorcism, as a way of combating doubt and of bolstering a crumbling belief in one objective and true universal reality.

A strong focus on validation may express, as well as augment, a general skepticism. There is a pervasive doubt about the value of knowledge claims, looking everywhere for flaws, errors, and possibilities of deception. Modern attempts to avoid religious dogma may have led to the other extreme of skepticism. A critical attitude toward knowledge claims, one's own as well as that of others, is a necessary part of scientific endeavor. When elevated to a dominating attitude, ruling the discourse of research, the quest for validation may, however, be self-defeating. A pervasive attention to validation becomes counterproductive and leads to a general invalidation. A research report that repeatedly and strongly stresses the validity of the findings may foster a suspicion in the reader. This may be the case if one hears something like the following in an ordinary conversation: "It is definitely true what I have told you; there is certainly nothing to be doubted; what I have told you is completely in accordance with the facts; there is no reason not to believe what I am telling you; I can prove every word I have said." The listener, who may not initially have been critical, may start becoming suspicious by the very preoccupation with telling the truth. Such a counterfactuality of strong and repeated emphasis on the truth of a statement may be expressed in the folk saying, "Beware when they swear they are telling the truth."

Rather than let the product, the knowledge claim, speak for itself, a legitimation mania may further a *validity corrosion*—the more one validates, the greater the need for further validation. By continually seeking valid proof, the quest for certainty and legitimate foundations may erode the very foundation that one is attempting to fortify. The modern preoccupation with verification may in some cases be scratching where it does not itch, with the scratching intensifying the itching as well as provoking itches where there previously were none. A modern legitimation and skepticism may feed on each other in a vicious circle. Some ways out of the validity paradox of legitimation mania and validity erosion may be suggested. First, the quality of the craftsmanship results in products with knowledge claims that are so powerful and convincing in their own right that they carry the validation with them, such as a strong piece of art. Ideally, the research procedures are transparent and the results evident, and the conclusions of a study are intrinsically convincing as true, beautiful, and good. Appeals to external certification, or official validity stamps of approval, then become secondary. In this sense, valid research would be research that makes questions of validity superfluous.

A stronger way out of the validation paradox is to live in ways that go beyond a pervasive distrust and skepticism of social interaction and the nature of the social world. This amounts to creating communities where validity does not become a primary question in social relations, neither in the scientific community nor in society at large. The question then becomes how we shall live so that we do not have to continually pose questions of validity.

REFERENCES

Altheide, D. L., & Johnson, J. M. (1994). Criteria for assessing interpretive validity in qualitative research. In N. K. Denzin & Y. S. Lincoln (Eds.), *Handbook of qualitative research* (pp. 485–499). Thousand Oaks, CA: Sage.

Becker, H. S. (1979). Do photographs tell the truth? In T. D. Cook & C. S. Reichardt (Eds.), *Qualitative and quantitative methods in evaluation research* (pp. 99–117). Beverly Hills: Sage.

Bernstein, R. J. (1983). *Beyond objectivism and relativism.* Philadelphia: University of Pennsylvania Press.

Cherryholmes, C. H. (1988). *Power and criticism: Poststructural investigations in education.* New York: Teachers College Press.

Cronbach, L. J. (1971). Test validation. In R. L. Thorndike (Ed.), *Educational measurement* (pp. 442–507). Washington, DC: American Council of Education.

Cronbach, L. J. (1980). Validity on parole: How can we go straight? *New Directions for Testing and Measurement, 5,* 99–108.

Eisner, E. W. (1991). *The enlightened eye.* New York: Macmillan.

Freud, S. (1963). *Therapy and technique.* New York: Collier.

Gergen, K. J. (1992). Toward a postmodern psychology. In S. Kvale (Ed.), *Psychology and Postmodernism* (pp. 17–30). London: Sage.

Glaser, B. G., & Strauss, A. L. (1967). *The discovery of grounded theory: Strategies for qualitative research.* New York: Aldine.

House, E. R. (1980). *Evaluating with validity.* Beverly Hills: Sage.

Kerlinger, N. (1973). *Foundation of behavioral research.* New York: Holt, Rinehart & Winston.

Kvale, S. (1976). Meanings as data and human technology. *Scandinavian Journal of Psychology, 17,* 171–180.

Kvale, S. (1989). To validate is to question. In S. Kvale (Ed.), *Issues of validity in qualitative research* (pp. 73–92). Lund, Sweden: Studentlitteratur.

Kvale, S. (1992). A postmodern psychology—A contradiction in terms? In S. Kvale (Ed.), *Psychology and postmodernism* (pp. 31–57). London: Sage.

Kvale, S. (1993a). Examinations re-examined—Certification of students or of knowledge? In S. Chaiklin & J. Lave (Eds.), *Understanding practice* (pp. 215–240). Cambridge: Cambridge University Press.

Kvale, S. (1993b). *Towards an educational rehabilitation of apprenticeship?* Unpublished manuscript, University of Aarhus, Denmark. (Revised translation of *En paedagogisk rehabilitering of mesterlaeren? Dansk Paedagogisk Tidsskrift, 1993, 41*(1), 9–18)

Kvale, S. (in press). Ten standard objections to qualitative research interviews. *Journal of Phenomenological Psychology.*

Lather, P. (1993). Fertile obsession: Validity after poststructuralism. *Sociological Quarterly, 34,* 673–693.

Lave, J., & Wenger, E. (1991). *Situated learning: Legitimate peripheral participation.* Cambridge: Cambridge University Press.

Lechler, P. (1982). Kommunikative Validierung [Communication validity]. In G. L. Huber & H. Mandl (Eds.), *Verbale Daten* (pp. 259–274). Weinheim, Germany: Beltz Verlag.

Lincoln, Y. S., & Guba, E. G. (1985). *Naturalistic inquiry.* Beverly Hills, CA: Sage.

Lincoln, Y. S., & Guba, E. G. (1990). Judging the quality of case study research. *Qualitative Studies in Education, 3*(1), 53–59.

Lyotard, J. F. (1984). *The postmodern condition: A report on knowledge.* Manchester, UK: Manchester University Press.

Miles, M. B., & Huberman, A. M. (1994). *Qualitative data analysis: A sourcebook of new methods.* Thousand Oaks, CA: Sage.

Mishler, E. G. (1990). Validation in inquiry-guided research: The role of exemplars in narrative studies. *Harvard Educational Review, 60,* 415–442.

Patton, M. Q. (1980). *Qualitative evaluation methods.* Beverly Hills: Sage.

Pervin, L. A. (1984). *Personality.* New York: Wiley.

Polkinghorne, D. (1992). Postmodern epistemology of practice. In S. Kvale (Ed.), *Psychology and postmodernism* (pp. 146–166). London: Sage.

Polkinghorne, D. E. (1983). *Methodology for the human sciences.* Albany: State University of New York Press.

Reason, P. (1994). Three approaches to participatory inquiry. In N. K. Denzin & Y. S. Lincoln (Eds.), *Handbook of qualitative research* (pp. 324–339). Thousand Oaks, CA: Sage.

Richardson, L. (1994). Writing: A method of inquiry. In N. K. Denzin & Y. S. Lincoln (Eds.), *Handbook of qualitative research* (pp. 516–529). Thousand Oaks, CA: Sage.

Ricoeur, P. (1971). The model of the text: Meaningful action considered as a text. *Social Research, 38,* 529–562.

Rorty, R. (1979). *Philosophy and the mirror of nature.* Princeton, NJ: Princeton University Press.

Rosenau, P. M. (1992). *Postmodernism and the social sciences.* Princeton, NJ: Princeton University Press.

Salner, M. (1989). Validity in human science research. In S. Kvale (Ed.), *Issues of validity in qualitative research* (pp. 47–92). Lund, Sweden: Studentliteratur.

Smith, L. M. (1990). Ethics in qualitative field research: An individual perspective. In E. W. Eisner & A. Peshkin (Eds.), *Qualitative inquiry in education* (pp. 258–276). New York: Teachers College Press.

Spence, D. (1982). *Narrative and historical truth. Meaning and interpretation in psychoanalysis.* New York: Norton.

Terhart, E. (1982). Interpretative approaches in educational research: A consideration of some theoretical issues—With particular reference to recent developments in West Germany. *Cambridge Journal of Education, 12,* 141–160.

Tschudi, F. (1989). Do qualitative and quantitative methods require different approaches to validity? In S. Kvale (Ed.), *Issues of validity in qualitative research* (pp. 109–134). Lund, Sweden: Studentliteratur.

Wahl, D. (1982). Handlungsvalidierung [Validation through action]. In G. L. Huber & H. Mandl (Eds.), *Verbale Daten* (pp. 259–274). Weinheim: Beltz Verlag.

— —

Steinar Kvale is Professor of educational psychology at the University of Aarhus, Denmark, Director of Centre of Qualitative Research the same place, and adjunct faculty at Saybrook Institute, San Francisco. He has written several articles on qualitative research and he has edited the books Psychology and Postmodernism *(1992, London: Sage) and* Issues of Validity in Qualitative Research *(1989, Lund, Sweden: Studentliteratur).*

CHAPTER 19

Emerging Criteria for Quality in Qualitative and Interpretive Research

—　—

Yvonna S. Lincoln
Texas A&M University

Not only are the boundaries of interpretive research as yet undefined, but criteria for judging the quality of such research are even more fluid and emergent. Developing criteria are nominated and cautions in applying them are discussed. The author also suggests two critical insights: The most promising of these criteria are relational, and they effectively collapse the distinction between quality (rigor) and research ethics.

Interpretive inquiry—especially as it is practiced in some fields of social science research—has been an accepted form of serious inquiry for a far shorter time than it has been for other social sciences (for instance, anthropology and sociology). Consequently, as its acceptance has been debated, it has been involved in intense cross-disciplinary discussions of what constitutes its quality criteria. I prefer to think of this issue of quality as a dialogue about *emerging criteria.* I label this discussion that way because I believe that the entire field of interpretive or qualitative inquiry is itself still emerging and being defined. There are far fewer fixed regulations in the discourse of interpretive scholarship than there are in more conventional forms of inquiry.

In the midst of this ongoing discussion, however, some scholars are arguing that interpretive research traditions have already moved beyond discussions of firm, fixed, or consensually derived criteria, which are declared foundational (or, at best, nonfoundational). As Smith (1993) points out, "The task for interpretivists is to elaborate what lies beyond epistemology and beyond the idea that there are special, abstract criteria for judging the quality of research" (p. 150), especially because "interpretivist[s] see criteria not as abstract standards, but as an open-ended, evolving list of traits that characterize what we think research should do and be like" (p. 153). These scholars have adopted a posture that is "antifoundational," that is, they argue that it has moved beyond, or stepped to the side of, rigid dualisms that characterize both empiricist and postempiricist inquiry (e.g., subject-object, true-false, objective-subjective; see, e.g., Smith, 1993, and Schwandt, 1995). But to argue that antifoundationalism avoids modernist and foundational dualisms is to sidestep an important issue, to wit, how *do* we separate good research from poor research across disciplines and traditions? That question still engages many scholars, both those seeking to do such research and those seeking to understand and to use it. And as compelling and seductive as Schwandt's (1995) call for practical rationality is (as an antidote to the epistemologic project of foundationalism), such community deliberation about *rightness* is not likely to prevail anytime soon. In fact, community deliberation about rightness—the exercise of practical rationality itself—suggests (as does Schwandt) that it has a "rhetorical" and "persuasive" (Smith, 1993, p. 16) character, which in turn suggests that listeners and dialogue participants have some standards (criteria?) by which they can judge the power or persuasiveness of various conversational and deliberative partners. We are consequently left with criteria determined by "a community of interpreters"—not far from where we are now. My own position is that conversations about criteria are important to the interpretivist community, if for no better reason than to engage and elaborate a complex and interesting dialogue and to create a space for a shared discourse wherein we might discover a new community of interpreters.

The first systematic consideration of criteria for new-paradigm inquiry was organized in 1981 by Bob Heinich, then the editor of the

TABLE 1   Criteria for Assessing Rigor or Trustworthiness in Research

Scientific Paradigm (rigor)	*Constructivist/Naturalistic Paradigm (trustworthiness)*	
Methodological criteria	Parallel Methodologic Criteria (Extrinsic)	Authenticity/ethical Criteria (Intrinsic)
Internal validity (Coherence)	Credibility (Plausibility)	Fairness
External validity (Isomorphism)	Transferability (Context-embeddedness)	Educative
Authenticity		
Reliability (Relicability)	Dependability (Stability)	Catalytic authenticity
Objectivity (Value-freedom)	Confirmability (Value explication)	Tactical authenticity
(Reliance on method)	(Reliance on data)	(Reliance on internal ethical system)

Educational Communications and Technology Journal. Bob commissioned a keynote address on rigor criteria for interpretive research; the invitees to the conference were all journal editors in education seeking guidance on how to judge qualitative studies submitted to them. That keynote address subsequently appeared in the *Educational Communications and Technology Journal* (Guba & Lincoln, 1982) under the title "Epistemological and Methodological Bases of Naturalistic Inquiry." Those guidelines essentially proposed a set of criteria, which resembled the four that guided conventional inquiry (see Columns 1 and 2, Table 1). These criteria were what we now understand to be "foundational," that is, they rested in assumptions that had been developed for an empiricist philosophy of research, and spoke to the procedural and methodological concerns that characterize empiricist and postempiricist research. Their primary use now, in my view, is to help students understand that interpretivist inquiry requires as serious a consideration of systematic, thorough, conscious method as does empiricist inquiry. I still use those methodological criteria to question doctoral students who are about to conduct dissertation research. These criteria act as reminders that seeking out multiple constructions of the world by multiple stakeholders has to be marked by serious, sustained searches for, and prolonged engagement with, those stakeholders and their constructions. Others of my colleagues seem to be less concerned with method, but disciplined inquiry is still characterized in my mind by thoughtful decisions about design strategies, including methods.

As a result of coming to understand the foundational nature of the original four criteria, Guba and I proposed five new criteria which took as their epistemologic basis the claims, concerns, and issues of the new paradigm, which by this time had been expanded and refined (Lincoln & Guba, 1985). These new criteria were highly reflective of the commitment of inquiry to fairness (balance of stakeholder views), to the learning of respondents as much as to the learning of the researcher, to the open and democratic sharing of knowledge rather than the concentration of inquiry knowledge in the hands of a privileged elite, and to the fostering, stimulation, and enabling of social action (see Column 3, Table 1; Guba & Lincoln, 1989).

Over the past decade, discussions of appropriate criteria have augmented more general debates about methodology. Scholars have taken up the issue both to defend their own work and to argue for new criteria. In retrospect, these proposals have made the field infinitely more complicated, but also infinitely more responsive, rich, and politically and ethically sensitive and complex. And this is where it begins to be interesting. The issues that scholars are proposing today make it clear that new paradigm inquiry is not, and never will be, second-rate conventional scientific inquiry. It is scientific inquiry that embraces a set of three new commitments: first, to new and emergent relations with respondents; second, to a set of stances—professional, personal, and political—toward the uses of inquiry and toward its ability to foster action; and finally, to a vision of research that enables and promotes social justice, community, diversity, civic discourse, and caring. As a result, any discussion of standards today necessarily signifies a radical shift in the vision of what research is, what it is for, and who ought to have access to it (Guba & Lincoln, 1989; Reason, 1993; Schwandt, 1995; Smith, 1993).

EMERGING CRITERIA

If one were to do a meta-analysis of these criteria, it would be quite clear that nearly all of the emerging criteria are relational, that is, they recognize and validate relationships between the inquirer and those who participate in the inquiry. This monism clearly brings the inquirer and those whose lives are being questioned into the kinds of communal contact that are not possible in more traditional inquiry, which posits a detached observer's distance between the inquirer and the subject of her inquiry. The various criteria that I wish to discuss, however, are distinctly addressed to different interpretive communities, which might be usefully described as more formal or more informal. Because of the specificity of the audience addressed, my discussion will move from the more formal toward the more intimate. I shall conclude with a discussion of several caveats that can be usefully inferred.

Standards for Judging Quality in the Inquiry Community

Elliott, Fischer, and Rennie (1994) presented a workshop at the Society for Psychotherapy Research meeting in Pittsburgh in 1993, which was dedicated to achieving some guidelines for judging qualitative research that is submitted for publication. In a document that they describe as an integration of "comments from panelists, audience, and a follow-up work group," they have proposed nine guidelines for publication. In the rationale for these nine guidelines, they observe the following:

> Diverse qualitative approaches, such as empirical phenomenological psychology, ethnography, qualitative discourse analysis, ethnomethodology, grounded theory, narratology, social action research, and symbolic interactionism, have all developed their own traditions of rigor, communication, and ways of working toward consensus. Qualitative research is conducted not to confirm or disconfirm earlier findings, but rather to contribute to a process of continuous revision and enrichment of understanding of the experience or form of action under study.
>
> The following guidelines are intended to characterize general traditions of publishability for qualitative research, guidelines to which all

authors hold themselves in principle, although the particular expressions of the traditions may vary. (Elliott et al., 1994)
Elliott and his colleagues (1994) have proposed that

[(1) manuscripts be] of archival significance. That is . . . [they] contribute to the building of the discipline's body of knowledge and understanding. (2) The manuscript specifies where the study fits within relevant literature and indicates the intended contributions (purposes or questions) of the study. (3) The procedures used are appropriate or responsive to the intended contributions (purposes of questions posed for the study). (4) Procedures are specified clearly so that readers may see how to conduct a similar study themselves and may judge for themselves how well the study followed its stated procedures. (5) The research results are discussed in terms of their contribution to theory, content, method, and/or practical domains. (6) Limitations of the study are discussed. (7) The manuscript is written clearly, and any necessary technical terms are defined. (8) *Any speculation is clearly identified as speculation.* (9) The manuscript is acceptable to reviewers familiar with its content area and with its method[s]. (emphasis added)

Please notice that most of us would agree that these are strong criteria or standards for the publication of any form of research, whether conventional or new paradigm. We might quibble about the relative openness of some of the wording, and we might suggest different ways of speaking about interpretive work, but in principle, Elliott and his colleagues have done a careful job of thinking through these guidelines. Their strength, however, is also their weakness: They bear a strong resemblance to quality criteria for conventional research, and in fact display no particular characteristics that would make them responsive primarily or only to qualitative or interpretivist issues. That is to say, any researcher, working in any paradigm that might be used in scholarly work, would almost surely assent to these criteria. Nevertheless, they are one attempt to provide additional clarity with respect to the disciplined nature of such work. The criteria proposed relate almost solely to the inquiry community (that is, to the knowledge production end of the research enterprise), but they are useful because they suggest how qualitative researchers have gone about answering the criticisms of the conventional community.

The statement of standards that Elliott and his colleagues (1994) developed have another weakness, however; this one is grounded in the "conceptual practices of power" (Schwandt, 1995). They are highly responsive to a situation described by Smith (1993, pp. 156-157), wherein the issue of criteria does indeed determine what will be presented and what will be published. And those things, Smith points out, have very clear implications not only for the social status of research knowledge, but also for the careers of social science researchers. Criteria viewed from this vantage point, particularly these criteria, which are aimed at publication, serve a strong exclusionary legitimation function within either the conceptual practice of power or the practice of conceptual power.

Positionality, or Standpoint Judgments

A second kind of quality criteria has to do with what I will label, as others have done, *positionality*. Positionality has been treated in the literature as though it were an epistemologic concern—and it most assuredly is—but I would argue that it is far more critical than simply being an epistemologic position, although that is assuredly important. Positionality, or standpoint epistemology, recognizes the poststructural, postmodern argument that texts, any texts, are always partial and incomplete; socially, culturally, historically, racially, and sexually located; and can therefore never represent any truth except those truths that exhibit the same characteristics. From the work of the standpoint epistemologists (Haraway, 1989; hooks, 1990, 1992, 1994), we can deduce that texts that claim whole and complete truth or that claim to present universal, grand, metanarrative, or generalizable knowledge (or knowledge that applies to all similar individuals or groups across time and across contexts) are themselves specious, inauthentic, and misleading. For standpoint epistemologists, only texts that display their own contextual grounds for argumentation would be eligible for appellations of quality and rigor. In this fashion, what has been treated as grounds for knowing becomes a standard by which all texts might be judged as quality or nonquality scholarship.

For standpoint epistemologists, a text that displays honesty or authenticity "comes clean" about its own stance and about the position of the author. The "immaculate perception" of the realist tale (van Maanen, 1988) is pointedly denied; texts that are not open about their social and cultural positions in the larger intertextual conversation are specifically interrogated and deconstructed to determine their situatedness. Detachment and author objectivity are barriers to quality, not insurance of having achieved it.

Community as Arbiter of Quality

The next set of criteria that are emerging as quality-cum-ethical criteria are a set I would group under the rubric of *community*. Although we might quibble about my name for this category, this particular set of standards does indeed reference the communitarian nature of research as it is reconceived in new-paradigm work. I label it *communitarian* because it recognizes that research takes place in, and is addressed to, a community; it is also accurately labeled because of the desire of those who discuss such research to have it serve the purposes of the community in which it was carried out, rather than simply serving the community of knowledge producers and policymakers. That is to say, it has much broader implications and uses than those to which most research has been directed in the near and far past. Among the scholars and theorists who are exploring community, I would nominate Palmer (1987) and Savage (1988).

Palmer (1987) is primarily concerned with the reestablishment of a sense of true community in academe, but in the process, he points out that the academic community's commitment to the traditional scientific paradigm's requirement of objectivity leads us to a stance of objectifying virtually all of our missions: teaching, inquiry, public service, and collegial relations. The consequences of such objectification of our social relations, he argues, have been a destruction of community and a perversion of research efforts. Only by abandoning the senseless commitment to what we now think of as objectivity can we reattain the state of being a learning community. The question he has posed in his work is: "How should we be thinking about the nature of community in the modern college and university?" The conclusion that he draws is that "epistemology is [not] a bloodless abstraction;

the *way* we *know* has powerful implications for the *way* we *live*" (Palmer, 1987, p. 22; emphases added). He goes on to elaborate the argument by noting that

> *every epistemology tends to become an ethic,* and that every way of knowing tends to become a way of living . . . [such that] the relation established between the knower and the known, between the student and the subject, tends to become the relation of the living person to the world itself . . . [and that] *every mode of knowing contains its own moral trajectory,* its own ethical direction and outcomes. (p. 22; emphases added)

Proposing that all knowing is relational and that objectivism (as one aspect of rigor in knowing and knowledge), with its analytic and experimentalist view of the world and persons in it, undermines community, Palmer suggests that objectivist knowing is essentially "anticommunal." That is, it subverts and effectively destroys the possibilities for community, except for that community dedicated to looking at the world in objectivist, abstract, analytic, manipulative, and experimentalist modes. Palmer suggests that new epistemologies might indeed create relational knowledge, the quality and rigor of which might be grounded in nonfragmenting, community-oriented ways of knowing. These might include, according to Palmer, feminist thought, Black scholarship, Native American studies, or ecological studies (Palmer, 1987, p. 24).

Savage (1988) moves the arguments about community specifically to the ethnographic research context. Savage is concerned not only with the devices or methods that we use to assure quality, but also with what quality itself might mean. Her answer is that quality research is that which "integrates research, critical reflection, and action"—a characteristic that she labels, from her work in Nicaragua, as *neighborliness*. She likens her position to those of liberation pedagogy and theology, which are themselves outgrowths of critical theory and action research. Again, we see the close connection between knowledge and the community from which it springs, and in which it is intended to be used.

Savage (1988) defines neighborliness as a "kind of praxis, a practical activity having a complex intellectual dimension, exercised for the sake of assisting the marginalized on a journey toward greater freedom and participation in common life" (p. 13). Neighborliness does not reject quantitative forms of proof, Savage says, but she agrees with Willis (1977, cited in LeCompte, 1993) that there is probably little that "reproduces something of the original" in such estimates of quality, and so ethnography typically spurns such forms of rigor and reliability (Savage, 1988, pp. 13-14). In aligning one strand of ethnography with the critical tradition—a move echoed by Kincheloe, McLaren, Carspecken, Willis, and others—Savage's intent is to place judgments of quality in the ability of research to link itself with "social action and social consequences" (p. 7). Thus research is first and foremost a community project, not a project of the academic disciplines alone (or even primarily).

The perspectives of Palmer (1987) and Savage (1988) move closer to the later arguments of Schwandt (1995) for creating dialogue and modes of discourse within interpretive communities, informed by moral reasoning as well as practical considerations. However, the emphases of Savage on action alongside and informed by inquiry, and of Palmer on the caring and trust within close-knit communities, reflect a somewhat broader sense of community than Schwandt explores at present.

Voice

Yet another criterion that is mentioned increasingly by researchers and theorists alike is *voice*. Attention to voice—to who speaks, for whom, to whom, for what purposes—effectively creates praxis, even when no praxis was intended. Patricia Hill-Collins, bell hooks, Dorothy Collins, and researchers from many disciplines have tackled the problem of voice: Who speaks for those who do not have access to the corridors of knowledge or the venues of the academic disciplines? LeCompte (1993) argues that it is the responsibility of serious qualitative research to "seek out the silenced because their perspectives are often counter-hegemonic" (p. 10). Research on voice and on the absence of voice or silencing must, Tierney (1993) argues, [maintain] traditional social-science standards of accuracy and representation, but it must also break down the shibboleths of disengagement and objectivity. Instead, postmodern research demands that the researcher be involved both with the "research subject" and with changing those conditions that seek to silence and marginalize. (p. 5)

This view of voice—voice as resistance against silence, as resistance to disengagement, as resistance to marginalization—echoes the cry for "passionate participation" (Lincoln, 1987) as a hallmark of quality in interpretive work and reflects earlier demands for any given text to demonstrate activeness, a committed stance on the part of the researcher, and a certain openness to multiple voices and interpretations of the work first proposed by Zeller (1986).

Thus voice not only becomes a characteristic of interpretive work, but the extent to which alternative voices are heard is a criterion by which we can judge the openness, engagement, and problematic nature of any text.

Critical Subjectivity

Yet another criterion is reflexivity, or critical subjectivity. Subjectivity goes under many names: critical subjectivity (Carr & Kemmis, 1986), transformative subjectivity (Frieden, 1989), and critical reflexivity. Although there is no general agreement on what the various forms of subjectivities or reflexivities might be, I will attempt to talk around the concept for the purposes of this work. Critical subjectivity or reflexivity is the ability to enter an altered state of consciousness (Heron, 1981; Rowan, 1981, p. 169) or "high-quality awareness" (Reason & Rowan, 1981) for the purpose of understanding with great discrimination subtle differences in the personal and psychological states of others. Further, such reflexivity is absolutely required to understand one's psychological and emotional states before, during, and after the research experience. Such reflexivity or subjectivity enables the researcher to begin to uncover dialectic relationships, array and discuss contradictions within the stories being recorded, and move with research participants toward action. Thus the words *transformative* and *critical* not only embody the action aspects of research, but also recognize the ability of meaningful research experiences to heighten self-awareness in the research process and create personal and social transformation.

Reciprocity

Reciprocity is a term I first encountered in the works of both Rowan (1981) and Reinharz (1979). Reciprocity as a characteristic of high-quality, rigorous qualitative interpretive inquiry is argued to be essential because of the person-centered nature of interpretive work. Rowan (1981), drawing on the work of Aaron Esterson, argues for this "science of reciprocities" because, quoting Esterson:

> Persons are always in relation [and therefore] one cannot study persons without studying the relations they make with others. . . . And the method used to observe must be one that allows us to study the personal form of relating. . . . The observer, with the cooperation of the other, constitutes himself as part of the field of study, while studying the field he and the other constitute. . . . [The researcher] must be able to reflect upon, and reason about, a reciprocity that includes himself as one of the reciprocating terms. (pp. 167-168)

McLaughlin and Tierney (1993) and I (1993) built on this reciprocity in our later work, arguing for the kind of intense sharing that opens all lives party to the inquiry to examination. But as far back as 1978, Shula Reinharz also dealt with reciprocity, characterizing high-quality research as a kind of "lover-model," wherein parties to the research effort and their relationships were marked by a deep sense of trust, caring, and mutuality.

Sacredness

The next criterion that is emerging is sacredness. The work of some of the feminist writers and the work of management specialists have begun, remarkably, to share some common themes. Merchant's *The*

Death of Nature (1983) and Schaef's *Women's Reality* (1981) both deal specifically with the relationship between feminism as an inquiry model and ethical and ecological concerns, or concern for the physical environment and its resources. Berry (1988) links not feminism, but rather emerging models and paradigms of science to ecological concerns in a way that recognizes and honors the ecological as well as the human. His concern is that in the destruction of the physical environment are the seeds for the destruction of the human spirit. Only by recapturing the sense of sacredness about that which nourishes and sustains us can we learn how both to inquire sanely and to live in peace.

This theme has been elaborated recently by Reason (1993), who argues that science has a sacred and spiritual character. The spiritual, or sacred, side of science emerges from a profound concern for human dignity, justice, and interpersonal respect. The sacredness in the enterprise of science issues from the collaborative and egalitarian aspects of the relationships created in the research-to-action continuum. Researchers who conceive of science in this way make space for the lifeways of others and create relationships that are based not on unequal power, but on mutual respect, granting of dignity, and deep appreciation of the human condition.

Sharing the Perquisites of Privilege

Brown (1993), in a recent "Point of View" piece in the *Chronicle of Higher Education*, makes a rather stunning admission when she says that she and her research respondent, "Mama Lola" (see Brown, 1992), both share in the royalties of the book whose life Mama Lola lives and whose life Brown chronicled in her eponymous book. Brown shares with her readers that when Mama Lola runs short of money, Brown contributes to the mortgage payment.

Lather (1995) has a similar situation in her work with women who live with HIV/AIDS. Although Lather does not contribute money to these women, she is very clear that the first publication—a desktop publication effort—will be for the women themselves, and that they will seek trade publication for a wider sharing of their story together:

that is, Lather, her co-researcher, and the women respondents in the HIV/AIDS support group with whom the two women have been working for 2 years.

Whereas Brown's (1993) sharing of the perquisites is a direct form of recompense for the story to which she has been allowed access, Lather's (1995) relationship is somewhat different. Brown acknowledges directly—through royalty payments split down the middle and through direct cash contributions to the running of Mama Lola's household—the debt that we owe as ethnographers, anthropologists, and qualitative researchers to the persons whose lives we portray. It is not a far leap to comprehend that the lives to which we have access account in no small part for the prestige we enjoy in the worlds we create and sustain via our research. I have written before (Lincoln, 1994, in press) about the question of who "owns" the lives we use, however sacredly and respectfully, for our research. For the somewhat dark side of research hides the fact that most of our research is written for ourselves and our own consumption, and it earns us the dignity, respect, prestige, and economic power in our own worlds that those about whom we write frequently do not have.

Lather's case is somewhat different, but it speaks to the sharing of perquisites nonetheless. It seems to me that Lather is trying, with her co-researcher and the participants, to re-create in textual form some of the complexity, horror, love, and anguish that the support group is going through, and at the same time inviting them to co-create with her a testament to their lives. When the desktop version of this text is created, the HIV-positive women will then begin to respond to what has been assembled from their stories. And the story is told largely in their own words. Although I have no information on royalties should their text become a trade book, it is clear that the women will have been enabled to create a living document about their lives, their struggles, their worries about their children—a personal and group history in which each of them will share some portion of ownership. In a sense, they will have gained power from the work which Lather and her co-researcher have undertaken on their behalf. Indeed, both of these models of ethnographic research begin to approximate very closely the world of true participant action inquiry, where the former subjects of research become active participants in reclaiming their own histories and re-creating their lives.

As we work with respondents in the future, we may have to "come clean" about the advantages that accrue to us as knowledge producers, especially the claim that we, and not they, are the genuine producers. Over time, this acknowledgment may prompt us to reconfigure our relationships not only with fieldwork, but also with our disciplines and our research participants. Imagine an academic world in which judgments about promotion, tenure, and merit pay are made on the basis of the extent of our involvement with research participants, rather than on our presumed objective distance!

SOME CAUTIONS ABOUT
THE EMERGING CRITERIA

I would like to advance a few cautions about this new work. First and foremost, specific criteria might apply to specific kinds or classes of research. To put it another way, any given criterion might have been extracted from a specific set of studies in which the proposer was engaged, and thus another inquirer might find limited utility or applicability for the specific criterion. It is untested whether this particular list would be widely or universally applicable to all qualitative or interpretive research. As the research group I cited earlier commented, different traditions might require different criteria, and indeed, we may be moving beyond criteriology and the search for uniform criteria. This will make our professional judgments harder but it has the potential to make our research more locally usable, as we might perhaps tailor our criteria to the community, or even better, permit criteria to grow indigenously as a natural consequence of the inquiry effort.

The second caution is that some of the criteria may be applicable at a certain stage of the inquiry but less applicable at another. I will use my own authenticity criteria as an example. Fairness could certainly apply to any and all forms of qualitative research and at any stage of the research. But one might be able to achieve catalytic or tactical authenticity only after ontological and educative authenticity have been reasonably fully achieved. In the same sense, and to use another example, voice (or achieving pluralistic voices) might reasonably be expected to occur throughout virtually all stages of an inquiry, but would grow increasingly important as consensus toward action in the social sense and construction of texts in the scholarly or community sense occurs. Thus the qualitative research community might well think about which criteria, at which stage, are the most useful and important, and to whom. Because new-paradigm inquiry directs our attention to multiple audiences and consumers and actors involved in cooperating on, directing, analyzing, creating, and using our research, we might usefully think about criteria for whom, and for what purpose.

The third idea to which I would like to draw attention is that all, or virtually all, of these criteria are relational. Reason and Rowan (1981) emphasized this idea when they pointed out that "any notion of validity must concern itself both with the knower and with what is to be known; valid knowledge is a matter of *relationship*" (p. 241, emphasis added).

The fourth caution I would advance is that just as the naturalistic/constructivist paradigm effectively brought about the irrelevance of the distinction between ontology and epistemology, so too does this paradigm and interpretive social science in general bring about the collapse of the distinctions between standards, rigor, and quality criteria and the formerly separate consideration of research ethics. In effect, many of the proposed and emerging standards for quality in interpretive social science are also standards for ethics. At the time of John K. Smith's gentle criticism of the so-called parallel, or foundational, criteria, I did not understand that standards for quality profoundly interacted with standards for ethics in inquiry. In work directed specifically toward the ethics of qualitative inquiry (Guba & Lincoln, 1989), we were able to generate five previously undiscussed issues in qualitative research, each of which enlarged the debate about standards to which qualitative inquiry might be held. Those were the problems of face-to-face encounters, for example, the necessity to build trust and rapport in what are sometimes short time frames; the virtual impossibility of maintaining anonymity in qualitative research under some circumstances; the problem of selecting and excluding material to be included in a case study; and the political and ethical pressure for open and honest negotiations around data collection, analysis, and presentation (Guba & Lincoln, 1989). None of these is particularly an issue of concern in conventional inquiry, and thus there are no federal guidelines for addressing them. This dissolution of the hard boundaries between rigor and ethics in turn signals that the new research is a relational research—a research grounded in the recognition and valuing of connectedness between researcher and researched, and between knowledge elites and the societies and communities in which they live and labor. Relationality is the major characteristic of research that is neighborly, that is, it is rooted in emerging conceptions of community, shared governance and decision making, and equity. Indeed, community (Stringer, in press) and neighborliness may be the most compelling metaphors for these emergent forms of inquiry and quality in inquiry.

CONCLUSION

What does all this mean? There is a very funny story in the hard sciences about a great physicist who gave a presidential address to a learned society sometime just before the turn of the century. He mourned in this address that new, young physicists had little to do but extend the decimal points out a few numbers farther. This speech occurred just before the work of Heisenberg, Bohr, and Einstein burst upon the world. The point of that story for me has always been that we never know when disciplinary or transdisciplinary challenges will arise, because the very nature of challenges is that they come from unexpected places.

We have a dialogue going now. It is about how we make judgments, how we can trust each other and the things we write. It is about creating certainty when life is about ambiguity. It is about what Karl Weick called creating "a little cognitive economy, and some peace of mind." We are not ready either to close down the conversation or to say farewell to criteria quite yet.

REFERENCES

Berry, T. (1988). *The dream of the earth*. San Francisco: Sierra Club Nature and Natural Philosophy Library.

Brown, K. M. (1992). *Mama Lola: A voudou priestess in Brooklyn*. Berkeley: University of California Press.

Brown, K. M. (1993, April 15). Point of view: Writing about "the other." *Chronicle of Higher Education*, p. A56.

Carr, W., & Kemmis, S. (1986). *Becoming critical: Education, knowledge and action research.* Philadelphia: Falmer.

Elliott, R., Fischer, C., & Rennie, D. (1994). *Evolving guidelines for publication of qualitative research studies.* Unpublished manuscript.

Frieden, S. (1989). Transformative subjectivity in the writings of Christa Wolf. In The Personal Narratives Group (Eds.), *Interpreting women's lives: Feminist theory and personal narratives* (pp. 172-188). Bloomington: Indiana University Press.

Guba, E. G., & Lincoln, Y. S. (1982). Epistemological and methodological bases of naturalistic inquiry. *Educational Communications and Technology Journal, 30,* 233-252.

Guba, E. G., & Lincoln, Y. S. (1989). *Fourth generation evaluation.* Thousand Oaks, CA: Sage.

Haraway, D. (1989). Situated knowledges: The science question in feminism and the privilege of partial perspective. *Feminist Studies, 14*(3), 575-599.

Heron, J. (1981). Philosophical basis for a new paradigm. In P. Reason & J. Rowan (Eds.), *Human inquiry: A sourcebook of new paradigm research* (pp. 19-36). New York: Wiley.

hooks, b. (1990). *Yearning: Race, gender, and cultural politics.* Boston: South End.

hooks, b. (1992). *Black looks: Race and representation.* Boston: South End.

hooks, b. (1994). *Outlaw culture: Resisting representations.* New York: Routledge.

Lather, P. (1995, April). *Creating a multi-layered text: Women, AIDS, and angels.* Paper presented at the Annual Meeting of the American Educational Research Association, San Francisco.

LeCompte, M. D. (1993). A framework for hearing silence: What does telling stories mean when we are supposed to be doing science? In D. McLaughlin & W. G. Tierney (Eds.), *Naming silenced lives: Personal narratives and the process of educational change* (pp. 2-9). New York: Routledge.

Lincoln, Y. (1993). I and thou: Method, voice, and roles in research with the silenced. In D. McLaughlin & W. G. Tierney (Eds.), *Naming silenced lives: Personal narratives and the process of educational change.* New York: Routledge.

Lincoln, Y. S. (1987, April). *The passionate participant vs. the detached observer.* Paper presented at the American Education Research Association Annual Meeting, San Francisco.

Lincoln, Y. S. (1994, May). *The sixth moment: Emerging problems in qualitative research.* Paper presented at the Annual Meeting, Society for Studies in Symbolic Interaction, Urbana, Illinois.

Lincoln, Y. S. (in press). The sixth moment: Emerging problems in qualitative research. *Symbolic Interaction Review Annual.*

Lincoln, Y. S., & Guba, E. G. (Eds.). (1985). *Naturalistic inquiry.* Thousand Oaks, CA: Sage.

McLaughlin, D., & Tierney, W. G. (Eds.). (1993). *Naming silenced lives: Personal narratives and the process of educational change.* New York: Routledge.

Merchant, C. (1983). *The death of nature: Women, ecology and the scientific revolution.* London: Wildwood House.

Palmer, P. J. (1987). Community, conflict, and ways of knowing: Ways to deepen our educational agenda. *Change, 19*(5), 20-25.

Reason, P. (1993). Reflections on sacred experience and sacred science. *Journal of Management Inquiry, 2*(3), 273-283.

Reason, P., & Rowan, J. (Eds.). (1981a). *Human inquiry: A sourcebook of new paradigm research.* New York: Wiley.

Reason, P., & Rowan, J. (1981). Issues of validity in new paradigm research. In P. Reason & J. Rowan (Eds.), *Human inquiry: A sourcebook of new paradigm inquiry* (pp. 239-250). New York: Wiley.

Reinharz, S. (1979). *On becoming a social scientist.* San Francisco: Jossey-Bass.

Rowan, J. (1981). "The leaves of spring" by Aaron Esterson: An appreciation. In P. Reason & J. Rowan (Eds.), *Human inquiry: A sourcebook of new paradigm inquiry* (pp. 167-171). New York: Wiley.

Savage, M. C. (1988). Can ethnographic narrative be a neighborly act? *Anthropology and Education Quarterly, 19,* 3-19.

Schaef, A. W. (1981). *Women's reality: An emerging female system in the white male society.* Minneapolis, MN: Winston.

Schwandt, T. A. (1995, March). *Farewell to criteriology.* Paper presented to the Quality in Human Inquiry Conference, University of Bath, U.K.

Smith, J. K. (1993). *After the demise of empiricism: The problem of judging social and education inquiry.* Norwood, NJ: Ablex.

Stringer, E. (in press). *Action research: A guide for practitioners.* Thousand Oaks, CA: Sage.

Tierney, W. G. (1993). Introduction. In D. McLaughlin & W. G. Tierney (Eds.), *Naming silenced lives: Personal narratives and the process of educational change.* New York: Routledge.

van Maanen, J. (1988). *Tales of the field. On writing ethnography.* Chicago: University of Chicago Press.

Zeller, N. (1986). *A rhetoric for naturalistic inquiry.* Unpublished doctoral dissertation.

— —

Yvonna S. Lincoln is Professor of Higher Education and Department Head, Department of Educational Administration, Texas A&M University. She is working on a book about dilemmas around policy when scientific discourses are no longer shared and when models of research compete and are in conflict. Her interests include methodology in qualitative research and the development of criteria for judging the products of such work. She is also the co-editor of Qualitative Inquiry *with Norman K. Denzin, with whom she also collaborated on the* Handbook of Qualitative Research.

CHAPTER 20

Confronting Anthropology's Silencing Praxis

Speaking Of/From a Chicana Consciousness

— —

Mónica Russel y Rodríguez

Metropolitan State College

In this article, the author explores how both normative and oppositional stances contribute to a silencing praxis in anthropology. She suggests that anthropology as a discipline and as an institution works hard to silence due to its history, its theoretical nature, and its methods that require static and uncomplicated single identities of its subjects and theoreticians. The practice and theory of anthropology contradict each other. Its practice demands an ethnographer-Native informer dyad, placing the ethnographer as the knower while only valuing the knowledge of the Native. Its theory values native knowledge and exalts diversity vis-à-vis cultural relativism. Opposing either theory or practice underscores the paradox. As a Chicana anthropologist, the author experiences a tricky conflation of these competing agendas. She recommends exposing these limitations and actively reclaiming the very voice and epistemology that has been denounced to persist in the method and efficacy of anthropology.

The Chicana among feminists, the feminist among Chicanos. The Chicano nationalist among Euro-Americans, the bridge builder among Chicano nationalists. Half Anglo, half Chicana. The newcomer in academe, the overeducated at home. The minority among the majority, the mainstream among raza. The binaries of my many identities are not so much a feeling of displacement for me, rather they bring a sense that I have many homes. These oppositional identities are not contradictions: They shape and are shaped by their analogue. They are powerful. Yet, I cannot always readily find those spaces. Oppositional strategies give way when they cannot afford me complexity, when those very spaces silence my voice.

As a theoretician, I often feel that I am the anthropologist among literary critics or cultural studies types: I provide the touchstone data to the occasional far-flung theory. The thing that confounds me in writing this article is that although I can see the utility of anthropology and I willingly occupy that position, I cannot find my place among anthropologists. For I have experienced myself among anthropologists not with a position but as absent, voiceless, nearly invisible. I see oppositional spaces in which power is generated from and in reaction to the norm. Yet, this oppositional stance only places me in other silencing locations.

In this article, I explore how both normative and oppositional stances contribute to a silencing praxis in anthropology. It seems to me that anthropology as a discipline and as an institution works hard to silence many of us, and I have difficulty transcending the demand to find a single identity—party line or oppositional—because anthropology, by its history, its theoretical nature, and its methods, requires static and uncomplicated single identities of its subjects and theoreticians. The normative practice and the theory of anthropology contradict each other. Its practice demands an ethnographer-Native informer dyad, placing the ethnographer as the knower while only valuing the knowledge of the Native.[1] Its theory values Native knowledge and exalts diversity vis-à-vis cultural relativism. Opposing either theory or practice underscores the paradox. As a Chicana anthropologist, I experience a tricky conflation of these competing agendas, agendas that leave me little space to stand.

Opposition is equally restricting and silencing, providing no refuge. Each stance that is oppositional to the conventional practice seems to be equally silencing, however, for different reasons. Opposition signals the role of the "authentic" Native, simultaneously appropriated and rejected from conventional anthropological paradigms. In rejecting the silencing norm, I seek out another space. Yet, these loci sustain the very idea of binary and static roles. I do not merely experience being ignored but being actively reshaped to fit into a mold and cannon that is so troubling.[2] Because the contemporary experience of ethnocentrism is based in a history of colonization, only as a strategy might I be willing to masochistically explore my inability to find a voice not to expose anthropology's neglect of feminists of color and other disenfranchised scholars but to interrogate anthropology, its practice and theory, showing how it actively silences.[3]

NORMATIVE ANTHROPOLOGY

A QUESTION OF THE KNOWER
The relationship between social scientist and object of study is one of unequal power. The underlying epistemology marks the anthropologist as knower and the Native as knowable, simple, able to be fully comprehended. The all too familiar binaries—ethnographer-informant, object-subject, Self-Other, Western-Native—persist despite anthropology's discussion of these demons of its colonial past. We have thoroughly criticized objectifying practices and theories in anthropology, a criticism meant to exorcise those demons. Indeed, this new stance is now so well documented as to appear to be a moot point, yet, it is not. In practice, the Native informer does not become subject. The Native informer is not acknowledged as knower or producer of theory. Henrietta Moore (1994, 1996) cogently reveals how the status of the knower is limited and determined within both empiricist and interpretivist paradigms—the two major schools of anthropological thought. Empiricist paradigms rest on objectivity, asserting that the world is knowable in a concrete way, thus configuring the Native as knowable and the objective observer as knower. Interpretivist paradigms see the production of ethnographic knowledge as mediated through the perspective of the person writing the ethnography. Hence, the interpretive lens and the authority that rests in authorship again sustains the anthropologist as active theorist, often replacing the Native as the central figure altogether (Moore, 1996).

An explosion of articles by scholars of color writing about their own communities, potential Native knowers that might be incorporated into anthropology, have been virtually ignored.[4] Dismissed and shunted off to what is supposed to be a lesser discipline—ethnic studies—anthropology ironically rejects the challenge that it is presumably well situated to take up: understanding representation, race, identity, and power in this postmodern world.[5] I suggest that being a Chicana anthropologist focusing on Chicana/ Chicano communities disrupts this division of the knower and the Native. Visweswaran (1994) comments on this peculiar exclusion of the theoretical contributions made by many scholars of color:

> I am not surprised that no inclusion of work done in ethnic studies or so-called indigenous anthropology is made in experimental ethnography, but I am dismayed. This, despite the fact these writings explicitly challenge the authority of representation . . . of themselves. Self writing about like selves has thus far not been on the agenda of experimental ethnography. To accept "native" authority is to give up the game. (p. 32)

The single status of ethnographer as objective knower not only corners the Native as the knowable, static, simple object but upholds the researcher as superior, civilized, and complex. Conversely, the criterion for being the objective knower is to be not-Native. The Native knower, or Visweswaran's "'native' authority," reveals this naked contradiction.[6] Although anthropologists of color are equally capable of writing good and bad ethnographies they/we are also well positioned to expose this division.[7]

Ana Castillo (1994), a Chicana writing about Chicanas, recognized the futility of working within existing anthropological paradigms in *Massacre of the Dreamers*. She identified a common, yet ironic, reality that the discipline of understanding culture does not provide insight for the Native knower. "At best I found ethnographic data that ultimately did not bring me closer to understanding how the Mexic Amerindian[8] woman truly perceives herself since anthropology is traditionally based on the objectification of its subjects" (p. 7). Castillo abandons anthropology and its tenets to position herself as a Chicana and theoretician and other Chicanas as knowers not as merely knowable. The question of how we see our multiple selves, in all our complexity, is sacrificed in the name of who can be the authentic or legitimate knower.

Many anthropologists have similarly questioned these complexities and challenges that are obscured or evaded by writing exclusively to or heeding critiques only from an academic community. This is usually couched as a dilemma facing only Native scholars as they identify the multiple audiences that might read their/our work.[9] I insist that this accountability should not be limited to the Native anthropologist but that Native anthropologists are well positioned to highlight this complexity of multiple audiences who are poised to disavow the knower-Native dyad. With notable exceptions, the intended reading audience for an ethnography about Mexican Americans rarely includes Mexican Americans. It is for this reason that Castillo (1994) asserted that anthropology does not provide insight for her, that it does not recognize Chicanas as knowers or theorists (see also Paredes, 1978).

The secondary feature that emanates from a normative paradigm of the knower anthropologist demands that the researcher also has one identity, a single subjectivity, and that is as the social scientist. Acknowledging the multiple subjectivities of the anthropologist and of the subjects and communities interrupts the knower-Native binary. To uphold the myth, the researcher must elide the power relationship with the communities in question (Zavella, 1993), which is especially noticeable if there are conflicting loyalties (see Visweswaran, 1994).[10] Abu-Lughod (1991) suggests that the epistemological structure of anthropology discourages us from directing our comments to more than one sense of who us/we might be. She is speaking of anthropologists who are "halfies" (people who are biracial, multiracial, or ethnic) and the dilemma they/we have in trying to figure out to which half of our apparent split subjectivities to write. However, I think her observations reflect the larger tensions felt by any anthropologist who identifies personally and politically with a community that is not exclusively academic, especially if class and access to economic power distinguish the two audiences. She describes the dilemma of being from two distinct communities.

> Halfies' dilemmas are even more extreme. As anthropologists, they write for other anthropologists, mostly Western. Identified also with communities outside the East, or subcultures within it, they are called to account by educated members of those communities. More impor-

tantly, not just because when they present the Other they are presenting themselves, they speak with a complex awareness of and investment in reception. (Abu-Lughod, 1991, p. 142)

I would further suggest that such dilemmas are good, that I/we should be aware of how our work will be perceived by various communities. Critical is that positioning and revealing of ourselves and our investments in the production of knowledge. Visweswaran (1994) names this "identifying ethnography," defining it as a practice "that asks that we exhibit and examine our alliances in the same moment" (p. 132).

Still, the production of knowable and definable contributions to the science of anthropology is valued over the theoretical and, paradoxically, highly espoused deconstruction of the object-subject relationship. Although anthropology as a discipline continues to fret over the power relationship inherent in its objectifying practices, actively dismantling that power is not rewarded. Displaying one's self as being politically or personally invested, as abdicating the presumption to define, and/or as being invested in the study of one's own community signals being not legitimate (Abu-Lughod, 1991; Lassalle & Pérez, 1997; Narayan, 1993; Weston, 1997). Although I could potentially be Chicana and anthropologist, to be a legitimate anthropologist, I should not study my own people. Kath Weston (1997) describes this delegitimizing feature of the "virtual anthropologist" who is not regarded as a "real" academician. In turn, to practice anthropology in the conventional, accepted manner, is to ask me and others to assume a position that cuffs ourselves into a paradigm that does not address what we really see. Arrested of insight and contribution, I would have to ignore the reality of my experience to privilege myself as a social scientist.

WANTING TO/TRYING TO BE THAT

KNOWER OR TO BE AN ANTHROPOLOGIST

I cannot think of a time in which anthropology and I regarded each other more critically than when I was on the market-the job market. Here, any identity I held became suspect and insufficient. I could not find an identity that would allow me to have a relationship, even an oppositional one, to anthropology. Again, an oppositional stance would, of course, give me a defined place in anthropology while shaping and being shaped by the discipline. Wanting to fit into the discipline from which I received three degrees, I tried to "be all that I could be" as an anthropologist. I was ready to sign up with the troops to ensure that I would be able to start paying off those college and graduate school student loans. I discovered that I could hold rank in two ways: perpetuate objectification and thereby uphold the practice of anthropology or become "the" Native scholar and thereby sustain the theory of anthropology.

The theory for my dissertation linked my insight from my family and communities with broader questions of class mobility, gender, sexuality, and race (Russel y Rodríguez, 1995). I drew from information from and participation with women I knew and with those who would become my friends.[11] I feared being disparaged as unscientific, self-reflexive, and indulgent. If I could have managed, I probably would have produced some generalizable laws of Chicana womanhood, but my mother was going to read my work, and the women I interviewed had already heard my conclusions. How could I spew, all chopped up and unrecognizable, the strength and ganas I saw in my mother and in my friends? How could I "Other" my mother? It was her comadre, Priscilla Salazar, telling me that I was "full of it," that I feared more than anthropologists telling me I was unscientific. Salazar is intelligent and well read, although she doesn't have a bunch of degrees. I would have to objectify women I knew and with whom I identified to save this social science. No, it wasn't just the scientific paradigm I had to watch out for, it was las comadres. They are knowers and theoreticians, and besides, they don't mince words. To become an authentic knower, I would have to ignore what I knew was a strength: the insight into both academic theory and local, Chicana women's theory.

Becoming the Native anthropologist was the other available space: oppositional yet well-defined, good benefits if I landed the right job. But I could not find a space for myself or my research. I found that the space I might use and that data I might wield were usurped by a system that is predicated on appropriating the knowledge and voice of the Other. My tentative legitimacy would be based on my ability to present myself as sufficiently Native. And neither I nor my research would satisfactorily stand still to be "authentic" Mexicanas.

NOT WANTING TO BE "THE" CHICANA

ANTHROPOLOGIST, ESSENTIALLY

The highly touted demand to assume the role of "the" Native scholar appears seductive to some, although many of us know that it provides no refuge (see Abu-Lughod, 1991; Limón, 1994; Rosaldo, 1989). Taking on the essentialized role and moral authority as "the" Chicana anthropologist is no oppositional stance that could dismantle the powers that I indict.[12] This would further the stereotype rather than confound it (Motzafi-Haller, 1997; Narayan, 1993). Virginia Dominguez (1994) makes the excellent observation that a few scholars of color are tapped by the academy to act as emblematic representatives of diversity. The hyperprivileged minority intellectual that she describes sustains the comfort of an overarching racist system. Dominguez challenges the epistemological roots that engender specific racializing practices.

> We . . . hyperprivilege (or at least allow our institutions to hyperprivilege) those targeted as "minority intellectuals." I am referring here to the hype about hiring "minority intellectuals"—the special interest, regulations, efforts, and even bidding wars that create an air of awkwardness about a great many of these efforts. (p. 334)

The existence of the hyperprivileged minority scholar allows for the visible presence and often pretense of racial diversity without having to substantively diversify as a discipline. This approach is a paradox in the ways that some minority academicians become the unwitting representatives of "their people" (Dominguez, 1994). The overall effect is the contradiction of seeking minority intellectuals but not really wanting to change in practice.[13] It is a means by which the participation of scholars of color as a whole is overlooked and simultaneously overdetermined (Fanon as cited in Bhabha, 1994).

OBJECTIFYING THE NATIVE AND THE NATIVE
SCHOLAR—OR HOW A SINGLE IDENTITY SILENCES

The elements of being Native and a Native scholar demand being highly integrated and highly exotic at the same time. The reification of Chicana/ Chicano stereotypes—of myself and my research—are both based on the very notion of what is Chicano. Both ask that chicanismo be presentable in a nice, palatable way that sustains Euro-Americans' comfort level. The demand to perform one's ethnicity as a scholar of color is simultaneously expected and abhorred. That is, to appear ethnic in the most outward manner is ideal. To be convincing and to perform one's ethnicity is implicitly and explicitly required. The stereotype, the ideal Chicano, would be like a "real" anthropologist, just Chicano. No theoretical contribution wanted or expected: simply race and ethnicity tacked on as an afterthought. To sustain the standing of the normative anthropologist against which one might be judged requires some fancy footwork because normative is such a multivalent position. Again, it requires me to ignore what I know to take the place of the legitimate knower. Furthermore, the fear and loathing of Chicanas and Chicanos (or of gays and lesbians, or both, or whoever is being made illegal that particular day) becomes palpable. Racism, sexism, homophobia, classism, and ableism get played out in who is considered good, legitimate, or even capable.[14] Taking on the role of a tamed Native (looks different maybe, checks an appropriate box) upholds rather than changes ideas of diversity.

In regard to race, one must look Mexican or not too Mexican, depending. I found early on that I could not be enough of a woman of color to satisfy; indeed, neither was my research sufficiently exotic. Much like Robert Alvarez's (1994) comments in his work "Un Chilero en la Academia," I did not fit the expected vision of a minority. Whereas some are too dark, I was too light. "If you are a woman of color, then so am I," I heard from one department chair on our first meeting, who launched into an anti-affirmative action diatribe. Thereafter, I felt that I could be seen as embracing a Chicana identity only for affirmative action benefits: After all, I could pass. More important, my contributions as a theorist of Chicana feminism plummeted to second or third place to my ability to play the part. I felt my tongue fall silent as I wondered how to position myself when that ground was not only disrespected but thought of as opportunistic, especially because I believe so fully and firmly in affirmative action programs.

The second reification of the Chicana/Chicano stereotype in anthropology is as a minority scholar. I spent my days trying to be/ become the diversity in an overwhelmingly male and Euro-American department. I so wanted the blessings of the institution that I probably would have become the hyperprivileged minority intellectual if I had been able to pull it off because I was so socialized in the system that created this exclusive space for me (see Dominguez, 1994). However, with the retreat of affirmative action policies and with substantive threats of altering the composition of academic institutions, such desire for diversity, even tokenized diversity, is increasingly distant.[15] Furthermore, I was hoping for recognition for the diversity in my scholarship, not for an essentialized, tokenized notion of my identity as Native. I tried to be a feminist, but I was told they already had one; my scholarship was apparently not needed. Here, I saw feminism not as a theoretical contribution or refinement to be respected but as a single position to be accounted for, tacked on, and checked off. It was a way to co-opt and silence at the same time. As the minority temporary instructor, I was marked by the very definition of minority as a blight on their high standards. Again, rather than see the potential theoretical contributions I might make, my identity became essentialized in the most striking way. In this way too, I was not merely set aside in binary opposition but was quarantined. I was incorporated into the departmental society only in the most referential way: simultaneously constrained and visible, partly appropriated but invisible in the mainstream.

In the meantime, students of color and other marginalized students came to me with stories of their hopes of going to graduate school being dismissed out of hand. One student who was in a small seminar class was incorrectly called María for an entire semester despite her rebukes to the professor that "not all of us are named María." Although becoming hypervisible to many students of color, I became increasingly invisible to a faculty that literally did not see me. Indeed, one common objection was that I did not integrate myself into the social fabric of the department. I did not attend the functions for those heralded scholars who espoused the very normative approach I found so troubling. I did not seem to endorse "real" anthropologists or "real" anthropology. However, I was also not seen even when I was present. I found myself attending meetings, conducting work in the main office, and encountering an occasional, "Why, I didn't even notice you!" I was the uninvited guest in someone else's home. I trod lightly, I shrank in the background, and, perhaps, I made myself invisible.

To speak and write as a scholar of color, in any case, is tolerated at best, feared at worst, and by and large not thought of as theoretically significant. One conversation at a research university presented this dialogue between me and another scholar regarding my publication options: "You see, I have to work with other scholars of Chicana feminist theory because it seems few anthropologists are well versed in it." "Well, of course you can write as many articles as you want for ethnic studies. We won't count it against you." Again, my contribution would be discounted out of hand, whereas my scholarship would be judged by many unfamiliar with and often disrespectful of discourses in feminist theory and ethnic studies. To be successful, I would be left to prove and validate my ability to endorse a single identity as a conventional anthropologist.

As an ethnographer, it became incumbent on me to play up the expected aspects of my research. For example, when I presented my research and the Chicanas I spoke with, anthropologists frequently insisted that these Chicanas were not authentic enough and that I had done a poor job in my research because they were not exotic enough; they seemed just like Euro-American women. This was cast as a methodological problem. To bend and shape my reading to please my audience left my research and me as the "authority" replicating the very processes of ethnic performance that I had found disconcerting.

FROM THE MARGIN TO

THE CENTER AND BACK AGAIN

How might I continue in such an ungracious discipline? I could see myself very much on the periphery. Yet, even the periphery has its own defined place. I use theory from a range of sources, specifically from literary criticism and film theory. I seek theories and models in textually innovative works, fiction, and poetry-places that many Chicanas identify in creating how we perceive ourselves. My use of Anzaldúa (1987) could hardly be peripheral. But here, I saw my space on the margins place me at the center and move me back out again.

Fragmented and poetic, Anzaldúa's (1987) commonly cited and heralded text about her Chicana experiences, *Borderlands/La Frontera* begins with an essay contextualizing the geopolitical, historical, and cultural terrain. Like Castillo's (1994) *Massacre of the Dreamers*, Anzaldúa uses methods and theories that parallel ethnographic sensibilities, illustrating that it is not the methods that distort Chicana images; rather, it is the deployment and reifying positionalities. Anzaldúa's essays draw from the textual approaches she ushered in with her coeditor Cherríe Moraga in their collection *This Bridge Called My Back* (Moraga & Anzaldúa, 1983). *This Bridge* provided an epistemological shift that located its authority neither in a scientific paradigm nor in a feminist standpoint that places itself in opposition to man (Alarcón, 1990). It favored using autobiographical and poetic practices as its basis for authority. This work established the possibility of seeing the subjectivity of women of color, which until then had not addressed women of color as knowers or as audience. Like so many others, *This Bridge* influenced my theory regarding, my practice of, and my writing about Chicana womanhood.

Oddly, using approaches identified as outside of anthropology—women's studies, ethnic studies, Chicana/Chicano studies, and cultural studies—unwittingly returned me to anthropology and placed some of my ideas squarely in its center. Discussions of subjectivity, experimental ethnography, and the use of poetics—if not poems—abound. How could that be? As noted earlier, the explosion of innovative texts is sustained in the name of the knower as theorist and the Native as not theorist. Although I certainly do not begrudge crediting the poetic elements of ethnography to heralded theorists such as James Clifford, George Marcus, and Clifford Geertz, what does distress me is the lack of attention to similar contributions from "Other" scholars (Gordon, 1988). Even the Native knower pioneers are rarely acknowledged as theorists. One can certainly imagine mainstream theorists, who may not even read or know the existence of marginalized theorists and theories, perpetuating this cycle of marginalization. Moreover, the advances in theory and method established by women such as Zora Neale Hurston, Ella Deloria, and Fabiola Cabeza de Baca have now been appropriated and reconfigured as experimental anthropology (Finn, 1995; Hernández, 1995; Lionnet, 1991; Rebolledo, 1995). Again, our contribution is both anticipated and ignored. I feel complicit in a system that asks me to identify and endorse the usual suspects, the "real" heroes of anthropology, while overlooking and participating in collective amnesia or collective disinterest in Native scholars. Ironically and not incidentally, the very terms that might describe my co-opted experience have been themselves appropriated into a postmodern lexicon.

Behar and Gordon's (1995) *Women Writing Culture* is a notable counterexample that acknowledges the theoretical and textual contributions of women scholars—Native knowers. Importantly, they place this collection in contrast to Clifford and Marcus's (1986) *Writing Culture* and their prefatory statement that dismisses outright feminist contributions. The contributors to *Women Writing Culture* study some of the foremothers of ethnography, detailing unconventional forms of writing and theorizing. However, the impact that Clifford and Marcus's *Writing Culture* made in anthropology underscores the ignorance of and continued disavowal of feminists and feminists of color. In effect, those earlier theoretical and textual contributions have been taken from the mouths and pens of women of color and made legitimate by Euro-American men. Promoted in Writing Culture as new textual practices rather than located in a political and historical context, even our own ways of understanding self and community become unrecognizable.

Yet, many anthropologists using far-ranging ideas of race, gender, class, and sexuality are published and cited. In this very article, I am able to cite and discuss the works of theorists who document the racializing and "othering" practices within anthropology. I see many brilliant scholars who identify and explore the inner workings of anthropology in this postmodern age. This notwithstanding, questions of legitimacy appear most starkly in hiring and tenure decisions, revealing the tentativeness in which many scholars are at once accepted and rejected (see Weston, 1997). Yet again, we are deftly usurped by the discipline. Even when this work is published and cited, it is validated in limited ways: published, yes; on course syllabi, perhaps; hired and tenured—not so quickly. It is not a coincidence that I understood how tenuous was my place in anthropology while on the job market, apparently so late in the game.

I see anthropology straining against the progressive and often radical efforts by marginalized scholars while presenting itself as the discipline of cultural diversity and analyses. Yet, anthropology manages to espouse, presumably above all other disciplines, a theory of culture and diversity while remaining so incredibly entrenched in a masculinist, heterosexist, and Eurocentric practice. The history of anthropology reveals the tricky double positioning that I experience and so effectively makes me think, "It must be me." How does it accomplish this? Again, I turn to the job market as a critical site of this duplicity.

There are two pervasive beliefs: One, any minority can write his or her own ticket to any position, and two, there is a simultaneous view equating being of color with being substandard, presumably as an unqualified quota hire. This is the first step toward the silencing act. It claims that anthropology values diversity among its colleagues and seeks diversity of theory. This second belief, that being of color is the same as being substandard, draws substantially from the unwillingness to see the Native scholar as knower and the failure to acknowledge or even be aware of the contributions of marginalized theorists and from contemporary expressions of racism. This diversity lip service obscures and mystifies a reality that I have observed; it is the alpha and the omega of my experience in anthropology. Based on those two premises, it leads me to the only logical conclusion that if I cannot find a voice, oppositional or otherwise, it must be because I am not good enough.

DIFFERENTIAL CONSCIOUSNESS

Thus, when I am questioned with "What makes your work anthropological?" I stand to ask this of myself. Indeed, I find that most theories I use do not emanate from anthropology precisely because they require me to take a problematic stance. Theories that are called anthropological also have parallels in or come from feminist theory, ethnic studies, and literary criticism—disciplines that have more seriously confronted colonial complicity. I cannot take a position theoretically, personally, or politically that requires me to silence myself or the women I know.

This ability to reposition myself has been the trick to my survival, but in my repositioning, I cannot be merely oppositional. Chela Sandoval (1991) writes about the need for such a perspective that can adequately respond to the multivalent constructs that have impinged on theorists of color. She explains,

> What U.S. third world feminism demands is a new subjectivity, a political revision that denies any one ideology as the final answer, while instead positing a tactical subjectivity with the capacity to recenter depending upon the kinds of oppression to be confronted (p. 14).

Sandoval conceptualizes this positionality, a tactic of U.S. Third World feminists, as "differential consciousness." More than oppositional consciousness, differential consciousness is a "kinetic motion that maneuvers, poetically transfigures, and orchestrates while demanding alienation, perversion, and reformation in both spectators and practitioners" (Sandoval, 1991, p. 3). The practice of differential consciousness in its mobility "requires grace, flexibility, and strength: enough strength to confidently commit to a well-defined structure of identity for one hour, day, week, month, year" (Sandoval, 1991, p. 3). Sandoval, a Chicana theorist, describes the common experience of not being able to find a single space or an oppositional voice. Yet more than reactive, Sandoval identifies differential consciousness, illustrating how it illuminates the practices of Chicanas I know and love, practices that I could see and experience but that eluded normative ethnographic approaches. Although these identities are well defined, they are also ever shifting and reconstituting. This requires the conventional ethnographic approach to interpellate one identity over others, simplifying complex and contradictory subjects in progress and, especially, obscuring power and various interstices of gender, race, and class.

Similarly invested in interrupting the stable object-subject relationship are literary critics such as Norma Alarcón. In her discussion of oppositional tactics, Alarcón (1990) unveils the power Chicanas claim in self-consciously seeking multiple positions in relationship to hegemonic feminism.

Multiple subjectivity is lived in resistance to competing notions for one's allegiance or self-identification. It is a process of disidentification with prevalent formulations of the most forceful theoretical subject of feminism. The choice of one or many themes is both a theoretical and political decision. (p. 366)

My experience in being unable to find a place among anthropologists as I experience normative anthropology is then a personal, theoretical, and political decision.

Given this terrain, I seek multiple subjectivity of audience and of myself, laying out the interstices and intersections as the strength of my work. The shift I and others, propose is to actively engage in the very intermediate space that is currently disavowed.[16] Denying the single, stable subject requires an explication of two or more moving actors: the Native knower and communities both as subjects in progress or continually transforming identities. The accounting of those relationships would obviate a claim on "fact" and "truth," looking more at how realities, identities, and perceptions are created and re-created. Achieving this would require an abdication of authority and an accountability that demands a more thorough interrogation of power and investment in particular identities. I draw parallels between Caren Kaplan's (1994) explanation of such accountability in a politics of location and the epistemological shift that could emanate from anthropology and that does appear in the work of virtual anthropologists (e.g., Davalos, 1996b; Motzafi-Haller, 1997; Weston, 1997).

Examining the politics of location in the production and reception of theory can turn the terms of inquiry from desiring, inviting, and granting space to others to becoming accountable for one's own investment in cultural metaphors and values. (p. 139)

Indeed, it is this very investment in cultural metaphors and values that Chicanas seek in the burgeoning Chicana literature, which could potentially be found in ethnography. I assert that autoethnography might have its place in that process inasmuch as we are highly invested in explicating the cultural metaphors and values that we espouse and those that we see espoused.[17] Although she is writing of feminism and I of anthropology, Kaplan (1994) further importantly indicates that scholars are not free from the responsibility of the interpretive acts in autobiography. Indeed, it would require us/me to reveal our/my power as interpreter rather than as emblematic speaker/ Native informant.

> Such accountability can begin to shift the ground of feminist practice from magisterial relativism (as if diversified cultural production simply occurs in a social vacuum) to the complex interpretive practices that acknowledge the historical roles of mediation, betrayal, and alliance in the relationships between women in diverse locations. (p. 139)

Chicana writers can and do take seriously that implicit power and privilege imbued in writing about ourselves. However, the process of revealing the power to define is critical. "Deconstructive ethnography allows one to view the process of asserting facts, to question at every moment what is being asserted as 'fact,' bringing a different epistemological process to bear on 'facticity'" (Visweswaran, 1994, p. 82). Being Native does not mean that this process, what Visweswaran (1994) calls deconstructive ethnography, is automatically, easily, or comfortably engaged. We must all work at revealing our assumptions and powers to define the discourse and the authority to assert "fact" (see Chabran, 1990).

It is not the essence of being Chicana or Native that encourages this questioning of fact or the indictment of authorial strategies.[18] I argue that the position that Chicanas and others are in provides an insight into the how authority, ethnography, Native, and knowledge interplay. The overlapping and contradictory identities imbued in being woman, person of color, and ethnographer provide an optimal position from which to demystify these elements (see, e.g., Kondo, 1990). Indeed, it may be the insertion of Native knowers, feminists, halfies, and virtual anthropologists that creates the epistemological conundrum.[19]

This position, seeking the transitory and multiple subjectivities, furthers our grasp of cultural production as we seek an increasingly complex understanding of postmodern life. Through autoethnography, we might explicate processes that have been eluding anthropology (Fischer, 1986; Hurston 1935/1978). It is not the nativeness of the anthropologist but the willingness to reveal the often uncomfortable contradictions of our identities that is at stake.

> A bi- or multi-ethnicized, raced, and gendered subject-in-process may be called upon to take up diverse subject positions which cannot be unified without double binds and contradictions. Indeed what binds the subject positions together may be precisely the difference from the perceived hegemony and the identity with a specific auto-history (Alarcón, 1994, p. 136).

Seeking a single space, a single voice, becomes increasingly problematic, its rejection perhaps the key to writing to multiple audiences and the means by which we can move toward textual practices that address these contradictions.[20] Chicanas and other U.S. Third World feminists have especially provided the most compelling examples of textual expression precisely because conventional practices fail to communicate their/our realities. The forms of radical textual practice I suggest include forms of autobiography and testimonials[21] but also fiction (Harrison, 1995; Visweswaran, 1994) and, furthermore, a multitude of forms that draw out relationships over the assertion of stable "fact." Privileging the relationships of author to various communities could provide a more enlightening context for understanding the multiple interpretations and investments in cultural metaphors (see, e.g., Alarcón's [1989] analysis of *la malinche* as a historical and contemporary metaphor). Rejecting linear chronologies, normative authorial strategies, and conventional views of history might more accurately reveal the constructedness of culture and history and the alliances they serve.

CONCLUSION

The conclusion is clear. We reside in a discipline that denies multiple subjectivity to researcher and Native and does so both theoretically and methodologically. The cognitive map of differential consciousness asserted by Sandoval (1991) reveals the complexities that Chicanas assume, not as objects but as speaking subjects, cognizant of our conditions. Chicanas engage in positioning that by its very nature eludes conventional anthropological theory and practice. By obviating and denying the multiple, overlapping, and occasionally competing identities of women of color, both as anthropological practitioners and as subjects of anthropology, we are required to take positions that are readily usurped by the mainstream. In this way, we are denied actual theoretical contribution while allowed to be only emblematic of the exotic Native. I do not desire to speak for my community (as is expected of the Native scholar). As yet, I cannot speak simultaneously of and from the community, but I look for a voice to be of the community without being a stereotype and from the community without further extending this silencing paradigm over my compañeras and compañeros.

The cost is clear. I seek strength in what is deemed a weakness. I must be a virtual anthropologist. My participation and contribution as an academician paradoxically threatens my role in the academy. Initially, when presenting this article, this contradiction saddened me, as I would not be a principal actor. I wrote,

> Further, by working so hard to move out of the deft configurations that silence I find myself spinning wheels to move ahead theoretically, cautiously navigating unchartered waters and wondering, again, maybe I am just not good enough (Russel y Rodríguez, 1996, pp. 12).

But you know what? Although the dynamic was important to name, to hell with it. Solving this paradigmatic conundrum is not ever going to put me in center stage. Still, and not unimportantly, it is my career, the cushy office, good benefits, and potential tenure that are sacrificed. On accepting this, for the time being at least, I must write and find strength as the Greek chorus commenting on this tragic comedy. I must apply and live differential consciousness, a praxis that rejects a single space in favor of stepping stones. I must theorize and embrace the contradictions. And it looks as if I am not going to be tapped to be the hyperprivileged minority intellectual, the Chicana diva. As much as I tried and as seductive as it looks, I know that it upholds the system it appears to challenge, a system that I question. It is in hybridity, being halfie, seeking both margin and center, and being virtual that I have a voice. Here theoretical, practical, and political opportunities release the stable object-subject to allow for ever-constituting forms of self and culture. This must be the continuously shifting differential consciousness I seek to theorize and practice powerfully as I continue to learn about Chicana feminism and gracefully by using in an hour, day, week, month, or year Chicana feminist tactics.

NOTES

1. I capitalize Native to remind the reader that this is a social construction and category rather than a question of nativity. As a Chicana, I, and many generations of my family, have been born in the United States, predating the time northern Mexico became the U.S. Southwest. However, as a group, Chicanas and Chicanos are not accorded the status of being "American" as we experience a panoply of exclusions and biases. As a biracial Chicana, I find my identity increasingly accorded as Native because I speak to and about undereducation, lack of health care, and underrepresentation even if I do not individually experience the more dramatic conditions of oppression.

2. I am spelling out the implications of normative anthropological theory and practice—the false promise of opposition and its concomitant binary positions. Here, we see loci of power determined within sets of relationships that, by their very definitions, cannot allow the voice of the Native knower. Disavowing the very structures that silence means that I repudiate the power and security that is promised within them. Job offers, tenure, authority, certainty, definitiveness—these are the features that seduce. My complicity with those silencing theories and practices, giving up my voice, would be handsomely rewarded. Desiring to be both Native and knower threatens that stability, relinquishes the rewards. Epistemologically acknowledging the Native knower is followed by a model of differential consciousness, accessing power and knowledge through a continuum and defining self through a spectrum of possibilities. It explores and explains not only why but how Native knowers who could potentially sit at the center of anthropological inquiry will not or cannot—at least at this time. It also prophesies the demise of an academic approach that privileges diversity of culture and Native thought but cannot explain its own increasing irrelevance in questions of race, sexuality, and gender.

3. This article examines the contradictions between the values and norms proscribed at the institutional level and my own individual experience especially while in the job market. What is intended is not a whining objection to the unfairness of the system but a definitive objection to the very contradictions that are espoused within it, because it is at the individual level that I experience most sharply those schisms that are otherwise tidily obscured. I will show how the written and unwritten rules of hiring, tenure, and publishing act as a concrete manifestation of that tension.

Drawing from Denis McQuail's (1983) *Mass Communication Theory*, I argue that this tension appears at three imbricating spaces: (a) the institutional level by valuing Native knowledge but prohibiting the existence of the Native knower; (b) the organizational level by the desire to hire minority faculty but not wanting diversity, often perpetuating racism within a prima facie effort to ameliorate racism; and (c) the individual level by the ways in which I must silence certain subjectivities—my specific experiences of race, gender, and class—to speak as a legitimate knower.

My point is that because being a Native knower is such a contradiction in the values and norms of anthropology and larger institutional practices, I, and others, experience this blatant rupture at the individual level, and we are encouraged to see those very contradictions as individual problems rather than as part of broader systemic and epistemological failures. It is not our nativeness or our identities—the quality of being Native—but the position of being Native that reveals these systemic ruptures. Yet, lest we cast this merely as a question of theory, I remind the reader that there are real implications and rewards for complicity in that system.

4. The fear of converging Native and scholar disrupts anthropology's premise and grounds for sustaining authority and superiority. Weston's (1997) essay, "The Virtual Anthropologist" illustrates the ways in which validity is stripped from scholars who "study their own," even when they do not always do so. Narayan (1993) ties anthropology's roots as a mechanism of colonization to the desire to maintain distinct categories of Native and scholar. Lassalle and Pérez (1997) write about the awkward expectation that Native scholars actually produce rather than comment on culture.

5. In one particularly painful job interview, a fellow anthropologist asked me to define and defend ethnic studies and thereafter suggested "that it is people like [me] who start race riots." Presumably, this particular "colleague" ascribed talking about and theorizing about the nature of race and racism as the same thing as advocating separatism. Many of us in ethnic studies do see the political side to our work and do aspire to incorporate equality as part of social change. However, I was not prepared for the anger and derision that was aimed at me, especially because I do not ascribe to race-based organizing, although my work does deal primarily with Chicana/Chicano communities. I cannot help but suspect that my work and my presence acted more as a lightning rod for this person's convenient, although inaccurately based, dismissal of ethnic studies.

6. Exposing these contradictions awakens the required suspended disbelief. In Helán Page's (1994) response to Virginia Dominguez's (1994) article on racialized practices in academe, Page refers to these practices as an example of claiming that "the Emperor has no clothes!" These perspectives are at once obvious and obscured by the ways in which contradictions are mutually overlooked. Revealing these contradictions is rarely rewarded, risks being kept out of the emperor's court, and is often regarded as impolite. Page (1994) nonetheless insists on the urgency of these observations. "In an era in which the extinction of our usefulness as anthropological experts is still a possibility, we simply cannot afford to pretend that transparently naked emperors are fully dressed" (p. 340).

7. Renato Rosaldo (1989) illustrates this point nicely in his work *Culture and Truth.* He explicates the distinction between the kinds of insights one might get as a Native scholar. His point is not that Native scholars have better insights but that we might be better positioned or more inclined to listen to the critiques of our subjects:

> I am saying neither that the native is always right nor that . . . the native ethnographer could never be wrong. Instead, my claim is that we should take the criticisms of our subjects in much the same way that we take those of our colleagues. (p. 50)

Patricia Zavella (1993) makes a similar point that it is the social positioning of the ethnographer that is at question rather than some Native essence that in and of itself creates better ethnographers. Moreover, she cites instances in which the term native does not mean the same thing as insider and notes that such relationships are complex.

I will argue that my Chicana feminism itself was an example of "outside within" status. Framed by larger historical forces and political struggles, identifying myself as a Chicana feminist meant contesting and simultaneously drawing from Chicano nationalist ideology and white feminism—being both insider and outsider within both movements and ideologies. (pp. 56-57)

8. Castillo (1994) uses Mexic Amerindian interchangeably with Xicana—an alternate spelling for Chicana or Mexican American woman. She uses both terms (Mexic Amerindian and Xicana) to emphasize the indigenous roots of Mexican American women, personally identifying her own history as specifically Mexica.

9. In upholding anthropological tenets, the question of the audience becomes paramount. Would I use the same language to articulate my notions of Chicana womanhood for Chicanas as I would for anthropologists (who can be, but are all too infrequently, the very same people)? To which part of my identity should I speak? Underscoring the dangers of blurring such audiences, bell hooks (1989) queries, "Dare I speak to the oppressed and oppressor in the same voice?" (p. 16). Any conversation between ourselves, entre nosotras, is certainly understood to be overheard and therefore shaped by and judged in relation to a conventional anthropological practice. Despite the ontological straits this puts me in, it is not a question that I can evade, nor is it a strait that any of us can or should ignore. The other facet of this question—"who is the audience?"—reveals the assumption that the Native would never read ethnographies. Different than the problem Castillo (1994) exposes (which was whether such ethnographies would resonate with Chicana audiences) is the reality that ethnographies are read and critiqued by Native scholars regardless of if they are written for us/them. When the Natives talk back, they/we are positioned to identify the assumptions that privilege the researcher as the paramount authority (see Rosaldo, 1986). Reminding us of this, Visweswaran (1994) writes, "With the loss of ethnographic authority, the subjects about who we write now write back, and in so doing pose us as anthropological fictions" (p. 9). Visweswaran sees how anthropologists have been believing in their own authorial strategies. Other theorists have been concerned with the distinctions between writing for Western and non-Western audiences (Moore, 1996; Narayan, 1989). Abu-Lughod marks this as a dynamic and often contradictory practice: She "argues that the split subjectivities of feminist and halfie anthropologists entail an uneasy traveling between 'speaking for' and 'speaking from,' creating new problems and strategies of audience" (as cited in Visweswaran, 1994, p. 131).

Lavie and Swedenburg (1996) also identify the discomfort engendered by simply being a Native who talks back within the daily working of an academic community.

These days, some of us from Out There live here, perhaps next door, and read and protest our neighbors' depiction of us. A few have Ph.D.'s in anthropology.... Some of us from Out There even sit in decision-making rooms with those who used to rely on our silence to ethnograph us. Many of our colleagues are still irritated by our ability to talk back, in multiple tongues: the languages of here, the languages of Out There, and the languages of the third time-space. For us, field and home blur, and sites of our research (what used to be roughing it in the field Out There) and sites of writing (what used to be the detached contemplation at home, Here) intermingle. Out There is still home. (p. 20)

10. Harding's (1987) work on feminist methodology suggests that we can interrupt the object-subject relation, epistemologically conceding that space, by more broadly defining who can be a knower, what can be known, and what counts for knowledge.

Although this solution is pleasing, in effect, it cannot happen. Visweswaran (1994) argues that despite feminist efforts to dismantle that inequity, the power inherent in ethnography cannot be avoided; hence, she titles her book *Fictions of Feminist Ethnography*. Even more than disavowing positivist methods that reinforce the object-subject split, my suspicion is that our discipline needs to play out the common (although somewhat more subtle) themes of colonization. The West maintains its superiority by continuously demonstrating its ability to define the Other. Lugones (1990) has provided a compelling theory of how we might still seek to understand other worlds but does not presume that such work is devoid of power. Furthermore, Lugones and Spelman (1983) detail precisely how researchers could create research questions and agendas with and among communities. Their suggestion resolves some of the power inequity already imbedded in what gets studied in the first place. Moreover, this positions people as knowers and theorists, not merely as informants.

11. The practice of drawing from personal experience is both rejected and accepted. Accepted at minimum are works such as Vincent Crapanzano's (1980) *Tuhami* and Clifford Geertz's (1988) *Works and Lives*. However, these authors persist as researchers-albeit more humanized researchers-in relation to their objects of study. Ruth Behar (1993, 1996) has been a strong and legitimizing force calling for and demonstrating the power of personal experience and autobiographical ethnography. Renato Rosaldo (1989) also explicitly uses his own personal experience to bring to light theory and analysis (see, especially, pp. 1-21). However, in *Translated Woman* (Behar, 1993) and in "Grief and a Headhunter's Rage" (Rosaldo, 1989, chap. 1), they again position themselves as researchers outside of their own communities. Moreover, prior to these works, both Behar and Rosaldo established themselves in more conventional ethnographic practices (e.g., Behar, 1991; Rosaldo, 1980). I hear many scholars strategizing or being counseled to write more "legitimate" work, leaving autoethnographic or personal work for after tenure. Similarly, I have been advised to write an "academic book." The point is clear: Autoethnographic writing and writing about one's own community is marked as interesting but not "real" work. Furthermore, such practices are only afforded those who have already established themselves as "legitimate" non-Native scholars in "legitimate" ethnographies.

12. As in Lassalle and Pérez's (1997) article, "'Virtually' Puerto Rican: 'Dis'-Locating Puerto Rican-ness and Its Privileged Sites of Production," I experience an expectation from many students to produce culture and represent Chicano nationalism in my identity, and my authenticity is questioned when I do not. Here, writing about culture and becoming the producer of culture blur. Lassalle and Pérez write about the expectation to become emblematic Puerto Ricans rather than scholars of Puerto Rican culture. Similar claims on my identity ask me to reject what I know as a woman, a feminist, and a biracial Chicana to assume the position of "the" Chicana writer within a Chicano nationalist framework. Doing so would ask me to ignore that I know as an anthropologist—an insight that critiques claims of nationalism and cultural change. The contradictions presented to Chicana feminists in relation to Chicano nationalism have been cogently reviewed and critiqued by critics such as Alarcón (1989, 1990), Fregoso (1993), and Rebolledo (1995) and by social historians such as García (1990) and Orozco (1990). Although the dynamics parallel each other, the difference between being required to be "the" Chicana anthropologist for academe and "the" Chicana writer for Chicano nationalism is that only academe holds power of being hired and tenured. Although I cannot evade questions of authenticity in academe, I could potentially avoid nationalist claims by simply ignoring others' judgments because they do

not determine my livelihood. Still, I choose to engage definitions of Chicano nationalism and concomitant ideas of Chicana-ness as political questions.

13. This is very much like the idea of tokenism that emanated from some affirmative action politics. Affirmative action's greatest detractors correctly point out conditions in which individuals seem to be hired not for their skills and knowledge but for the grossest reduction of their identities as minority hires. The hyperprivileged scholar is indeed a kind of tokenism that produces not change in the system but a perception of openness. At the time I am writing this article, I fear that some affirmative action legislation will erase even the traces of tokenism, wherein there is not even a discussion of race, identity, and qualifications. I find this absence of discussion or even contention much more frightening than accusations of tokenism. I find the uneventful exclusion of African Americans and Latinas/Latinos from law schools more frightening than the admittedly imperfect status quo.

14. This article was initially written for "Ethnocentrisms Within: Women of Color, Lesbians, and Women With Disabilities Look at Anthropology," an invited session by the Committee on the Status of Women in Anthropology for the 1996 annual meetings of the American Anthropology Association. This panel beautifully addressed the common delegitimizing experience that women of color, lesbians, and disabled anthropologists must confront (see Davalos, 1996a; Juárez, 1996; Kasnitz, 1996; Newton, 1996; Russel y Rodríguez, 1996).

15. Dominguez's (1994) article, "A Taste for 'the Other,'" was written prior to the onslaught of anti-affirmative action legislation and policies proposed and enacted in California and Texas, specifically in the University of California system and at the University of Texas law school but also throughout the country. Hyperprivileging is a practice that asserts that with the superstar minority hire, racism is taken care of. However, what seems worse is the dismantling of affirmative action with the suggestion that it is no longer needed, that we are on an equal playing field, and that individuals will be hired according to "quality." What is defined as quality problematically replicates a racist system. Although affirmative action may have created hyperprivileged scholars, at minimum, ideas of what counts as quality were more visible although certainly not ideal.

16. I believe that these spaces that Sandoval (1991) and Alarcón (1990) theorize are similar to those suggested by Bhabha's (1990, 1994) notion of third space and time-lag, Lavie and Swedenburg's (1996) third time-space, some components of hybridity (as in Weston, 1997), and Anzaldúa's (1987) mestizaje and frontera/borderland.

17. In anthropology, I see that autoethnography's increasing popularity is indeed a common recourse to epistemological problems (Reed-Danahay, 1997; Trotter, 1992). Autoethnography is heralded by some literary critics as a bridge from autobiography to explication of the author's position within a cultural context. Lionnet (1991) describes autoethnography as "the process of defining one's subjective ethnicity as mediated through language, history, and ethnographic analysis" (p. 166). Here, we can understand the construction and interpretation of culture as a process, not as static stereotypes that often confound ethnographic practice. It seems a most direct way to "demonstrate the basic humanity of [the autoethnographer's] people to an audience of readers" (Deck, 1990, p. 239). For those of us concerned with the presentation of communities of color in the United States and elsewhere where our humanity has often been denied, this is a critical contribution. Many scholars in anthropology have already engaged in autobiographical or autoethnographic approaches as the roots of their theory building (Frankenburg & Mani, 1996; Romero, 1992) or as a means to interpret

anthropological questions (Lavie, 1993; Rosaldo, 1989). Too frequently, we use this approach at a cost. It is a place that I claim and see other Chicana anthropologists, such as KarenMary Davalos (1996a), claim even when it is disregarded.

18. This untenable position—that the Native researcher has better or more accurate insights—I think is more often than not used as a straw man to deflect critiques made about different positionings (Rosaldo, 1989) or different perspectives that scholars of color might claim. Certainly, researchers such as Gwaltney (1980/1993) in his often highly compelling book *Drylongso* do suggest that he, as an African American doing research in an African American community, has better insight into the data. Still, I think that the overall assertion is not in being of color; rather, it is in the different implications our identities hold in the process of ethnography.

19. Alarcón provides a compelling interpretation of a Kafka tale describing the battle of a woman fighting between two antagonists.

> She has two antagonists: the first presses her from behind, from the origin. The second blocks the road ahead. She gives battle to both. To be sure, the first supports her in her fight with the second, for it wants to push her forward, and in the same way the second supports her in her fight with the first, since it drives her back. But it is only theoretically so. For it is not only the two antagonists who are there, but she herself as well, and who really knows her intentions? Her dream, though, is that some time in an unguarded moment—and this would require a night darker than any night has ever been yet—she will jump out of the fighting line and be promoted, on account of her experience in fighting, to the position of umpire over her antagonists in their fight with each other. (Arendt as cited in Alarcón, 1994, p. 128)

The woman, like the Native knower, situated between two fighting antagonists, is the reason that there is a battle at all. "The fact that there is a fight at all is due to the presence of the [wo]man. Her insertion, her inscription break up the motion of the force, their linearity" (Alarcón, 1994, p. 128). Leaving the battle to become umpire refutes the logic of woman's insertion into the battle. Similarly, Native knowers cannot simply disengage from fighting for voice and for unessentialized inclusion—although we might want to be promoted on account of our experience in fighting. Such a promotion to umpire evades the issue that it is the presence of the Native knower that begs the contradictions.

20. Rosa Linda Fregoso (1993) expounds on film as a medium for questioning the presentation and consumption of Chicana/Chicano culture. Her readings of Euro-American hegemonic and Chicano hegemonic culture within filmic representations provide a context for understanding the more creative, although much less popular, works by directors such as Lourdes Portillo. Similarly, Barbara Harlow (1987) explores how resistance writings must differ from traditional texts, "experiment[ing] with structures of chronological and temporal continuity" (p. 85) in the effort to redress historical and power inequities. I am suggesting that seeing ethnography as poetry or as a story does not sufficiently challenge the historical and social contexts, especially when it concerns communities of color in the United States. Furthermore, we would do well to consider much more radical textual practices.

21. The testimonial is a notable rhetorical form within ethnographic strategies, disallowing facile relationships of knower-known, social scientist-native, and theory-practice. Promising what might be a perspective from the margins and challenging conventional boundaries of representations, testimonials became a favored genre for political commentary in Latin America (Sánchez, 1995). Self-generated testimonials

appear especially in resistance narratives such as Alicia Partnoy's (1986) *The Little School: Tales of Disappearance and Survival in Argentina.* The more popular form, the mediated testimonial (e.g., Burgos-Debray's [1984] I . . . Rigoberta Menchú) relies on an intermediary such as an ethnographer. The investment in representation by the producers of mediated testimonials creates a unique dynamic between speaker and ethnographer. Beverley's (1987) description of the mediated testimonial in his "Anatomía del testimonio" includes features that interrupt the simple ethnographer-informant relationship. Among them are (a) the sense of collective that marks a testimonial as representative of a larger, marginalized group; (b) the sense of survival and urgency that often accompanies testimonial; and (c) the narrator's use of the ethnographer to reconfigure his or her representation politically and historically. This locates the narrator as actor and the ethnographer as more akin to recorder than researcher. Testimonials, however, are mediated by the recorder, and that mediation includes power and positioning in representation and interpretation. The objectives and motivations are significantly more complex in testimonials. Whereas the narrator of a testimonial may assert "an active and conscious effort to counter other representations" (Sánchez, 1995, p. 13), the ethnographer may endeavor to collaborate with this counterrepresentation, or he or she may ironically represent or realign it to fit more conventional discourses. The power over representation, production, and interpretation necessarily remains in the hands of the ethnographer, regardless of the narrator's intent.

REFERENCES

Abu-Lughod, L. (1991). Writing against culture. In R. G. Fox (Ed.), *Recapturing anthropology: Working in the present* (pp. 137-162). Santa Fe, NM: School of American Research Press.

Alarcón, N. (1989). Traddutora, traditora: A paradigmatic figure of Chicana feminism. *Cultural Critique, 13*, 57-87.

Alarcón, N. (1990). The theoretical subject(s) of *This Bridge Called My Back* and Anglo-American feminism. In G. Anzaldúa (Ed.), *Making face, making soul = Haciendo caras* (pp. 356-369). San Francisco: Aunt Lute Press.

Alarcón, N. (1994). Conjugating subjects: The heteroglossia of essence and resistance. In A. Arteaga (Ed.), *An other tongue* (pp. 125-138). Durham, NC: Duke University Press.

Alvarez, R. R., Jr. (1994). Un chilero en la academia: Sifting, shifting, and the recruitment of minorities in anthropology. In S. Gregory & R. Sanjek (Eds.), *Race* (pp. 257-269). New Brunswick, NJ: Rutgers University Press.

Anzaldúa, G. (1987). *Borderlands/La frontera: The new Mestiza.* San Francisco: Spinters/ Aunt Lute.

Behar, R. (1991). *Santa María del Monte: The presence of the past in a Spanish village.* Princeton, NJ: Princeton University Press.

Behar, R. (1993). *Translated woman: Crossing the border with Esperanza's story.* Boston: Beacon.

Behar, R. (1996). *The vulnerable observer: Anthropology that breaks your heart.* Boston: Beacon.

Behar, R., & Gordon, D. (Eds.). (1995). *Women writing culture.* Berkeley: University of California Press.

Beverley, J. (1987). Anatomía del testimonio. [Anatomy of the testimony] *Revista de crítica literaria,* 13.

Bhabha, H. (1990). The third space: Interview with Homi Bhabha. In J. Rutherford (Ed.), *Identity: Community, culture, difference* (pp. 207-221). London: Lawrence & Wishart.

Bhabha, H. (1994). *The location of culture.* New York: Routledge.

Burgos-Debray, E. (1984). *I . . . Rigoberta Menchú.* London: Verso.

Castillo, A. (1994). *Massacre of the dreamers.* New York: Penguin.

Chabran, R. (1990, May). *Culture and truth: The encounter between rhetorical anthropology and Chicano studies.* Paper presented at Chicano Cultural Studies: New Directions, University of California, Santa Barbara.

Clifford, J., & Marcus, G. E. (1986). *Writing culture: The poetics and politics of ethnography.* Berkeley: University of California Press.

Crapanzano, V. (1980). *Tuhami: Portrait of a Moroccan.* Chicago: University of Chicago Press.

Davalos, K. (1996a, November). *Decolonized selves and writing: A strategy for women of color in anthropology.* Paper presented at the annual meeting of the American Anthropology Association, San Francisco, CA.

Davalos, K. (1996b). La quinceañera: Making gender and ethnic identities. *Frontiers, 16*(2/3), 101-127.

Deck, A. A. (1990). Autoethnography: Zora Neale Hurston, Noni Jabavu, and cross-disciplinary discourse. *Black American Literature Forum, 24*(2), 237-256.

Dominguez, V. R. (1994). A taste for "the Other": Intellectual complicity in racializing practices. *Current Anthropology, 35*(4), 333-347.

Fischer, M.M.J. (1986). Ethnicity and the post modern arts of memory. In J. Clifford & G. Marcus (Eds.), *Writing culture: The poetics and politics of ethnography* (pp. 194-233). Berkeley: University of California Press.

Finn, J. L. (1995). Ella Cara Deloria and Mourning Dove: Writing for cultures, writing against the grain. In R. Behar & D. Gordon (Eds.), *Women writing culture* (pp. 131-147). Berkeley: University of California Press.

Frankenberg, R., & Mani, L. (1996). Crosscurrents, crosstalk: Race, "postcoloniality," and the politics of location. In S. Lavie & T. Swedenburg (Eds.), *Displacement, diaspora, and geographies of identity* (pp. 273-293). Durham, NC: Duke University Press.

Fregoso, R. L. (1993). *The bronze screen: Chicana and Chicano film culture.* Minneapolis: University of Minnesota Press.

García, A. (1990). The development of Chicana feminist discourse, 1970-1980. In E. DuBois & V. Ruiz (Eds.), *Unequal sisters* (pp. 418-431). New York: Routledge.

Geertz, C. (1988). *Works and lives: The anthropologist as author.* Stanford: Stanford University Press.

Gordon, D. (1988). Writing culture, writing feminism: The poetics and politics of experimental ethnography. *Inscriptions, 3/4*(8), 7-24.

Gwaltney, J. L. (1993). *Drylongso: A self portrait of Black America.* New York: New Press.

Harding, S. (Ed.). (1987). *Feminism and methodology.* Bloomington: Indiana University Press.

Harlow, B. (1987). *Resistance literature.* New York: Methuen.

Harrison, F. V. (1995). Writing against the grain: Cultural politics of difference in the works of Alice Walker. In R. Behar & D. Gordon (Eds.), *Women writing culture* (pp. 233-245). Berkeley: University of California Press.

Hernández, G. (1995). Multiple subjectivities and strategic positionality: Zora Neale Hurston's experimental ethnographies. In R. Behar & D. Gordon (Eds.), *Women writing culture* (pp. 148-165). Berkeley: University of California Press.

hooks, b. (1989). Choosing the margin as space of radical openness. *Framework, 36,* 16-24.

Hurston, Z. N. (1978). *Mules and men.* Bloomington: University of Indiana Press. (Original work published 1935)

Juárez, A. (1996, November). *You poor oppressed Mexicanas! Cultures, stereotypes, sexisms, and feminisms.* Paper presented at the annual meeting of the American Anthropology Association, San Francisco, CA.

Kaplan, C. (1994). The politics of location as transnational feminist critical practice. In I. Grewal & C. Kaplan (Eds.), *Scattered hegemonies: Postmodernity and transnational feminist practices* (pp. 137-152). Minneapolis: University of Minnesota Press.

Kasnitz, D. (1996, November). *Marginal bodies, marvelous lives: Women with disabilities within the academy and without.* Paper presented at the annual meeting of the American Anthropology Association, San Francisco, CA.

Kondo, D. K. (1990). *Crafting selves.* Chicago: University of Chicago Press.

Lassalle, Y. M., & Pérez, M. (1997). "Virtually" Puerto Rican: "Dis"-Locating Puerto Rican-ness and its privileged sites of production. *Radical History Review, 68,* 54-78.

Lavie, S. (1993). "The one who writes us": Political allegory and the experience of occupation among the Mzeina Bedouin. In S. Lavie, K. Narayan, & R. Rosaldo (Eds.), *Creativity/Anthropology* (pp. 153-183). Ithaca, NY: Cornell University Press.

Lavie, S., & Swedenburg, T. (Eds.). (1996). *Displacement, diaspora, and geographies of identity.* Durham, NC: Duke University Press.

Limón, J. (1994). *Dancing with the devil: Society and cultural poetics in Mexican American south Texas.* Madison: University of Wisconsin Press.

Lionnet, F. (1991). Autoethnography: The An-Archic style of *Dust Tracks on a Road.* In D. LaCapra (Ed.), *The bounds of race* (pp. 164-195). Ithaca, NY: Cornell University Press.

Lugones, M. (1990). Playfulness, "World"-Travelling, and Loving Perception. In Gloria Anzaldúa (Ed.), *Making face, Making soul = Haciendo caras* (pp. 390-402). San Francisco: Aunt Lute.

Lugones, M. C., & Spelman, E. V. (1983). Have we got a theory of you! Feminist theory, cultural imperialism, and the demand for "The Woman's Voice." *Women's Studies International Forum, 6*(6), 573-581.

McQuail, D. (1983). *Mass communication theory.* London: Sage.

Moore, H. (1994). *A passion for difference: Essays in anthropology and gender.* Bloomington: University of Indiana Press.

Moore, H. (Ed.). (1996). *The future of anthropological knowledge.* New York: Routledge.

Moraga, C., & Anzaldúa, G. (Eds.). (1983). *This bridge called my back.* New York: Kitchen Table: Women of Color Press.

Motzafi-Haller, P. (1997). Writing birthright: On native anthropologists and the politics of representation. In D. Reed-Danahay (Ed.), *Auto/Ethnography: Rewriting the self and the social* (pp. 195-222). New York: Berg.

Narayan, K. (1989). *Storytellers, saints, and scoundrels: Folk narrative in Hindu religious teaching.* Philadelphia: University of Pennsylvania Press.

Narayan, K. (1993). How native is a "native" anthropologist? *American Anthropologist, 95,* 671-686.

Newton, E. (1996, November). *"Be unspeakable and unspoken": The status of lesbians in anthropology.* Paper presented at the annual meeting of the American Anthropology Association, San Francisco, CA.

Orozco, C. (1990). Sexism in Chicano studies and the community. In T. Córdova (Ed.), *Chicana voices: Intersections of class, race, and gender.* Colorado Springs, CO: National Association of Chicano Studies.

Page, H. (1994). Response to "A Taste for 'The Other' ": Intellectual complicity in racializing practices. *Current Anthropology, 35*(4), 340-342.

Paredes, A. (1978). On ethnographic work among minority groups: A folklorist's perspective. In R. Romo & R. Paredes (Eds.), *New directions in Chicano scholarship.* La Jolla, CA: Chicano Studies Monograph Series.

Partnoy, A. (1986). *The little school: Tales of disappearance and survival in Argentina.* San Francisco: Cleis.

Rebolledo, T. D. (1995). *Women singing in the snow: A cultural analysis of Chicana literature.* Tucson: University of Arizona Press.

Reed-Danahay, D. (Ed.). (1997). *Auto/Ethnography: Rewriting the self and the social.* New York: Berg.

Romero, M. (1992). *Maid in the U.S.A.* New York: Routledge.

Rosaldo, R. (1980). *Ilongot headhunting, 1883-1974: A study in society and history.* Stanford, CA: Stanford University Press.

Rosaldo, R. (1986). *When natives talk back: Chicano anthropology since the late '60s* (Renato Rosaldo Lecture Series Monograph: Vol. 2, series 1984-1985). Tucson: Mexican American Studies and Research Center, University of Arizona.

Rosaldo, R. (1989). *Culture and truth: The remaking of social analysis.* Boston: Beacon.

Russel y Rodríguez, M. (1995). *Renegotiating responsibilities, transforming culture: Gender, sexuality, and class in the contestation of Chicana womanhood.* Unpublished doctoral dissertation, University of California, Los Angeles.

Russel y Rodríguez, M. (1996, November). *Performing one's ethnicity/Speaking from the community.* Paper presented at the annual meeting of the American Anthropology Association, San Francisco, CA.

Sánchez, R. (1995). *Telling identities.* Minneapolis: University of Minnesota Press.

Sandoval, C. (1991). U.S. Third World feminism: The theory and method of oppositional consciousness in the postmodern world. *Genders, 10,* 1-24.

Trotter, M. A. (1992). *Life writing: Exploring the practice of autoethnography in anthropology.* Unpublished master's thesis, University of Illinois, Urbana-Champaign.

Visweswaran, K. (1994). *Fictions of feminist ethnography.* Minneapolis: University of Minnesota Press.

Weston, K. (1997). The virtual anthropologist. In A. Gupta & J. Ferguson (Eds.), *Anthropological locations: Boundaries and grounds of a field of science* (pp. 163-184). Berkeley: University of California Press.

Zavella, P. (1993). Feminist insider dilemmas: Constructing ethnic identity with "Chicana" informants. *Frontiers, 13*(3), 53-76.

——

Mónica Russel y Rodríguez received her Ph.D. from the University of California, Los Angeles, in 1995. Her dissertation was titled Renegotiating Responsibilities, Transforming Culture: Gender, Sexuality, and Class in the Contestation of Chicana Womanhood. *She is assistant professor of Chicana and Chicano studies at Metropolitan State College of Denver. She continues to research and write on representations of authenticity and authority in ethnic studies and anthropology.*

AFTERWORD

——

Thus do the readings in Part Five bring the *QI Reader* full circle, back again to our three goals. These essays reflect cutting-edge work in the field. They present a critical framework for interpreting and evaluating new work. They show how reflexive methodological work can contribute to critical political, moral discourse.

The field of qualitative inquiry is open-ended. The future cannot be predicted, its outlines barely glimpsed. Still, there is no turning back. The distinctions between epistemology, ontology, ethics, and aesthetics have blurred, collapsed. We are on the edge of a new interpretive moment, and in that moment, new understandings will emerge. Old issues will take on new life. Issues previously unimagined will become problems. We anticipate that these new discourses will find their way into the next edition of the *QI Reader*.

SOURCES

— —

Belgrave, Linda Liska, and Kenneth J. Smith. (1995). Negotiated Validity in Collaborative Ethnography. *Qualitative Inquiry, 1*(1), 69-86.

Bochner, Arthur P. (2000). Criteria Against Ourselves. *Qualitative Inquiry, 6*(2), 266-272.

Brady, Ivan. (1998). A Gift of the Journey. *Qualitative Inquiry, 4*(4), 463.

Ceglowski, Deborah. (2000). Research as Relationship. *Qualitative Inquiry, 6*(1), 88-103.

Creef, Elena Tajima. (2000). Discovering My Mother as the Other in the *Saturday Evening Post*. *Qualitative Inquiry, 6*(4), 443-457.

Dunbar, Christopher, Jr. (1999). Three Short Stories. *Qualitative Inquiry, 5*(1), 130-140.

Fine, Michelle, and Lois Weis. (1996). Writing the "Wrongs" of Fieldwork: Confronting Our Own Research/Writing Dilemmas in Urban Ethnographies. *Qualitative Inquiry, 2*(3), 251-274.

Halley, Jean. (2000). This I Know: An Exploration of Remembering Childhood and Knowing Now. *Qualitative Inquiry, 6*(3), 349-358.

Jones, Stacy Holman. (1999). Torch. *Qualitative Inquiry, 5*(2), 280-304.

Kvale, Steinar. (1995). The Social Construction of Validity. *Qualitative Inquiry, 1*(1), 19-40.

Lincoln, Yvonna S. (1995). Emerging Criteria for Quality in Qualitative and Interpretive Research. *Qualitative Inquiry, 1*(3), 275-289.

Nowak, Mark. (2000). Two Microethnographies. *Qualitative Inquiry, 6*(1), 129-132.

Pelias, Ronald J. (2000). Always Dying: Living Between Da and Fort. *Qualitative Inquiry,6*(2), 229-237.

Richardson, Laurel. (1997). Skirting a Pleated Text: De-Disciplining an Academic Life. *Qualitative Inquiry, 3*(3), 295-303.

Richardson, Miles. (1999). The Anthro in Cali. *Qualitative Inquiry, 5*(4), 563-565.

Ronai, Carol Rambo. (1999). The Next Night *Sous Rature*: Wrestling with Derrida's Mimesis. *Qualitative Inquiry, 5*(1), 114-129.

Russel y Rodríguez, Mónica. (1998). Confronting Anthropology's Silencing Praxis: Speaking Of/From a Chicana Consciousness. *Qualitative Inquiry, 4*(1), 15-40.

Smith, Kenneth J., and Linda Liska Belgrave. (1995). Negotiated Validity in Collaborative Ethnography. *Qualitative Inquiry, 1*(1), 69-86.

St.Pierre, Elizabeth Adams. (1997). Circling the Text: Nomadic Writing Practices. *Qualitative Inquiry, 3*(4), 403-417.

Travisano, Richard V. (1998). On Becoming Italian American: An Autobiography of an Ethnic Identity. *Qualitative Inquiry, 4*(4), 540-563.

Weems, Mary E. (2000). Windows. *Qualitative Inquiry, 6*(1), 152-163.

Weis, Lois, and Michelle Fine. (1996). Writing the "Wrongs" of Fieldwork: Confronting Our Own Research/Writing Dilemmas in Urban Ethnographies. *Qualitative Inquiry, 2*(3), 251-274.

NAME INDEX

——

SUBJECT INDEX

ABOUT THE EDITORS

––

Norman K. Denzin is Distinguished Professor of Communications, College of Communications Scholar, and Research Professor of Communications, Sociology and Humanities at the University of Illinois, Urbana-Champaign. He is the author of numerous books, including Screening Race: Hollywood and a Cinema of Racial Violence, Interpretive Ethnography, The Cinematic Society, Images of Postmodern Society, The Research Act, Interpretive Interactionism, Hollywood Shot by Shot, The Recovering Alcoholic *and* The Alcoholic Self, *which won the Charles Cooley Award from the Society for the Study of Symbolic Interaction in 1988. In 1997 he was awarded the George Herbert Award from the Society for the Study of Symbolic Interaction. He is past editor of* The Sociological Quarterly, *coeditor of* The Handbook of Qualitative Research, 2/e, *coeditor of* Qualitative Inquiry, *editor of* Cultural Studies—Critical Methodologies, *and series editor of* Studies in Symbolic Interaction.

Yvonna S. Lincoln is Professor of Higher Education and Department Head, Department of Educational Administration, Texas A&M University. She is coeditor of Qualitative Inquiry *with Norman K. Denzin, with whom she also collaborated on the* Handbook of Qualitative Research, 2/e, *and coauthor of* Effective Evaluation, Naturalistic Inquiry, *and* Fourth Generation Evaluation. *She is editor of*

Organizational Theory and Inquiry *and coeditor of* Representation and the Text. *She has been the recipient of numerous awards for research, including the AERA Division J Research Achievement Award, the AIR Sidney Suslow Award for Research Contributions to Institutional Research, and the American Evaluation Association's Paul Lazarsfeld Award for Contributions to Evaluation Theory. She is the author of numerous journal articles, chapters, and conference presentations on constructivist and interpretive inquiry and on higher education administration.*

ABOUT THE CONTRIBUTORS

— —

Linda Liska Belgrave is Associate Professor in the Department of Sociology at the University of Miami. Her primary research and teaching interests include social gerontology and medical sociology, particularly the experience of and responses to chronic illness, and research methods.

Art Bochner is Professor of Communication and codirector of the Institute for Interpretive Human Studies at the University of South Florida. He is coauthor of Understanding Family Communication *(Allyn & Bacon) and coeditor of* Composing Ethnography *(Alta Mira) and of the AltaMira book series on* Ethnographic Alternatives. *He has published more than 50 articles and monographs on close relationships, communication theory, and narrative inquiry in the human sciences. His current research explores ethnographic practices in the public domain, institutional depression in higher education, and love on the Internet.*

Ivan Brady is Distinguished Teaching Professor and Chair of Anthropology at the State University of New York at Oswego. A former President of the Society for Humanistic Anthropology and Book Review Editor of the American Anthropologist, *he is currently developing a new version of his book on* Anthropological Poetics *(1991). His poetry has appeared in various books and journals, including* Reflections: The Anthropological Muse *(edited by I. Prattis, 1985),*

Cultural Studies↔Critical Methodologies, Pendulum, Anthropology and Humanism *(Quarterly), and* Qualitative Inquiry.

Deborah Ceglowski is Assistant Professor of Early Childhood Education in the Department of Curriculum and Instruction and the Center for Early Education and Development at the University of Minnesota. Her research interests include early childhood policy, researchers' relationships with those they study, and using short stories as research text. She is currently heading a team of community researchers investigating how parents and children describe childcare in rural and urban Minnesota.

Elena Tajima Creef teaches in the Women's Studies Department at Wellesley College. She is the author of Imagining Japanese America *(New York University Press, forthcoming) and numerous articles on Asian American women and culture. She is currently writing a creative nonfiction book titled* Notes of a Fragmented Daughter *about identity, Asian mothers, and growing up "hapa" (mixed-race) in the multiple places she learned to call "home" in North Carolina, southern California, and Japan.*

A former alternative education teacher, **Christopher Dunbar, Jr.** *is Assistant Professor in the Department of Educational Administration at Michigan State University. Dr. Dunbar earned his PhD in Educational Policy Studies from the University of Illinois Urbana Champaign. He has published articles in* Qualitative Inquiry, Cultural Studies, *and* Theory Into Practice.

Michelle Fine is a professor of social psychology, urban education, and women's studies at the Graduate School and University Center, City University of New York. Her research interests revolve broadly around the questions of social injustice, especially in her work with public high schools, prisons, and youth in urban communities. Fine's research is typically participatory, with youth and/or activists, drawing from feminist, critical race, and critical theories. Recent books include The Unknown City: Lives of Poor and Working Class Young Adults; Speedbumps: A Student Friendly Guide to Qualitative Research; *and* Construction Sites: Excavating Race, Class,

Gender & Sexuality in Spaces For and By Youth *(all co-edited with Lois Weis).*

Jean Halley is a doctoral student in the sociology program of the Graduate School and University Center of the City University of New York. She is currently finishing her dissertation, a social history exploring 20th century ideologies of adult-child touch in the United States. She has taught full-time for the women's studies program at Hunter College of the City University of New York. She has also taught as an adjunct instructor for the women's studies program, the film and media studies program, and the sociology program at Hunter College and Queens College of the City University of New York. Currently, Halley is a writing fellow helping to develop writing across the curriculum at Hunter College. She holds a master's degree in theology from Harvard University.

Stacy Holman Jones received her PhD in Performance Studies from the University of Texas, Austin. She is Assistant Professor in the Department of Communication at the University of South Florida. Her work has appeared in Qualitative Inquiry, Text and Performance Quarterly, *and the* Journal of Contemporary Ethnography. *She has also published a book titled* Kaleidoscope Notes: Writing Women's Music and Organizational Culture.

Steinar Kvale is Professor of educational psychology at the University of Aarhus, Denmark; Director of Centre of Qualititive Research the same place; and adjunct faculty at Saybrook Institute, San Francisco. He has written several articles on qualitative research and he has edited the books Psychology and Postmodernism *(1992, London: Sage) and* Issues of Validity in Qualitative Research *(1989, Lund, Sweden: Studentliteratur).*

Mark Nowak's collection of ethnographic poems and photographs, Revenants, is recently out from Coffee House Press. He is editor of Xcp: Cross Cultural Poetics (http://bfn.org/~xcp) *and teaches at the College of St. Catherine in Minneapolis.*

Ronald J. Pelias *teaches performance studies in the Department of Speech Communication at Southern Illinois University. His most recent book is* Writing Performance: Poeticizing the Researcher's Body *(Southern Illinois University Press).*

Laurel Richardson *is Professor Emeritus of Sociology and Visiting Professor of Cultural Studies in Education at The Ohio State University. Her book,* Fields of Play: Constructing an Academic Life, *was honored with the Society for the Study of Symbolic Interactionism Cooley Award. Her current project is an autoethnographic exploration of the intersections of race, class, ethnicity, family, and gender.*

Miles Richardson *is the Doris Z. Stone Professor in Latin American Studies at the Department of Geography and Anthropology, Louisiana State University. Poetry apart, he finds that his titles get longer as he gets closer to 70 (which is pretty close), to wit: Louisiana State University Press has accepted for publication* Being-in-Christ and Putting Death in Its Place in Spanish America and in the American South: An Anthropologist's Account. *He is currently at work on* Re(pro)claiming the Anthropocentric Voice in Postmodern Discourse.

Mónica Russel y Rodríguez *is currently working on her forthcoming book,* Pura Mestiza: Gender, Mixed Race, and Nation in Mexican America. *She is teaching in the Anthropology Department and in the Latin American Studies Program at Northwestern University. Comments and correspondence can be sent to mryr@northwestern.edu.*

Carol Rambo Ronai *is Assistant Professor at the University of Memphis. She is currently working on three books: one from life history materials with striptease dancers* (Striptease as Resistance), *which is being revised; one using life history materials with adult survivors of childhood sexual abuse; and one that will outline and explore the layered account as a methodology.*

Kenneth Joseph Smith's *teaching and research interests are in the areas of social psychology, mental disorder, and gerontology. He regularly teaches undergraduate courses in the sociology of mental health,* *culture and personality, collective behavior and social movements, and social psychology. At the graduate level, Dr. Smith offers seminars on the subjects of qualitative research and social psychology. His recent publications are studies on subjects such as the return migration of black retirees to the South, membership in a community mental agency, survivors of Hurricane Andrew, and African American caregivers of Alzheimer patients. He is currently Professor Emeritus and lecturer in sociology at the University of Miami and Barry University, as well as Vice President of the Society for the Study of Symbolic Interaction (2001-2002). Smith received his AB from the University of Dayton, the MA from The Ohio State University, and the PhD from Duke University.*

Elizabeth Adams St.Pierre *is Associate Professor of Language Education and Affiliated Professor of both the Qualitative Research Program and the Women's Studies Department at the University of Georgia. Her research interests focus on the work of language in the construction of subjectivity in women and on troubling the traditional categories of qualitative inquiry during her investigations.*

Richard V. Travisano *teaches sociology at the University of Rhode Island. Presently he is writing poetry on just about anything, and prose about Rhode Island shellfishermen, and about his growing up Italian in Waterbury, Connecticut.*

Mary E. Weems *is a performance poet, playwright, and an activist artist educator. Weems earned a PhD in Education at the University of Illinois, Urbana-Champaign. Her book,* I Speak from the Wound in My Mouth: A Political Act, *is forthcoming from Peter Lang.*

Lois Weis *is the author and/or editor of numerous books and articles relating to social class, race, gender, schooling, and the "new" economy. Her most recent publications include* Speedbumps: A Student Friendly Guide to Qualitative Research *(with Michelle Fine);* Construction Sites: Excavating Race, Class, and Gender Among Urban Youth *(with Michelle Fine); and* Beyond Black and White *(with Maxine Seller). Lois sits on numerous editorial boards and is a former editor of* Educational Policy.